A treatise on social theory

VOLUME ONE

A treatise on social theory

VOLUME I: THE METHODOLOGY OF SOCIAL THEORY

W. G. Runciman, F.B.A.

FELLOW OF TRINITY COLLEGE, CAMBRIDGE

CAMBRIDGE UNIVERSITY PRESS

CAMBRIDGE
LONDON   NEW YORK   NEW ROCHELLE
MELBOURNE   SYDNEY

Published by the Press Syndicate of the University of Cambridge
The Pitt Building, Trumpington Street, Cambridge CB2 1RP
32 East 57th Street, New York, NY 10022, USA
296 Beaconsfield Parade, Middle Park, Melbourne 3206, Australia

First published 1983

Printed in Great Britain at the University Press, Cambridge

Library of Congress catalogue card number: 82–4493

British Library Cataloguing in Publication Data
Runciman, W. G.
A treatise on social theory
Vol. 1: The methodology of social theory
1. Sociology
I. Title
301   HM51
ISBN 0 521 24906 6 hard covers
ISBN 0 521 27251 3 paper back

The author and publisher would like to thank the following for permission to reproduce material in this volume: Angela Carter for the poem on pages 223–4 from *Japanese Snapshots*, © Angela Carter 1971; Rex Features Ltd. for the photograph on page 61; Culver Pictures Inc. for the photograph on page 233; Professor Claude Levi-Strauss for the photograph on page 257; the B.B.C. Hulton Picture Library for the photograph on page 271.

A treatise on social theory

For Ruth

VOLUME I

The methodology of social theory

Contents

Preface

The idea of this treatise was initially conceived in the summer of 1966. In the years between then and now, I have incurred more- obligations than I could possibly hope to list to a great number of colleagues, pupils, correspondents, symposiasts, reviewers and friends. I must apologize collectively to them for not acknowledging individually the discussion and advice from which I have benefited at their hands. But I am fully aware how much I owe to all of them for it.

I must apologize also to readers who may be familiar with what I have written on these matters already, since on some topics I repeat without qualification, while on others I flatly contradict, arguments which I have set out in print elsewhere. I can only ask such readers to accept that I am now putting forward as systematically as I am able to do views of which I have come to be sufficiently persuaded that except on points of detail I am unlikely to revise them again. This treatise is not going to be the full and definitive treatment of its subject which in 1966 I dreamed that I might one day be able to achieve. But I have come to the reluctant conclusion that it would not be significantly improved if I were to delay the start of its publication yet further. My hope is that Volume II will be completed by 1985 and Volume III by 1990. But each volume can, in any case, be read independently of the one or two still to follow.

The delay since 1966 is due in large part to my having decided to combine my academic career with a career in business. I wish that I could feel entitled, like Namier in his Preface to *The Structure of Politics at the Accession of George III*, to quote Gibbon's dictum that 'the Captain of Hampshire Grenadiers has not been useless to the historian of the Roman Empire'. But I am in any case aware that the chairmen of companies are not always wiser than university professors. I have learned much about the workings of social institutions from my experience of what is misleadingly called the 'real' world. But the extent to which I am a better sociologist for being at the same time a practising capitalist should be left to my readers to judge rather than to me.

My particular gratitude is due to Jon Elster, Alan Ryan and John Torrance for comments on the preliminary version of this volume which have saved me from many errors and infelicities; to Bernard Williams, who very kindly read two separate versions and whose criticisms were of exceptional value; to Patricia Williams, whose editorial counsel and patience have been of the greatest help throughout; to the Council of Trinity College, Cambridge for the award of a Fellowship under Title B and the facilities for research which go with it; to Lesley Flaherty, who has typed and retyped successive drafts with unfailing cheerfulness; and above all to my wife, to whom the work as a whole is dedicated in the knowledge that without her understanding and support I could never have undertaken it at all.

Trinity College, Cambridge
December 1981   W.G.R.

I

Introduction: the nature of social theory

§ 1. The debate between those who affirm and those who deny that there is a fundamental difference in kind between the sciences of nature and the sciences of man has continued without resolution for more than two hundred years. If the arguments to be put forward in this volume are correct, the debate can for practical purposes be regarded as closed. But to show this is not so much to arbitrate among the contending parties as to rewrite the terms in which the debate ought initially to have been framed. My principal argument to this effect can be summarized in a sentence: there is no special problem of explanation in the human sciences, but only a special problem of description. Properly defined, explanation and description can be distinguished both from each other and from either the reportage of facts or the advocacy of values; and this in turn facilitates not only the analysis of the concept of understanding but the demarcation of methodological questions from either philosophical or technical ones. But how is this claim itself to be construed? The sciences of man have evolved in not only historical but methodological subordination to the sciences of nature, and this has meant among other things that the twentieth-century social scientist, whatever his* views on the scope and nature of his subject, cannot help being driven by the relative paucity of his results to the fear that he may be forever excluded from the enchanted garden in which the fruit of the tree of knowledge can be seen hanging so much closer within reach. He cannot but ask himself not simply how his methodological problems are to be solved but whether they are not problems of an altogether different order from those of the sciences of nature. He needs to know, in other words, in just what sense his difficulties *are* methodological in the first

---

* Or of course hers: in the absence of a singular pronoun covering both sexes, I propose for convenience to use 'he', 'him' and 'his' to denote both hypothetical researchers and their presumptive readers, whether male or female.

place. How is he to tell a problem of technique from a problem of epistemology? And until he does, how can he settle the appropriate sense to be given to the terms 'explanation', 'description', 'fact', 'understanding' and the rest?

It does not immediately follow that theories of human behaviour must be philosophical in some way in which theories in the natural sciences are not, since if it turns out that the difficulties which are peculiar to the human sciences can, after all, be construed as no more than technical, then the contribution which methodological discussion can make to them will be limited to the elucidation of the logic of accepted scientific practice. But this conclusion cannot itself be construed as no more than technical. Even those who deny a fundamental difference between the sciences of nature and the sciences of man cannot deny that the question arises at all. This is itself already a difference; and if we ask how the difference comes about, the answer is not in dispute between rival methodological schools. It comes about because the study of self-conscious human behaviour is itself self-conscious human behaviour, and the differences between the two sides in the long debate can all be categorized in terms of the conclusions which they hold to follow, or not to follow, from that fact.

To speak of two sides is, no doubt, an oversimplification. Those who have affirmed that the difference between the sciences of nature and of man is fundamental have done so on many different and often incompatible grounds. Already in the nineteenth century some, like Dilthey, who held that the human sciences are marked off by their subject-matter, were attacked by others, like Windelband, who held that they are marked off by their method. Many who have agreed in rejecting the Positivist account of the social sciences have disagreed both over the interpretation of the doctrines attributed to it and over the diagnosis of the errors to which those doctrines are alleged to lead. On the other side, those who have held that the study of man is a natural science like any other have in practice interpreted that belief in altogether different ways: it is enough merely to contrast the anthropological method expounded by Radcliffe-Brown with that expounded by Lévi-Strauss. Those few authors who have succeeded in making a lasting contribution to the debate have for the most part done so, as Max Weber did, only by occupying and holding a limited area of the middle ground against attacks directed from either flank. Yet to the methodologist, as opposed to the historian, this diversity of opinions poses less difficulty than might appear, for much of it can itself be accounted for by the persistent compulsion of one side to reject all of the recommendations of the other, however innocuous and even sensible some of them may be. The tacit assumption which has time and again bedevilled the progress of social theory is that both scientific Naturalism and philosophical Idealism either stand or fall as a whole; and this has been linked in turn with a recurrent tendency on the part of the practitioners of the human sciences to regard some one favoured method as the paradigm by reference to which their presuppositions can be vindicated. But the house of science has many mansions. If B. F. Skinner, author of *The Behaviour of Organisms* as well as *Walden Two*, is right about the way to predict the conditioned responses of bar-pressing rats, this does not make R. G. Collingwood, author of *Roman Britain* as well as *The Idea of History*, wrong about the way to reconstruct what went on in the minds of those who designed Hadrian's Wall.*

In any case, much mutual recrimination among social scientists over the 'scientific' standing of each other's work has rested on a limited, if not downright ignorant, conception of what in fact takes place within the sciences of nature. Methodologists of social theory may not need to know just how molecular biologists, oceanographers, mechanical engineers or inorganic chemists set about their research in the way that they may need to know just how art historians, political scientists, econometricians or demographers do. But they must divest themselves of any general preconception about the relative uniformity of the sciences of nature in contrast to the sciences of man. There is more in common between some human and some natural sciences than between many pairs of both. Not only biology but geology furnishes more illuminating parallels for the sociologist, anthropologist or historian than classical mechanics. Here too, the progress of social theory has often been diverted and sometimes retarded by the influence of mistaken analogies drawn from the most immediately fashionable of the sciences of nature. In the eighteenth century, it was bound to be tempting to think of society as a machine, and in the nineteenth as an organism. In the twentieth, it is bound to be tempting to think of it as a communication network. But the gap between analogy and reduction is still too wide to be spanned by the assertion, true as it may be, that social theorists have more to learn from cybernetics than from either engineering or physiology. Neither the substantive nor the methodological problems which are peculiar to the sciences of man will be solved just by drawing analogies to the sciences of nature.

---

* Although he was: Collingwood's hypothesis that the curtain was designed to screen the approach of troops assembling for a sortie through the sally-ports has been overturned by the discovery that the road running parallel to the inner side of the wall was built a century later. But that is the way science proceeds.

To whatever extent, on the other hand, the problems of the human sciences *are* analogous to those of the natural, the question whether those of the human sciences are technical or epistemological is effectively answered. If the analogy holds, it follows that the problem in question does not arise from the original difference that the one set of sciences is, but the other is not, dealing with self-conscious behaviour. Thus if, for example, the multifarious difficulties surrounding the notion of causality appear to the social scientist to be the impediment barring him from a satisfactory account of human behaviour, he needs to show in what way they are different from and more intractable than those which have not, after all, prevented the emergence of well-tested explanations in biology, chemistry and physics. Philosophers of science are no more nearly unanimous on such awkward questions as the logic of disposition concepts and counterfactual conditionals than they are on causality itself. But practising sociologists, anthropologists and historians have, fortunately, no need to be able to answer them before addressing themselves to the question what, if anything, marks off the practice of the sciences of man from the practice of the sciences of nature as different in kind.

§2. To put the question in this fashion at all may invite the objection that I am already assuming a part of what I claimed to be going to demonstrate. But it assumes no more than that there is *a* difference between science, whether of man or nature, and non-science. It carries no more implication about the kind of difference it is than about the position of the human sciences in relation to it. No doubt arguments can be advanced to diminish the epistemological status conventionally accorded to science but denied to metaphysics or religion. But if science has nothing to teach us, then there is nothing to learn. The lecture-room sceptic, here as elsewhere, cannot be controverted in his own terms. But the social theorist confronted with the claim that all aspiration to inter-subjectively testable knowledge of the workings of the world is illusory can reply with perfect seriousness that he only wishes he had as many illusions as his colleagues in the Faculty of Engineering.

This rejoinder is at the same time quite compatible with a more modest degree of scepticism. To hold that there is a difference between science and metaphysics, or science and art, or science and the absence of any would-be systematic observation and reasoning about the world in which we find ourselves, involves no necessary commitment to the doctrines of Positivism. The arguments to be put forward in this volume are quite compatible with a reminder that science itself, when studied as a human activity, has certain affinities with religion; that no empirical observation is free of presuppositions; that progress in science is not progress towards any goal of final knowledge, but only away from a relatively less learned ignorance; and that not only the substantive discoveries of science but even its most deeply entrenched procedural rules are beyond a certain level not merely provisional but arbitrary. Still less controversial is the assertion that study of the actual course of scientific discovery discloses a wide and consistent discrepancy between the course of the research which led to it and the logic in terms of which its outcome will later be rationalized. But none of this deprives the idea of science of its meaning. The revolution in ideas which led to quantum mechanics or special relativity is still in another category from that which led to abstract painting or *musique concrète*. There need only be *some* additional constraint within which the natural or social scientist exercises his discretion for art to be marked off from science as an activity different in kind.

This difference is linked in turn to the familiar contrast between discovery and creation. It is true that to the degree that progress in art proceeds by way of advances in technique it too proceeds by discovery: the painters of the Italian Renaissance were no less significantly dependent on the discovery – or, strictly, rediscovery – of perspective, or the architects of the Gothic cathedrals on the discovery of the vault, than twentieth-century molecular biologists on advances in X-ray crystallography. But we still cannot speak of the history of art as cumulative in the way that we can speak of the history of science. The contrast may not be as clear-cut as has sometimes been assumed by Positivist philosophers of science. But it is not wholly spurious. The successes of science may be both historically fortuitous and methodologically provisional, but some, at any rate, of its failures are irredeemable. It is not simply a matter of academic fashion that phlogiston theory, or humoral physiology, or phrenological explanations of criminality have yet to return to favour.

Yet this, as methodologists of all persuasions will acknowledge, is not the end of the matter. For even when the validity of the – or at least a – contrast between science and art or metaphysics has been accepted, it can be used to make the status of the social sciences seem more problematic rather than less. If the history of science is narrated as, so to speak, an ontologist's story, then the social sciences should fit well enough into it: it has merely been a matter of finding out whether there are or aren't such things in the world as action at a distance, photons, biological species, the collective unconscious, perfect competition, schizophrenia, totemism, stateless societies and so on. But methodological questions cannot simply be reduced to ontological. We cannot bypass the difficulty of analysing the kinds of knowledge at which social scientists claim to have arrived. Are we really to say that Marx discovered (in Engels's phrase) the 'law of the development of human history' in the same sense that Newton discovered the laws of motion? Or that Malthus discovered that population increases geometrically if unchecked in the same sense that Theodorus of Cyrene discovered the irrationality of $\sqrt{3}$? Or that Marshall discovered the elasticity of demand in the same sense that Harvey discovered the circulation of the blood?

These are, at least for the moment, only rhetorical questions. But they are already symptomatic of the ambivalence which seems inherently to attach to the claims of the social sciences to be sciences. Is it not, after all, puzzling that Marx's writings should still be read by sociologists at all? No physicist, unless also a historian of physics, reads the writings of Newton, or needs to. No biologist needs to read Darwin's *Origin of Species*. Yet Marx, and his commentators, and his commentators' commentators are read and reread a century after his death quite as though *Capital* made no more pretence to be a work of science than, say, Carlyle's *Sartor Resartus*. A possible answer is that Marx's discoveries still stand intact and no further advance has yet been made on them. But this will hardly do. Not only have there indeed been modifications and advances, but it is in any case impossible that a social theory framed both in and for mid nineteenth-century Europe should be directly applicable to circumstances and events of a kind which its author could not conceivably have foreseen. It is this which makes it plausible to regard Marxism, as so many of both its adherents and its detractors do, not as a scientific theory about the workings of human societies so much as a metaphysics in terms of which to view them, coupled with a programme by means of which to change them; and is not this enough by itself to show that the sciences of man and of nature are different in kind?

Yet even if it is agreed that Marxism is both a metaphysics and a programme, and that this is why it continues to be debated as widely and as vehemently as it is, it does not follow that social science is inherently 'ideological' in some sense that natural science is not. Celestial mechanics was ideological in the time of Copernicus and Galileo; geology was ideological up to and including the time of Lyell; biology was ideological in the time of Darwin and, later, of Lysenko. They ceased to be so not just because the opponents of certain of their findings came to change their politics but because the grounds of those findings were such that they had in the end to change their beliefs. No doubt those findings and therefore beliefs must, like all scientific findings and beliefs, be regarded as susceptible in principle to some sort of possible revision. But in this there is no distinction between the sciences of man and of nature. Some further argument needs to be adduced before it is claimed that twentieth-century debates over wage-push versus cost-pull inflation are inherently more 'ideological' than sixteenth-century debates over the number of Jupiter's moons.

§3. Here already, however, three related objections are likely to be put forward by those who deny the methodological unity of natural and social science. First: have I not chosen examples to suit my case which presuppose, but do not by any means demonstrate, that there is no divide between nature and culture? Second: am I not simply avoiding the whole question of cultural relativism by which the force of my examples is effectively undermined? And third: do I not assume a sense of 'ideological' which ignores the fact that the social sciences, unlike the natural, are not and cannot be value-free?

To the first objection, the answer is that no more need be assumed at this stage of the argument than that there are some empirical questions about human behaviour which are empirical in the same sense and to the same degree as in any science of nature. To say this is not covertly to define 'behaviour' to exclude what those who deny the methodological unity of natural and social science rightly claim to be distinctive of it: it is not to talk merely of automatic reflexes and neurophysiological events. Whatever may be the difficulties in specifying what it is that is distinctive about human behaviour, even the most distinctively human forms of it do still lend themselves to some straightforward questions of observation and measurement. Historians may not yet be able to agree about the causes of the First World War, but none of them (as Clemenceau is reported to have said) maintains that it was caused by the Belgian army's invasion of Germany. Demographers may not yet be able to account satisfactorily for the remarkable rise in population which took place in England and Wales between the end of the eighteenth and the end of the nineteenth centuries; but none of them, even in the absence of public registration of births and deaths for the earlier part of that period, claims that it actually went down. Psychologists may not yet be able to define, let alone to explain, schizophrenia; but none of them disputes that there is a distinctive condition – porphyria – which is brought about by the presence of a dominant autosomal gene and commonly manifests itself in the third decade of life through behavioural symptoms which sometimes lead to its being mistakenly diagnosed as a 'schizophrenic' illness. Sceptics about the impossibility in principle of a science of man are perfectly entitled to point to the limitations of our knowledge of human behaviour by comparison with our knowledge of the workings of purely physical systems. But they are not entitled to infer from these limitations that nothing whatever is as well known, in a 'scientific' sense of 'known', about human behaviour as about the movements of the galaxies or the properties of the nucleic acids.

To the second objection, the answer is not, as it has sometimes been argued to be, that the doctrine of cultural relativism is self-refuting, but only that it is self-defeating. To deny that universal validity attaches to any claim to knowledge advanced by members of a 'scientific' culture is not to be committed to a claim that this proposition itself is universally true. But it is to deprive all academic enquiry of its (admittedly self-set) purpose. There is in practice no escape for either the natural or the social scientist from a correspondence conception of truth. This again is not a simple matter of logic. Any discussion of truth-conditions raises issues which are, and are likely to remain, controversial among philosophers. But to assert that 'copper expands on heating' or 'the Battle of Hastings was fought in 1066' is true – or for that matter false – is to presuppose a relation of some kind between observation-statements and the state of the world. The nature of this relation is a further question which the practising sociologist can well afford to leave to the philosophers of science. But he cannot, whatever his view of the nature of it, afford to do without a distinction between statements which assert something to be true by virtue of there being such a relation and statements which do not. Among the observation-statements which he makes will no doubt be the statements both that what is held to be true on one side of the Pyrenees is held to be false on the other, and that what it means to say of a statement that it is true is held to be one thing in one Department of Philosophy and another in another. But neither he nor his fellow-sociologists from rival theoretical schools will dispute that 'what it means to say of a statement that it is true is held to be one thing in one Department of Philosophy and another in another' is true if and only if what it means to say of a statement that it is true is held to be one thing in one Department of Philosophy and another in another.

To the third objection, the answer is that it has relevance to what has been so far said only if it is the case that every observation-statement about human behaviour logically entails, or is entailed by, some value-judgement; and the onus is on anyone who holds this to demonstrate it. It is not in dispute that there is in practice a connection between observation-statements and value-judgements in the sciences of human behaviour for the simple reason that we do all have standards of value which apply to the behaviour of ourselves and other people but not to the behaviour of inanimate objects (their applicability to animals being itself a matter of one's values). Nor is it in dispute that statements of the form of observation-statements may on closer inspection turn out to be value-judgements; or that many value-judgements are dependent on empirical assumptions which, if discarded, would require the value-judgement to be revised; or that the practice of social science raises issues of policy about which different people's value-judgements are likely to conflict; or that many social scientists will, in the absence of definitive evidence, incline to believe what best accords with the value-judgements to which they are committed; or that a social scientist's initial choice of topic for study, even if not psychologically determined by his moral or political values, is a value-judgement of a kind in itself. But from none of these assertions does it follow that no statement of purported fact about human behaviour can be value-neutral – that is, true (if true) or false (if false) irrespective of what the sociologist who states it holds to be morally, politically or aesthetically good or bad.

In stating and dismissing these three objections, I do not pretend that the philosophical questions underlying them are not serious. Nor do I pretend that anything said in this volume will bring those questions closer to resolution. But to the methodologist, as opposed to the philosopher, of social science, discussion of them is necessary only to the extent that the practice of social science would be modified if one rather than another answer to them is thought to hold. There are many contentious issues in the philosophy of the social sciences, and on many of them philosophical as well as merely technical discussion can be of demonstrable benefit even to the least philosophically-minded of their practitioners. But practising social scientists need no more be inhibited from doing research at all by their inability to provide a cast-iron refutation of cultural relativism than their colleagues in the Faculty of Engineering by their inability to provide a cast-iron proof that the world has been in existence for longer than half an hour. The considerations which make relativism plausible may make the construction of explanatory, descriptive and/or evaluative theories of human behaviour problematic in a way that theory-construction in natural science is not. But this does not require practising sociologists, anthropologists and historians to abandon their conviction that they can report at least some of it as a matter of fact independently of rival conceptions of the nature of human agency, rival accounts of what it means to claim of a proposition that it is trans-culturally valid, or rival doctrines of the role in social science of moral and political value-judgements. They would have to do so only if it were to be convincingly demonstrated to them that nothing whatever which they have succeeded in reporting as having happened or been the case can be treated as factual in the same sense and to the same degree as the findings which natural scientists report and which are accepted as such by their fellow-practitioners even from rival theoretical schools.

§ 4. To say that the study of human behaviour is at least to some degree an empirical and not a purely philosophical matter is not, perhaps, to say very much. Indeed, it may be that not even the most radical Idealists* have ever seriously believed that a rise in the population of England and Wales or the German army's invasion of Belgium are not matters of fact but of ideological interest or metaphysical speculation. The more formidable charge of the Idealists is that the would-be sciences of human behaviour consistently fail to live up to their own conception of what constitutes a science: they fail, that is, to achieve the cumulative theoretical progress, or even the first decisive rupture with common sense, which marks off the activity of science from the casual inductive empiricism by which ordinary people order and classify their world and the other people in it. Where, the Idealists will ask, in all the centuries in which attempts have been made to study social behaviour scientifically, have theories deserving of the name been found? What is 'sociological theory' except history without the dates? What is 'anthropological theory' except a compendium of travellers' tales? What is 'economic theory' except glorified book-keeping?

The last of these questions is particularly provocative, since of all the sciences of human behaviour economics is by general consent the most fully developed and the most firmly established, and its history from the days of Quesnay and Adam Smith can be (and often has been) told in terms of a cumulative extension of observation, development of theory, diagnosis and correction of previous error and refinement of technique. But it can also be told as a sequence not of scientific discoveries but of ideological shifts whereby the concepts of money, labour, value and trade are redefined to fit the institutions and interests of each succeeding period. Even with hindsight, it is difficult to retell the history of previous disputes between rival schools in such a way as will convincingly fit the model of cumulative test and revision. On the cumulative view, the

* By 'Idealists' is meant simply those sometimes designated 'anti-Naturalists' – those, that is, who deny the methodological unity of the sciences of man and of nature. The label thus includes Collingwood, although he himself repudiated it. But it has no more to stand only for the doctrines of Hegel and his followers than 'Positivist' has to stand only for either Comte and his followers on the one hand or the members of the Vienna Circle on the other.

Utilitarians and Physiocrats of the eighteenth century* should have been advancing mutually exclusive theories, each offering a distinctive explanation of the same set of facts about the contemporary processes of production, distribution and exchange, and it should long since have become clear which theory was, and which was not, vindicated by the evidence. But it hasn't. It is all very well to ask which was right: the view that the role of money in the economy is to generate purchasing capacity which in turn elicits production, or the view that money is merely the medium of exchange which cannot of itself create value since only exchanges with the land itself are absolutely profitable and trade reduces in the end to barter. There is no clear-cut answer. These are not questions of the same kind as questions about the role of the heart in the circulation of the blood or the nature of resistance to an electrical current. They are questions about (among other things) the nature of human needs and the meaning of 'value' to the people whose 'needs' they are. And these, surely, are questions of philosophy rather than science.

Yet it would again be a mistake to conclude from this objection that the social sciences are not, let alone that they can never be, sciences. To this kind of scepticism, salutary as its impact may be, there are two answers. The first is that the history of the physical and biological sciences can equally well be told in terms of ideological shifts rather than conclusive observations and decisive experiments. The second is that although there may be an additional difficulty common to all the social, but none of the natural, sciences, it does not follow from it that no theoretical progress, in the 'scientific' sense of theory, has been or can be made in them at all. On the contrary: once the problems of reportage and description (in the sense in which I shall be using those terms) are seen for what they are, it becomes all the easier to see that problems of explanation are in principle the same in the sciences of man and of nature.

The objection, accordingly, is valid only against a methodology which no practising social scientist needs to defend. The idea that the progress of knowledge must be characterized by conclusive observations and decisive experiments has by now been overtaken by both the history and the philosophy of science. Not only have the natural sciences been seen not to have proceeded as the stereotype suggests, but the old-fashioned idea of an external world impinging itself on the unprejudiced consciousness of the enquiring empiricist has been abandoned by practitioners and methodologists alike. The difficulty only arises because an unspoken

*On whom see Mark Blaug, *Economic Theory in Retrospect*[2] (1968), Ch. 1 ('Pre-Adamite Economics').

assumption of this kind did often inform the scepticism both of scientific Naturalists and of philosophical Idealists, who in the one case despaired at and in the other case rejoiced over the apparent inability of the sciences of man ever to turn themselves into the sort of activity which natural science was mistakenly supposed to be. Of course, the sciences of man cannot be 'scientific' if large areas of the natural sciences are not 'scientific' either. But many, if not quite all, of the supposed contrasts between the two simply disappear under more careful examination. No doubt economic theory is culture-bound; but Galileo's Law breaks down over distances not negligible in proportion to the radius of the earth. No doubt Physiocrats and Utilitarians differed in their chosen prescriptions for the economies of their place and period; but population geneticists have differed widely in their prescriptions for ensuring what they regard as the genetic well-being of the human race. No doubt sociologists are unable to predict the future course of technological innovation and changes in the mode of industrial production; but biologists are unable to predict genetic mutation and the future evolution of species. No doubt the political relations between nation-states are immune to controlled experiment; but so are the courses of the stars. No doubt metaphysical and even theological differences underlay the arguments of the eighteenth-century economists about the concept of surplus value; but the arguments about basalt among eighteenth-century geologists between 'Neptunists' and 'Vulcanists' were far from unconnected with what they believed to be implied by the text of the Book of Genesis.*

To say that the sciences of man have progressed less far and less fast over the last 200 years is no doubt still true, provided that the necessary revision of the old-fashioned stereotype of science has not been taken so far as to rob the notion of scientific progress of meaning altogether. But it is not difficult, with hindsight, to see why. The exaggerated hopes, as we can now see them to have been, of the Encyclopaedists are not evidence for saying that no theoretical insights transcending common sense have yet been attained. It is one thing to say that economic theory has not fully resolved the differences by which the Utilitarians and Physiocrats were divided. It is quite another to say that economic theory has made no progress whatever since Quesnay, and that we nowadays understand nothing more about the flow of goods and services in a monetarized market economy than he did. Indeed, the way in which the vocabulary of common sense itself has been changed testifies in economics no less than in physics or chemistry to the size of the breach

* The example is taken from Charles Coulston Gillespie, *Genesis and Geology* (1951).

with the common sense of previous ages which has been made. The eighteenth-century wage-earner had, we may safely take it, no clearer conception of multipliers, indifference curves and liquidity ratios than he had of gravitational pull or focal length or molecular excitation. There is no call to deny that in the case of economics there has been less progress since, and that there remain difficulties of a further kind. But nor is there any call to pretend in the face of economic theory that there is no such thing.

§ 5. The nature of the distinction which needs to be drawn can best be brought out by taking as an example the economy most remote from our own which still fulfils the conditions which make it plausible to speak of an 'economy' at all. The sociologist who studies the economies of ancient Greece and Rome can hardly fail to be aware of the differences which mark them off from the economies of eighteenth-, let alone twentieth-, century Europe. But he will at the same time be aware that he is in a better position to understand their workings than the ancients were. He will recognize, for a start, that they lacked the concept of an 'economy'.* But he will not therefore conclude that theirs was not an economy any more than that because they lacked the concept of 'malaria' they never died of it. Roman landowners might not – indeed, it seems reasonably clear from such evidence as has come down to us that they did not – calculate the net yield on agricultural land relative to the other forms of capital investment open to them. But it was, in fact, low; and this in part explains why the ancient economy followed the course which it did. Similarly, the Roman economy was characterized by the absence of wage-drift inflation under long-term stability of interest rates, and this too helps to explain what did – or, no less interestingly, did not – happen to its rate of growth over the period when the potential for significant expansion can be argued with hindsight to have been most evidently present. The conclusions of this kind at which the twentieth-century researcher is able to arrive are not affected one way or the other by the fact that the ancient Romans themselves did not arrive at them and could not even have expressed them in the language available to them at the time. On the contrary: the gap between the twentieth-century researcher's account and the Romans' own is a measure of the breach with common sense which has been achieved.

But is the twentieth-century researcher not, perhaps, guilty of ana-chronism? How (it might be asked) can he justify the imposition of

---

* See M. I. Finley, *The Ancient Economy* (1973), on which this section is principally based.

categories wholly alien to those of the people whose self-conscious behaviour he is claiming to account for? To this, the answer is that he may, indeed, be guilty of imposing anachronistic categories – sociologists often do, and are. But when they are, it is not because it is necessarily illegitimate to apply to other people's behaviour theoretical terms which they neither would nor even could have applied to it themselves. It is illegitimate only if the application of such terms assumes that they did when they didn't. If the twentieth-century researcher tells his readers, for example, that the Pisistratids of Athens in the sixth century B.C. invested government capital in rural development in preference to international trade, he is certainly guilty of anachronism, since his assertion entails the possibility that a statesman of the period could have posed the alternatives to himself in these terms. But if he tells us that from the third century B.C. onwards the Romans created an increasingly artificial cost-benefit imbalance between regions by progressively withdrawing the supply of corn to Rome from the hands of private contractors and the free play of the market, he will, provided that the evidence supports his case, be correct irrespective of whether or not the Romans could have put it to themselves that that was what they were doing. If our objector continues to maintain that all that has been achieved is to carry out the Romans' 'glorified book-keeping' for them, he may. But even this phrase implicitly concedes that there is more than 'unglorified' book-keeping involved – or in other words, that the twentieth-century researcher's account rests on the invocation of at least some rudimentary concepts and propositions of economic theory.

It may still be said that the anachronistic account is inadequate by itself. But I have not sought to suggest otherwise. Nor have I sought to deny that sociologists must begin by reporting the behaviour which they have chosen to study in terms which the agents themselves could agree. The basis of the twentieth-century researcher's account of the ancient Roman economy rests on the evidence of his sources for acts of buying and selling, borrowing and lending, mortgaging, foreclosing, hoarding, taxing, bequeathing, etc., which taken together constitute the 'economy' about which he writes. Only then can he go on to rephrase his findings in theoretical terms which will enable him to explain the behaviour which his sources report to him. But in so doing, he is no differently placed from his colleagues in natural science, whose observations are likewise translated for the purpose of explanation into theoretical terms which are in no sense given to them with or by the observations themselves. It is possible, and indeed likely, that the theoretical terms will themselves be revised or replaced at a later stage. But this is not because they are theoretical; it is more likely to be because they are not theoretical enough.

'But this still ignores the difference that in the sociological case the observations are of behaviour which has meaning to the agents. Acts of purchase and sale, etc., are more than interactions of molecules.' Indeed so. But they are not therefore out of reach of theoretical terms. The fact that they have meaning creates an additional problem, or set of problems, for the sociologist; it exposes him, as we shall see, to the risk of a category of mistakes which his colleagues in natural science will never have the occasion to make. But the meaningfulness of behaviour does not render it inexplicable. On the contrary, the additional difficulty which it raises is not to do with explanation at all.

THE CONCEPT OF UNDERSTANDING

§ 6. To the question 'where then does this additional difficulty reside?' the readiest answer is 'in the need for the observer to understand human behaviour and not (or not merely) to explain it'. But what then is to count as understanding? That subjective meaning is a distinctive feature of human behaviour is uncontentious. What is contentious is whether it follows that the logic of explanation is different in the sciences of man from the sciences of nature. To this, my answer is: no, not the logic of *explanation*. But the recourse to italics reveals that the question is likely to prove misleading if phrased, as it generally is, in such a way as to invite a simple yes or no. It can be answered adequately only when the concept of understanding has itself been broken down into what I shall from now on refer to as its primary, secondary and tertiary senses. The first of these is the understanding necessary for the reportage of what has been observed to occur or be the case; the second is the understanding of what caused it, or how it came about; and the third is the understanding necessary for its description in the special sense here given to that term.*

For this purpose, it is best to start from the other end – that is, to ask not 'what does it mean to understand a person's actions (or thoughts, or feelings, or words)?' but 'what does it mean to *mis*understand them?'. In a poem by Roy Fuller, there occurs the line: 'The filthy aunt forgotten in the attic' – which one critic, at least, took to refer to 'a painting, of

---

* Although special in that it is at variance with much of conventional usage, it is neither original nor unique: the decision to adopt it was significantly influenced by S. Toulmin and K. Baier, 'On Describing', *Mind* n.s. LXI (1952).

course'. But the poet meant a *real* aunt (unless, that is, you think he is lying when he tells us so). So the critic had misunderstood, as might an archaeologist who failed to realize that what he took to be a weapon of war was a cosmetic implement, or an ethnographer who failed to realize that what he took to be a serious ritual was a piece of play-acting, or a musicologist who failed to realize that what he took for a semiquaver in the composer's manuscript was an inkstain. But it is a different matter altogether when the observer has quite well grasped what went on, yet still declares himself baffled by it. When Collingwood tells us that he was provoked into his study of the nature of history by his inability to understand what could possibly have been in the mind of the designer of the Albert Memorial,* he does not mean that he was unable to say what 'designing the Albert Memorial' means, or even to say what were the influences which prompted the designer to design it. He means that he could not answer for himself the question: how could it have seemed to the designer of the Albert Memorial that the *Albert Memorial* was the memorial to design? And he realized that until he had answered it to his satisfaction he must have failed to understand what the designer's thoughts and feelings ('really') were.

Some, including Collingwood himself, have been led by puzzlements of this kind to conclude that the researcher must somehow recreate in his imagination the state of mind which he at first finds baffling. But this is true only in the sense that no researcher can understand an action without understanding the terms in which it is characterized by the agent – which is trivial. If this means that no researcher can understand an action which he had never been in a state of mind to perform himself, it is false (or if true because that is what 'understanding' is defined to consist in, then leading to the totally self-defeating conclusion that nobody can ever understand anybody else). It may be that Collingwood, if he was to remedy his bafflement, had to come to understand more than he had about the taste of the Victorians, their attitudes to the monarchy, the origin and course of the Gothic Revival, and so on. But he did not need to have served an apprenticeship in an architect's drawing-office or to have been born before 1830 or even to have familiarized himself with the intimate details of the personal life of Sir George Gilbert Scott.

Nor is the matter one of evaluation. No doubt Collingwood found the Albert Memorial ugly. But his bafflement was that of the historian, not merely of the critic. His task was to understand the state of mind in which the Albert Memorial could be thought beautiful by its designer and those

* See his *An Autobiography* (1939), Ch. 5.

who commissioned him, whether or not he found it beautiful too. It is true that to do so he must have had the capacity, at least to some minimal degree, for aesthetic appreciation: he must at some time or other have himself sensed beauty of some kind in something. But to say this is only to restate in other terms the point that the observer must always understand the meaning of the terms in which agents themselves characterize what they think, feel, say and do. A man blind from birth cannot be said to understand the meaning of colour terms even if he has been taught by other cues in the behaviour of those who can see to apply the terms on occasion correctly; and if Collingwood had been totally without the capacity to see anything as either beautiful or ugly, then even though he might apply these terms 'correctly' too, we should have to say that he was using them without really knowing their meaning. But it goes without saying that he did; and only because he did was he able to put his methodological problem to himself in the first place.

The lesson to be learnt from Collingwood's problem, therefore, is not that the sociology of art, or of anything else, depends on some procedure whereby the observer identifies himself with the agent whom he is studying. Still less is it that understanding in any of its three separate senses entails that the observer is committed to a value-judgement one way or the other about what he observes. It is that the agent is privileged in his own awareness of what he thinks, feels, says and does in a way which goes beyond what is covered by understanding in the primary sense. Not only does he understand, subject to the possibility of exceptional circumstances to be considered later on, what he thinks, feels, says and does; he also understands in the tertiary sense *what it is like* to think, feel, say and do it. Marc Bloch, in *Le Métier d'Historien*, which he began to write in the Autumn of 1940 after the Fall of France, asked himself 'Did I truly know, in the full sense of that word, did I know from within, before I myself had suffered the terrible, sickening reality, what it meant for an army to be encircled, what it meant for a people to meet defeat?'* And it is a question of the kind which is as familiar to all but the most insensitive observers of ordinary social life as it is to the academic sociologist, anthropologist or historian. To Bloch's particular question my own answer would have to be: no. I have been in the army, but not in war and still less in defeat, and if I had been my response to his remark would no doubt be coloured by the relevant memories of my own. But in another sense, I understand him very well – much better than Collingwood understood the designer of the Albert Memorial. I am

---

* Eng. trans. as *The Historian's Craft* (1954), p. 44.

not recreating Bloch's experience, and I hope I never shall. But the sense of understanding which I have from Bloch derives precisely from what he conveys about the difficulty of describing it, of conveying what it was like. To say of an experience such as this 'It was worse than you could possibly conceive' is to say just what will most effectively bring home to the person who has *not* experienced it the degree to which it transcends what he has.

Notice, however, how little this has to do with understanding in the secondary, explanatory, sense. An account of this kind may, in certain contexts, have a role to play in answering the question 'what brought it about?'. Bloch might for example wish to account for his subsequent feelings and conduct by reference to the severity of the impact of defeat. But to do so he does not need to convey what it felt like. It is enough for him to report that the impact was severe and to demonstrate that it was so severe as to upset the plans or inhibit the motives by which his subsequent behaviour would otherwise have been guided. Explanation does always presuppose understanding in the primary sense: if the writing of *Le Métier d'Historien* is to be explained, at least in part, by Bloch's need to assuage the impact of defeat – which is what he tells us himself – then to understand the explanation his readers must understand what it means to say that Bloch was 'in' the army which the Germans defeated and what events are referred to by the term 'the Fall of France'. But he need not even ask himself the question 'what was it *like*?'; and there is no reason to suppose that if he did he would have a better explanation of Bloch's behaviour than he has already, any more than Collingwood, if he once came to feel that he ('really') understood what it was like to design the Albert Memorial, would thereby have added anything to the perfectly satisfactory explanation at which he could already have arrived in terms of the influences which prompted Sir George Gilbert Scott to design it when he did. The fact, however, that practising sociologists, anthropologists and historians are often trying both to describe in this sense and also to explain helps itself to explain why it is that the distinction between explanation and description has not been clearly recognized. The historian of the distant past, no less than the anthropologist who returns from an exotic and alien culture, is concerned to convey to his readers not simply the course of a sequence of reported events, or even a set of more or less well-tested concatenations of cause and effect. He is also concerned to convey the nature of the institutions and practices by which the lives of the people whom he has been studying are governed in the way in which those institutions and practices were perceived and experienced by them. But it is only the latter, not the former, which is peculiar to the sciences of human behaviour and poses methodological difficulties separate from the difficulty of explaining why what happened happened as, when and where it did.

When, therefore, a twentieth-century writer on the social structure of ancient Rome speaks of his need to understand the institution of, say, chattel slavery, he should be taken to mean this in all three senses. He must in the first place be sure that he has not misread his evidence in such a way as would lead him to misreport what has actually taken place: he must have established that the Romans did buy and sell people as things. In the second place, he is likely to have some idea about the causes of the origin and continuation of their practice of doing so. But if he goes on, in the third place, to discuss the nature of Roman slavery in such a way as to reveal that he is unaware that not only miners and factory hands but bankers, doctors and naval captains could all be of servile status, then he will be guilty of misunderstanding in the tertiary, descriptive, sense. He may not be reporting anything which is inaccurate or offering any explanation of an event, process or state of affairs which is not validated by his evidence, yet at the same time be failing to convey to the reader what the institution of slavery was like in terms of the possibilities known to be inherent in it by the members of the society in which it operated and was recognized as legitimate. The methods by which misunderstanding of this kind can be diagnosed will have to be treated in greater detail later on. But for the purpose of the argument at this stage, it is enough that it should have been shown that the accounts of the nature of human institutions and practices given by sociologists, anthropologists or historians do frequently expose them to the risk of it.

The difficulty in clearly formulating the distinction between the three senses of understanding is made worse (and not only in English) by the different uses to which the word 'explain' can be put. It is often said that not all explanation is causal; and to the extent that the question 'why?' is not always a request for a cause, this is a sensible reflection of ordinary speech. But there comes a point at which flexibility of usage borders on punning. It is unhelpful to talk of 'explaining' the structure of the Roman élite, or the legal relations between masters and slaves, or the institution of *peculium*, or the practice of manumission, if by that is meant simply saying what they were; and it is more unhelpful still if what is meant is saying what they were like. The most useful rule by which to be guided in practice, therefore, is simply to ask which of four questions – 'what?', 'why?', 'what like?' or 'how good or bad?' – is being answered by any sociologist, anthropologist or historian* who talks of explaining, describing, appraising, elucidating, making sense of, giving an account of, exploring the nature of, grasping, gaining an insight into, analysing, weighing up, interpreting, etc., any chosen event, process or state of affairs.

§7. The need for precision in terminology is no less acute where the subject under discussion is an individual action than where it is an institution or practice. I suggested earlier that the ingredients of what we now refer to as 'the Roman economy' are individual acts of buying, selling, borrowing, lending, etc., as understood by those who carried them out; and this claim I take to be uncontentious even to those opponents of so-called 'methodological individualism' who wish quite rightly to insist on the presence of at least some emergent properties predicable of institutions but not of individuals. It would, however, be palpably mistaken to treat these individual actions as devoid of social meaning. Any act of sale or purchase is not merely a physical, or even a psychological, fact but a social one. To report, therefore, that such an act has taken place is to presuppose an explanation at another level of the words and gestures constitutive of it. The observer of such an act could in theory – and if unfamiliar with the culture, might very well in practice – ask himself the question 'why are these words being spoken and these gestures being made?'; and the answer would be that it is because the one person is buying, and the other selling, the article which is the subject of their discussion. But from the standpoint of the practising sociologist, anthropologist or historian whose concern is with the words and gestures only to the extent that they do have a social meaning, what requires to be explained is an action or a set of actions as such. His need is to understand in the primary sense what the action is; to understand in the secondary sense why it has, or how it comes to have, been done; and to understand in the tertiary sense what it was like for the agent to do it.

The third, admittedly, is not relevant or necessary in all contexts. If I am puzzled by your putting out your hand, I may need to ask you both why you are putting out your hand (or better, what you are doing in putting out your hand), and on receiving the reply that you are, say,

---

* What (it might be asked) is the difference between these three? Methodologically, there is none. But they do differ markedly in the kinds of questions about human institutions and practices which they ask and the techniques which they use to answer them. It would be as eccentric to label Gibbon's *Decline and Fall of the Roman Empire* a work of sociology as to label Frazer's *The Golden Bough* a work of history or Marx's *Capital* a work of anthropology.

performing the action of signalling, to ask you to explain why you are signalling. But once you have told me that you are signalling because there is a vehicle behind you whose driver would not otherwise know that you are about to turn right (and have gone on, if required, to tell me that you are about to turn to your right because that is the way to where you want to go), I am unlikely to want to ask you 'what is it *like* to signal that you are about to turn right?'. All this means, however, is that signalling of this kind is so far conventional that the state of the mind of the agent performing it is, in the absence of special circumstances, unproblematic. In a context where signalling has to do with, say, cheating at cards I might well want to ask you what it was like. I would want to ask because cheating is, by definition, not a socially conventional action – if it were, it wouldn't be cheating – and I wished to understand what it was like knowingly to act in violation of the convention and, more broadly, how a social convention of this kind impinges on the sensibilities of someone who is nevertheless prepared to violate it.

'But for *that* sort of understanding, one goes to novels, not sociology.' Yes, one may. But not necessarily. The point is not that description of what an action, or a practice, or an institution, or even the mores of a whole society, is or was like is not part of the sociologist's task; it is that the novel, fictional though it is, can perfectly well perform the function of sociology. Novels *are* sociology to the extent that their authors make them so. This too is a topic to which I shall be reverting at greater length in Chapter 4. But I introduce it here because it may help to elucidate the difference between understanding in the primary, secondary and tertiary senses. Someone who says after reading Proust '*Now* I understand what is meant by the decadence of upper-class society in the Paris of the *belle époque*' is not suggesting that he needed to be taught the meaning of the term 'decadence', or that he regarded the behaviour in question as inexplicable. Nor, indeed, is he suggesting that he was incapable of evaluating it. He means that he needed to come to understand what it was like to belong to a period and milieu such as Proust describes, just as Collingwood needed to come to understand what it was like to belong to a period and milieu in which the Albert Memorial was the memorial to design, and the twentieth-century writer on ancient Rome needs to come to understand what it was like to belong to a society in which doctors, bankers and naval captains could all be slaves.

§8. If the concept of understanding is to be dissolved in this way into three, what are the implications for the concept of rationality? To many practitioners as well as philosophers of social science, rationality is central to any satisfactory account of human behaviour, and the attempt to provide one will succeed or fail to the degree that the behaviour under study can be brought within its scope. But once the distinction has been drawn between reportage, explanation, description and evaluation, it is evident that rationality has a useful part to play in the last three only. Explanatorily, its use is perhaps most familiar to social scientists in the models of consumer choice and entrepreneurial strategy formulated by theorists of market economies. Descriptively, a good example of its use is furnished by E. R. Dodds's *The Greeks and the Irrational* (1951), which, Dodds tells us, grew out of a young man's coming up to him in the British Museum and saying of the Parthenon sculptures that he was unmoved by them because they seemed to him 'so terribly *rational*, if you know what I mean'. Evaluatively, its use is integral to moral or political theories in which it is defined as a desirable goal in itself and social choices and policies are assessed as good or bad in accordance with their conformity to it. But at the level of primary understanding, behaviour is neither rational nor irrational as such. It might, perhaps, be objected that since man is by definition a rational animal the presupposition of rationality is or ought to be built in to the terms in which any or all human actions are conceptualized from the outset. But this suggestion makes no difference to the methodology of primary understanding. It is only as valuable as the explanations, descriptions or evaluations of particular reported items or sequences of presumptively rational behaviour to which it leads.

To say this is not to rule out the possibility that there are some people so constituted that their behaviour has to be reported as, so to speak, beyond the pale of reason entirely. Not merely is the visiting sociologist unable to make head or tail of the peculiar things which they say and do, but their fellow-members of their own society also categorize them as radically ununderstandable. But to report an item or sequence of behaviour as radically ununderstandable is to say that it is so inaccessible to any possible explanation, description or evaluation as to fall outside the definition of 'behaviour' altogether; and to report a belief as radically ununderstandable is to say that it consists of statements which assert no propositions, and therefore that it is not a belief at all. Perhaps, indeed, the difficulty arises only beyond the point at which explanation is not sociological but physiological – where, that is, 'irrationality' as a theoretical term applied to merely deviant or unorthodox behaviour gives way to the attribution of an innate or imposed incapacity to perform the mental functions which are within the repertory of all normal members of the species. It is not as if any real-life sociologist has ever, or ever will, come back from the field with a report of a whole society which is 'irrational' in the sense that its institutions and practices are utterly ununderstandable in the primary sense. This claim must stand open to challenge by anyone who wishes to advance an example which undermines it. But I have yet to find one. There is an often-cited fictional one of Wittgenstein's in which we are asked to suppose a society whose members appear to value piles of wood according to the height of the pile irrespective of the base area and therefore the total quantity, in the manner (the parallel is Wittgenstein's own) of the so-called 'Wise Men of Gotham'.* But the society does not in fact exist, any more than the inhabitants of Gotham (which does) ever in fact joined hands round a thorn bush to keep a cuckoo in it. And even if it did, there is nothing in Wittgenstein's account to suggest that the visiting sociologist could not report what its members were doing in terms understandable in the primary sense by us and acceptable in principle to them. Indeed, the example presupposes it, for the sociologist's puzzlement only arises from his observation that they really do value wood on this basis. Why they do, what it is like for them to do it, and whether it is good or bad that they should, all remain to be discussed; and much real-life ethnography consists in seeking explanations and descriptions of reported behaviour which is at first sight just as hard to explain and describe as this, whether the hoarding of aragonite stones by Yap Islanders, or the collecting of autographs of professional entertainers and athletes by European or American schoolchildren. Such examples are salutary not because they force a decision on the rationality or irrationality of the behaviour reported but because, on the contrary, the behaviour has to be correctly understood in the primary sense before it can be explained, described or evaluated with the help of 'rationality' or any other theoretical concept.

A different objection might be that irrationality may have to be invoked at the level of primary understanding where different things that 'they' are observed to say or do are palpably inconsistent with each other. What is the visiting sociologist to say of them if they assert p one minute and not-p the next, or if after choosing A in preference to B and B in preference to C they then choose C in preference to A? But to this, the answer is that at the level of primary understanding there is nothing more he *can* say once he has given his report that this is what they indeed say or do. He may well acknowledge that it raises both technical problems of interrogation and philosophical problems of verification: when his native informants insist that 'we worship a God who is at the same time

* L. Wittgenstein, *Remarks on the Foundations of Mathematics*[3] (1978), Pt.I, §§ 149–51.

three persons and one person', he may be equally at a loss to devise a supplementary question with which to cross-check the ostensible content of the belief or to formulate a criterion by which to decide whether it can possibly be assigned a truth-value. But he adds nothing to his report by saying that the assertion that anything can be both one and three of the same thing at the same time is irrational. If they are truthful in what they say they believe, he must accept that they have some reason of their own for believing it; and if they are not joking or dissembling in the mutually inconsistent choices which they appear to make, he must accept that something has motivated them to violate the principle of transitivity of preferences. At this level, the concept of rationality is dispensable if not positively misleading. For the purpose of primary understanding, all beliefs should be treated as rational, but no actions.

To test this dictum, think of what is (to you) the most irrational belief that you know of anyone's holding and the most rational action that you know of anyone's doing and ask yourself what difference it makes to your primary understanding to categorize them as such. To me, the most irrational belief which I know of anyone's holding is the belief that there exists an omnipotent and at the same time benevolent God. It is a belief which I have discussed from time to time with highly intelligent fellow-members of my own society who sincerely subscribe to it. The discussion always ends, after a predictable detour through the so-called Free Will Defence, in an impasse where I am left with nothing more to say than that for God to permit the avoidable suffering which he does isn't *my* idea of benevolence. But this doesn't lead me to want to deny that my interlocutors do believe that there exists an omnipotent and benevolent God. It only leads me to realize that I have not understood that belief in either the secondary or the tertiary sense.

When it comes to actions, the most rational action which I know of anyone's doing is buying cheap – the exemplary action, together with selling dear, of 'economic man'. But to say that someone is observed to choose a cheaper article in preference to a dearer equivalent is made no more convincing as a report of the preference observed by adding that it is by definition rational to do so. The choice has still to be explained and described, as does the choice of someone else who, however perverse it may seem, buys the dearer equivalent in preference to the cheaper.

In practice, rationality is often invoked for the purpose not of advancing understanding in any of its three senses but of soliciting the reader's agreement to an evaluation. A person who tells another that it is 'irrational' to spend so much money on clothes, or bear continuing grudges for trivial slights, or to want to be married in church despite being an unbeliever, or to smoke cigarettes although knowing that they cause cancer of the lungs, is not telling him what he is doing, or why, or what it is like, but that his actions are a case of what the speaker regards as culpable folly. Similarly, a sociologist who tells his readers that election to office is a more rational device than succession by inheritance, or that it is irrational to make homosexuality punishable by law, or that the economy would be more rationally organized on socialist than on capitalist principles (or vice versa), is saying that according to his values officeholders ought to be elected, homosexuality legalized and the economy organized along socialist (or capitalist) lines. He is, of course, perfectly free to do so and to support those judgements with explanatory and descriptive arguments in which the concept of rationality may also appear. But this is not to be confused with explaining or describing, and still less with reporting, it as such.

'But you must still admit, value-judgements aside, that you find some actions more irrational, and some beliefs less rational, than others.' Yes I do. But that tells you something about me, not them. It tells you that I lack a theory with which to explain and/or describe them. It does not even tell you how remote they are from those with which I, and by implication you, are most familiar. It is a reaction provoked no less by institutions and practices within my own society than by those of the ancient Romans or the modern Azande. To me, the Zande practice of consulting the poison-oracle before deciding where to plant the groundnuts involves beliefs no more irrational, and actions no less rational, than the practice in which I was brought up myself whereby an education in such peculiar skills as the translation of Shakespearean blank verse into Sophoclean iambics was held to be a sensible preparation for a career in British government or industry. But a remark of this kind is in itself no contribution to the understanding, in either the secondary or the tertiary sense, of either of them. It serves only as a reminder that any and all institutions and practices, once understood in the primary sense, have to be explained and described with the help of theories and concepts which may be just as elusive where the actions and beliefs are closely similar to the researcher's own as where they are so profoundly dissimilar that it may require months of fieldwork or documentary research before even primary understanding can be achieved.

The moral of these examples, therefore, is twofold. It is not just that the concepts of rationality and irrationality, however useful a role they may perform in explanatory, descriptive or evaluative theories, have no role at the level of primary understanding. It is also that primary understanding requires for that very reason a mixture of both sympathy and detachment. To report all actions as equally irrational is to refuse to take any institution or practice, however familiar, for granted: it is to have mastered what the French aptly call the *technique du dépaysement*. Conversely, to report all beliefs as equally rational is to refuse to judge them ethnocentrically: it is to take seriously the people who hold them. To approach them in this spirit does not commit the researcher to accepting or rejecting either the explanations or the descriptions (or, for that matter, the evaluations) of the institutions and practices which the people in question may offer themselves. But it does commit him, and is meant to commit him, to accepting their own primary understanding of what it is that they do.

ANALYSIS OF ACTIONS

§ 9. But are we really to say that agents always know what they are doing? Surely not. Even if action is defined for the practising sociologist's purposes in terms of the meaning which agents give to their behaviour, it can hardly be denied that people do a great many things which they do not know that they are doing and which someone else may be in a position to tell them that they are doing whether they know it or not. You may be twitching your leg, accumulating a fortune and breaking your mother's heart without being aware of any of them. But it would be perverse of you to claim that you weren't once it had been pointed out to you by an honest and qualified observer that you were. The standard response in the face of examples like these is to say that not all the things which a person does can be classed together: what an agent brings about, or achieves, or has happen to him, is not properly speaking an action of his. But this is not enough to dispose of the problem. The practising sociologist, having conceded that not everything which is done by the agents whom he has studied is an action, is entitled for his purposes to assume, and even to insist, that every action which *is* done by them is – by definition – done intentionally. But he is not entitled to assume that his agents can never be mistaken about what they are (intentionally) doing and he or some other observer be in a position to tell them so.

The simplest cases are those where someone has either misperceived his physical environment or misjudged his bodily movements. Thus you may honestly say 'I am steering for the lighthouse' but I may know that the lighthouse is a mirage: or you may think that you have put the third finger of your left hand on your right knee, but I may so successfully have confused you in the course of our game of 'Simon says' that you have unwittingly put the third finger of your right hand on your left knee. But the cases of interest to the sociologist are those where the agent is mistaken about the aspects of the context of his action which are themselves, in addition to his intention, constitutive of it: you cannot, for example, be said to be signing a cheque in the absence of financial institutions which enable the piece of paper on which you write your signature and your instructions for payment to fulfil the conditions which make it a cheque. The example is a trivial one of the kind frequently used to illustrate either or both the difference between a movement and an action and the social nature of conventional norms. But as with so many features of human behaviour, it is more important not to forget the truisms which attach to these differences and, more important still, the consequences which follow from them. If in the light of the examples which I have used I repeat the question 'Do agents always know what they are doing?', the answer which suggests itself is: yes, except where they are mistaken about something *about* the action which is constitutive of it.

The same answer cannot, on the other hand, be given about reasons for actions; or if so, then only because 'reason' is being used to stand for intention as opposed to motive. As I have remarked already, 'why did you put out your hand?' and 'what were you doing in putting out your hand?' may be two ways of asking the same question; and the same holds for 'what was your reason for putting out your hand?' and 'what was your intention in putting out your hand?'. Where they are, the second of each pair is preferable not because it is necessarily a more natural turn of phrase but because it helps to clarify the distinction between what someone does and why he does it or what it is like for him to do it which is fundamental to this discussion. 'Signalling' is an action, and to specify an action is in the ordinary way to account for the bodily movements which, together with both the agent's intention and such features of the social context as may be relevant, make the action what it is. Explanation proper – proper, that is, to the practice of sociology, anthropology and history – can then begin with the question 'why *signalling*?'; and here, although the agent may have one or more reasons which he will advance in reply, they do not have the privileged status of his intentions. The observer may, it is true, want sometimes to accord it in practice: when, in the example I have been using, you tell me that you are signalling because you are about to turn right and the road to the right is the one which leads to where you wish to go, I am unlikely to want to contradict you without special excuse. But it is not difficult to construct examples in which a special excuse is present. Such examples do not depend only on the ambiguity of the notion of wanting, although it is true that there are circumstances in which agents may plausibly be claimed to know what they are doing but not what they want. Nor do they depend on the no less problematic notion of self-deception, although I would expect most readers to agree that it can be correctly applied to some accounts of their reasons which other people give (although not, of course, to oneself, except in the past). Reasons lack privileged status because if offered as explanations of actions and the intentions constitutive of them they stand, either directly or indirectly, for motives; and about these, agents can be thoroughly mistaken (and often are).

Lest this claim should itself be misunderstood, I should perhaps make it clear that to deny privileged status to agents' accounts of their motives is not thereby to absolve the observer from taking account of them. This was the conclusion drawn by those early Behaviorists who, in their reaction against the reliance of an earlier generation of psychologists on the evidence of introspection, dismissed accounts of mental states of any kind as not only untestable but unnecessary, since behaviour is to be explained in terms of cause–effect relations between stimulus and response, and it is immaterial to such explanations what may or may not go on in between, whether physiologically or phenomenologically. But this was no less a mistake in the other direction than were the earlier presuppositions which the Behaviorists sought to overthrow. Not only do explanations in terms of stimulus and response require some account of what goes on inside the agent (or, as agents become in Behaviorist theory, the organism) if the different effects of similar stimuli on different agents are to be accounted for without circularity or regress. But why in any case throw relevant evidence away? There are countless occasions on which agents' accounts of their motives furnish the observer with information not otherwise available to him. How can you possibly discover, unless he tells you, that Professor X's secret reason, i.e. motive, for going to the international sociological conference in Paris next spring is his wish, and therefore his intention in the further sense of design or plan, to see his mistress? But he knows, because he knows that he would not otherwise go to the trouble of writing the paper on which his acceptance of the invitation to attend the conference depends. Or at any rate he thinks he knows. For it is possible that he might be mistaken, since if the counterfactual conditional is never tested he cannot be *certain* that he might not have decided to write the paper and go to the conference after all. This is not just a matter of his capacity for critical self-analysis. Agents can never be certain, and in many cases will be at a loss even to guess, which of several concomitant motives for a given action was the decisive one; and the observer of their behaviour may well guess better than they can, whether simply because he has known the particular person long and well or because he has a well-tested explanatory theory of behaviour, whether Behaviorist, Freudian or what you please, which entitles him to proffer an informed diagnosis such as the person would not be qualified to make for him. But the material for the diagnosis still includes the person's own assessment of his motive, which, whether it is right or wrong, is necessarily relevant to it; and unless the person chooses to divulge it, it remains directly accessible only to himself.

§ 10. This emphasis on motive may seem to carry the implication that identification of motives is essential to the explanation of human behaviour; and so, with certain necessary qualifications, it does. But it does not carry the implication that sociology is for that reason reducible to psychology. It implies only that it is dependent on it.

It is often said that the reducibility of one science to another is an empirical matter in any case, so that the question whether sociology is reducible to psychology is best left to be resolved in the course of future research. But reducibility is itself a problematic concept. The reducibility of sociology to psychology is a different matter from the reducibility of chemistry to physics; and reducibility of concepts is a different matter from reducibility of laws. To claim that sociology is strictly – or, as it is sometimes put, in a 'strong' or 'hard' rather than a 'weak' or 'soft' sense – reducible to psychology is to claim both that the sociological terms featuring in any validated empirical statement could be replaced without loss of meaning by psychological terms and that any such statement positing a non-fortuitous conjunction between one and another social fact could be shown in turn to be linked to a corresponding regularity at the psychological level. But this would not put sociologists, anthropologists and historians out of business. If through some as yet unimagined empirical discoveries all conjunctions of social facts were to turn out to be consistently linked to, and thus derivable from, some set of laws featuring only psychological terms, then the terms in which statements of social facts were couched would presumably come to be synonymous with those of the psychological laws. In that event, sociological concepts would survive only as less cumbrous than their psychological equivalents, rather as psychological terms themselves would, if psychology had in turn been reduced to physiology, survive only as less cumbrous than the detailed accounts of brain-states known to correspond to them; and explanations of social facts would all rest on a specification of the psychological states of designated individual persons. But however startling the discoveries which the sciences of man may hold in store, they can hardly do away with the need for sociological terms whose purpose is precisely to designate the relations between, as opposed to the properties of, individuals; talk of societies, institutions and practices will not become redundant even if sociological theories can somehow be shown to be merely special cases of psychological theories. There is no need for practising sociologists, anthropologists and historians to make up their minds in advance about the likelihood of its happening or the consequences for them if it does. It is not because of its implications for arguments about reducibility* that they have to concern themselves from the outset with the relation of attributions of motive to the explanation of social facts.

Their necessary concern with motives follows simply from the truism that action, thought and feeling can be attributed only to individuals and not to the collectivities constituted by them. The explanation, or even just the report, of a social event, process or state of affairs may and probably will have reference to many things other than the self-conscious behaviour of designated persons. But it must include such a reference, even if only implicitly, if it is to belong to sociology at all, and there will necessarily be a relation of extensional equivalence between the propositions asserted in the explanation or report and the set of propositions, including those attributing self-conscious behaviour to the relevant persons, which must be true if the report is to be accurate and its explanation valid. No sociological proposition can be asserted which does not involve a claim that (among other things) certain individual human actions took place; and unless these are supposed to have been unmotivated altogether, the claim that the actions were performed presupposes the operation of motives of some kind. This does not involve any further claim as to whether, or how, attributions of motive furnish sociological explanations with a condition of success. Explanation in sociology, as elsewhere, is a function of the context in which the question 'why?' is asked, and there are – as we shall later see – any number of successful explanations of events, processes and states of affairs which say nothing about motives whatever. But they would nonetheless collapse if their assumptions, however deeply implicit, about motive were to be shown *not* to hold.

So stated, the basis of the sociologist's concern with individual psychological states is scarcely controversial. But it is by reference to such states, even where the reference is only implicit, that not only explanations but

---

* On which see e.g. D. H. Mellor, 'The Reduction of Society', *Philosophy* LV (1982), and the references there cited.

reports of social events, processes or states of affairs are typically vindicated when challenged. To the rival observer who denies that a social fact occurred as it is claimed to have, the researcher will naturally reply by setting out his evidence; and this evidence will consist of observations or records of people having thought, felt, done and said things in a designated context. His claim that an outlying province was in a state of rebellion, or religious observance was on the decline, or a system of kinship was matrilineal, or a governing party was voted out of office, rests on his ability to demonstrate that individual provincials were taking up arms, that the number of churchgoers decreased over a given period, that all members of a kinship system traced their descent through females only, and that individual electors cast their votes in some ascertained proportion in favour of the opposition. These individual actions cannot, of course, be abstracted from the social context which gives them their meaning. But once again, a claim about the social context can be vindicated only by the researcher's pointing to the evidence for other concomitant – or, more usually, antecedent – individual actions. In so doing, he need in no way be seeking to reduce sociological terms to psychological: there is no inbuilt suggestion of an intensional equivalence between the initial proposition which the rival observer has challenged and the accounts of individual behaviour which are invoked in its defence. His invocation of them is simply a practical consequence of the truism that thought, feeling and action are attributes of individual agents only.

There is, however, one further consequence which becomes apparent when not merely his report but his explanation is challenged. The challenge may, as I have implied already, be directed to a necessary or sufficient condition claimed to hold which is not sociological at all. If, for example, the researcher maintains that a strike wave has been caused by a heat wave – or, as a correspondent to *The Times* actually put it in August of 1911,* to 'prolonged and unremitting solar bombardment' – then his evidence that the sufficient condition held will be drawn from meteorological and not sociological records. But even here, where the presumptive cause is a physical one, the explanation falls down if it cannot withstand the objection that there is no adequate reason to believe that the occurrence of the presumptive cause could actually have motivated individual agents so to act that the report that there was an outbreak of strikes can be shown to be correct. At this point, the appeal to motives is inescapable. It is in this sense that psychology of some kind or other

* See K. J. G. C. Knowles, *Strikes* (1952), p. 157.

is presupposed even by a sociology which deals only in collectivities and institutions and the relations between them. Again, there is no necessary suggestion of reduction, but only of dependence. Sociology, from this point of view, can best be regarded as psychology plus social history, just as biology can be regarded as chemistry plus natural history.* The analogy is not to be pressed too closely, and it raises questions about the role of laws in sociological as opposed to biological explanation to which I shall have to return in Chapter 3. But it helps to bring out the methodological point that sociology, however many empirical generalizations it may be able to validate which link the occurrence of one social fact with another, depends for the answer to the question why these generalizations hold on an account both of the evolution of social institutions on the one hand and of the dispositions and potentialities of individual agents on the other. Sociology cannot produce laws except in so generous a sense of 'law' as to admit any *ceteris paribus*, non-fortuitous conjunction as lawlike. But it can and does consume them. It is true that psychologists do not, at least for the present, have sufficient knowledge of the human mind to be able to say in any strict sense what motives are. But this does not alter the degree of sociologists' dependence on presumptive truths about them.

§ 11. Enough has, I hope, been said by now to suggest in outline what I take to be the nature of the sociologist's (or anthropologist's or historian's) task. But an example may bring out more clearly the relation between the four distinguishable aspects of it which are dealt with separately and at greater length in the chapters which follow.

Consider further the example of a wave of strikes. 'Strike' is already a term specific to societies in which labour is formally free, and it presupposes that within such societies concerted action is possible among groups of workers who have contracted to sell their labour to an employer, whether private or public, on specified terms, and who now agree among themselves to withdraw that labour. This, we could say, is what 'strike' means. For the sociologist to apply it, therefore, in reporting a particular sequence of behaviour is to claim that he is right so to understand that behaviour in the primary sense: if he has failed to realize that the labour force is not formally free or that the workers concerned were not in fact acting in concert, then he cannot be said to have discovered what it is that they were doing, however accurately he has recorded their words and movements. But if he is right to report them as 'striking', then he can go on to try to answer the question why the wave

* J. J. C. Smart, *Philosophy and Scientific Realism* (1963), Ch. 3 ('Physics and Biology').

of strikes should have come about. He may have all sorts of possible answers in his mind, including the meteorological. But for them to count even as would-be explanations, two things must hold. First, they must specify what the difference would have been if the antecedent condition singled out in the context of the attempted explanation had not in fact obtained; second, they must be based on a presumptive theoretical grounding for a *ceteris paribus* causal generalization guaranteeing that the condition singled out can be counted on to produce this observed effect. In the case of the sociologist who seeks to explain an outbreak of strikes, the condition singled out and the presumptive theory underlying it may be any one of a very wide variety, depending on what it is about the outbreak which is puzzling him. Is it that it covers so many industries, or regions? Is it that the strikes are so frequent, or so protracted, or both? Is it that they appear to relate so little to wages, or so much? Is it that they occur when times are good (and workers presumably contented)? Or that they occur when times are bad (and workers presumably less well able to afford to go without the wages they would have earned)? And so on. The list could be extended almost indefinitely. Indeed, it may even be inapposite to suggest that it depends on what the researcher is puzzled by, for he may not, as it happens, feel puzzled in the least but be seeking merely to show his readers that what he takes to be the conventional explanation (as it might be, 'political agitators') is untenable when the evidence is more closely examined. But in each case, the explanation actually proffered will conform to a common logical pattern and will be vulnerable in principle to objections of a common kind. Whatever antecedent conditions it singles out, it will collapse at once if it can be shown to rest on a misunderstanding (in the primary sense) of what it sets out to explain; or if the counterfactual conditional which it implies can be shown to be false; or if one or more of the presumptive generalizations (including those about individual motives) on which it rests can be shown not to be grounded in some sort of testable and at least provisionally unfalsified theory.

Suppose, however, that it passes all these tests as well as it is reasonable ever to expect. Suppose that the sociologist's report of the events which constitute the wave of strikes is convincingly supported by the evidence; that the different accounts by workers and employers are sufficiently in accord; that the pattern of variation in strike activity is such as to furnish the controlled comparisons which justify the attribution of causal importance to the antecedent conditions singled out; that the implied counterfactual is well supported by evidence of correlation between strike activity and plant size, or unionization, or social isolation, or technological change, or whatever it may be, which can be drawn from other places and times; and that the motives of the workers who are claimed to have gone on strike because, and only because, the stipulated conditions obtained are unproblematic. Is that all that we should expect the researcher to say to his readers? Surely not; or not unless he has also, in the course of it, managed to convey some sense of understanding in the tertiary sense – some understanding, that is to say, of what it was *like* for those who *were* so motivated as to go on strike under the reported conditions to come to decide to do so. What did they think they were ('really') doing? That they thought they were deciding to withdraw their labour is enough to furnish the explanandum from which the researcher has begun. But it is not enough to convey to the reader an adequate sense of *their* sense of the context within which their actions took place and of the nature of the institutions and practices of the society, region, industry, community and plant as experienced by them. What were their ideas of their relations with their workmates, their supervisors and their union officials? What was, to them, the nature of the sense of grievance or discontent to which they were giving expression? These questions are not answered by even the most rigorous degree of secondary understanding except to the extent that the topics which they raise feature among the counterfactual conditionals and presumptive generalizations on which the validated explanation depends; and even then, they will not so feature in a way which answers them completely. Yet the sociologist who is unable to answer may fairly be told that he writes of things which he knows little or nothing about – 'knows', that is, in the sense that Evans-Pritchard knows about the Azande but you and I do not, or that Bloch knows about the 'sickening reality' of defeat in war but you (or at any rate I) do not, or that in the words of the Book of Exodus 'Ye know the soul of a stranger, seeing ye were strangers in the land of Egypt', or that a writer born and brought up in the Indian community of Trinidad can say of himself on visiting India proper 'I know, for instance, the beauty of sacrifice, so important to the Aryans.'*

Nor is this all. For the sociologist, even if he is concerned only with the most general and impersonal aspects of industrial relations, must be aware that the concerted withdrawal of labour in a market society raises issues of justification and legitimacy. The strikes may or may not be thought by the employers affected to be a breach of contract in the sense defined by the law. But even where questions of legality are irrelevant –

---

* V. S. Naipaul, *India: a Wounded Civilization* (1977), p. 4.

where, say, the wave of strikes is bound up with the expiry and renegotia-
tion of periodic agreements between employers and employees – those
involved will have views about the seriousness of the grievances cited,
the fairness of the conditions under which collective bargaining takes
place and consequently the justifiability (or not) of a concerted withdrawal of labour. These feelings too may feature in the explanation of
the strikes if it is they which differentiate this particular state of affairs
from those where, although conditions were otherwise similar, the wave
of strikes did not in fact occur. But the researcher cannot but ask himself
in addition whether the behaviour he has explained and described *is*
justified. He will, if his fieldwork and/or documentary research has been
properly done, have established the grounds on which the strikers held
that their behaviour was justified and the grounds on which their employers held that it was not. He can hardly help, therefore, having a view
of some kind, however tentative, about which side was or wasn't acting
in such a way as to bring about a better or worse outcome. He may, of
course, not choose to say anything about it, just as he may choose only
to explain and not to describe, or vice versa. But he cannot deny that the
question is both meaningful and relevant. No sociologist, even the most
successfully *dépaysé*, can plausibly claim that he has no answer whatever
if he is asked whose side he would have taken, and why, if he had himself
been involved as a participant in such a way that his own decision would
have influenced the course of events.

It might be said that in choosing this particular example, I have chosen
a field of social behaviour where contentious evaluative issues are salient.
But the same distinctions and arguments apply, and can easily be shown
to apply, over the whole field of social theory. Even in the study of so
relatively apolitical a topic as, say, the family, reportage, explanation,
description and evaluation lead into each other in much the same way.
It is possible, no doubt, to concern oneself only with one and not another.
Books have, at one extreme, been written with the purpose of using the
relevant branch of finite mathematics to generate an exhaustive typology
of kinship systems, just as they have been written at the other extreme
with the purpose of denouncing the institution of the family for its alleged
inhibition of human freedom.* But to give an account of any chosen
system of kinship and family relations is, at the minimum, to report it
under a designation which raises the explanatory question why it is of
this type and not another; this raises in turn the descriptive question what

* Contrast Harrison White, *An Anatomy of Kinship* (1963), with D. G. Cooper, *The
Death of the Family* (1971).

a system of this type is like, either in particular or in general, for those who are brought up within its rules; and this raises in turn the evaluative question about the merits or demerits, the success or failure, of it or others like it in bringing about what the researcher holds to be good or bad for the society concerned.

§ 12. Questions of all four kinds are, accordingly, ever-present in social theory, whichever it may be that the individual sociologist, anthropologist or historian chooses to take up in any particular case. Yet at the same time, however easily they may merge into one another in the course of an enquiry which does not deliberately restrict itself to only one or two of them, they remain questions altogether different in kind. To see this still more clearly, the readiest way is to contrast the nature of the discretion which the researcher retains in the course of answering them. That he does retain discretion even in the kind of enquiry which most closely conforms to the Positivist model of science does not, I assume, need to be further argued. It is not only that even the simplest report of an event, process or state of affairs cannot be expressed in a language free of presuppositions. It is also that it may be located at widely different points along the axes of time, space (both geographical and social) and generality. It may be dated relative to days, years or epochs; it may be placed relative to primary groups, sub-cultures, nation-states or even human society as a whole; it may be specified relative to particular detail, intermediate generalization or the highest level of abstraction. Even before the process of explanation is underway, therefore, any account which is put before the reader is permeated with the consequences of the exercise of a prior discretion. Yet by the very fact of putting forward an explanation of his reported observations at all, the researcher has imposed on himself a twofold constraint. He is constrained by the evidence both in the sense that he has assumed a relation of some kind between the observation-statement he has put forward and the state of the world, and in the sense that he must accept that his explanation stands or falls with the counterfactuals entailed by it.

He is, to be sure, constrained by the evidence also in whatever description he may offer of what the reported sequence of events or state of affairs was like for those involved in it; but in a different way. He must not include in his description any report which can be shown *not* to be accurate. But the choice of reports to include, and of terms in which to express them for this purpose, is still an open one. Additional criteria of selection and emphasis have to be brought to bear which are not given by the evidence, even when every report which might conceivably be relevant is to hand. Nor can the choice be made by taking refuge in the privilege to be accorded to agents' own accounts of what they think and feel, for the sociologist cannot simply reproduce these without commentary. If he holds, as he may, that they do constitute the best description by which the reader can be given a sense of 'what it was like', he has still to argue it. It is not even enough that his own commentary on their description should be demonstrably compatible with it, for although it must indeed be so – in a sense to be explored more fully in due course – this still leaves him a discretion which is literally infinite: there is an infinity of reports which he could put forward about the event, process or state of affairs which he is describing which neither assert anything which can be shown to be inaccurate nor phrase anything in such a way that the agents themselves would not be willing to accept it. Explanations, it could loosely be said, are discretionary before the evidence is in, but descriptions are still discretionary after.

Evaluations, on the other hand, remain discretionary forever; or at least, they remain discretionary to all but those who subscribe to a cognitivist theory of ethics according to which it is itself a matter of fact whether individual actions or social institutions or practices are good or bad.* Yet at the same time, even the sociologist who does not subscribe to a cognitivist ethics will accept that any particular value-judgement which he makes may require to be modified by what his empirical investigations may disclose. Not, of course, that his basic values themselves will require to be modified: the Whig who judges all social institutions as good or bad according to whether they enlarge or diminish individual liberty, or the Marxist who judges them according to whether they augment or reduce the revolutionary potential of the working class, can continue to apply his chosen criteria whatever may or may not take place in the future or be discovered to have taken place in the past. But these judgements are not made in a vacuum. They attach to the motives, or the consequences, or both, of individual actions, and whatever the values to which they may appeal, it is always possible that some circumstance might come to light which would show that the motive, or the consequence, of the action was not what it had seemed and the judgement could as a result no longer be applied to it. Evaluation, therefore, remains discretionary, but in conception rather than application. The researcher

* 'Cognitivism', like 'Idealism', has more than one connotation in philosophical discussion: what is meant by its use here is that sociologists are bound to accept that evaluation is discretionary unless they are able to refute the assertion that 'there are no objective values' in the sense expounded by J. L. Mackie, *Ethics: Inventing Right and Wrong* (1977) – which they will certainly not be able to do on sociological grounds alone.

who allows his personal values to intrude into the account which he puts before his readers must accept that he may very well find himself in a position where he cannot persist in that part of his account without incoherence. But nothing in what he discovers need ever force him to conclude that the evaluative theory to which he subscribes is on that account mistaken. In both explanation and description, the evidence, although it can neither vindicate nor impose any single authoritative account, can still put some theories, at any rate, out of court; in evaluation, it can do so only to the extent that the researcher lets them – to the extent, that is, that he chooses to put his values at risk by advancing a concrete judgement which a reassessment of the evidence might overturn.

It takes little familiarity with the writings of sociologists, anthropologists and historians to be aware how often and how intricately the four are intertwined. In any full-length account of a complex event, process or state of affairs, the writer's purpose is likely to encompass reportage, explanation, description and evaluation alike. He is likely, that is, to want not only to persuade the reader that the events, processes or states of affairs which he has chosen to report came about as he reports them and for the reasons or causes which he has put forward, but at the same time to convey to the reader his idea of what it was like for the participants and to bring the reader round to his view of them as good or bad. But however intricately the four are connected in his account, it will always be possible in principle for the reader to disentangle them. In practice, the disentanglement is often made more difficult than it need be by the language and style in which the work is couched. But the distinction between them is no less fundamental to the methodology of social theory simply because a particular author obscures it, whether deliberately or not.

§ 13. I have said already that the distinction is a matter of context, not of syntax; and this, indeed, is one reason why it is harder to apply in practice than the discussion of it in principle might lead one to expect. But a very simple example will show just how radical a difference the context may make. Suppose that I say of someone's behaviour that it was 'psychotic'. I am going beyond a (mere) report of what the person said or did. But am I giving an explanation, a description or an evaluation? It can quite well be any of them. I may mean that the behaviour was caused by a clinical condition documented under the heading 'Psychosis' in the dictionary of psychological medicine which I have chosen to consult. Or I may mean that although I am well aware that the agent concerned is not clinically psychotic, the behaviour strikes me and the agent likewise as remarkably *like* that of a psychotic. Or I may mean that the behaviour evinced so callous a disregard for the feelings of other people that it was as though only a clinical condition could account for it, but since it is clear that the person was not in such a condition the behaviour is to be condemned as bad. The example may seem a trivial one. But there are many standard terms in the vocabulary of sociology which can, and do, oscillate in this way according to their context and the purpose of the researcher who uses them. 'Democratic', 'alienated', 'prejudiced', 'deviant', 'bourgeois', 'tribal', 'charismatic', 'imperialist' and any number of others can be used equally readily to explain, to describe and to evaluate, and for the reader to tell which he may have to consider not simply the phrase or sentence in which they appear but the whole passage and even, sometimes, the whole work. It is hardly surprising, therefore, that the distinction has not been so clearly perceived or so closely discussed within the literature of social theory as my argument suggests that it should.

Notice also that analysis of the distinction calls for more than a simple invocation of the conventional distinction between facts and values. Evaluation, naturally enough, belongs on the side of values; and reportage and explanation belong on the side of facts, provided that 'facts' are recognized to be defined as such by presuppositions which the observer has brought to them. But description belongs neither with the one nor with the other. The test of a good description is not whether it 'fits the facts', for the researcher's problem in framing it lies in choosing between different reports all of which are in accord with his own or some other trusted observer's observations and none of which would be rejected as inaccurate by those whose behaviour is being described. But nor is his choice between them a matter of his personal values, contingently relevant as they may be. Describing is a form of utterance marked off equally, on the one hand, from saying what happened and why and, on the other, from making a claim that it was either a good thing or a bad one.

The criteria by which a description is to be tested are equally distinctive. Their distinctiveness may be masked by the use of terms which are colloquially applied with the same readiness to explanation: thus, it may seem as natural to speak of a description as of an explanation as, say, valid or well founded or persuasive or convincing. But the last two of these are perlocutionary terms, not illocutionary ones; and the first two carry the implication that descriptions can be either true or false, which strictly they cannot. The descriptions given by sociologists, anthropologists or historians, although they may consist of statements of fact, are not to be construed as statements of fact themselves: they must not misreport, misidentify or misname anything, but that is all. Once these conditions are satisfied, the criteria which apply to them are of a different kind. If they fail, it is because they can be shown to be, for example, over-simplified or ahistorical or exaggerated or ethnocentric. None of these, with the possible exception of 'exaggerated', has a direct bearing on truth-value, and even 'exaggerated' is more likely to have reference to failings of selection and emphasis than to lack of correspondence between observation and report. Nor, equally, are any of these terms tied logically to an evaluation of whatever actions are being described; although the two may be connected in practice – exaggeration, for example, may well be deployed for the purpose of encouraging the reader to approval and praise or disapproval and blame – the conclusion would be modified neither in kind nor in degree by a modification or even a reversal of the author's values. Yet these terms, and the criteria to which they appeal, are directly relevant to passage after passage in the writings of socio-logists, anthropologists and historians even in cases where the reader may not only share the author's values but also agree with the author's explanation of why the actions reported and described occurred.

That they are not relevant in this way to the writings of natural scientists goes, I take it, without saying. No doubt there is a sense in which the natural scientist too may be concerned to say what states of affairs or sequences of events are or were like and to describe them from one rather than another point of view. But this has nothing to do with a standard of good or bad description which appeals, whether directly or indirectly, to what the subjects of the description might have to say about it themselves. It is not that this difference by itself need amount to very much; as always, it is more a question of what follows from it. Not even the most radical Behaviorist will deny that human beings do, but natural objects do not, have thoughts and feelings. What he will say is that no methodological conclusion is to be drawn from it except that this gives sociologists an advantage over their colleagues in the physical and even the biological sciences who cannot, for both better and worse, submit the objects of their studies to verbal questionnaires. Against this, however, the sociologist may fairly reply that the advantage is not unmixed, for it exposes him (as I remarked already in Section 5) to the risk of mistakes of a kind which his natural-scientific colleagues will never have the occasion to make. Worse still, it imposes an additional task upon him whose difficulty far outweighs such advantage as he may gain from being able to ask his subjects, who all too often will mislead him, and perhaps themselves, about what they are doing. His colleagues (including his Behaviorist colleagues in his own university department) may still rejoin that he is making too much of it. But the answer, in the present context, is that the methodological problems of description in sociology turn out to require a chapter to themselves as long and in some ways more difficult to write than the chapter on explanation.

'But what you say adds nothing to what has been said many times by methodologists of the Phenomenological, Hermeneutic or *Verstehende* schools.' No. It adds a great deal. I must emphasize as strongly as I can from the outset that although the authors commonly classified under these labels have indeed said many interesting things about the way in which meaning is given to action and the way in which sociologists can – or beyond a certain point, cannot – discover or capture or intuit or perceive or penetrate or reconstruct that meaning, none to my knowledge has drawn the inferences which I am concerned to argue here. None has discussed the problem of description in the way that I have formulated it and all have treated the problem of understanding in a way which ignores, if it does not actually confuse, the distinction between reportage, description, explanation and evaluation which I am concerned to eluci- date. The indisputable fact that human actions have meaning to their agents means neither that they have to be 'understood' instead of ex- plained nor that their explanation is rendered impossible. True, it follows from the fact that meanings are constitutive of human actions that they must be correctly understood in the primary sense if a valid explanation, or understanding in the secondary sense, is thereafter to be arrived at. An incontrovertibly useful contribution of sociologists of the so-called 'ethnomethodological' school* has been to point out how difficult primary understanding can be even – or perhaps all the more – within an observer's own period and milieu, and how hazardous it may therefore be to take the data of speeches, interviews and suchlike at face value. But it does not follow that explanation of human actions must follow different methodological rules, or appeal to different criteria of validity, from explanation of everything else.

It is this view that the distinctive problems of the social sciences are problems of description and not of explanation which accounts for the order of Chapters 3 to 5. Where 'describe' is used in a looser or less specialized sense than here, it may seem natural to think of the sociologist as first describing Roman slavery, the Fall of France, a wave of strikes or Zande poison-oracles, and then going on to explain and/or evaluate

---

*See e.g. Harold Garfinkel, *Studies in Ethnomethodology* (1967), or Jack D. Douglas, ed., *Understanding Everyday Life* (1971).

them. But much the less ambiguous term for the first operation, or stage, on which the others depend is reportage (including, where appropriate, narration). This is the stage at which the facts are stated, the observations listed or the story told. It cannot be the first stage of all, either in logic or in practice, once it is acknowledged that 'facts' can never be defined independently of presuppositions imposed on their observations by even the most clear-eyed and least prejudiced observers. But for the purpose of methodological analysis of the sociologist's task, that task may be taken to begin with the reportage or narration of the event, process or state of affairs for which there has then to be offered an explanation and/or a description and/or an evaluation which can secure the assent of rival observers of any and all theoretical schools. In some instances, it may actually go no further than reportage alone. The researcher whose curiosity is sufficiently limited, or terms of reference sufficiently circum-scribed, may wish to go no further than to report that Kish begat Saul who begat Jonathan; or that in 1956–57 86% of salaried male employees in the private sector of British industry were members of an occupational pension scheme; or that heroic *chansons* in the vernacular were in circula-tion in Northern France from the middle of the eleventh century. The distinctions sometimes drawn between social research and (mere) 'fact-finding', or between sociology and (mere) 'sociography', or between anthropology and (mere) 'ethnography', or between history and (mere) 'chronicle', all make the same point. But I shall assume from now onwards that researchers' goals are more ambitious than this. I shall assume that the practising sociologist, anthropologist or historian who has reported the occurrence of an event, process or state of affairs will then go on to offer an explanation of why it came to occur as it did, to describe what it was like for those involved in it and to evaluate it at least to the minimal extent for which I shall be arguing in Chapter 5. I take them in this order not because researchers necessarily follow it, let alone because no other order is possible. It is entirely for methodological convenience that I assume that researchers explain before they go on to describe, and describe before they go on to evaluate.

TWO KINDS OF VALUE-JUDGEMENT

§ 14. At this point, there may have occurred to some readers an objection along the following lines: I said in Section 2 that I reject the claim that the social sciences are not and cannot be value-free; yet this whole discussion of the nature of the sociologist's task is permeated with blatantly evaluative terms. I have talked not merely of logical consistency and empirical correspondence between reportage and fact, both of which already invoke a standard of value, but also of misunderstanding, exaggeration, ahistoricity and suchlike, and even of 'good' descriptions as contrasted with 'bad'. Does not, therefore, the practice of sociology as here defined involve the application not of some ultimately 'objective' scientific procedure but, on the contrary, of choices made by reference to the values which the sociologist brings to it?

The claim that judgements of logical and/or scientific validity are value-judgements is familiar alike from nineteenth-century German debates about scientific method and twentieth-century debates within the Anglo-Saxon tradition of analytical philosophy; and unless 'value' is so defined as to rule it out, the claim is impossible to deny. But it does not constitute an argument against the doctrine of value-neutrality *within* the social sciences, for this would, as I remarked in Section 3, require a demonstration that a sociological proposition accepted as true is true only as a function of some other proposition involving the moral, political or aesthetic values by which human behaviour is judged good or bad. It might still be argued – and sometimes is – that the criteria of accuracy and validity as applied in the sciences of nature cannot be applied at all in the sciences of man. But this is an argument of another kind, which I have rejected already on other grounds. Where claims of accuracy and validity *are* made, whether in the natural or the social sciences, they can be overturned only by reference to criteria which are internal to the practice of science as such. It is not an argument against accepting a scientific explanation as valid to say that accepting it as valid implies a commitment to the value of validity. There is admittedly a difference between the purported statements of fact put before their readers by natural and by social scientists to the extent that the latter may – and quite often do – denote the events, processes or states of affairs which they are concerned to report in terms which betray the intrusion of moral, political or aesthetic values. But their appeal to scientific accuracy is not undermined thereby. A demographer of right-wing (or perhaps Trotskyist) sympathies may want to say that the population of the Stalinist dictatorship exceeded 200 million by 1940 where his colleague of left-wing sympathies may want to speak of it as the population of the Soviet people's democracy. But neither of them is guilty of bad demography unless it turns out that the population of the country to which both are referring in their chosen terms was in fact as little as, or less than, 199,999,999.

The criteria by which descriptions are to be judged do, as I have been at pains to insist, raise issues which are peculiar to the social sciences.

But they too are internal to the practice of those sciences, just as are the criteria of reportage and explanation which are common to the natural and the social sciences alike. A description of a social institution which omits a feature of its workings which would be held by its members to be essential to the tertiary understanding of what it is like is, for that reason, a bad description. But this is no more a moral or political judgement about the goodness or badness of the institution as an institution than is a judgement that a purported statement of fact is true or false. It is always possible that there remains a contingent connection between the badness of bad sociology and the sociologist's own moral, political and aesthetic values; if he misreports the population of the Soviet Union for the purpose of mounting a polemic against the birth-control policies of its government, or misexplains its treatment of the Kulaks for the purpose of exonerating Stalin from responsibility, or misdescribes the ideology of Leninism for the purpose of presenting it in a more or less favourable light, then it is true to say that his sociology is bad because of the influence of his values. But this is a matter of psychology, not logic; and it happens precisely through the intrusion of non-sociological values which have been permitted to override the internal values of sociology. Such examples, far from undermining the doctrine of value-neutrality within sociology, serve only to illustrate it.

This autonomy of standards does, however, work both ways. There is no inconsistency if a person who, as a sociologist, is scrupulous in telling the truth, the whole truth and nothing but the truth is equally scrupulous about refraining from doing so either publicly as a citizen or privately as a spouse, parent, colleague or friend. Here again, there are always contingent connections. The sociologist who believes that certain forms of social organization are more conducive than others to the practice of good sociology and the advancement of science generally may on that account work, as a citizen, for the promotion, maintenance and diffusion of those forms. But he may equally well not. Even if he believes, as some do, that an 'open' society is best for the advancement of science, he is not debarred, simply because he is himself a scientist, from opposing or even subverting his own society in the pursuit of some other political aim. The values of science are not political values unless scientists make them so. A sociologist who publishes findings which convincingly support the hypothesis that inherited differences in measured intelligence vary significantly according to sex and/or race may – depending on *your* political values – be a bad citizen although a good scientist, just as may have been, in your eyes, the physicists who made the atomic bomb.

Conversely, it is a mistake to suppose that a piece of research is ever necessarily the worse simply because of its obvious contingent connection with the researcher's extra-scientific values. Gibbon, for example, was demonstrably wrong about the role of the early Christians in the decline and fall of the Roman Empire, and no reader of *The Decline and Fall* can fail to be aware of the extent to which his fine eighteenth-century disdain for their obscurantism and bigotry underlay and influenced his point of view. But he might have turned out to be right. His values explain (psychologically) the kind of explanation which he sought to uphold; but they have no bearing (logically) on the reasons for which that explanation has not proved possible to sustain when more adequately tested than he was either willing or able to test it. Similarly, no reader of *Capital* can fail to be aware of the degree of Marx's detestation of what he saw as the evils of nineteenth-century capitalism. But that is not what makes him either right or wrong about its workings and consequences. It is often difficult for the reader of works such as these not to be influenced likewise by either agreement with, or dissent from, the author's extra-scientific values. Catholic readers of Gibbon are almost bound to be more sceptical of Gibbon's conclusions than confirmed anti-clericals like himself. Defenders of capitalism are almost bound to be more sceptical of prognostications about its internal contradictions and impending overthrow than committed socialists who share Marx's detestation of it to the full. But it is no more the case in the sciences of man than of nature that a proposition is more likely to be either true or false because more or less people hope more or less passionately that it is. Indeed, there are well-known cases in the history of social science where a discovery has been made only because the investigator who made it was persuaded in advance that he would find the opposite of what he then did. Charles Booth was prompted to make the studies of poverty in late Victorian London for which he is remembered by the conviction that the extent of poverty was being exaggerated by critics from the Left;* but he then found that its extent was, in fact, greater even than many of the Left had supposed. It is itself a contingent question whether those findings in the sciences of man which have best withstood refutation have been those which were more or less directly inspired by a conscious prejudice on the researcher's part.

The interaction between academic and political values is, admittedly, a great deal more complex than is brought out by a passing reference to Gibbon, Marx or Charles Booth. It is, for example, quite possible for a body of research which has been consciously inspired by a set of pre-

* See T. S. and M. B. Simey, *Charles Booth: Social Scientist* (1960), Ch. 3.

conceived political values to be resisted even by critics whose political values are ostensibly the same. But this sort of case is as much an illustration of the logical gap between political value-judgements and scientific hypotheses as it is of the psychological connection between political preconceptions and the way in which scientific hypotheses are received. Let me take as an example a topic to which I shall return in Volume III. There is a substantial body of research which demonstrates that there has been a widespread and consistent difference between 'working-class' and 'middle-class' families in twentieth-century Britain in modes of behaviour, outlook and speech. Much of this research has been carried out by sociologists whose sympathies are overtly of the Left, and implicit both in the design of the research and the presentation of the results there has been an evaluation to the effect that the social system which generates these differences discriminates in favour of middle-class families at the expense of their working-class counterparts. This evaluation, moreover, has been widely held to be directly supported by the research results. For if the way in which the social system works serves to exclude the children of working-class families from education, both formal and informal, of the kind most advantageous in the competitive and differentiated society in which they live, then not only are they not to be reproached by critics who share the middle-class values for being as they are but, on the contrary, it is the duty of middle-class critics to work for the ending of the discrimination which makes them so. But this view itself has been subjected to vigorous criticism. Does it not (it has been asked) rest on an unquestioned presupposition that those brought up in the working class are so far incapable of choosing their own life-style and bettering their own condition that only middle-class reformers can enable them to do so? And is not this presupposition at the same time both ignorant and patronizing? Why should it be supposed that working-class people ought to want to share the standards of the middle class? Oughtn't those who wish to change the existing system to be seeking to encourage and propagate the outlook and values of the working class rather than to instil into working-class families the outlook and values of their middle-class commentators? And oughtn't research on these topics to be concerned, therefore, not with the effect of a system dominated by middle-class values on a presumptively passive and inadequate working class but with the innate capacity of the working class for the conscious advancement of its own cause?

Here, it might plausibly be said, there is an inextricable fusion of fact and value not merely in the psychology of researchers and their critics but in the practice of the research itself; and this example has, indeed, been used on occasion in support of arguments directed against the doctrine of value-neutrality. But here too, whether in the practice of research or in the criticism of it, the interaction of scientific and political values can be shown to be contingent only. Let me assume, for methodology's sake, that the reported differences between working-class and middle-class families are sufficiently well documented to be acceptable as matters of fact, whatever difficulties may remain about the categorization of families under these two heads and the admitted frequency of borderline cases. If we then go on to ask for an explanation of these differences, it is undoubtedly the case that the question may, depending on how it is framed, lead to the pursuit of a number of different lines of research; and it is undoubtedly the case also that the choice which different sociologists make is conditioned by values which they hold over and above the values internal to the practice of science. But the sociologist who chooses to ask the question 'why do working-class families fail to follow the habits, and accept the standards, which lead to personal advancement as defined in middle-class terms?' can be shown to be doing bad sociology only if in the course of his answer to it there is implied a claim that working-class families do or don't, can or can't, or under certain conditions would or wouldn't behave in a way which (if the critics from the other side are right) the evidence would not in fact support. For what, after all, does their criticism rest on? Their objection that the framing of the question in this way is ignorant and patronizing has force precisely because it carries a counter-claim to the effect that a *good* sociologist would realize that working-class people do not have to behave in the way that the question, so framed, presupposes that they must; and this counter-claim is itself one which only further and different sociological research can vindicate. The objection is not that the proper answer depends on statements of political preference in the absence of empirical study, but that a better empirical study would show the question to be wrongly put. Of course, there will continue to be the possibility of disagreement about what sort of research will, if carried out, have most effect in promoting the changes which the researcher would like to see. But neither side in the debate will deny that the answer to *this* question depends, obviously enough, on a further judgement of a different kind.

§ 15. 'But if the link between scientific and political values is only a contingent one, why make such heavy weather of it?' A fair question. The controversy on this topic has continued much longer than it should if the matter is as simple as the previous section made it appear. Mere reassertion that all the arguments which have been advanced against value-neutrality within sociology can be shown to be misconceived is not a substitute for an account of why it is that they have not been seen to be so.

A part of the answer lies in the degree to which the questions about which sociologists, anthropologists and historians are most deeply concerned, both as researchers and as citizens, are at once uncertain and complex. Since there are without doubt many practising social scientists who do, in the absence of definitive evidence, incline to believe what best accords with the value-judgements to which they are committed, it is tempting to say that even if the connection between their beliefs and their values is not a logical one, it might as well be. What distinguishes a 'left-wing' from a 'right-wing' account of, say, the Industrial Revolution is not just a preference for one kind of regime or society rather than another, or even a sympathy with the underprivileged and dispossessed and a suspicion of those set in authority over them; it is also a consistent disposition to give the benefit of the doubt to those reports and explanations of the relevant events which will, if accepted, be most likely to incline the uncommitted reader to agree that the underprivileged and dispossessed are deserving of sympathy and, more generally, that collective forms of social organization are to be preferred to individualistic. The author will be a better propagandist, as well as a better sociologist, if he makes it clear that the acceptance of his explanation does not logically depend on a prior agreement with his values, for nothing is less persuasive to the uncommitted reader than to realize that a purported explanation so set out as to appear to be valid whether right-wing readers like it or not is in fact so constructed that 'valid' has to be construed to mean 'valid-for-left-wing-readers-only'. But where the connection between the explanations put forward and the values to which the author is committed is as uniform and pervasive as it is apt to be on topics like this, it will not be surprising if the effect on some readers, at least, is to obscure the realization that it remains nevertheless a contingent one.

This realization is often made more difficult still by the fact that the author may himself deny it. But once the grounds of the denial are made explicit, the contingent nature of the connection will emerge once again. The most persuasive of such denials have been those which rest on the admitted difference that moral and political standards apply only to the behaviour of human beings and claim on the basis of this that, as it is sometimes put, the sciences of human behaviour are therefore necessarily 'value-relevant'. The weakness of this argument, however, is that it glosses over the difference between the inevitability of what is still a contingent relevance on the one hand and a logical connection on the other. It simply does not follow from the fact that sociologists, anthropologists and historians all do have moral and political values of their own that when they study behaviour to which those values are relevant they are thereby necessarily committed to one set of concepts, topics, hypotheses or explanations in preference to another. It is true that their choice of concepts is indeed a choice: it is not dictated by their evidence so much as the other way round. But again, it does not follow from the fact that it is not dictated by the evidence that it must be dictated by their values. Explanatory presuppositions are one thing; evaluative presuppositions are another. To bridge the gap between them by subsuming both under what Max Weber called *Wertideen* leads merely to a dilemma, for if that is what 'value-relevance' is about then the natural sciences are 'value-relevant' too; but the point of introducing the notion in the first place was to account for the way in which the relevance of 'values' to human behaviour distinguishes the role which they inevitably play in the sciences of man from the role which they cannot possibly play in the sciences of nature.

There is, however, a further reason why the link between scientific and moral, political or aesthetic values has so often been misconceived. It is because so little attention has been given to the distinction between evaluation and description (as opposed to explanation). If even explanations in sociology are often couched in such a way as to make it appear that they are necessarily connected with the sociologist's values, how much more likely must it be that sociologists' descriptions will appear so. But it is just as important to mark off description from evaluation on the one side as from explanation on the other. It may be that in the works of sociologists, anthropologists and historians the contingent connection between their values and their descriptions is even more blatant than the connection between their values and their explanations. But it is still only contingent. The author whose purpose is to persuade his readers to take the side of the underprivileged and dispossessed will no doubt be at pains to describe their sufferings in such a manner as will best succeed in doing so. But if his values lead him to romanticize or oversimplify or otherwise misdescribe those sufferings, then the reader who realizes that he has done so will be put off once again. What is more, if the description is well enough done then even the reader who still does not share the author's values will have no choice but to accept it. If a right-wing reader of a left-wing account of the sufferings of the hand-loom weavers in the early decades of the Industrial Revolution holds that those sufferings were outweighed by the eventual benefits which industrialization brought to the working class at large, this does not logically (and may well not psychologically) require him to dissent from a description which brings home to him just how much more severe those sufferings were than he had previously understood (in the tertiary sense). To claim that acceptance of the description entails acceptance of the evaluation is to claim that the reader cannot say without self-contradiction that the hand-loom weavers, although they did suffer in the manner so vividly and authentically described, had no legitimate claim on the government of the day to do more than it did to alleviate those sufferings. Now I would not, as it happens, want to say that myself. But I cannot see how it would be self-contradictory if I did. And the moment that any such pair of assertions is admitted to be sayable without self-contradiction, the claim that description and evaluation are *necessarily* connected must collapse.

THE PROBLEM OF REFLEXIVITY

§ 16. More generally, the distinction between reportage, explanation, description and evaluation can help to dispel much of the difficulty held to arise from the inherent reflexivity of social theory; and this in turn makes it possible for a better answer to be given than I gave in Section 2 to the question why there are classics of social theory which continue to be read long after they are written. Where their content is purely explanatory, there will be no difference between them and classics of natural science: to the extent that the concepts and theories which they propound are accepted as valid, they will have passed into the textbooks and only the historian of the subject will have reason to read them at all. If, however, they are descriptive also they may continue to be read for much the same reason that novels continue to be read. I have said that novels are themselves sociology to the extent that their authors make them so; and the converse of this is that descriptive sociology can (and, some would say, should) have all the long-term readability of good novels. Where the work has a significant evaluative content as well, this may help to keep it in print still longer. But this is apt to depend on the extent to which the moral and political judgements which it seeks to uphold are felt still to be relevant to subsequent generations of readers. Polemical sociology, like polemical fiction, may turn out to date all the more quickly on that account.

It is not, therefore, simply because social scientists are instances of their own subject matter that the construal of the work of the 'classical' social theorists seems so often to be bound up with a familiarity with their lives and times. These are not of any greater intrinsic interest than the lives and times of the heroes of physics or biology: the achievements of Newton or Darwin or Einstein prompt just as many questions about what they thought they were doing and why they did it as do the achievements of Marx or Durkheim or Weber. But it does not seem in the same way necessary to answer them before claiming to know what it is that Newton, Darwin and Einstein discovered about the laws of motion, the evolution of species, and general and special relativity. The writings of Marx, on the other hand, could be said to make sense only in relation to his personal reactions to German philosophy, French politics and British economics, and his conception of the role which he sought to perform within a society whose collapse he at once predicted and desired. The writings of Durkheim could be said to make sense only in relation to his personal response to the dangers to social cohesion which he saw in the joint effects of industrialization and the decline of the Church. The writings of Weber could be said to make sense only in terms of his personal commitment at once to academic liberalism and political nationalism as perceived by a self-styled bourgeois in Wilhelmine Germany. Once, however, their descriptions and evaluations are distinguished from the explanations with which they are bound up, the biographical questions which they raise can at the same time be disentangled from the methodological ones. Methodologically, their explanations depend neither on their descriptions of their own societies from their personal point of view nor on their evaluation of them in the light of their personal moral or political ideals. But since their descriptions and evaluations have a continuing interest as well, not only their own works but the works of their biographers and critics continue – quite rightly – to be read.

Of all the 'classical' social theorists, Weber is probably the most instructive example because of the unusual extent to which his wide-ranging substantive interests were matched by his awareness of the methodological problems posed by them – an awareness which itself further compounds the problem of reflexivity. There can be few, if any, of his readers who have turned back to his Inaugural Lecture delivered at Freiburg in 1895 from his denunciation of 'prophets of the chair' delivered to the closed session of the *Verein für Sozialpolitik* in 1914 without a sense that professors in glass houses ought not to be throwing stones. How are we to construe the writings of an author whose precepts about the neutrality of science are so much at variance with his practice? When Weber insists, for example, as he does, that the concept of 'charisma' in the sense which he gives to it is 'value-free', how are we to reconcile this with those passages in his writings which betray an unmistakable preference for the charismatic leader over the bureaucrat, and the readily documented connection between changes in his view of charisma and changes both in German politics and in his own personal life? These questions, however, are only biographically, not methodologically, problematic. If 'charisma' is a less useful theoretical concept in the sociology of politics than Weber hoped or supposed, this is not because he preferred charismatic leaders to bureaucrats or vice versa. If his use of it is more closely bound up with his own political attitudes than at first appears, this may make his writings more illuminating rather than less as a source from which the reader may gain a sense of what politics in Wilhelmine Germany were like. If his favourable view of it lends support to a doctrine of *Führerdemokratie* which could be used to legitimate the evils of Nazism, this commits no one else who does not share the initial preference to a similar view. The three distinguishable aspects are of course bound up together in his work as we have it, and the historian of social theory whose concern is to establish what exactly Weber meant has to take account of all of them. But the sociologist of a later period and a different milieu can extract what is useful to him without having to resolve the biographical questions which only raise in their turn the question whether the biographer's own life and times may not need to be examined in order to make sense of *his* way of writing a biography of Weber.

§ 17. The sociology of sociology, therefore, although it poses difficulties for its practitioners additional to those which face the sociologist or historian of natural science, does not force the conclusion that sociology itself cannot be practised without an infinite regress. There may, in principle, be a sociology of the sociology of sociology, and then a sociology of the sociology of the sociology of sociology, and so on. But any work of sociology, whether a sociology of sociology or of any other human institution or practice, can be judged by the internal standards of science independently of questions about how it itself came about, what it is like, and whether the doing of it is a good thing or a bad one.

This is not to deny that a discussion like this one is, no less than the substantive social theory which is to follow it, a product of the period and milieu in which it is written. No reader of this treatise will fail to be aware that it could not have been written in any century but the twentieth or in any culture outside the Western European intellectual tradition. But this obvious fact of the sociology of sociology is of no help in determining whether or not its arguments are sound. It would be equally mistaken to suppose that they must be sound because they come at the end of a long and triumphant evolution of 'rationalized' social theory as to suppose that they cannot be sound because their presuppositions and purposes must by definition be as parochial as those of any of the social theorists of the past. It is a fact of sociology, or if you prefer of history, that there was not and could not be either a history of historiography or a sociology of sociology until a certain stage of development of social thought. But that fact can be accommodated within the methodology set out in this volume without any need to modify either the criteria for, or the relation between, reportage, explanation, description and evaluation.

Consider the explanatory aspect first. Why is it that the beginnings of a reflexive sociology can be traced no further back than the eighteenth century? A question so phrased cannot but betray the perspective of hindsight: it is only with hindsight that Vico's *Scienza Nuova* of 1725 becomes a 'landmark' in the history of Western thought, or that we can ask what was lacking in the *Politics* of Aristotle which distinguishes it in kind from a 'modern' work of political science. But that does not mean either that the question is not a genuinely explanatory one or that an answer to it is impossible in principle. It is, as I have argued already, characteristic of sociological explanation that it requires the invocation of theoretical terms unavailable to those to whose behaviour they are to be applied; and this holds no less of the history of people's ideas about their history than it does of the history of their economic and political institutions or, for that matter, of their technology and their physical science. I do not claim to know the answer to my own question. Nor, indeed, do I believe that anyone else knows it. But historians of ideas (and/or 'sociologists of knowledge') have gone some way towards finding it out. What is more, those who have been most successful in doing so have been precisely those most concerned to challenge the kind of implicit evolutionism which views the history of the sciences, whether of nature or of man, as tending inevitably towards the state which they happen to have reached by the author's lifetime.

When it comes to the descriptive aspect, it follows likewise from what I have argued already that the concepts – or lack of them – of the writers of earlier periods must have priority over those of the self-consciously reflexive sociologists of the present day. But there is nothing improper in drawing a contrast between the two. On the contrary: the mistake which invites the charge of 'ahistoricity' is precisely the mistake of describing the social thought of an earlier period as though it carried implications which could be rephrased without distortion in the idiom of a later age. To understand in the tertiary sense the social theory of the writers of ancient Rome, it is necessary to be aware that they themselves were *not* aware of the need to describe the society in which they lived from any other than what we would now regard as a limited and unrepresentative point of view. It is true that in Plautus's comedies, or Tacitus's histories, or Petronius's *Satyricon* there are speeches put into the mouths of characters drawn from the whole range of Roman society. But their purpose is rhetorical, not sociological. When Plautus gives us the remarks of a slave about the miseries of slavery, or Tacitus the remarks of a mutineer about the burdens of military service, or Petronius the remarks of a parvenu about the pleasures of wealth, the one thing they are *not* doing is the sort of novel-writing which I have said can be classed as sociology. Again, I make no claim to know *why* they are not. It is just as difficult to explain why realism in art appears only when it does as it is to explain the same about experimentalism in science. It is more difficult still to resolve the further question whether or not there is some specifiable causal connection between them. But there is nothing about it which need inhibit the sociologist from describing a society distant in time or place in a way which conveys to the reader what it was like by means of a contrast with the assumptions and concepts of his own. Indeed, there *is* no other way except to suggest to the reader that he go off and do his own fieldwork or documentary research for himself.

In the same way, the evaluative aspect poses no problem to which the solution is not already implicit in the previous argument. There is a sense in which any history of science is a history of heroes and villains, not because it is the business of the historian to pass judgement on the virtues or vices of the thinkers of the past but because the internal criteria of science discriminate by definition between those whose ideas have – for better or worse – been 'good' ideas and those whose ideas have been 'bad'. To single out Marx or Durkheim or Weber as social theorists of 'classic' status is avowedly to make an evaluation of them: it is to say not only that they have been influential but that they have deserved their influence. But it is not to say anything about the goodness or badness of their influence on society as opposed to their influence on sociology as practised within it. To those who subscribe to a further presupposition whereby a moral or political value attaches to the practice of sociology, the further conclusion will of course follow. I have already conceded that if a society whose workings are being systematically studied by some of its members is for that reason a better society than one which is not, then it must be true to say that whoever is thought to study it well (by academic standards) is thereby doing good (by political standards). But nobody, whether practitioner or reader of such studies, is required simply by choosing to practise or read them to subscribe to the further presupposition. This aspect of the reflexivity of social theory does not, therefore, any more than either of the others, raise any further methodological difficulty.

CONCLUSION

§ 18. There remains only one more preliminary question to be answered before I go on to examine the separate methodological issues raised by reportage, explanation, description and evaluation in more detail, and that is the question of the status of these remarks themselves. This chapter has claimed (to recapitulate) that there is no special problem of explanation in the sciences of man, but only a special problem of description; that the concept of understanding needs to be dissolved into not just two, but three; that for the purpose of primary understanding all beliefs should in the first instance be treated as 'rational', but no actions; that agents always know what they are doing, but not why, except where they are mistaken about something about their action which is constitutive of it; that sociology is inherently dependent upon, but not for that reason strictly reducible to, psychology; that explanatory, descriptive and evaluative sociology, however closely combined in practice, are always distinguishable in principle; that the relation of academic to political values in sociology is contingent, not necessary; and finally, that the problem of the reflexivity of sociology can, like substantive social theory in general, be satisfactorily accommodated within the framework of the fourfold distinction between reportage, explanation, description and evaluation. But how are these dogmatic-sounding assertions to be classified? Are they propositions within sociology, or outside of it?

The answer is that they are neither. They should be construed as guides to practice – maxims with the help of which sociologists, anthropologists and historians may be enabled better to succeed in what they set out to do. They are not technical maxims; they do not tell researchers how to conduct their research. Rather, they tell them what conditions their research must fulfil if its results are to be accepted as uncontroversial by fellow-practitioners from rival theoretical schools. Only a set of criteria which is neutral between substantive theories can distinguish between those disagreements which can, in principle at least, be settled by further research and those which can be settled only within the framework of a presupposition, or set of them, which no appeal to the evidence could ever directly disconfirm. It is still true that no substantive research is or could be innocent of presuppositions which are neither derivable from nor testable against it. But it is, as we shall see, possible to draw a workable distinction between presuppositionlessness (*Voraussetzungslösigkeit*) and theory-neutrality. When this has been done, it will be easier to see not only what distinguishes good theories from bad ones but also why so relatively little of what is written by social scientists under the rubric of 'theory' leads either to the unquestioned discovery of new social facts or to what is accepted by all rival schools as a better explanation, description or evaluation of old ones.

If, however, these maxims are more than technical, they are at the same time less than philosophical. Not only does this volume not presume to teach practising sociologists their job, but it does not pretend to advance by a single step the resolution of any of the disputes among philosophers of science on which its arguments touch, as they are bound to do, at many points. Indeed, it is one of its principal purposes to enable practising sociologists, anthropologists and historians not to ignore but, so far as possible, to bypass those disputes without damage to their substantive research. This relatively modest ambition may seem in contradiction with my opening claim that if my arguments are correct, the long debate between those who affirm and those who deny that there is a fundamental difference of kind between the sciences of nature and the sciences of man can be regarded as closed. But that claim was made from the viewpoint strictly of the methodologist, not the philosopher, of social science. To the philosopher, there are no doubt many issues in the relations between the social and the natural sciences which still are, and are likely to remain, controversial. But I believe that the arguments advanced in this volume are of a kind which lead far enough and no further into the philosophy of social science for sociologists, anthropologists and historians who accept them to proceed with their work without further misgivings about its vulnerability to methodological criticism; and in the two volumes to follow I shall myself be acting on that belief.

2

Reportage in social theory

§ 1. Once the maxim 'no observations without presuppositions' has come to be accepted as a truism, no practising sociologist, anthropologist or historian, however little interested in methodological as opposed to merely technical questions, will conduct his researches as though all he has to do is to record the facts of human behaviour as they are to be found out there in the world by an observer sufficiently diligent to track them down and sufficiently open-minded to let them speak for themselves. Research may, admittedly, still seem like this to the researcher who only wants to know who begat the begetter of Saul, or what percentage of salaried male employees in England and Wales were in occupational pension schemes in 1956–7, or whether any heroic *chansons* in the vernacular were in circulation earlier than the year 1000. But it would be a mistake even for him to suppose that methodological questions arise only after he has come upon whatever item or sequence of behaviour it is that interests him. For what has led him in the first place to say that that is what it is? Might there not be other designations under which he could report it also, or instead?

The first of these questions can be answered only by an adequate account of what I have called understanding in the primary sense – the sense, that is, in which to *mis*understand is, e.g., to take a cosmetic implement for a weapon of war, a piece of play-acting for a serious ritual or an inkstain for a semiquaver. To claim to have avoided such misunderstanding is to claim to have discovered what is or was going on, as distinct from and preliminary to discovering why it is or was going on as, where and when it is or was. But the line between the two has to be drawn by the researcher. There is no brute level of analysis above which his categorization of his observations is discretionary and below which it is mandatory. A practising sociologist who wants to know why someone is chopping wood, opening a door or pointing a gun will no doubt be content to ignore the (to him) trivial question of the nature of the physical movements constitutive of those actions and the criteria by which the actions are identified as such. But as I have pointed out already, any report that an action has taken place presupposes an explanation at another level of the words and gestures constitutive of it. To say 'He is chopping wood' is to answer the question 'Why is he moving his limbs in that way?', just as to say 'It is a semiquaver' is to answer the question 'Why is there a mark on the paper like that?' I dare say no practising sociologist (*pace* Weber, who uses it as an example, together with door-opening and gun-pointing, in the opening pages of *Economy and Society*) has ever in the whole history of the sciences of man had reason to treat the observation of a man chopping wood as problematic. But it would not be difficult to construct an example in which he would be misled by failing to do so; and in the case of 'pointing a gun' there is a great number of contexts in which not only sociologists but courts of law may go seriously wrong if the reported observation is unquestioningly taken as given.

Once it is accepted that agents themselves are to be held to know what they are doing except in those relatively unusual cases where they are ignorant of something constitutive of it, then provided that they are prepared to tell the enquiring fieldworker the truth he has only to ask them. If I ask you 'What are you doing with the gun?', you may reply 'I didn't know I had it in my hand', in which case I shall report 'He/she held the gun as though pointing it at the rabbit'; or you may reply 'Because I wanted you to think that I was aiming at the rabbit', in which case I shall report 'He/she pointed the gun as though aiming at the rabbit'; or you may reply 'Why do you think – can't you see I'm aiming at the rabbit?', in which case I shall report that I have observed you aiming a gun at a rabbit and then go on to ask you why you are doing *that*. Yet even in this simple example, my report that you aimed a gun at a rabbit presupposes that certain questions not explicitly asked about what it is to aim a gun could all have been satisfactorily answered. Not only are there problems in framing a watertight definition of 'aim', but in any case all activities with meaning to their agents are recognized by those agents as subject to contextual constraints. The agent may choose to violate the constraints; but that too can only be done by first recognizing that they are there. There are ways and ways of aiming guns; there are times and places for doing it; and there is nowhere a society in which there is no way, time or place for doing it which could not be regarded as calling for special comment by which the report that a gun was being aimed might need to be qualified.

It is not, therefore, the ostensible simplicity of an action which makes its reportage unproblematic, but its relation in the mind of the person performing it to the intention, in its context, in terms of which it is defined. To marry someone, for example, is to do something less simple in a number of ways than to aim a gun at a rabbit. But that does not mean that a sociologist who reports that X has married Y has any more reason to doubt that that is 'really' what has happened than in the case of the ostensibly simpler act. He has still to make sure that he is not somehow being taken in – that he has not been watching a rehearsal or a practical joke or the making of a film. But he has to do that anyway as part of what is involved in understanding in the primary sense, and it is no more inherently difficult in the one case than the other. The report of a marriage may suggest more questions of an explanatory and/or descriptive and/or evaluative kind than does the report of the aiming of a gun at a rabbit. But if those who have apparently been marrying each other have confirmed to the enquiring fieldworker that that is indeed what, so far as they are concerned, they have been doing, then unless he has failed to master the language sufficiently to have grasped the meaning of 'marry' in their dictionary he can in practice treat the report of the marriage as uncontroversial and go on from there to ask whatever explanatory, descriptive or evaluative questions may interest him about the form and history of the ceremony, the feelings of the participants, the particular circumstances which brought them together, or the desirability of their union.

Nor is a report any more controversial if the action observed is unusual or even unique. In my own society, so far as I am aware, it has never happened that anyone has tweaked the Prime Minister's nose in public. But if someone does, and is seen to do so in broad daylight by reliable witnesses, then however puzzling the explanation, however difficult to describe the state of mind of the person who was so motivated as to do it, and however contentious its evaluation as good or bad, there will not be anything problematic about the report. It does not matter that the term 'tweak' is even less precise than 'aim'. I cannot tell you exactly what physical movements in relation to another person's nose are necessary and sufficient to vindicate the report, if challenged, that a case of tweaking has been observed. But if one day in 1919 at the Versailles Conference M. Clemenceau had said to Mr Lloyd George 'I am going to tweak your nose!' and had thereupon gripped Lloyd George's nose between the thumb and forefinger of his right hand (or left – either would do) and turned them smartly to the right (or left), thereafter releasing his grip and returning his hand to his side, then it would for any purpose that a practising sociologist, anthropologist or historian might have in mind be a fact that the British

Prime Minister's nose had been tweaked. And however startling the fact, it is neither more questionable if it only happens once nor less questionable if it is subsequently repeated.

What is problematic about the reportage of human behaviour is only rarely the relation between physical movements and the intention with which they are performed. It is much more often the relation between the intention and the context which gives the intention, and therefore the action, its meaning. Practising sociologists seldom if ever need to specify the conditions which turn the observation of gestures and noises into the identification of actions which can then be reported as matters of fact. They do, however, need to be sure that in making the transition they have correctly pitched the level at which the report identifies the action as such. They must not read so much into their observations that their reports of it go beyond the correct relation of it to the context which makes it the action it is into a pre-emptive explanation, description or evaluation of that action. But at the same time, they must not leave so much out that the identification can successfully be challenged by a rival observer as a misunderstanding in the primary sense.

§ 2. Here, for example, is a photograph which, since I cannot run you the film in full, I must ask you to accept as an appropriate still extracted from a sequence of a person doing a rain-dance. The assertion that it *is* a rain-dance is of course not purely empirical, if by that is meant that the observation of the person's gestures and dress is by itself enough to vindicate the claim that it is a rain-dance which he is dancing (or for that matter, that he is dancing at all). But he says that he is doing a rain-dance, there is no reason to suppose that he is lying and his performance is well within the rules which are relevant for the dancing of rain-dances. With that information, you have only to look at him to be satisfied that there is nothing controversial – whatever your explanatory hypothesis of the cause of such behaviour, your sense (or lack of it) of what rain-dancing is like for those who do it, or your moral, political or aesthetic values – in the report that on the date in question a rain-dance was being performed.

But wait. The date is the drought of 1976, the place is Bournemouth and the name of the man is John Morley. He has managed a little rain for the Bournemouth Water Company (or so he says), but he thinks that if the drought is really to be ended a lot more people in other parts of England should do some rain-dancing too. Well, fair enough. But some readers may, like myself, be reminded of the Jewish joke about the mother who is telling one of her friends about 'my son, the captain': sure enough, there is the son in his nautical jacket and cap, his talk of 'abaft' and 'astern',

'ahoy!', 'belay there!' and all the rest of it; but the friend says, 'So to you he's a captain. To me he's a captain. But to captains is he a captain?' Likewise: to rain-dancers is it a rain-dance?

The question is not to be dismissed as purely verbal. No doubt we *can* say, if we want, that it is a rain-dance whoever is dancing it, provided that it is being danced correctly and that the person doing it, being of sound mind, etc., knows it to be a rain-dance. But might it be more accurate to report Mr Morley as *demonstrating* or *attempting* a rain-dance? If you or I were to go and practise as shamans among the Tapirapé Indians of Central Brazil (among whom women can be shamans as well as men)* and were to find that we were able to practise with some limited success, could we claim to *be* shamans in the same sense that we would report of *other* Tapirapé shamans that they are shamans? If a Mid-western housewife on return from a world tour starts performing the Japanese tea ceremony every day, correctly and with conviction, can we report her without qualification as 'performing the Japanese tea ceremony'? And if we think we can but the Japanese tell us we can't, can we say that we are right and the Japanese wrong? If and only if the agents in question are, so to speak,

* See Charles Wagley, *Welcome of Tears* (1977), p. 197.

entitled to their declared intentions can the actions defined by reference to those intentions be accepted by the observer as such.

Nor is this the only way in which the observer might, on further reflection, wish to qualify an initial report that he has observed a rain-dance. For just as he may have assumed too readily that the person performing it is qualified to be performing it according to the conventions which give it its meaning, so may he also have assumed too readily that where the person *is* qualified the performance does not need to be questioned as such. What about the familiar phenomenon which is sometimes referred to by sociologists as 'role distance'? Suppose that the film is of a native-born Indian performing a rain-dance as, where and when rain-dances have been performed by his tribe since time immemorial, but that at the end of the performance, when the observer has switched off his cine-camera, he turns round and lowers one eyelid in what the observer cannot but understand in the primary sense as not merely a blink but a wink. Can the observer continue to sustain his report that he has observed a rain-dance? The answer can only be 'yes' if the wink is for some reason *not* to be understood as signalling the absence of the intention which makes Mr Morley's performance (if he is, indeed, properly qualified) a 'real' one.

The relation between an agent's intention and the context which gives the intention its meaning is, accordingly, problematic at both ends: the observer has to be sure that he knows all that he needs to know about the context *and* the intention. He cannot be expected, in his report, to list all of the things which might be true but are not, and would, *if* true, compromise his assertion that an act of X-ing was what he observed. But he can, and should, be expected to have considered seriously the possibility that he has been confronted with a case which a rival observer might call in question. The most widespread, the most routine, the most familiar actions – giving a present, say, or issuing an order – are surrounded at both ends by a sort of penumbra where the present may cease to be a present and the order an order. It need not be a question of the gross misunderstanding which takes cosmetic implements for weapons, play-acting for serious rituals and inkstains for semiquavers. Rather, the difficulty is that presents shade over into exchanges or displays, and orders into requests or threats. Neither intentions nor their contexts are by any means always clear-cut. The researcher must both identify the agent's intention and establish that the agent is not mistaken about something constitutive of the action which he or she is (intentionally) performing. But there is never any way of being absolutely certain either about somebody else's intentions or about the absence of contextual ambiguities which would require the observer to say that the agent does not know precisely what he or she is doing. This is no argument for scepticism about the possibility of reportage at all, for it implies no unwillingness to accept that sociologists' reports, non-presuppositionless though they may be, can correctly be claimed to assert a relation between their observations of behaviour and the behaviour observed which is either true or false. But it does serve as a reminder that the distinction between reported behaviour and the explanation, description or evaluation of it is not between straightforward empirical observations on the one hand and subtle theoretical speculations on the other. It can just as well be the observations which are speculative and the theories which are straightforward. The danger is then not that an observation is wrongly explained (or described or evaluated), but that the explanation is of something which wasn't there to be explained – let alone described or evaluated – in the first place.

§ 3.   This danger extends to the further aspect of behaviour which, where it is relevant, has in practice to be treated by the observer as constitutive of the actions observed in the same way as the agent's intention: the agent's beliefs. As we shall see, beliefs can also be treated as causes of actions. But that they are sometimes constitutive of actions is not a statement which, I assume, any reader will find controversial: if the priest has lost his faith in God, or Mr Morley secretly believes that his rain-dance cannot possibly affect the weather, they cannot be reported as 'praying to God' and 'rain-dancing' without a qualification to that effect, and what the Pope was doing in the year 816 in 'anointing' Louis I of France was a matter of what he believed to be God's role as well as his own.

Practising sociologists, anthropologists or historians do not need to be able to answer the philosophical question what it is that belief consists in. But they do need to be able to say whether the presence of it is constitutive, or causal, or neither, of the behaviour they are studying. They also need to distinguish between belief *that* and belief *in*. Often, it is true, the second involves the first: the native informant who says 'I believe in God the Father Almighty' means – if he or she does mean it – that so far as he or she is concerned there exists a supreme, omnipotent Being who made us all. But belief in what one is doing may be a question simply of accepting convention and eschewing role distance rather than of subscribing to the text of a creed. An atheist priest cannot be reported as praying to a deity who is not there for him to pray to, but an atheist colonel can perfectly well be reported as performing the consecration of the regimental colours in the church of the regimental town. To believe in a ceremony is not necessarily to believe any proposition to be true other than the proposition that the ceremony has some kind of purpose or value. The sociologist who has failed to understand that the colonel does *not* have to subscribe to what the priest is apparently saying will, therefore, misreport it if he does so in terms which imply that the colonel does.

On the other hand, it will be just as much of a mistake if he refuses to attribute to those whose actions he has observed a belief which they do in fact hold. A Zande who believes in witchcraft believes that there really are witches, that various misfortunes can be and often are caused by their agency and that one or more of his neighbours can quite well be one. The rival observer who tries to explain away what Evans-Pritchard reports of the Azande by speaking of their practices as though their talk of witches was merely metaphorical or symbolic has, as it were, insisted that the semiquaver is an inkstain when it isn't.* It does not matter at this point whether the native informant has a word corresponding to the English 'belief'. Nor does it matter whether the English-speaking sociologist has doubts of his own about the universal validity of 'Western' logic. Negation is a cultural universal, whatever else may or may not be, and there never has been or will be discovered a society in which there is not the possibility of one person's asserting something or other to be the case and another person's refusing to accept the assertion as correct.

The practising sociologist's most troublesome difficulty is, once more, to adduce sufficient evidence of the appropriate kind to dispel the scepticism of the rival observer. What is the small child 'really' doing in talking to the doll, the Archaic Greek in setting food before the corpse, the urban pedestrian in walking round the ladder, the Neoplatonist in anointing the dagger with a weapon-salve, the Zande in consulting the poison-oracle and the neurotic in confessing to a psychoanalyst? In every one of these cases, there are not merely two possibilities but three. Each of these agents may neither believe nor disbelieve the propositions which, if they did believe them without qualification, would require the observer to report that there had occurred, and therefore called to be explained, described and evaluated, a performance informed by adherence to them. The child may only believe that the doll *might* come to life, the Archaic Greek that the souls of the dead *may* have a need for food, the pedestrian that it *could* be a sensible precaution against ill luck to walk round the ladder, the Neoplatonist that it is not *wholly* implausible that the vital spirits of the congealed blood should reunite with the victim's body, the Zande that the poison-oracle *appears* to be reliable and the neurotic that

---

* See E. E. Evans-Pritchard, *Theories of Primitive Religion* (1965), p. 110, as well as his *Witchcraft, Oracles and Magic among the Azande* (1937), *passim*.

it is worth giving Freudian therapy a *try*; and in the same way, Mr Morley may harbour *occasional* doubts about the causal efficacy of rain-dancing. It makes no difference how far the belief in question strikes the observer as 'rational' or – at this stage – how far its context and implications are understandable to the observer in either the secondary or the tertiary sense. What is needed is no more (but no less) than a primary understanding of the dictionary meaning of the relevant belief, a recognition that cases of semi-belief are at least as readily to be expected as unquestioning conviction or total scepticism, and a specification of the observations ancillary to the observation of the action which furnish grounds for asserting the belief, or half-belief, constitutive of it to be present or not. This is seldom as easy as it sounds, as even a limited and haphazard reading of works of sociology, anthropology and history will quickly demonstrate. Too often, what purports to be a report either of a belief as such or of a set of actions of which a belief may or may not be partly constitutive is pitched at a level where a pre-emptive theory is already built in. The imposition of observer's categories may not be illegitimate in itself. But it becomes so where it involves the attribution to the agents on whose thoughts, words and deeds a report is being made of assumptions or capacities which are not in fact theirs. The rival observer who continues to refuse to allow that the Azande mean what they say about witches must adduce some evidence other than his own beliefs about witchcraft before discarding Evans-Pritchard's conclusion that his informants are themselves to be believed and that 'witch' does mean to them what its dictionary definition suggests that it should.

'But to ascertain and report what you call the "dictionary" meaning of a belief is itself more than a matter of direct observation.' Admittedly so. It will no more do for the sociologist to report only 'my informant believes whatever it is that they mean when they say that they believe in God the Father Almighty, and the words "Father Almighty" mean whatever their dictionary says' than to report 'they are doing whatever "marrying" means in their culture'. But the enquiring fieldworker can arrive at a primary understanding of the dictionary meaning without bringing to bear either the underlying theoretical concepts on which explanation may turn out to depend or the deeper insights into the nuances of its implications in 'their' minds which may be necessary for the purpose of description. As it happens, I am not at all sure how best to construct either a demonstrably valid explanation or a convincingly authentic description of what it is that churchgoers in my own society are doing when they recite the Nicene Creed. But I have no hesitation in reporting them as asserting – if they are, indeed, believing Christians – a conviction of the existence of a single, supreme, supernatural power in the sense given in the Oxford English Dictionary. No doubt my report takes for granted much that a visiting fieldworker from an alien culture could not possibly infer by observation alone. But so, likewise, may the identification of inanimate objects and natural events. To report that 'they' do, as a matter of fact, believe in God and that certain of their actions cannot be understood in the primary sense if that fact is not recognized as such is not to lay claim to an 'understanding' not fully in accordance with the same procedures and criteria which obtain where the behaviour is as simple and straight-forward as you please.

There is, it is true, another set of problems which is associated with the criteria for establishing what 'they' mean when they assert a belief and which has been influentially expounded under the rubric of 'indeter-minacy of translation'.* Quine's paradigm example is of the fieldworker ignorant of a native language and lacking either translator or lexicon who has to establish whether 'they' mean by 'gavagai' just what he means by 'rabbit' and has therefore to devise some set of questions which can be put to 'them' under different selected circumstances in order to eliminate any possible indeterminacy between rabbits and, as it may be, rabbithood, rabbit stages or rabbit parts. Now there can be no question that the indeterminacy of translation does pose technical difficulties for the practising sociologist, and not just for the linguist, semanticist or philo-sophical logician: how can he make *certain* that the native aiming the gun at what 'they' call the 'gavagai' is not trying to shoot the numinous aura of rabbithood which, according to 'their' metaphysics, is instantiated in this particular scurrying creature? But it is not a difficulty which undermines the possibility of primary understanding of alien beliefs altogether. On the contrary: it only arises because of the possibility of coming to understand that 'they' mean 'numinous aura of rabbithood' and *not* 'rabbit'. There remains the purely philosophical problem posed by the fact that it should be possible at all for us either to master new languages or to recover the illocutionary force of what is said by other native speakers of our own, and a satisfactory account of what makes it possible has somehow to be formulated without an appeal to the very same notion of meaning which it seeks to elucidate. But the hard-pressed fieldworker does not have to call off his research until he is able to say how he comes to be able to do what he knows very well that he can – that is, in Quine's own phrase for it, 'settle down and learn the language directly as an infant might'. He will recognize that he may still, at the conclusion of his fieldwork, be in

* W. V. Quine, *Word and Object* (1960), Ch. 2.

doubt whether one of Evans-Pritchard's Nuer informants who tells him *'gän liakä Kuoth'* means that he believes in a higher Spirit in quite the same sense that Lord Hunt, in the last sentence of his account of *The Ascent of Everest* (1953), tells his readers that 'There is no height, no depth, that the spirit of man, guided by a higher Spirit, cannot attain'. But this is not because the very notion of a 'dictionary meaning' of a term like 'spirit' is unworkable. The fieldworker will be fully aware, whether he is studying Lord Hunt and his co-religionists, the Nuer, the Neoplatonists, the Archaic Greeks or anybody else, that it may not be possible to specify the content of those beliefs in such a way as to satisfy all rival observers that he has so far exhausted their meaning as to be able to claim complete understanding. Quine is quite right to point out that bilingual translators can still translate differently from each other, just as native speakers of a common language can use the same words and phrases in different ways. But to the rival observer who invokes Quine on indeterminacy in order to discredit the fieldworker's claim to have understood that 'they' do at any rate believe in the existence of a 'higher spirit' in a recognizable dictionary meaning of 'spirit', he can fairly reply by quoting from a rival philosopher to the effect that 'Meaning, under any theory whatever, cannot be *in principle* subjective because meaning is a matter of what is *conveyed* by language.'* All sorts of technical pitfalls may beset the enquiring fieldworker of the kind which attend any attempt at primary understanding of rain-dances, marriage ceremonies, rabbit-shoots, collective affirmations of religious creeds or anything else. But it is Quine's own methodological maxim that 'assertions startlingly false on the face of them are likely to turn on hidden differences of language', and Quine's own comment on his maxim that 'one's interlocutor's silliness, beyond a certain point, is less likely than bad translation – or, in the domestic case, linguistic divergence'. There is no ammunition here for phenomenological sceptics of the practical possibility of primary – as opposed to secondary and/or tertiary – understanding of anyone's beliefs but one's own.

Reassurance about the possibility of reporting alien beliefs will not by itself resolve the difficulties which may stand in the way of determining just how far a stated belief is to be taken literally, or how far those who stated it can be said themselves to understand what exactly they are saying. It is not just that they may be sceptical or half-hearted. In addition, they may be knowingly and even deliberately unclear. The diligent fieldworker may by the end of his researches conclude not only that his native informants neither quite believe nor disbelieve what they

* Michael Dummett, *Frege* (1973), p. 83 (author's italics).

tell him, but even that they sincerely believe without knowing quite what it is that they say they are believing. An informant who claims to believe in a God who is at the same time three persons and one person may hold it as a further tenet of his faith that his beliefs should not be capable of logical or empirical validation, just as an informant who says he believes that the quantum principle excludes transitions from one electron orbit to another by arbitrarily small interactions within the electromagnetic field may admit that he is too ignorant of physics to know exactly what it is that he is claiming to hold to be true. But for the purpose of reporting them, the enquiring fieldworker needs only to have established that they *are* beliefs and that the terms 'God' and 'Trinity', like 'quantum principle', 'electron orbit' and 'electromagnetic field', do have an ascertainable dictionary meaning to which his native informants subscribe, whatever further difficulties of explanation and description they may also raise.

§4. It might be objected here that I have glossed over the extent to which the extensive ethnographic literature on ritual and symbolism is not only substantively but methodologically contentious. Not only do practising anthropologists differ among themselves about how these indispensable terms are to be defined; they also offer their readers very diverse accounts of what is 'really' going on in games, processions, entertainments, celebrations, rites of passage and suchlike. To agree precisely what 'their' actions mean to 'them' is just what rival observers of the same noises and gestures may find most difficult. If one asserts and the other denies that, say, what they are observing is an instance of the composition and/or performance of a 'work of art', is not their disagreement a theoretical disagreement which has to be settled before and not after the report that it was or wasn't 'art'? Before it is asked why 'they' symbolize X by Y and what it is like for them to do so, does it not have to be established what it *is* to symbolize one thing by another? It cannot simply be a matter of asking a native informant, since it may well be that they do it unreflectingly and without even possessing in their dictionary a concept translatable on the most generous interpretation as 'symbolism'. If pressed for elucidation of their intentions and beliefs, they may only reply with a myth which merely raises again the very same questions in the hard-pressed fieldworker's mind.

Now there are undoubtedly many institutions and practices documented in the ethnographic record which are more difficult to report to the satisfaction of rival observers, even after intensive fieldwork, than raindances, marriages or rabbit-shoots. But the more exotic the practice, the more useful the rule that the actions of which the practice consists should be designated by reference only to the intentions and beliefs which *are* constitutive of them. Primary understanding goes no further than the point where noises and gestures can first be labelled as actions because of the meaning to 'them' which makes them so; and 'meaning' here carries no weightier presuppositions than those necessary to distinguish clapping the hands from applauding a performance (sincerely or not), or dragging a stick across the sand from drawing a picture (artistically or not). Since the agent's account is privileged, it follows that the complexity of the ritual or symbolism and the degree of the observer's difficulty in conceptualizing it are immaterial to the status of that account as a report. Nor does it matter for the purpose of reportage how reflective an answer the native informant gives to the question 'what are you doing?'. Mr Morley may offer a lecture on the history, symbolism and latent social function of the rain-dance where a native-born performer who takes rain-dancing as a matter of course would go no further than to tell the enquiring fieldworker that it is a dance which the fellow-members of his tribe perform when they want it to rain. But no rival observer will quarrel with the report that they are rain-dancing. There may, no doubt, remain puzzlement about the significance of rain-dancing in their culture as a whole. Particularly if it is related to a more elaborate ceremonial cycle which is in turn bound up with a system of related myths, the question 'yes, but what are they *really* doing in rain-dancing?', or 'yes, but what is the *full* meaning of the rain-dance to them?' will require an excursion into its history, symbolism and latent social function which the unreflecting native informant will be quite unable to provide and of which Mr Morley's version cannot be taken on trust. But these are theoretical questions, whether explanatory or descriptive, about which the agents do not have the same degree of privilege as attaches to their initial assertion that they are rain-dancing. They are, and are bound to be, controversial questions because of the difficulty of testing the claims of rival schools, or even of establishing how they could possibly be tested: however plausible a Durkheimian suggestion that 'they' are 'really' expressing social solidarity, or a Freudian suggestion that they are 'really' acting out un-conscious desires, or a Collingwoodian suggestion that they are 'really' performing a work of art, or a Lévi-Straussian suggestion that they are 'really' seeking to reconcile conceptual oppositions, enormously much more supporting evidence and argument will be needed before agree-ment that one or another theory is the right one can possibly be reached than before deciding that the possibilities of misunderstanding in the primary sense can be discounted and that it is a 'real' rain-dance, whatever else there may be to be said about it. But the number and difficulty of

further questions left unanswered by the (mere) report to that effect make
no difference to its status as a report on a par with 'it's a real marriage',
'he's really aiming the gun at the rabbit', 'Clemenceau really did tweak
Lloyd George's nose' and 'they really do believe in God'.

It is, admittedly, true to say that the primary understanding of ritual
and symbolic language and behaviour involves a process of *decoding* in
a way that understanding of more straightforwardly literal behaviour
does not. But this is a difference only of degree. Indeed, one of the
conclusions which can be drawn from Quine's arguments about the
indeterminacy of translation is that the enquiring fieldworker is committed to an exercise in cryptographic technique even where he is
concerned with nothing more than establishing the correspondence between the natives' 'gavagai' and his 'rabbit'. The distinction between
primary and either secondary or tertiary understanding still holds. The
pattern of colours on the piece of cloth attached to the stick of wood
which the uniformed man is carrying up the aisle is as meaningless as
the scratches on the tablets unearthed at Pylos until it has been understood that it is the flag of the local regiment in the first case and an
inventory recorded in Linear B in the second. The second may be an
exercise in 'decoding' in a more strictly technical sense, but in both it is
a matter of recovering the constitutive intentions and beliefs which made
the colours or scratches what they are under a sociological definition.
Similarly, to 'decode' a *roman à clef* is to come to understand in the primary
sense that when the author wrote 'Madame de X' he in fact meant to
designate the real-life Madame de Y. But to 'decode' the myth of Asdiwal
as an expression of the strain inherent in a system of patrilocal but
matrilateral cross-cousin marriage* is an exercise in secondary, not
primary, understanding: it is to offer an explanation of why the content
of the myth is what we understand it in the primary sense to be. And
to 'decode' the metaphorical style of Flaubert by teasing out parallels and
overtones which can then be read back into his text is an exercise in
tertiary understanding: it is to offer a description of what the *oeuvre* is
like from the viewpoint of a reader as fully immersed as was Flaubert
himself in the nuances of the language in which it was composed.

Art, ritual, symbolism, ceremonial and such do undoubtedly pose
formidable difficulties of interpretation for sociologists, anthropologists
and historians, whatever interpretation 'interpretation' is given. But the
important methodological issue is neither the philosophical problem of

---

* Claude Lévi-Strauss, 'The Myth of Asdiwal', Eng. trans. in Edmund Leach, ed., *The
Structural Study of Myth and Totemism* (1967).

meaning on one side nor the technical problem of decipherment on the other. It is the problem of defining and preserving a criterion of theory-neutrality whereby the reportage of 'their' intentions and beliefs can be set out in terms acceptable to any rival observer who accepts that 'they' are truthful and of sound mind. In practice, one question leads inexorably to another: are they slaughtering the animal? Yes; but are they sacrificing it to a deity? Yes; but are they making an exculpatory thank-offering to the deity? Yes; but are they at the same time symbolically identifying the animal with the deity to whom the meat is being offered in exculpation and thanks? Yes; but do they really believe that the deity would have punished them if they failed to make the sacrifice in the ritually proper way? Yes; but have they ever systematically tested that belief? Well – no, but ... and we are already embroiled in all sorts of theoretical controversies about the nature of alien belief-systems before having settled our report of what it is they were 'really' doing in plunging the knife into the animal's throat in the first place. They may have been performing a sacrifice at least as unarguably as Mr Morley was performing a rain-dance. But whether 'sacrifice' is a term of reportage *alone* depends on how it is defined and used.*

THE CHOICE OF TERMS

§ 5. Thus far, I have mostly spoken as though the observations which sociologists report to their readers are all of actions as such. But of course they are not. Not only do they range over events, processes and states of affairs which will be reported in terms of emergent properties not predicable of individual actions as such, but they extend to signs, artefacts, traces, memorials and any number of things whose relation to observable actions is indirect and often obscure. To understand them in the primary sense is still to be able to specify the intentions and beliefs constitutive of them. But how is this to be done? The cosmetic implement which might be a weapon and the semiquaver which might be an inkstain are relatively clear-cut cases. It is true that to see a piece of metal as a strigil is to impose on it a presupposition about the possible habits and purposes of an agent who might have fashioned or used it, just as to see the mark on the paper as a semiquaver is to impose on it a presupposition about the possible tastes and conventions of an agent who might have composed or performed it. But in these examples the choices at the level of reportage are manageably narrow ones.

* Cf. G. S. Kirk, 'Some Methodological Pitfalls in the Study of Ancient Greek Sacrifice (in particular)', *Entretiens sur l'Antiquité Classique* [Fondation Hardt] XXVII (1981).

Imagine yourself, on the other hand, an archaeologist of the thirtieth century A.D. faced with this:

How much do you have to be able to say about it in order to satisfy a rival observer that you have understood it in the primary sense? It is an advertisement from a twentieth-century newspaper – so far, so good. But it will no more do to stop at the point of saying 'It is an advertisement for whatever "All Races" took "Humpty Dumpty on Ice" to be', than at the point of saying 'My informant believes whatever it is that they mean when they say that they believe in God the Father Almighty' or 'they are doing whatever "marrying" means in their culture'. Enough has still to be specified about the agents' intentions and beliefs and their context for the practising sociologist (or in this case, archaeologist) to be able to make it clear to his readers that Humpty Dumpty is a pantomime, the pantomime tradition extends in the culture in question to performances on skates, and the society is one in which the admission to public entertainments of persons classified according to certain legal rules as belonging to different 'races' is not to be taken as a matter of course. Such a report still says nothing about why pantomimes in general or Humpty Dumpty in particular were performed, let alone about what kind of account the audience might give of what it was like or what if any justification there may be for a society in which the race of the members of the audience is of any relevance to their admission. But it already involves the classification of the object in question not merely as a 'newspaper advertisement' but as a newspaper advertisement for one particular kind of thing (a public entertainment), and one particular kind of that kind of thing (a pantomime), and one particular kind of that kind of that kind of thing (a pantomime performed on skates); and it also involves the classification of the society not merely as one in which people pay to watch pantomimes on skates, but as a racially segregated one in which segregation does not always extend – but sometimes does or might – to attendance at public entertainments.

Talk of 'classification' here is a little premature, since to report an observation in such a way as to justify the claim to have understood it in the primary sense hardly calls for the elaborate exercises in taxonomy which may be necessary in the development of an explanatory (or descriptive or evaluative) theory. Yet to designate anything under any heading whatever is to categorize it as being one kind of thing as opposed to at least one other. To say no more than that 'Humpty Dumpty' stands for a pantomime is already to presuppose a drawing of perhaps debatable distinctions. Where reportage alone is at issue, the implicit classification need not be either rigorous or exhaustive: the accuracy of the report does not depend on specifying the exact relation of pantomime to opera buffa, musical comedy, vaudeville, farce, Punch and Judy shows, etc. But it does rest on the researcher's grounds for disposing of any suggestion by a rival observer that there is an alternative designation which should have been preferred to it by the criterion and for the purpose of primary understanding. The standard test of a classification in science generally is its capacity to generate explanations more powerful than their competitors, and in the sciences of man this extends to the further purposes of description and evaluation as may be called for. But the first test of the implicit classification underlying any reportage of human behaviour is that it should discriminate with sufficient precision within the range of possible intentions (and, where relevant, beliefs) which in the given context may be constitutive of the event, process, state of affairs, sign, artefact, trace, memorial, etc., which has been either directly or indirectly observed. The thirtieth-century archaeologist's first question, when confronted with what is in fact an advertisement from an issue of the *Capetown Times*, is: 'What does this mean that people were *doing*?' To answer it, he has to tell his readers enough to amount to a report but not so much as to imply, and still less to pre-empt, an explanation, description or evaluation. He may have all sorts of theories of his own about the origin and transmission of the pantomime as an art form, the wider repercussions in the sensibilities of its audience of its symbols and conventions or its use by a ruling élite to distract the members of a subject population from their proper awareness of social injustice. But if he is to claim it as a fact about South African society in the middle of the twentieth century that among its institutions and practices was the advertised performance on ice rinks before segregated audiences of the particular kind of theatrical entertainment known as 'pantomime', he must use these terms in a way which cannot be construed as doing more than identifying the intentions and beliefs of the performers, the audience and the public authorities which make 'Humpty Dumpty on Ice for All Races' a case of what he reports it to his readers as being.

§6. Yet no two independent observers will ever give identical reports of the same event, process or state of affairs, even if both subscribe with equal conviction to the methodology of reportage set out in this chapter. Nor will the differences between their two reports derive solely from philosophical disagreement over the scope and import of the concepts of intention and belief on the one hand or technical disagreement over the amount of fieldwork necessary to rule out special circumstances on the other. Even if they agree on both of these, they will still have had to make choices of terminology and presentation over which methodological arguments may arise. Here are five examples of different kinds in ascending order of difficulty:

(i) Both observers are watching the same exchange of shots between two armies. But one asserts and the other denies that it is a 'battle'. The disagreement is not over whether the combatants are 'really' fighting, since both are satisfied that it is more than a (mere) tourney, manoeuvre, feint or display. It is over whether it is as much of a fight as to count as a battle and not a (mere) brush, skirmish or fracas.

This is a borderline dispute of the kind that can be safely resolved by fiat. No doubt there will always be room for disagreement over how much of a fight is a battle, as over how large a cottage is a house, how small a book is a pamphlet or how numerous a group is a crowd. But the rival observers need only settle on some purely conventional dividing-line for the report to become uncontentious between them.

(ii) Both observers have witnessed the same handshake between two old friends who have met after an interval. But one reports them as 'performing the conventional ceremony of greeting' and the other as 'mutually acknowledging the duration of their parting'. There is no disagreement about the agents' intentions in grasping each other's hands. It is not as if one observer asserts but the other denies that they are, say, sealing a bargain or exchanging congratulations. But nor is it as if the two reports were reports of the same intentions and beliefs.

This sort of example is a little more contentious, not because it could be shown that either report is incompatible with the agents' own account of what they are doing but because of a possible implication that one rather than the other corresponds more nearly to what the agents might report of themselves. But any action can be reported under a number of alternative designations according to the aspect of it with which either the agent or the observer may be principally concerned. Provided that the chosen designation can indeed be shown to be acceptable in principle to the agents as consistent with their intentions and beliefs, the multiplicity of other possible designations is no argument against the choice of any particular one of them. Only if there is doubt about the absence of special circumstances which might require the designation to be qualified is one observer entitled to argue that the other's choice is not merely less relevant to his particular interests but unacceptable as the basis for a would-be theory-neutral report.

(iii) Both observers have discovered that in Ashoka's India there were roving ambassadors employed by the monarch to exercise intermittent plenipotentiary powers on his behalf in the outlying regions. But one is, and the other is not, prepared to designate them *missi dominici* on an analogy with the empire of Charlemagne. There is no accusation of mistranslation amounting to misreportage, as when the Spanish chroniclers designated as *mercatores* the Inca '*mindaláes*'* who were not in fact doing at all the same thing as contemporary European 'peddlers', '*Kaufmänner*', '*pieds poudreux*', 'broggers' or 'chapmen'. But there is a disagreement over the application of a term originating in one society to an ostensibly similar institution or practice independently evolved by another.

This is a case of the kind where the very similarity of 'dictionary' meaning may turn out to be deceptive. To report to Charlemagne that Ashoka too has what Charlemagne calls *missi dominici* or to Ashoka that Charlemagne too has what Ashoka calls *dhamma-mahāmāttas* may be a helpful elucidation *ad hominem*; but it cannot be claimed that the two are precisely equivalent to each other. Yet to appear to equate the two in this way is misreportage only if the dictionary meaning assigned to both ('roving ambassadors. . .' etc.) can be shown not to fit. Undoubtedly further research will disclose a number of differences in what they did and how they did it, and perhaps a too ready assimilation of the two carries a risk that they will be misexplained or misdescribed on that account. But that is immaterial to the theory-neutrality of the report that Charlemagne and Ashoka did both employ persons in roles the vernacular terms for which are equally compatible with the same extended definition given in answer to a request for a 'dictionary' meaning.

(iv) Both observers have been watching one of the celebrated 'potlatches' of the Kwakiutl Indians of the North-West Pacific coast. But one gives and the other refuses to accept the equation of 'potlatch' with 'agonistic prestation'. There is no doubt in either of their minds that it is a real potlatch – the natives are not just rehearsing or putting on a show for the tourists. But although 'gift-giving' and 'competing' are both demonstrably consistent with the declared intentions and beliefs of the agents there is still room for disagreement whether these are the aspects

*On whom see F. Salomon, 'Systèmes Politiques Verticaux aux Marches de l'Empire Inca', *Annales* XXIII (1973).

of the 'potlatch' which can uncontentiously be treated as constitutive of it.

In a case such as this one, there is a double difficulty. First, the proffered equivalent comes uncomfortably close to both explanatory and descriptive pre-emption: to say that it is a case of 'agonistic prestation' is to imply both that their motive in gift-giving is emulation and that this kind of gift-giving has more of the feel of Philip of Burgundy outdoing his nobles by giving his own Gargantuan feast at Lille, or Cleopatra outdoing Antony by dissolving her pearl in vinegar,* than of a normal exchange of presents between groups or persons proud, as is only natural, of their own largesse. Second, the potlatch is so much more complex an event than a rain-dance or a marriage that the interrelation of the individual actions of which it is composed is itself debatable: it needs, for a start, to be demonstrated and not assumed that the intentions and beliefs of the different participants are consistent with each other. Here, therefore, it is true to say that theory-neutrality can only be preserved by a form of designation which, as it were, decomposes the vernacular term. It is a matter of reportage that the natives are giving away, or in some instances destroying, accumulated possessions. It is also a matter of reportage that they are knowingly engaged in competition with the members of other clans. But if 'agonistic prestation' is to be equated with 'potlatch', then 'potlatch' will have to be conceded to be a theoretical term for 'us', even though it may be used as a term of straightforward reportage by 'them'.

(v) Both observers have been reading a narrative history of political and military events in England and Scotland between 1640 and 1645. But one reports those events as a 'civil war' and the other as a 'revolution'. They are not in dispute over the dates, places and outcomes of any of the battles that took place, and not even in their most sceptical moods does either of them seriously argue that the contending armies were not fighting for sovereignty over the kingdom. But they do disagree over whether the violent transformation of the society which undoubtedly occurred is or is not to be designated 'revolutionary'.

This type of disagreement is thoroughly familiar in polemics between historians of rival theoretical schools, and it is the less likely to be resolved the more complex the event, process or state of affairs over which it has arisen. But in this example, the two alternative terms are not on the same theoretical footing. If the dictionary meaning of 'revolution' specifies that it is a transformation brought about, sociologically speaking, from below,†

---

* These parallels are taken from Johan Huizinga, *Homo Ludens* (Eng. trans., 1950), Ch. 3 ('Play and Contest as Civilizing Functions').

† Which it does: the O.E.D. gives (under III.7) 'A complete overthrow of the established government in any country or state by those who were previously subject to it.'

then to apply it is to pre-empt at least a part of the explanation of what both observers agree to have occurred. 'Brought about from below' is a phrase in which a causal hypothesis is implicit already, and which may, depending on how it is used, carry descriptive and/or evaluative overtones as well. But to say that a war is a 'civil' war is (merely) to report that the fighting is between members of the same society: it may be a revolutionary civil war or it may not. There is, accordingly, nothing to prevent the disputants in this example from agreeing as a matter of reportage that a civil war was fought between 1640 and 1645 but disagreeing whether the social composition of the warring factions and the role of their constituent groups was such as to vindicate the further claim that it was a 'revolutionary' one.

All these different examples are typical enough of disputes which do frequently arise between practising sociologists, anthropologists and historians. They are sometimes less easy to resolve than my comments may suggest. But where they are, it is all the more important that the disputants should draw a clear-cut line between reportage and either explanation, description or evaluation. For otherwise, they can hardly fail to find themselves engaged in one of those dialogues of the deaf in which all the evidence brought to bear is presented to the reader in terms so firmly embedded in the presuppositions of one or another incompatible 'paradigm' or '*Problematik*' as to pre-empt all possibility of subsequent agreement. The danger, moreover, is present no less to the robust empiricist concerned only to get as close to the facts as he can than to the philosophically-minded theorist sensitive to all the implications of such topics as indeterminacy of translation, methodological individualism, value-relevance and the logic of counterfactual conditionals. The precaution to be taken is therefore twofold. It is not just that terms like 'potlatch' and 'revolution' have to be used in a way which makes clear whether or not they carry pre-emptive theoretical implications going beyond the intentions and beliefs constitutive of the agents' observed behaviour. In addition, clarification is necessary for terms like 'interpret' and 'understand' themselves. If an anthropologist tells his readers that, say, 'Preliterate societies are characterized by complex rules of marriage that can often be interpreted directly as power brokerage', the reader has somehow to have it made clear to him whether marriage rules and power brokerage are to be held to be matters of reportage only and 'direct' interpretation to be equated with primary understanding, or whether this is a claim for the validity of a reductionist explanation in which the causes of the restrictions observed to operate on potential marriage partners are traced to relations of power between the kinship groups to which the potential marriage partners belong.

There is no rule which the reader can apply to settle this question. It is the author who has to make it clear which kind of a claim is being made. Even if the intentions and beliefs constitutive of the actions of which the institution or practice is composed are unproblematic in themselves, it may not be obvious that its designation by the chosen term is a matter only of understanding in the primary sense. As the example of 'sacrifice' showed, it is often impossible to establish without ancillary argument how far a standard sociological term can be construed as a term of reportage alone. For this reason, I have chosen for more extended discussion two which have been mentioned already and which are, apart from their substantive interest, instructive in what may at first sight seem the unlikelihood that the second should be so very much less straightforward than the first: 'slavery' and 'magic'.

§7. I cited slavery in Section 4 of Chapter 1 in order to illustrate the difference between understanding in the primary, secondary and tertiary senses, and I assumed for that purpose that a report that the institution of slavery has been found to exist in a society is unproblematic. It is true that there is, as always, a possibility of primary misunderstanding. When, for example, in the nineteenth century the British sent recruiting officers up from the Gold Coast to Nigeria to offer bounties to potential trainees for their West African Force, they were mistakenly supposed by 'them' to be seeking either to buy slaves or to bribe slaves to run away from their existing owners.* But for the purpose of reportage, the question is only whether persons are legally and customarily owned by other persons or not. For the purposes of either description or evaluation, slavery is no doubt a very different thing not only between societies but within them. The experience of the trusted business agent of a wealthy Roman senator who is on the verge of manumitting him is, from his point of view, overwhelmingly more like that of other free Romans than it is like that of the chained, beaten and half-starved slave-gangs on the *latifundia* which the very same senator also owns. But it can hardly be a mistake to report that both are examples of slavery.

And yet: even if there is no dispute among rival observers about the existence of slavery in ancient Rome, could it not still be objected that it varies so much between one society and another as to cast doubt on any assimilation under a common term of the ownership of chattel slaves

---

* The example is taken from Jack Goody, 'Slavery in Time and Space', in James L. Watson, ed., *Asian and African Systems of Slavery* (1980), pp. 33–4, on which I have drawn for much of this section.

in Roman law and the ownership of slaves in, say, African societies where the conception of property embraces kinship relations and slavery is a form of adoption? The difficulty is not one of translation. It would make no difference if the argument were conducted entirely in Latin or an African language. It is that there is no common dictionary meaning of 'ownership' itself. It is not enough to distinguish slavery from helotry, peonage, indenture, penal incarceration, corvée labour, military conscription or tied tenancy. Even if all observers can agree that none of these involves ownership of persons as chattels, they may still disagree over resemblances and differences between the kinds of rights in, or over, other people which different forms and conceptions of slaveowning may involve. Among the Ila of what is now a part of Zambia, the essence of slavery was designation as born outside the village and absorption into the owner's kin-group, and slaves who lived long enough in the same village came to be regarded as no longer property. In the Ottoman Empire, the essence of it was entry into relationship to the Sultan in person, so that the obverse of the unfreedom of slavery was the privilege of office: until the system broke down, the military and administrative élite of the empire were slaves. In nineteenth-century Nepal, although the essence of slavery was ownership in an absolute, exclusive and complete sense, slaves could and indeed had to retain their caste, so that a household slave ranked higher in the fundamental ritual hierarchy of purity and pollution than even the richest untouchable.

But these and other such variations, whatever their implications may be for the explanation, description or evaluation of the society of which they are reported, do not undermine the use of 'slavery', defined explicitly as ownership of people, across the whole of the range. For they are, after all, variations in forms of what is still distinguishable from other forms of subordination by virtue of its assimilation of persons and the way they are treated to the other kinds of things that are bought, sold, pledged, discarded, bequeathed and given away. That the exercise of property rights is often restricted by law or custom is immaterial. The use which owners are permitted to make of animals which belong to them may likewise be restricted. Just because locally-born household slaves in the Comoro Islands could be sure of not being sold, it does not follow that they were not owned by their masters any more than it follows from the requirement that a Roman who had killed one of his slaves should perform an act of ritual purification – which he need not for the killing of an animal – that he did not own people and animals alike. Nor does it matter whether slaves are individually or corporately owned, or used for productive or non-productive purposes, or given their freedom by manumission or adoption, or acquired by purchase or by capture, or conceded or denied a family life of their own. None of this gives a rival observer grounds on which to dispute that 'slaves' are all, by virtue of being the property of others, deprived of their own discretion over the use of their bodies, time, work, skills and capacity for relations of kinship, marriage, parenthood or social intimacy in general.

A definition of slavery in terms of ownership does not eliminate the possibility of borderline cases. But they will be innocuous cases which can be settled by fiat and distinguished unambiguously from metaphorical parallels. Where, for example, a historian of race relations calls Indian indenture in Mauritius 'a new system of slavery', the term may be both descriptively and evaluatively apposite. But to report or, therefore, to explain it as such would be a primary misunderstanding of the same kind as to take literally a reference by the 'Great King' of Persia to his satraps as 'my slaves' or to equate the early Islamic non-servile *chākars**** with the servile Ottoman Janissaries. Similarly, when a mediaeval abbot of Vézelay says of one of his serfs 'he is mine from the soles of his feet to the crown of his head'† it would be a primary misunderstanding to construe this as an assertion that the man was not a serf but a slave. The genuine borderline cases are those in which either the relationship is transitional (as when a captured pawn may be ransomed, or a debt-slave is working his way to freedom) or there is a form of ownership so far curtailed by law and/or custom as to reduce the difference between slavery and freedom to vanishing-point. When, in the Roman case, the emperor Justinian remarked that tied tenants (*coloni adscripticii*) had come to be practically indistinguishable from agricultural slaves, he did not mean, any more than Bloch's abbot of Vézelay, that slaves had become serfs or serfs slaves: although it may be a valid explanation of the decline of slavery in the later Roman Empire to say that the progressive denial of rights to *coloni* created a functionally equivalent substitute, this does not imply that the difference in law and custom had disappeared altogether. But in the Chinese case, where chattel slavery was a firmly established practice within the context of strong patrilineages and widespread peasant poverty, there was a category of female dependents who, although bought as chattels for use in unpaid domestic service, were in some parts of China, at least, explicitly and automatically accorded the status of lesser daughters. Rival observers may, therefore, disagree over whether these *mui jai* were slaves of a kind always conceded kinship rights by their

---

* On whom see M. A. Shaban, *Islamic History: a New Interpretation* II (1976), Ch. 4.
† Quoted by Bloch in his *Feudal Society* (Eng.trans., 1961), p. 265.

owners or adopted daughters acquired by purchase. But it does not pre-empt a subsequent explanation, description or evaluation to report the practice in the one way or the other. Slavery defined in terms of owner-ship of persons by persons is still a term of reportage which can be applied by observers of the Ila, the Ottomans and the Nepalese as well as of ancient Greece and Rome, the Caribbean, Brazil and the Southern United States.

The objection may still be maintained that this is not the most useful way of defining slavery. But usefulness is always relative to some further theoretical purpose. Once the category of involuntary labour on behalf of others is to be further sub-divided, it is entirely permissible to separate, say, formally free wage-labour from all other types and then to classify the other types by reference not to ownership/non-ownership of persons but to degrees of rightlessness which in turn correlate with ownership at different points and in different ways. This will have the effect of bracketing some relatively privileged slaves with some junior kinsmen and indentured apprentices while marking off the chattel slave proper from the outsider introduced into a household as the corporate property of a lineage, and it may well be that the explanation, description and/or evaluation of the societies in question will be better advanced thereby. Indeed, it might even happen that observers of all rival schools came in the end to agree that the concept of 'slavery' defined in terms of ownership was of so little value that it could be discarded altogether without in any way inhibiting the further progress of substantive research. But that would be a very different matter from discarding it in the face of a methodological argument that it never was or could be used theory-neutrally in the first place.

§ 8. With magic, on the other hand, the case is very different.* It is true that sociologists, anthropologists and historians have often reported observations of the practice of 'magic' at times and places where the evidence permits the intentions and beliefs constitutive of the agents' practices to be clearly specified. Why not, therefore, frame a working definition along the lines that in 'magic' agents believe in the existence of unseen powers, their intention is to manipulate (rather than to worship, implore or propitiate) those powers and the rules governing the attempted manipulations exclude any systematic test of its efficacy? And why not then dispose of borderline cases by fiat? This time, however, it cannot be done.

The difference is that in the case of owning people, as in that of fighting

* For this section I have drawn particularly on John Skorupski, *Symbol and Theory* (1976).

battles, the necessarily arbitrary discrimination between borderline cases is immaterial to the grounds on which the observer's claim to understanding in the primary sense is based; but in the case of manipulating unseen powers, it is critical to it. The alternative report which the rival observer proffers will not only draw the boundaries of 'magic' differently but in so doing will modify the designation applied to the constitutive intentions and beliefs held to be common to all 'magical' practices. The dispute might, in the event, hinge merely on rival definitions of 'manipulate' and could accordingly be resolved by adopting criteria so general that any attempt to bring about a change in the course of natural or human events can be accommodated within it: understanding in the primary sense would then rest on the observer's satisfying himself merely that he had not failed to rule out the possibility that 'they' might be joking, play-acting, demonstrating, experimenting, etc. But if 'manipulation' is to be used to designate literally *any* attempt to cause something to happen, 'magic' ceases to serve the purpose for which it was originally introduced as a would-be standard sociological term. Most of the sociologists, anthropologists and historians who have used the term in their writings have wanted, in designating an observed practice as 'magical', to mark it off alike from 'science' on the one hand and 'religion' on the other, magic being generally seen as non-systematic manipulation, science as systematic manipulation and religion as systematic non-manipulation. Their difficulty, however, has been that these designations can be used as terms of reportage acceptable to all observers only if, once the borderline has been drawn, they are exclusive. They may admittedly coincide in the sense that the event, process or state of affairs may involve more than one of them, or in the sense that the agents whose behaviour has been observed may at different times practise all three. But the same action must not at the same time be reported as a manipulation and not, or as systematic and not. Magic, however defined, is exposed as a term of more than reportage if two observers, both of whom are satisfied that they have sufficient evidence to claim understanding in the primary sense and agree the accuracy of each other's field-notes, still disagree in a way that they cannot jointly dismiss as a purely verbal borderline dispute over what is or is not to count as an instance of it.

This, however, is just what happens. The disagreements between rival observers are not over where to draw borderlines or even over whether 'magic' could, for convenience, be redefined in some narrower sense which would restrict its reported occurrence to a small number of designated societies whose members share a common set of precisely specified beliefs. They are over which of the practices that are agreed to involve the intention of, and belief in, influencing the course of human or natural events are to be bracketed with which. In this case, unlike the reportage of a pantomime on skates, classification is neither premature nor irrelevant. Thus Frazer, in *The Golden Bough*, is explicit that magic is 'barren' by definition: anything that has passed or, presumably, could pass systematic test is not magic but science. But from this it must follow that much of medicine is to be labelled magical, for relatively little of it has been subjected to systematic test and relatively few of its practitioners have been able to give an adequate rationale for all the treatments which they have prescribed. At the same time, Frazer's insistence that manipulation of impersonal powers is to be contrasted with pleas for assistance addressed to personal powers has to accommodate the fact that impersonal powers may be invoked by incantations amounting to pleas and pleas may be addressed to personal powers as a means of manipulating the course of events. Frazer's views do not need to be taken as definitive. But variants of the distinction as drawn by other 'classical' authorities have scarcely fared better. Durkheim's variant continues to maintain a distinction not only between magic and religion on the grounds that magic has neither a church nor a conception of sin but also between magic and science on the grounds that science is on the profane or secular side of the line between what is 'sacred' and what is not; but the differences are then blurred to the point of invisibility by his continuing also to insist that – in his own words – '*la foi qu'inspire la magie n'est qu'un cas particulier de la foi religieuse en général*' and '*la pensée scientifique n'est qu'une forme plus parfaite de la pensée religieuse*'.* A third form of the distinction, which goes back to Tyler's *Primitive Culture* (1871), retains the distinction between magic and religion in terms of the personal nature of the powers to whom the religious believer addresses his prayers while distinguishing magic from science in terms of the magician's unreflecting belief in a form of causal relation between talking about things and acting on them which the scientist rejects as untested; but this requires us to bracket, for example, Christian baptism with magic while still leaving us with the difficulty that much medicine and agronomy and a good deal of other 'science' is unreflecting and untested too. Yet a fourth approach, combining parts of Tyler with parts of Durkheim and resting on the observation that much ostensibly 'magical' ritual is purely symbolic, distinguishes between magical and non-magical manipulation in terms of an acceptance of unsystematic empiricism as 'rational' (e.g. planting crops where previous generations have planted them, but without knowing why) and a dismissal

*Emile Durkheim, *Les formes élémentaires de la vie religieuse* (1912), pp. 577 and 613.

of 'magic' as not being literally believed in by those who practise it (e.g. pressing the elevator button several times when in a hurry); but this merely takes us back where we started, for the problem of understanding such behaviour in the primary sense is precisely that of distinguishing that which *is* informed by a belief of a particular kind from that which isn't.

These continuing difficulties in arriving at a definition of 'magic' which would be mutually acceptable to all rival observers do not in themselves show the attempt to be misconceived. But they do show that the different agents' intentions and beliefs cannot all be lumped under a single rubric. It *may* be possible to frame a definition which discriminates both precisely and consistently among all the varieties of haruspication, faith-healing, sorcery, incantation of spells, ritual purification, symbolic identification of substances, propitiation of divinities, initiation ceremonies, prophecy, witchcraft, *defixio*, lucky charms, sacramentalism, demonic possession, thaumaturgy, astrology, communion with spirits and shamanism which have by now been documented in the historical and ethnographic record. But such a definition will have gone well beyond a theory-neutral reportage of cases whose claimed similarity to each other can be vindicated by direct reference to the agents' own intentions and beliefs in the contexts in which they have been observed.

Nothing in all this prevents the use of 'magic' for explanatory, descriptive or evaluative purposes. But where it is being so used, it must not be so phrased as to appear to be passing as a term of reportage alone: the implicit theory and the definition tailored to it must be made explicit. The sociologist who has an explanatory hypothesis about the psychological need underlying rituals for the avoidance of danger may quite legitimately want to use 'magic' to connect the behaviour of the deep-sea (but not lagoon) fishermen of the Trobriand Islands as observed by Malinowski, the Acapulco divers who cross themselves before each plunge from the cliffs, and the soldiers of all ages who have carried talismans with them into battle; the sociologist who sees a descriptive parallel between the atmosphere generated by widely different forms of symbolic behaviour associated with the promotion of communal effort may quite legitimately want to use 'magic' to assimilate work-dances, crop-festivals, ship-launchings and academic sociology conferences; the sociologist concerned to disparage beliefs not vindicated by empirical test of the relative success of different means to common ends may quite legitimately want to use 'magic' to bracket government economic policies of which he disapproves with folk medicine. But the assertion that 'they are practising magic', although couched in the form of an ostensible report of observed behaviour, should not be construed as relating to the observations made in the same theory-neutral way as 'it is a rain-dance', or 'they are getting married', or 'he is aiming a gun at a rabbit', or 'Clemenceau tweaked Lloyd George's nose', or 'they believe in God', or 'they are fighting a battle', or 'it is an advertisement for an unsegregated performance of a pantomime on skates' or 'they own slaves'.

THE BOUNDS OF REPORTAGE

§9. In the ordinary case, appeal against the alternative designation of events, processes or states of affairs put forward by a rival observer will be to the intentions and beliefs of the agents as these are reported by themselves: the only exceptions will be those unusual cases where the agents can be shown to be ignorant of something constitutive of their actions. But this principle would be too restrictive if erected into a methodological directive governing the criteria of legitimate reportage. It is perfectly possible for the observer to report 'their' actions in terms which 'they' do not possess without thereby overstepping the boundary of reportage into the territory of explanation, description or evaluation. The sociologist who wants to report a case of what he calls 'patrilineal segmentation' is well aware that the members of the society in question do not conceptualize their system of kinship in terms like these any more than they talk about the salt which they eat in a term equivalent to what we call 'sodium chloride'. How astonished Evans-Pritchard would have been if one of his Nuer informants whom he had questioned had replied by taking a twig and scratching in the sand a diagram like the one below:

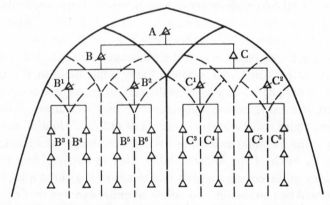

But unless the rival observer can produce evidence to show, as it might be, that despite appearances sons, or sons' sons, come to form separate lineages with their own names and rituals and reciprocal ceremonial relations, the assertion that patrilineal segmentation has been observed among the Nuer may be counted as a report which, if conveyed to 'them', would be allowed by them to be entirely consistent with their own way of putting it.

The criterion of what 'they' would agree to accept can, moreover, be invoked without the practising sociologist's needing to be drawn into philosophical debates about what exactly it is that synonymy consists in. It is true that in an example such as 'sodium chloride', to induce 'them' to accept the term involves acquainting them with knowledge of a kind which we possess but they may not: it is only by virtue of the discoveries of chemistry that the equivalence is established, in contrast to the synonymy which obtains between, say, 'bachelor' and 'unmarried man'. But to the practising sociologist, what matters is not the nature of the difference between synonymy of these two, or any other, kinds but only 'their' readiness to accept that 'patrilineal segmentation' does apply to what 'they' do without their having to be told anything else about 'our' explanatory, descriptive or evaluative theories of kinship. And once they do accept it, then whatever objections the rival observer may raise about what *he* regards as the gratuitous intrusion of alien jargon, the sociologist who finds 'patrilineal segmentation' a useful term of reportage is entitled to present it to his readers as such.

Conversely, he is equally well entitled, on grounds of convenience, to discard a term of reportage of 'theirs'. If, for example, he is studying the social structure of eighteenth-century Spain, he will hardly be in a position to dispute the designation of certain adult males by the census-takers of 1787 as *hidalgos*. He has no grounds for suspecting them of misreportage; they are not mistaken about something intrinsic to the applicability of the designation like the person who says 'It's a lighthouse' when it is a mirage or 'It's a cheque' when there aren't the institutions which would enable the piece of paper ever to be exchanged for cash. But when he discovers, as he will,* that whereas every adult male in the Basque provinces is designated 'hidalgo', less than 1% of them are so designated in the centre and south, he may well feel something to be amiss. This is not a problem about the dictionary meaning of *hidalgo*. '*Hidalgo*' is etymologically a *hijo* (or *filho*) *de algo*, or 'son of something', which is to say a member by birth of the lower nobility. But so remarkable a regional discrepancy in the census suggests that to report it without qualification might indeed be tantamount to a failure of understanding in the primary

* Cf. Raymond Carr, 'Spain', in A. Goodwin, ed., *The European Nobility in the Eighteenth Century*² (1967), pp. 44–5.

sense. In fact, the answer to the discrepancy lies in the relation between inherited status and the reconquest of Spain from the Moors; and the researcher who has come to realize it is perfectly justified, if he so chooses, in abandoning 'their' term of reportage in favour of terms of his own which, while still acceptable in principle to 'them', may encapsulate in a way that *hidalgo* does not that feature of the context of the terminology of eighteenth-century Spain which leads to an otherwise incomprehensible regional discrepancy in the census.

§ 10. Difficult as some decisions of this kind may be, the limit of reportage has still not been reached. Under certain conditions, a yet further degree of relaxation is permissible. There is no objection in practice to terms of 'ours' which do explicitly carry explanatory, descriptive or evaluative presuppositions if they can be introduced in such a way that propositions embodying them can still be construed by the reader as if they were only reports. It remains essential that the theoretical purpose and the definition tailored to that purpose be made explicit. But if they are, even terms which the rival observer may regard as not merely controversial but thoroughly misconceived can nonetheless be allowed to stand. The test is not synonymy in 'their' terms, but the demonstrable possibility of transposition *salva veritate* into whatever alternative terms the rival observer may prefer.

Perhaps surprisingly, this holds even where the purpose is descriptive. It remains true that, as I have already argued, agents' own accounts are privileged in sociological description in a way in which in explanation they are not. But as we shall see in Chapter 4, where the criteria of misdescription are analysed in more detail, it would be a mistake to suppose that agents cannot honestly misdescribe what they have thought, felt, said or done. There is always the possibility that rival observers (who may also be participants) will disagree over descriptive terms as well as over explanatory or evaluative ones; and where they do, it may be equally possible to transpose them in a way which leaves the theory-neutrality of the reports which they embody intact.

Consider, for example, the term 'Renaissance'. On the one hand, it is commonly used to denote the period from roughly the fourteenth to the sixteenth centuries A.D. during which there took place in Western Europe, and particularly Northern and Central Italy, a revival of classical art and learning, the articulation of an individualistic and secular ethic and the emergence of city-republics embodying what we would now call the 'modern' conception of the state. But its point is not simply to designate that period and whatever events and processes can uncontroversially be reported as having taken place in it. It is also to convey the descriptive implication that those events and processes were like a rebirth. A rival observer who disputes the use of the term need not be disputing that there did take place a conscious revival of classical art and learning, etc., but merely that the metaphor of 'rebirth' is appropriate to it. The reason why the term has passed into common use is that it has come to be generally accepted that the agents whose observed behaviour is covered by the designation, whether or not they actually conceived of their actions in terms of a metaphor of rebirth, were nonetheless aware of a relationship between their institutions and practices and those of the Roman past. If in the course of further research it were to turn out that, say, Petrarch did not write in imitation of Horace or Machiavelli in commentary on Livy, that the *capitani del popolo* had no sense of recreating in their office and its functions the old *tribuni plebis*, that the orators of the period did not take Cicero and Quintilian as their models or the architects and their patrons Vitruvius, that Federigo da Montefeltre knew nothing of Greek or Latin literature and that Alfonso the Great's enthusiasm for antiquity is an invention of later historians, then the term ought to, and no doubt would, be discarded forthwith. But as it is, there is an abundance of evidence for the claim that not only the scholars but also the statesmen of the period were imbued with an intention of, and belief that they were, recreating both the artistic and the political achievements of their pre-decessors in ancient Rome after the period which came with hindsight to be designated the 'Middle Ages', and it is the demonstrable accuracy of reports to that effect which authenticate the descriptive use.

On the other hand, however, there is much less agreement among rival observers as to whether the events and processes which took place in China under the Sung Dynasty between roughly the eleventh and the thirteenth centuries A.D. were such that the metaphor of rebirth is apposite there too. There was admittedly an advance, which was also in part a revival, of learning; there was a restoration of political stability through the re-establishment of central control over the large landed proprietors who had benefited during the 'Middle Empire' from the breakdown of the militia system and enforced restriction on private landholdings introduced under the T'ang; there was a return to the classical tradition of secular thought which amounted to a reversal of the protracted dominance of Buddhism; and there was a conscious attempt to exploit and disseminate the discoveries in metallurgy, medicine, time-keeping, mathematics and chemistry inherited from the past. But there was no resurrection of ancient models such as took place in the European Renaissance, for in China they had never been so far forgotten; there was no previous period sufficiently analogous to the European 'Middle Ages' to justify the description of the emergence from them by a metaphor of rebirth; there was no institution sufficiently closely corresponding to the Church which in Europe had not only rivalled but displaced the earlier culture; and the restoration of political forms which had broken down in the middle of the eighth century was a successful recentralization of a country always liable to political fragmentation, not a recreation in the sense that the Italian city-republics were a recreation of the classical *poleis*. The historian or sociologist of China, therefore, who does, as some do, wish to use the term 'Renaissance' to designate the events and processes which took place under the Sung is well aware that there are rival observers who will reject it. But in so doing, these others do not need to be disputing either that there did take place an advance, which was also in part a conscious revival, of learning, etc., or that it is these particular events and processes which the term 'Sung Renaissance' is being used to designate. They remain free to reject the descriptive presupposition as misconceived while accepting as accurate reports framed in terms which imply, and are meant to imply, that presupposition.

Where the presuppositions are instead (or in addition) evaluative, transposition *salva veritate* will be still more readily feasible, since the designation used will be bound to permit the disentanglement of its ostensive meaning from the value-judgement implicit in it. This, as I conceded in Section 8 of Chapter 1, is not always as easy in practice as it sounds in principle. But in the ordinary case, the use of an evaluative term does not prevent the assertion in question from functioning as a simple report which the rival observer can accept as accurate even if he is wholly out of sympathy with the evaluation presupposed. Consider, for example, the designation of an employment policy as a practice of 'discrimination'. Nothing prevents the rival observer from agreeing that on the given definition the policy *was* discriminatory while rejecting the presupposition that if so it must therefore be a bad one. Nor does it matter whether the definition is generally adopted either in law or by custom by the members of the society within which the practice has been observed. If a sociologist who is studying employment practices in his own or any other society observes in the field that employers take on men in preference to women and whites in preference to blacks to a degree greater than can possibly be attributed to chance, then even if this involves no breach of the legislation in force in the society governing equality of opportunities he is still quite entitled to state as a matter of reportage that 'discrimination' occurs with a specified frequency; and the rival observer who regards such practices as excusable and/or inevitable and/or positively desirable can still accept the frequency of occurrence as a matter of reportage which can be checked in the same way as reportage of wage-rates, labour turn-over, distribution of the labour force by size of firm or any other such less emotive and, at first sight, more objectively measurable feature of the economy in question.

Where, finally, the underlying presupposition is explanatory, the problem of consistency with 'their' terms barely arises at all. If, in the example which I used in Chapter 1, the ancient Romans lacked the concept of malaria this in no way undermines its value in explaining what happened to the inhabitants of the Pontine Marshes, and if they lacked the concept of inflation this in no way undermines its value in explaining what happened to food prices during the third century A.D. as the silver *denarius* progressively declined in value. A rival observer who rejects a proffered explanation will, naturally, be reluctant to use as a term of reportage a designation whose explanatory presuppositions he believes to be invalid. He will not mind 'their' being reported as including 'sodium chloride' in their diet because its synonymy with 'salt' is theoretically uncontroversial, whereas he may well be much less happy with the attribution to 'them' of, say, 'collective neurosis' even if his own observations are not in conflict at the level of understanding in the primary sense. The test remains, however, whether transposition *salva veritate* is possible; and if it is, the rival observer should be prepared to accept as a term of reportage even a term pre-emptive of a theory which he believes to be generative of invalid explanatory hypotheses.

As an example chosen to bring out the possibility of transposition *salva veritate* despite irreconcilable theoretical disagreements of all three kinds, consider the term 'exploitation'. Explanatorily used, it commonly presupposes a commitment to a labour theory of value; descriptively used, it commonly presupposes a conviction that 'they' were at least implicitly aware of a common interest against their employers; evaluatively used, it commonly presupposes a moral criterion whereby the extraction of surplus value from the employees who created it by their labour is wicked. Yet a rival observer who shares none of these presuppositions can despite this transpose the reportage of the occurrence of 'exploitation' *salva veritate* into his own alternative terms. Suppose that the rival observer subscribes to a Pigovian rather than a Marxian theory of labour economics. For him, 'exploitation' is therefore to be defined in terms of the following diagram:*

---

* See A. C. Pigou, *The Economics of Welfare* (1920), p. 512 n.1.

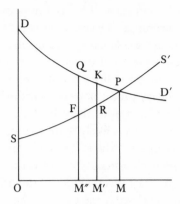

Here PM is taken to be the general wage-rate resulting from free competition in a market economy, while RM′ is the rate most profitable to employers acting in combination as opposed to QM″ which is the rate most profitable to workers. If RM′ is paid then, for Pigou, 'unfairness' is the excess of PM over RM′ and 'exploitation' the excess of KM′ over RM′. This way of looking at it may again be as remote from 'theirs' as would be a labour theory of value. But provided that the appropriate values of wage-rates can be assigned, then a report to the effect that particular groups of workers were or were not being exploited on a given occasion can be accepted as accurate by the Marxian observer too, just as the Pigovian observer can accept as accurate a report that, say, there has been a 'heightening of the rate of exploitation' when to him the better way to phrase the same admitted social fact would be to say that 'as a result of a well-judged investment in more sophisticated technology an increase in per capita output has been achieved'. The two of them are not required to agree on whether either of their conflicting theories marks a scientific advance analogous to that which licenses the designation of 'salt' as 'sodium chloride', or on whether one or other of them is better fitted to convey to their readers what the experience of the employees whose wage-rates they are reporting was like for those employees themselves, or on whether one allocation of investible resources as between capital investment and higher wages is more or less of a good thing or a bad thing than another. But nothing prevents their agreeing that the other is perfectly capable of reporting observed cases of what he chooses for reasons of his own to call 'exploitation' in a manner which passes the tests both of understanding in the primary sense and of accuracy of correspondence with what has in fact occurred.

§ 11. There does now come a point, however, beyond which a restriction needs once again to be imposed. This is the point beyond which the criteria of reportage become, as it were, submerged too deep for recovery under the pre-emptively explanatory, descriptive or evaluative presuppositions of the terms used to designate the events, processes or states of affairs observed. It might still be maintained that terms which risk overstepping the boundary can, if it seems worthwhile, be rescued by a stipulative redefinition which pulls them back out of danger. But as we saw in the case of 'magic', this is likely to undermine the purpose of their introduction in the first place. 'Magic' can be defined in such a way as to function as a theory-neutral term only by retreating from the problem of categorizing together or apart certain kinds of intention and belief which, in their context, throw up borderline cases of the kind which cannot be resolved by fiat. And in the same way, there is a multitude of terms commonly used to designate events, processes and states of affairs which must, if they are to retain the original purpose of introducing them, pre-empt explanation, description or evaluation to an extent which makes transposition *salva veritate* unattainable.

Consider, from this point of view, the term 'feudalism'. Like 'Renaissance', it has passed into common currency, and there may seem little that is controversial about its use to designate the fusion of benefice and vassalage as observed in certain parts of Western Europe during the so-called Middle Ages and as first so labelled in the early eighteenth century by the Comte de Boulainvilliers. It is true that even on the most restricted definition, it is still open to a rival observer to challenge the reportage of particular instances on the grounds that it has not been established that this *was* a granting of landholding on the basis of continuing ownership by the grantor coupled with entry into bonds of commendation and protection between grantor and grantee. But once the necessary understanding in the primary sense has been achieved, there may seem no reason to treat as contentious talk of a 'feudal' society or an age of 'feudalism'. Unfortunately, however, the use of these terms is very much more problematic than this. It is not merely that numerous sociologists, anthropologists and historians of widely differing theoretical persuasions have wanted to apply them to societies remote in both time and place from those that Boulainvilliers had in mind,* but that the explanatory, descriptive and evaluative presuppositions carried, and meant to be carried, by them are disputable in a way which can be settled neither by fiat nor by reference to the intentions and beliefs of the agents themselves.

*Cf. e.g. the bibliography in J. S. Critchley, *Feudalism* (1978), pp. 192–205.

It is immaterial to the methodological argument which of the disputants are in the right and which in the wrong. In Volume II, I shall have to return to several of the substantive issues about social relations, social structure and social evolution which the concept of feudalism raises. But for the moment, I am concerned only to show that there is a clear-cut boundary beyond which the incompatible presuppositions of rival observers cannot be reconciled for the purpose of reportage by transposition *salva veritate* into each others' terms. The claim that the fusion of benefice and vassalage constitutes a distinctive form of social organization already carries, in the absence of special explanation to the contrary, a presupposition that the society in question is one in which power rests on land-ownership and sovereignty is decentralized. If vassalage is fused with benefice, this must be a function at once of need and possibility – need on the part of vassals for lords and of lords for vassals, and possibility both in the sense of political institutions and military technology (or lack of them) permitting the decentralization of sovereignty and in the sense of a system of production permitting the extraction of a surplus from a dependent peasantry. But by now we are well beyond the point at which disputes over borderline cases can be resolved without compromising the possibility of transposition. No doubt we *can* stipulate that 'feudalism' is to designate the system embodying those, and only those, fusions of benefice and vassalage which can be reported as such to the satisfaction of all observers of certain parts of Western Europe during the Middle Ages. But this is almost as much of a retreat from any problem of substantive sociology as 'It is an advertisement for whatever "All Races" took "Humpty Dumpty on Ice" to be', 'they are doing whatever it is that is called "marrying" in their culture' or 'my informant believes whatever it is that they mean when they say that they believe in God the Father Almighty'.

The denial that transposition is feasible can best be tested against the designation as 'feudal' of the one society which has been held by qualified observers most closely to resemble the Western European case: Japan. It has been argued among others by Bloch himself that the salient characteristics of the European fusion of benefice and vassalage are also present in Japan: viz. (in Bloch's words), 'A subject peasantry; widespread use of the service tenement (i.e. the fief) instead of a salary, which was out of the question; the supremacy of a class of specialized warriors; ties of obedience and protection which bind man to man, and within the warrior class, assume the distinctive form called vassalage; fragmentation of authority leading inevitably to disorder; and, in the midst of all this, the survival of other forms of association, family and state...'* What is more, 'they' have a word for it themselves: *chigyō*. Why, therefore, is it not a matter of reportage that Japan, like Western Europe, passed, as Bloch holds, through a 'feudal' phase?

The difficulties, however, begin to emerge even on inspection of the notion of vassalage itself, for the 'ties of obedience and protection' which bound man to man under the *chigyō* system were, as Bloch was aware, simply not the same as those of Western Europe. In the first place, in Japan, despite the continuance of a titular monarchy, the 'chain of vassalage' came to an end before reaching the throne, whereas in Europe the monarch stood at the visible apex of the hierarchy of commendation. Secondly, multiple fealties were virtually unknown in Japan, where the ties of vassalage were much more those of a quasi-familial obedience to the lord than of a quasi-contractual relationship of homage. Thirdly, by comparison with Europe, legalism remained rudimentary in Japan, where there were no vassal courts. Fourthly, the people of Japan, geographically isolated as they have been throughout their history in a way that applies to no country in Europe, were imbued with a degree of national consciousness which not merely was absent among the peoples of Europe during the 'feudal' age but can be argued to be positively inconsistent with the pattern of loyalties engendered by the fragmentation of Europe during the period in which the institution of the fief evolved.

These difficulties are compounded as soon as we go on to ask what is implied in the notion of feudalism as a 'phase'. There will be no dispute that in Japan, as in Europe, the historical period within which the designation is plausible is bounded at either end by periods characterized by economic, social and political institutions very different in kind. But to seek to apply Bloch's extended definition to the Japanese case raises the question when precisely it is that the characteristics which he lists were so far salient in Japan as to license the claim that it was passing through a 'feudal' phase. The *chigyō* system evolved from the previous *shōen* system under which local lords collected dues directly from their subject peasantry; but they were then doing so within a continuing framework of central institutions inherited from the eighth-century Taihō Codes. When this framework broke down in the Sengoku period, it was a breakdown which could as well be designated 'civil war' as 'feudalism'. The Tokugawa Shogunate, which followed the progressive reunification of the late sixteenth century, retained the fusion of benefice and vassalage to the extent that half the Tokugawa lands themselves were granted to their so-called 'bannermen' (*hatamoto*) while the 'outside' (*tozama*) lords

* *Feudal Society*, p. 446.

controlling the North-East and South-West of Japan were left in seigneurial control of their own domains, taxing their own peasantry, raising and maintaining their own armies, and decreeing their own law. Yet at the same time, the Shoguns instituted the beginnings of a salaried bureaucracy, a national standing army, periods of enforced residence by the regional lords and their families in the capital city, a network of police informers stretching over the whole of the country, and a monopoly of the minting of gold and silver coinage. Even in the Sengoku period, the fact that there was a word which appears to translate readily into English as 'fief' is no more a justification for labelling the system 'feudal' than the fact that in neighbouring Korea there was a social group of *chungin*, which translates readily into 'middle men', is a justification for talking about the existence of a Korean 'bourgeoisie'. Even the relationship of vassalage itself could be viewed not as intrinsic to the *chigyō* system so much as perpetuating in a new form the relationships already present in the pre-Taihō Yamata state between the 'vassal clans' (*miyatsuko*) and the Sun Line. How, therefore, can the term 'feudalism' possibly be used to designate the form of social organization of Japan at any period in such a way that the rival observer who disagrees can accept it as if it were a matter of reportage alone?

Thus it is not simply that any attempt to apply a term coined in, and for, Europe to the very different culture of Japan is bound to submerge the criteria of reportage under the explanatory, descriptive or evaluative presuppositions of the researcher who has chosen to apply it. It is that 'feudal' cannot be divested of pre-emptive theoretical overtones if only because the purpose of emphasizing the significance of a fusion of benefice and vassalage is to carry them; and this being so, propositions about any society to which it is applied can no longer function as reports transposable *salva veritate* into the terminology of rival observers from different theoretical schools. The boundary-line has accordingly to be drawn at whatever point the designations embodied in a set of report-like, theory-neutral-seeming propositions can no longer pass this test.

§ 12. Reports of human behaviour, therefore, can be accepted as factual by rival observers, even from different theoretical schools, if but only if two conditions are satisfied: first, that they are not pre-emptive of any subsequent explanation, description or evaluation of the event, process or state of affairs of which the report is made; second, that they are demonstrably accurate in what they assert of not only the words and gestures but the intentions and beliefs, in their context, of the agents of whose behaviour the event, process or state of affairs consists. The two cannot, however, be treated independently of each other, since appeal to a criterion of accuracy presupposes already that the boundary between reportage and explanation, description or evaluation has itself been drawn. In order, therefore, to make it easier to distinguish in practice between misreportage attributable to inaccurate observation and mis-reportage attributable to theoretical pre-emption, I propose to introduce another hypothetical person alongside the rival observer. This second person, to whom I shall refer from now on as the 'recording angel', is supposed to have been present at and throughout whatever event, process or state of affairs is under discussion, but to have brought to it no explanatory, descriptive or evaluative presuppositions of any kind. He has no views at all about such questions as whether the labour theory of value is valid, or whether the metaphor of rebirth can authentically be applied to the so-called 'Sung Renaissance', or whether a racially dis-criminatory employment policy is morally unjustifiable or not. He is only, as it were, the keeper of a videotape library so comprehensive and so detailed as to put him in a position to see and hear everything that an enquiring fieldworker could ever have wanted to see or hear. Thus, the kind of thing that he can pass on to us as requested does not merely include who begat the begetter of Saul, what proportion of salaried male employees in England and Wales were in occupational pension schemes in 1956–7 and whether any heroic *chansons* in the vernacular were in circulation before 1000. It extends also to a knowledge of how much is omitted from Bismarck's memoirs about the events leading up to the Franco–Prussian war, what figure the population of Baghdad reached under the Abbasid Caliphate, whether the French fired first at Fontenoy, who wrote the letters of 'Junius', whether Athens was walled before the Persian invasion,* and what name Achilles (if he existed) assumed when he hid himself among women (if he did).

Even this modest list may invite two related objections. First, it is surely misleading to imply that the accuracy of a sociologist's report is always to be assessed as though it were a matter of arithmetical precision. Second, even where so limited a criterion *is* the appropriate one, the recording angel has still to be credited with some knowledge of the inner states of the agents whose behaviour is preserved for posterity on his videotapes, and this must surely involve him in theoretical speculation sufficient to defeat my purpose of introducing him as a hypothetically authoritative source for what 'really' took place.

---

* Which Herodotus and Thucydides both say that it was, but modern archaeologists have been unable to confirm.

There is, however, nothing controversial in an admission that accuracy is a criterion relative to the purpose for which it is sought. Total accuracy is an unattainable ideal in any empirical science, whether natural or social. What matters to the practising sociologist is not that his reports should be absolutely precise, or even as precise as is technically feasible, but that they should be precise enough for his subsequent explanations, descriptions and evaluations. For example: if the Occupational Tables of the Census of Population of the United Kingdom for 1951 are as accurate as they are set out to appear, then there were in that year two clergymen of the Church of England, four solicitors, four doctors, one dentist, ten opticians, twenty-three chiropodists and thirty-four qualified accountants all under sixteen years of age.* We do not need to send the enumerators back into the field for a recheck before dismissing these figures as nonsense. Yet what purpose could be in the mind of a practising sociologist, anthropologist or historian of any theoretical school which would require this palpable inaccuracy to be corrected before the Occupational Tables in the 1951 Census could be put to use in an explanation, description or evaluation of the social structure of mid twentieth-century Britain? Or again: if I read in a textbook history of Japan that that country was 'completely cut off from international commerce' in the Tokugawa period, I do not dismiss its author as a liar or a charlatan just because I happen to know that there was, in addition to the Dutch enclave at Nagasaki, one *daimyō* who conducted a quite extensive trade with Korea. Nor is the hypothetical demographer in Section 14 of Chapter 1 to be seriously reproached for reporting as 'a population of two hundred million' a population which the recording angel knows to have been only 199,999,999. Yet there are, by contrast, cases where the dotting of i's and crossing of t's is quite literally of decisive importance. In, for example, R. B. Merriman's *Life and Letters* of Thomas Cromwell, two letters are printed in which Cromwell appears to be blackmailing priors of monasteries which he saved from suppression; but the fact is that the originals are in a handwriting which is not that of either Cromwell or any of his clerks, so that Merriman's transposition of them into print involves an inaccuracy amounting to serious misreportage.† The recording angel, accordingly, is not committed to a rigid criterion of perfect accuracy without reference to context. But nor is he committed to any other criterion derived from presuppositions which rival observers will not necessarily share. He is merely there to tell

* See David C. Marsh, *The Changing Social Structure of England and Wales 1871–1951* (1958), p. 163 n.1.
† The example is taken from G. R. Elton, *The Practice of History* (1967), p. 76.

us as much as we say we need of what we could in principle have seen and heard for ourselves.

So far as knowledge of agents' inner states is concerned, the recording angel has no special privilege. Although he can observe their behaviour on his videotapes in every aspect and from every angle, he has to infer its constitutive intentions and beliefs from their outward manifestations, as any and all observers have to do. He does not know the soul of a stranger or the beauty of sacrifice or the terrible, sickening reality of defeat in war. He only knows the dictionary meanings of the words which the agents use and the manner and context in which they use them. He can go back to his archives, if we ask him to, for videotapes of the behaviour of other people than those with whom we are immediately concerned, and he has at his disposal every technique by which observation of their actions might be extended and refined. But that is all.

Here are two examples, of which the first is from a French sociologist (Marcel Granet) writing about early China and the second from an English historian (Arthur Bryant) writing about the Napoleonic Wars:

(1) The authority of tradition, the solemnity of the festival, the importance of the rites and the number of those who took part in them all combined to give the holy orgy an unusual emotional force. How intense must have been the emotions animating the crowd!

(2) Far away in England the mail-coaches drawn up on the parade outside the General Post Office in Lombard Street were decked – men, horses, carriages – with laurels and flowers, oak leaves and ribbons. Presently, the lids thundered down on the mail-bags and the waiting horses pawed the ground, the guards sounded their horns, and the news of the fall of Ciudad Rodrigo went radiating outwards down a dozen great trunk roads, through cheering towns and villages where every heart leapt for an instant in the glow of a single common pride.

Both are couched in a language more rhetorical than scientific: the reader's assent is being solicited by means not only of their content but of their style. But whatever their authors' purposes in so couching them, they have, nonetheless, to be construed in the first instance as reports. They are accurate if, and only if, the emotions animating the crowd *were* intense, and every heart *did* leap for an instant. So: were they or weren't they? did they or didn't they? The authors can't really know. But the recording angel does. And an appeal to him suggests, at least to me, that the answer is no in both cases.

The inaccuracy of Granet's report does not reside in the use of 'must have been' as such. If, for example, he were to report (as a demographer working on the figures given by Marco Polo has in fact done) that the population of Hang-chou in the late thirteenth century 'must have been' between five and seven millions, then provided that his inferences from Polo's figures and Polo's figures themselves were correct the assertion would rank without qualification as an accurate report: there is no reason to suppose that the precise figure in the recording angel's archives is inconsistent with it. But there is every reason to doubt whether the recording angel's videotape of the holy orgies would confirm that there was quite the degree of collective emotion among the participants which Durkheimian theories of the *conscience collective* presuppose. The 'must' is supported neither by logical deduction nor by empirical observation recorded in the sources. That *some* emotion animated the crowd is plausible enough. But the claim to intensity is (I would suggest) likely to be inaccurate to the point of fiction: if we were to have access to the recording angel's videotapes I would not (would you?) be prepared to wager that Granet's report would be vindicated as such.

Bryant's report is similarly suspect, but with the difference that it is infected not with the presuppositions of Durkheimian sociological theory but with a patriotic fervour which the recording angel, who is not an Englishman, is not going to share. We may fairly assume that if Bryant's documentary sources depict pawing horses bedecked with flowers the recording angel's videotape will confirm them. 'Thundering' lids on the mail-bags, although possibly a little overpitched, would probably be acceptable as accurate if we could hear the original sound reproduced. Whether or not there were precisely a dozen trunk roads is no more important than whether the Occupational Tables of the 1951 Census are inaccurate as to the ages of two clergymen, four solicitors, four doctors, ten opticians, one dentist, twenty-three chiropodists and thirty-four accountants. But *every* heart leaping for an instant? Or even *nearly* every heart? Surely not. What may, perhaps, pass as a venial exaggeration in a loyal address from the hustings must be accounted an inaccuracy amounting to misreportage in a work of historical scholarship.

Like any other such device, the recording angel carries the argument of this chapter no further forward by himself. He can only arrive at conclusions which have been programmed into him already. But he is not to be taken merely to embody the lowest common methodological denominator of all the accumulated reports of sociologists of rival Behaviorist, Structuralist, Phenomenological, Marxian, Durkheimian, Weberian, Utilitarian or other schools. Nor, on the other hand, does he embody just the trivially *a priori*. His usefulness resides in the help which his archives can in principle provide for rival observers who need to establish whether their dispute is about the accuracy of each other's reports or (or as well) about the acceptability of each other's theories.

§ 13. Furthest in the other direction from inaccuracy resulting from miscomputation is the kind of misreportage which arises from *misnaming*. It is true that names, or labels generally, cannot themselves be true or false; only propositions can. It is also true that roses smell as sweet under any other name; practising sociologists have no need to concern themselves with philosophical arguments about sense and reference and the possibility of exceptions to Leibniz's Law of transposition *salva veritate* between pairs of names denoting an extensionally identical nominee. There is an obvious need to be careful not actually to confuse one person with another: a historian of the Crusades who reports that Baldwin invested Baldwin with the county of Edessa in the autumn of the year 1100 – which he did – needs to know which Baldwin is which, and a historian of sixteenth-century Spain needs to know that Cardinal Ximenes and Cardinal Cisneros are not two men but one. But these are simple technical problems: they raise no methodological issue. Yet names can be chosen and deployed in the service of purposes which go well beyond reportage alone. Was, for example, the 'Indian Mutiny' not more than a mutiny? Was the 'Peasants' Revolt' not less than a revolt? Are the 'People's Democracies' either popular or democratic? Even the proper names of places and persons may be so used that although the propositions in which they feature are demonstrably true the rival observer will want them reworded. If I report the reconstitution of Germany in 888, I can expect to be told by some pedant that I should have called it not Germany but 'East Francia', and if I report the birth of Trotsky in 1879, I can expect to be told that I should have called him not Trotsky but 'Bronstein'.

Quibbles of this kind may seem to take the proper pursuit of accuracy to the point of silliness. If readers are to be told what happened in or to do with the territory of Germany/East Francia, or what was said or done by Bronstein/Trotsky, their concern is whether the recording angel would confirm the reports about them which they are being invited to accept, not whether there is for other reasons a choice of names wherewith to designate them. But to say this is not enough to exorcize the preemptive overtones which the work or passage may carry if one is chosen in place of another. In evaluative contexts, the underlying purpose is likely to be the more easily detectable the more strongly the author's prejudices are held: a historian who calls Hitler 'Shicklgruber' is even more obviously seeking to disparage him than a historian who calls

Napoleon 'Bonaparte', and a historian who calls 'The American Civil War' 'The War between the States' may safely be presumed to be on the side of the Confederacy. But there may be a less immediately visible, yet no less significant, difference in the overtones insinuated by an author who speaks of black South Africans as 'Bantu' or of Rosselón as 'Roussillon' or of Cicero as 'Tully' or of Beatrice Webb as 'Lady Passmore'. If reportage alone were at issue, the difference would be trivial. But it isn't. The choice of a name is for a purpose, and the purpose is likely to be the intimation, if not actually the pre-emption, of an explanation, description or evaluation dictated by a theory to which not all rival observers need subscribe.

Pre-emption becomes, moreover, progressively more likely the further the chosen label from a proper name. Indeed, once the name is not strictly a name but a nickname or title, it may carry an overtone which turns out on examination to amount to misreportage as such. If I choose to call Prince Charles Edward 'the Young Pretender', I may mean only to imply that this was the designation normally applied to him by the citizens of the country to the throne of which he was a claimant; I may not be voicing any preference of my own for the Hanoverian Succession. But suppose my researches were to disclose that he – Charles Edward – had formally waived his claim to the throne in a hitherto unknown document in 1787: ought I not to stop calling him 'Pretender'? Conversely, if I accept 'Kenneth I' as the correct designation for the Scottish conqueror of the Picts, am I not committed to the perhaps inaccurate report that what he – Kenneth MacAlpin – did in 843 was to establish what can properly be called a Kingdom of Scotland? It is perhaps, depending on the context, a matter of no more than verbal convention which can accordingly be settled by fiat. But I might, on the other hand, be fairly accused of so using 'Kenneth I' as to be no less guilty of misreportage than were the seventeenth-century European travellers to Japan who mistakenly labelled the *daimyō* 'kings', or the geographer Strabo, writing in the first century A.D., who misreported the Bacchiads who ruled Corinth in the seventh century B.C. as 'tyrants'.

The problem is seldom if ever a very serious one. Where it arises, it can be resolved easily enough by putting the potentially contentious name into quotation marks, thereby signalling to the reader that the author's purpose is denotation alone and that the chosen name can innocuously be replaced by another. Although this technique has in practice to be sparingly used if the printed pages with which the reader is confronted are not to be clouded by swarms of inverted commas, it will at least ensure that the hackles of rival observers are not so far raised as to impede the progress of substantive research. But however easily soluble it may be, the problem is one which brings out yet again the importance of defining as clearly as can be done the line between reportage on one side and explanation, description or evaluation on the other. Names may be theory-neutral in themselves. But in use, they have to pass the same test of transposability which, if they are so used as to fail it, will disclose to the reader that the line has been crossed, whether wittingly or not.

SUB-TYPES AND VARIANTS

§ 14. Reportage has so far been discussed as though it were, so to say, a one-off exercise. I have made it clear that it extends beyond statements about individual actions. But I have not yet considered the criteria for assessment not merely of single reports to the effect that a rain-dance, marriage, rabbit-shoot, pantomime or battle has been observed to occur, but for connected sequences of reports which follow rain-dances, marriages, rabbit-shoots, pantomimes, battles, or successions of them over their course – in other words, for *narratives*.

At this point, the criteria of art and science diverge sharply. In art, there are criteria for narratives as such. There are good stories and bad stories. Good stories have a beginning, a middle and an end; they have a whole range of purposes irrelevant to science – whether to amuse, frighten, sadden, excite or elicit any variant or combination of such emotions; they have their own standards of relevance dictated by these purposes; and they can be judged by whatever standards of composition or style may be advanced by literary critics of different schools. But in social science, there is no purpose to be served by sequences of reports apart from the contribution which they make to the explanation and/or description and/or evaluation of some sequence of human behaviour or some institution or practice so constituted. They must of course be accurate – or rather, accurate to the degree of imperfect precision which the explanation, description or evaluation to which they are to lead requires. But there are only two reasons for sociologists, anthropologists or even historians to string reports together in a sequence isomorphic to the temporal sequence of what they report: either because the sequence itself is to be explained, described or evaluated, or because it explains, describes or evaluates something in its turn.

In case this claim is disputed by those for whom, as they are apt to put it, Clio is a muse, let me make it clear that there is no contradiction. Nothing prevents a work of sociology, anthropology or history from

being a work of art as well as of science, any more than anything prevents
a natural-scientific treatise from being written, as at one time they used
to be, in verse. If a naval historian's account of the Battle of Midway can
make a rattling good yarn, so can an astronomer's or a physicist's account
of the solar eclipse the observation of which confirmed Einstein's theory
of special relativity. How dramatic, if well told, is the story encapsulated
in J. E. Littlewood's note to Bertrand Russell of 1919: '*Dear Russell*,
Einstein's theory is completely confirmed. The predicted displacement
was $1''.72$ and the observed $1''.75 \pm .06$. *Yours J.E.L.*'! Science, whether
social or natural, can be so practised and recounted as at the same time
to meet the criteria of art. But it is neither better nor worse as science
on that account, whether its tasks are only, as in natural science, reportage
and explanation or whether they are or may be extended, as in social
science, to description and evaluation as well.

Here then are three stories, each consisting of connected reports in
temporal sequence which are all, to the best of my knowledge and belief,
true:

1. In 1415, Frederick Hohenzollern, Margrave of Brandenburg, was
   made an Elector of the Empire, and in 1525 Albert Hohenzollern,
   Grand Master of the Teutonic Order, was made Duke of East Prussia.
   In 1614, the Rhineland territories of Cleves and Mark fell to the
   Electorate of Brandenburg and in 1618 East Prussia did likewise. In
   1701, the Electorate was raised to a Kingdom by the Emperor Charles
   VI. In 1713, Frederick William I became King and in 1720 he added
   West Pomerania to his Kingdom. Over the course of his reign, the
   population grew to more than 2 million, the army to some 80,000 troops
   and the annual revenue of the crown to 7 million thalers. Frederick II,
   who succeeded in 1740, conquered Silesia and added the territory of
   West Prussia including the Netze District and Ermland to his Kingdom by agreement with Austria and Russia. Over the course of his
   reign, the population grew to more than 5 million, the army to some
   150,000 troops and the annual revenue of the crown to 23 million
   thalers. Following the outbreak of the French Revolution and the
   subsequent European war, Prussia gained South Prussia in 1793 and
   New East Prussia including Mazovia in 1795, and after a mixture of
   losses and gains between 1795 and 1815 acquired Rhine-Westphalia
   at the Congress of Vienna.

2. Festus Sam Okote-Eboh was born in the old Warri province of Nigeria
   and educated at the Baptist School in Sapele. After his schooling, he
   was first a municipal clerk and then a teacher. In 1935 he joined the
   Bata Shoe Company. He was promoted first to accountant and chief
   clerk in Lagos and then to deputy manager of the Sapele branch. After
   the War, he went into business on his own and became a timber and
   rubber merchant and the owner of a chain of schools. In 1951, he was

elected to the Western Region House of Assembly. In 1954, he became a Member of the Federal Parliament for Warri and national treasurer of the National Council of Nigeria and the Cameroons (later National Council of Nigerian Citizens). In 1955, he was appointed Minister of Labour and in 1957 Minister of Finance. In 1959, during the election campaign, he was attacked by Action Group newspapers for corruption. He continued to be Minister of Finance until January 1966, when he was kidnapped in the military coup d'état. On January 21, 1966, his body was found in a shallow grave 30 miles outside Lagos, riddled with bullets.

3. On November 4, 1854, Florence Nightingale reached Scutari. On the 5th, she and her party of nurses were escorted to the Barrack Hospital. She found that she had been allotted six small rooms and a kitchen for her party of forty, with no furniture, no food, no medical supplies and no bedding. All the doctors but one ignored her, and she refused to allow her nurses to go into the wards without authorization. On the 6th, the wounded from Balaclava began to arrive at Scutari, but even by the 9th she had managed to accomplish no more than to be permitted to provide invalid food from her own stores on the requisition of a doctor. Only on the 9th, after the arrival of a further influx of sick and wounded, did the doctors turn to her. The wards were by now over-flowing and the arrivals were laid down on unwashed verminous floors. There were no pillows, blankets, screens or operating tables. She estimated that there were over 1,000 men suffering from acute diarrhoea for whom there were only 20 chamber pots. In the second half of November, Mr Stafford, M.P., who had come to Scutari on a private visit of inspection, tried to get the lavatories cleaned; both the Senior Medical Officer and the Military Commandant refused. The wards were cleaned only by her purchase of 200 scrubbing-brushes from Constantinople. At the beginning of December, when the arrival of another 500 sick and wounded was announced, she engaged 200 Turkish workmen on her own responsibility and at her own expense and that of *The Times* to repair and clean two further wards to receive them. She supplied all the utensils, including knives, forks, spoons and towels, arrowroot and port wine. 'We felt', said one of the men she received, 'we were in heaven.'

Each of these stories offers an answer to a question beyond the mere request for a report of what happened over the course of four centuries of Prussian history in the first case, the lifetime of a single Nigerian in the second and a few weeks of the Crimean War in the third. The first offers an explanation even though no such words as 'because', 'effect', 'result' or 'consequently' appear anywhere in it. The second offers a description even though it is innocent of a single metaphor, simile or even adjective relating to the experiences of the person whose life it describes. The third offers an evaluation even though nothing in it entails either that Florence Nightingale's behaviour is to be commended or that the authorities' behaviour is to be deplored. They may or may not be good stories in themselves. That is up to you. But as sociology, their point is that the sum of the reports of which they are composed answers an unspoken question. If you want to know how it came about that by the first half of the nineteenth century Prussia, which might appear to be one of the unlikeliest candidates to become the preponderant power in Germany, had grown to a size which made it the vehicle for German unification itself, then one possible answer is to tell you that it grew by a haphazard sequence of territorial and therefore demographic and economic accretions whose cumulative effect was unrecognized at the time. If you want to know what the transition from colonial dependence to independent statehood, and from independent statehood to civil war, was like for those Nigerians who lived through it, one possible answer is to give you the authentic life-story of a Nigerian whose career exemplifies it particularly vividly. If you want to know how good a person Florence Nightingale was not merely in her compassion and courage but in her discretion and efficiency, one possible answer is to give you an account of what she did in Scutari between the beginning of November 1854 and the end of the year.

Although the time-span covered in these three examples is very different, this difference is not related to their difference of purpose. A story can imply an explanation, a description or an evaluation, or all three, quite independently of the location of the reports which constitute it on the axes of time or space or generality. In practice, its location will relate to its purpose to the extent that there is a particular contrast, or range of contrasts, which gives the story its point: a story which embraces the whole of the globe, goes back to the dawn of mankind and deals in cultures or civilizations as its protagonists implies an answer to very different kinds of questions about why it all came about in the way that it did, how it was experienced by its protagonists and whether it was a good thing or a bad one from a story which is focussed on the thoughts, words and deeds of a single person over a few brief moments at a particular spot. But this still leaves entirely open the nature of the purpose, or mixture of purposes, which the story serves.

It is true to say that a narrative of a kind is implicit in any report of behaviour. I may present you with a single photograph depicting Mr Morley in Indian dress, or a single diagram depicting the system of patrilineal segmentation observed among the Nuer. But neither depiction is strictly synchronic. A story attaches alike to Mr Morley's rain-dance, which has a beginning and an end and requires that his gestures follow a specified sequence, and to the kinship system of the Nuer, in which the social relationships between fathers and sons, and brothers and brothers, have to follow a specified sequence too if the report is to hold. For my purpose, however, this narrative element can uncontentiously be incorporated within whatever is involved in the primary understanding of the behaviour observed. Just as a report of the simplest action presupposes an answer at a different level to the question why the particular sounds were uttered and gestures made, so it presupposes a narrative in which certain sub-units of behaviour have followed a sequence but for which the action would not be the action it is. It follows that if the observer has wrongly assumed this sequence to have been what it was not, he will be misreporting what he thought was a rain-dance as a rain-dance, or what he thought was a marriage as a marriage. But this is a separate matter from the deliberate linkage of reports of actions with one another. Here, likewise, it is true to say that reportage can never be strictly synchronic: even a set of reports all phrased in the so-called ethnographic present will have to incorporate an arrangement of the actions reported into a temporal sequence of a kind. In these cases, however, the risk of misreportage arises not because a sequence of a kind is implied, but because of what the sequence implied may presuppose in its turn about the explanation, description or evaluation of itself. What then arises, once again, is the risk of obscuring the frontier at which reportage has been left behind and explanation, description or evaluation have begun.

§15. Furthermore, reportage is not a one-off exercise in place any more than in time. To concede that all actions are unique (since no two contexts are identical in all respects) is not to undermine the theory-neutrality of the claim that slaves were owned by the Ila, the Ottoman Turks and the Nepalese as well as the Romans or that battles were fought at Thermopylae and Midway as well as Hastings. Once given that there are at least some designations which can be applied across time and place without a rival observer's being able to show that the report framed in terms of them either misunderstands the actions reported in the primary sense or pre-empts their explanation, description or evaluation, then reportage must be admitted to cover at least some cases of multiple occurrence. Just as the specification of temporal sequence yields the particular form of reportage called narrative, so the specification of multiple occurrence yields the particular form of reportage called *generalization*.

'Generalization' is a term habitually used by sociologists, as by others, to carry the implication of something more than the mere haphazard joint occurrence of the same institution or practice. The reader may fairly expect, when confronted by it, some suggestion that the set of independent reports which make it up have more in common than just the occurrence of actions which can be understood in the primary sense as equivalent to each other. There is a hint, and often more than a hint, of prevalence or tendency, a tacit quest for regularity or uniformity which might one day end in the discovery of universal laws. But just as reports in sequence may suggest, without actually pre-empting, an explanation, description or evaluation of what they narrate, so may reports in conjunction suggest, without actually pre-empting, an explanation, description or evaluation of what they juxtapose. Generalizations about human behaviour, whether in terms of recurrent similarities in different contexts or recurrent conjunctions in similar contexts, can be allowed to stand or fall, like narratives, by the criteria of reportage alone. The rival observer is always free to question the purpose for which a particular generalization has been assembled: if the reader is told that, say, complexity of social organization correlates with economic output across a stated range of societies in the historical and ethnographic record, the presumption must be that the researcher telling him so has in view some sort of causal hypothesis and underlying theory which will account for the connection. But that does not prevent the reports of which the generalization consists from being construed in the first instance, at any rate, as theory-neutral. The rival observer who wishes to challenge it can do so only by showing one or more of its constituent parts to be inaccurate or to involve a misunderstanding in the primary sense. The validity of the explanation to which they may be a prelude is not yet in question.

An objection of a different kind which the rival observer may make – and often does – is that the definition of the terms in which the generalization is couched has been tailored to fit it. But this too is a criticism of the purpose to which it is to be put rather than of the accuracy of its constituent parts. Pre-emptive taxonomy is another matter to which I shall have to return (in Section 18). But even where the definitions employed are, and are admitted to be, so framed as to presuppose some explanatory, descriptive or evaluative theory this will not necessarily impugn the accuracy of the reports as such. If the rival observer can show that what 'they' have been doing is not the same in each case then an inaccuracy will indeed have been exposed: if 'feudalism' is defined in terms of a fusion of benefice and vassalage, and vassalage in terms of what it means in the context of Western Europe, then it is inaccurate, as we have seen, to report it of Japan. But if 'their' behaviour demonstrably fits the definition given, and the transposition *salva veritate* is demonstrably feasible, then theory-neutrality has been preserved.

Notice also how little accuracy has here to do with numerical precision – or at least, for as long as reportage alone is at issue. A social psychologist seeking, for example, to test under experimental conditions the textbook generalization that people tend to engage in activities which maintain their rank within the group of which they are members may be much exercised by whether a statistically significant number of his subjects continue to do so even when he has tampered with their motives by engineering a temptation to them to behave otherwise. But he is by then a long way across the boundary between reportage and explanation. To assert merely that people of certain kinds tend to behave in certain ways under certain conditions is not in itself to presuppose anything about the motives which cause them to do so or the extent to which they are influenced by the conditions specified. The assertion will probably strike its readers as a truism. But the more textbook generalizations about human behaviour strike their readers as truisms, the more strongly is the possibility of theory-neutral reportage of multiple occurrence across a range of times and places confirmed.

§ 16. There is, however, one special kind of sociological generalization which raises a separate problem of accuracy of its own: the *aphorism*.

Some aphorisms about human behaviour belong unequivocally with art, not science, and gain their point only because they are by intention sarcastic, humorous, cynical, extravagant, ironic, polemical, etc. A crackerbarrel saw about human nature (like Kin Hubbard's 'when a feller says "it hain't th' money but th' principle o' th' thing", it's th' money') or a pseudo-worldly epigram about manners and morals (like Balzac's *'Quand on connaît Paris, on ne croit à rien de ce que s'y dit et l'on ne dit rien de ce que s'y fait'*) is not to be solemnly construed by the reader as a would-be sociological generalization any more than a story about an Englishman, a Scotsman and an Irishman in a railway carriage as a would-be psychological theory of differences in national character. But when, for example, La Rochefoucauld tells us that we forgive those who bore us but not those whom we bore, he is asserting something which depends for its impact not merely on its charge of paradox but on a recognition by the reader that it is sufficiently accurate to rank as a genuinely informative observation, or even a modest discovery, about social behaviour. The rival observer may object that the observation is culture-bound, the terms in which it is couched imprecise, and the selection of evidence implied by it neither systematic nor impartial.

But can he seriously maintain that it is no more than a literary *jeu d'esprit* grounded nowhere in experience that he and other observers can replicate? He may, perhaps, seek to dismiss it as merely a passing *aperçu*. But then: *on s'est quand-même aperçu de quelquechose*!

The difference between an aphorism like La Rochefoucauld's and a generalization like those to be found in textbooks of sociology is not so much that it is less precise – it may, on the contrary, be more so – but that its accuracy does not rest on the strength of its claim to generality, even where it is so phrased as to make it appear so. To say that people tend to behave in such-and-such a way is to invite the reader to think of cases where they do not. Hedged about by *ceteris paribus* as such a generalization is bound to be, it will lose whatever point it has if the reader can instantly think of numerous counter-examples. Generalizations about human behaviour may not need to be universal before they can qualify as such. Nor indeed can they be without access to the recording angel's archives. But they do need to make more ambitious claims of multiple occurrence than 'here and there' or 'now and again ...'. La Rochefoucauld's aphorism, on the other hand, does not lose its point simply because his readers can think of numerous examples where we don't forgive those who have bored us and do forgive those whom we bore. It constitutes, if it does, a modest discovery about social behaviour because it is an accurate report not of what always, or even nearly always, happens but of what sometimes can and in practice does more often than the unreflecting reader has hitherto supposed.

The aphorist's skill, accordingly, resides not in the care and perseverance with which he seeks out counter-examples, like the ethnographer combing the globe for societies where the incest taboo is not to be found, but in his perspicaciousness in detecting forms or manifestations of behaviour which the scrutiny of rival observers has overlooked. The reader who catches an accompanying hint of an explanatory hypothesis will probably turn out to be right: just as the claim that complexity of social organization is correlated with economic output implies some sort of causal connection between the two, so the claim that we forgive those who bore us but not those whom we bore implies some sort of causal connection between feelings of shame or resentment and awareness of having talked in such a way as to be regarded as boring. Indeed, its impact derives in part from its contradiction of the secondary understanding presumptively attributed to the unreflecting reader. But as stated, it is to be construed as reportage on no different a level from even the most platitudinous of textbook generalizations. The assent of the rival observer does not depend on his acceptance of La Rochefoucauld's explanation, whatever it may be, of what he has understood in the primary sense to be going on in the *salons* of pre-Revolutionary France. It depends only on his agreeing that on a sufficient number of occasions to warrant the assertion of a modest generalization the realization that one is being bored by an interlocutor is accompanied by feelings of tolerant superiority while the realization that one is being a bore is accompanied by feelings of resentment and shame.

Aphorisms of this kind may, and often do, originate in the mind of the discoverer as a derivation from a theory at which he has arrived on other grounds and which the rival observer may reject. When, for example, a twentieth-century Marxist historian of Western European art (John Berger) tells a television audience that 'Men look at women. Women look at men looking at them', he is drawing their attention to what he regards as a symptom of the subordinate position of women, and their systematic exploitation by men, in the societies whose portrayal of women in art he has been studying. But his presumptive explanation might be invalid and the reported observation accurate nevertheless. It is not a report which, in practice, we can conclusively test. But the recording angel is well placed to check it for us, since he can look up the expression on the face of every man and woman who has ever glanced at one another in the societies which Berger has in mind. And if the recording angel confirms that there was, on balance, the difference that most of the women's glances at the men were intended to appraise the men's reactions to them whereas most of the men's were concerned only with their appraisal of the looks of the women, then the aphorism would be justified as one of those genuinely informative observations which amounts to a modest discovery transposable *salva veritate* between Marxist and non-Marxist observers, whatever the explanation may turn out to be and whatever the further nuances which may call to be described.

Of all sociologists, the one whose generalizations and narratives alike are most often phrased as aphorisms is Tocqueville. The pages of *Democracy in America* and *The Ancien Régime and the French Revolution* are studded with them. Some are unmistakably evaluative (as when he says of the French people that it has 'transported the tastes of a slave into the very practice of its liberty; as incapable of ruling itself as it has shown itself stubborn in resistance to its teachers'); some are straightforwardly explanatory (as when he accounts for the lesser eagerness of the French than the Americans for general ideas in politics by saying that the social condition of France caused its people 'to conceive very general ideas on the subject of government, whilst its political constitution prevented it from correcting those ideas by experiment'); some are primarily descriptive (as when he says of the 'charms' of equality that 'the noblest hearts are not insensible to them and the vulgarest spirits exult in them'); and some are, ostensibly at least, mere reports of joint occurrence (as when he observes that 'religious peoples and trading nations entertain peculiarly serious notions of marriage'). In practice, the disentanglement of their explanatory, descriptive or evaluative content may require much care and subtlety. But all of them purport to rest on reported observations, whether of Tocqueville's own or of other authorities on whom he is prepared to rely, sufficiently accurate to qualify as contributions to social science. Do religious peoples and trading nations entertain peculiarly serious notions of marriage, or don't they? The rival observer will, no doubt, raise a host of familiar difficulties: are the institutional rules which constitute and regulate the institution of 'marriage' the same in all the cases? how can 'serious' be defined by derivation from 'their' intentions and beliefs alone? aren't *all* peoples 'religious'? doesn't the comparison of more and less 'peculiarly' serious presuppose acceptance of a pre-emptive theory? But there is no reason in principle why a claim of this kind must be incapable of passing the tests which would license its status as a report. And if it does, it should be treated as such: it should not, simply because it is phrased as an aphorism, be dismissed as less 'scientific' than a report couched in the language of the comparative ethnographer working from a cross-cultural data bank stored in an electronic computer or the historical demographer presenting statistics of life-expectancy in the form of numerical tables.

The converse, however, holds true as well. It would be equally mistaken to attribute to Tocqueville a superior understanding of human behaviour simply because his observations are more pithily phrased. They may well have a greater impact on the reader than the solemn recital of case-studies by the cross-cultural ethnographer or the pedestrian enumeration of frequencies by the historical demographer. Imagine yourself, for example, reading Tocqueville's dictum about the reluctance of democratic societies to engage in wars and their determination in continuing them in Washington D.C. in 1950 when President Truman's advisers were unable to get from Congress the modest increase in defence spending which they wanted until, under the impact of events in Korea, the defence budget was suddenly and effortlessly tripled. It would be as hard not to feel some *frisson* of recognition as it would if, say, at Teheran or Yalta or Potsdam a few years earlier you had been happening to read his prophecy that America and Russia each seemed 'marked out by the will of Heaven to sway the destinies of half the globe'. But reports are accurate, just as explanations are valid, descriptions authentic and evaluations coherent, independently of the degree to which the reader is struck by them. Their perlocutionary effect is a matter for the literary critic, not for the methodologist of social theory.

§ 17. But there are other ways than narratives on the one hand or generalizations on the other in which a set of independent observations may be so reported as to form a *pattern*; and where they are, it is harder still to judge whether theory-neutrality has, or could have, been preserved. Consider, from this point of view, a hypothetical sociologist of the mid twentieth century whose particular interest is in hierarchies of social prestige among face-to-face groups and who reports to his readers three findings, as follows:

In the first example, he has been carrying out a study of a medium-sized industrial company in England, and has observed in the course of it that the head of the company addresses his colleagues and subordinates differently according to their rank relative to his own. The deputy managing director is addressed by an abbreviated Christian name, department heads by Christian name in full, senior clerical staff by surname alone, foremen and trade union convenors as 'Mr', the shopfloor by surname alone, junior clerks and secretaries by Christian name alone and the nightwatchman by an abbreviated Christian name. There are, no doubt, some exceptions and discrepancies, but the sociologist has satisfied himself (and could satisfy any rival observer) that these usages are modal. Accordingly, he reports his observations in the form of Table 1 showing the form of address used by the head of the company to employees according to rank, assigning them for the purpose to one or other of seven distinguishable ranks and assuming for the sake of convenience (and also to respect anonymity) that each person is called 'Michael Smith'.

	Rank of ALTER		Modal Form of Address
	1	–	'Mike'
	2	–	'Michael'
EGO rank 1	3	–	'Smith'
(managing director):	4	–	'Mr Smith'
	5	–	'Smith'
	6	–	'Michael'
	7	–	'Mike'

Table 1

In the second example, the sociologist has been doing his fieldwork in a Hindu village in Central India and has been informed by the members of each of seven mutually acknowledged, hierarchically ordered castes that certain degrees of contact with those of lower rank are held to be ritually polluting. On further enquiry, confirmed by observation, he learns that there are six levels of interaction which are permissible to a person of equal or higher rank but prohibited for a person of lower rank: in ascending levels of pollution these are first, touching the person's child; second, touching the person; third, using the person's pipehead; fourth, touching the person's brass utensils; fifth, serving fried food; and sixth, serving boiled food. Accordingly, he reports his observations in a table of the form of a perfect Guttman scale, like Table 2.

	Rank of ALTER	Level of interaction					
		1	2	3	4	5	6
	1	np	np	np	np	np	np
	2	np	np	np	np	np	p
EGO rank 1	3	np	np	np	np	p	p
(highest caste):	4	np	np	np	p	p	p
	5	np	np	p	p	p	p
	6	np	p	p	p	p	p
	7	p	p	p	p	p	p

p = polluting
np = non-polluting

Table 2

In the third example, the sociologist has been asking adult men in a medium-sized New England town to tell him about their putative willingness to have members of different occupations in relations of greater or lesser social propinquity to themselves. His interest, once again, is in persons of high rank and to identify them he singles out those who answer 'upper class' to the question 'If you were asked to use one of these four names for *your* social class, which would you say you belonged in – the middle class, the lower class, the working class or the upper class?' He then hands them a list of seven occupations – physician, high school teacher, electrical engineer, janitor, truck driver, street sweeper and factory foreman – and asks them to tell him whether they strongly agree, agree, disagree or are undecided about their willingness to have a physician, etc., in the following seven relationships to them: son-in-law, father-in-law, closest personal friend, person to invite to supper, person to visit with regularly, member of a common social club and next-door neighbour. He next scores the answer on a scale ranging from 7 to 35 in accordance with a weighting which assigns 1 to 'strongly agree', 2 to 'agree', 3 to 'undecided', 4 to 'disagree' and 5 to 'strongly disagree'. Each of the 25 respondents' scores are transformed according to the formula $z_i = \dfrac{X_i - \bar{X}}{S}$ where X_i is one of the seven scores, $\bar{X}$ is the mean of a given respondent's seven scores and S is the standard deviation of the mean. The resulting distribution of z scores for a given respondent therefore has a mean of 0 and standard deviation of 1. For convenience of presentation, the sociologist multiplies each z score by 100 and adds 500 and then publishes his findings in the form of a table like this:

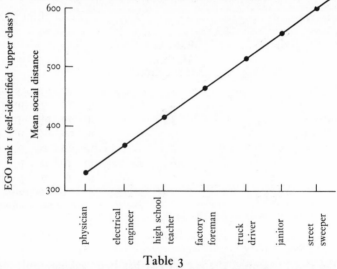

Table 3

Some readers may already be suspicious about the sources for these examples; and if so, they are right – up to a point. The first is adapted from the humorist Stephen Potter's *One-Upmanship* (1952);* the second is a doctored version of an article published in 1960 by Pauline M. Mahar in the journal *Sociometry*; and the third is a still more heavily doctored version of findings reported by Edward O. Laumann from a study done in Cambridge, Massachusetts, in 1963 and published under the title *Prestige and Association in an Urban Community* (1966). But all three are, even as I have presented them, perfectly possible findings, and that is all that is needed for the methodologist to ask: if they aren't (mere) reports, what are they? There is nothing more intrinsically problematic

---

* See p. 50 n.1 on 'Farr's Law of Mean Familiarity'.

about a pattern than about a one-off event, whether a performance of Humpty Dumpty on ice for all races or the outbreak of the Third World War. Nor is it relevant to bring in philosophical questions about the ontological status of the patterns: tables like these obviously stand at a further remove from the events which generate them, but so do the pointer readings of physical science. The only reason to deny them the status of reports would be that a rival observer could convincingly argue that they embody a misunderstanding in the primary sense of the intentions and beliefs of the agents observed. There have, as always, to be considered the possibilities of the kind which I discussed in the opening sections of this chapter: might they be joking? or, do they all attach the same meaning to the attribution of rank, caste or job title? But the same holds likewise for the one-off events. There needs to be some additional reason advanced before the rival observer is entitled to be more sceptical of the sociologist's report simply because the observations reported form no matter how striking a pattern.

Notice that in the first example, even though taken from a source not merely unscholarly but facetious, there is nothing whatever to invite the rival observer's scepticism. The forms of address are unambiguous and the ranks, both of ego and his subordinates, are institutionally defined in a way acknowledged by all the native informants. It may be that none of them has observed that the forms of address modally used by the person of highest rank fall into quite so symmetrical a pattern. But once it is pointed out to them, they can hardly fail to agree; and once they do, what ancillary observation can the rival observer adduce which would undermine the accuracy of the report?

In the second example, by contrast, the rival observer is likely to be less easily satisfied. He may accept that the community studied can be ranked into seven transitively-ranked castes or sub-castes which 'they' all acknowledge as such. But he will suspect that the levels of interaction held to be polluting fall into the pattern of a Guttman scale only because they have been preselected for the purpose; and he will be right. These are not the only interactions which fall under 'their' criteria of purity and pollution. Rather, they are the only ones which will yield the pattern shown. Yet does even so highly selective a presentation entail that the table cannot be construed as a report? Provided that the sociologist's procedures are explicit and replicable, on what grounds can the rival observer object that theory-neutrality has been violated? It is standard practice across the whole range of the natural and social sciences to try a good fit: a researcher who plots his data on a logarithmic graph, or rotates his axes in a factor analysis, is not pre-empting the explanation, description or evaluation of what he reports. There is no presupposition underlying it which prevents transposition *salva veritate* in accordance with some alternative terminology and procedure.

What, then, of the third example? Here, the rival observer will be more recalcitrant still, for the data have been not just selectively presented but deliberately manipulated and even, it could fairly be said, artificially manufactured. The seven occupations along the bottom line are seven out of twenty-three about which respondents were asked; but the other sixteen fall nowhere near the straight line shown. In any case, the so-called 'mean social distance' of the vertical co-ordinate is an artefact in a double sense: first, it reflects not observed but hypothetical behaviour; and second, it is given a numerical expression in accordance with rules invented by the researcher for himself. How, therefore, can it possibly be claimed that the pattern so neatly presented to the reader is given in nature as a matter for the enquiring fieldworker to discover and report? Yet even here, the rival observer will be hard put to show in what respect the pattern presented is inaccurate as a report or for what reason it cannot be transposed *salva veritate* into a terminology of a different kind. It is true that the translation into a numerical score of what 'they' have been observed to do and say involves a Procrustean conceptualization of the researcher's own into which 'their' responses have been forced. But it still does not follow that there is being put to the reader something other, or more, than a report which rival observers can all go out into the field and check for themselves.

There is indeed a serious methodological moral to be drawn. But it is not a moral about the reportage of patterns as opposed to anything else. It is a moral about construal of the researcher's purpose in reporting them. In actual practice – that is, the practice of professional publication and debate – examples like these *are* more controversial than reports of the number of salaried male employees who were members of occupational pension schemes in 1956–7. No doubt even here, there may be a rival observer wanting to argue about, say, the precise criteria for 'membership', or the inclusion of directors of enterprises as 'employees'. But these will be boundary disputes of the innocuous kind. The controversial nature of these three examples of patterns, by contrast, becomes clear as soon as the reader asks the obvious and sensible question: 'what are these observations being reported to me *for*?'. In these examples, the sociologist's interest is taken at the outset to be in 'hierarchies of social prestige'. But what are they? Under what presuppositions do researchers claim to recognize one out in the field? The sceptical reader who has been given the uneasy feeling that these pretty-looking tables are somehow putting something over on him is fully entitled to ask whether that part of the evidence which has not so much fallen as been actively pushed into a striking pattern does not accord rather too well with some pre-emptive theory of the researcher's own. The plausibility of the rejoinder will not depend on the researcher's ability to argue that the pattern reported was, as it were, waiting for him to find it, as in the first example, rather than having to be picked out by him, as in the second, or constructed by him, as in the third. In all three, the rival observer's charge is that the pattern, although not in itself pre-emptive of an explanation, description or evaluation, is being *used* in support of an explanation, description or evaluation which is to follow; but at that point, the researcher must be able to convince not only the rival observer but the sceptical reader whose reaction is to say 'yes, but that isn't what *I* would have chosen as evidence in studying hierarchies of social prestige'.

This objection is not one which can be brushed aside with the comment that all definitions are arbitrary. Consider the familiar example of IQ, or 'measured intelligence' as defined by the battery of Stanford-Binet tests, which has been shown time and again to fit remarkably closely to the pattern of the normal (Gaussian) distribution. The scores, and their replicability, are a matter of reportage: any number of rival observers can try it out for themselves and they will all get much the same pattern of results. But they are not bound to agree that what they have been measuring is 'intelligence'. Those who do think so are likely – perhaps under the banner of 'operationalism' – to defend themselves by saying that they are at liberty to define 'intelligence' as whatever it is that Stanford-Binet tests test. But it won't do. For if its definition is really an arbitrary matter, why not argue that 'intelligence' is measured by speed over 1500 metres (adjusted, as the Stanford-Binet tests are, for age)? The 'operationalist' defence is plausible only to the extent that there are convincing theoretical arguments for supposing that continuing research will disclose, in the light of a much extended knowledge of human cognitive and intellectual processes and capacities, that those tapped by Stanford-Binet tests correlate significantly with the rest. Otherwise, what possible justification is there for claiming that Stanford-Binet test performance is what intelligence *is*?*

It is still true to say that all three of the tables set out above can be vindicated as reports. But they cannot be vindicated as reports acceptable

---

* I have borrowed here from N. J. Block and Gerald Dworkin, 'IQ: Heritability and Inequality, Part I', *Philosophy & Public Affairs* III (1974), pp. 331ff.

to any rival observer as reports *of a hierarchy of social prestige*, for that would require either the acceptance of a theory of the observer's which was so well validated as to dictate the meaning of the phrase to 'us' and 'them' alike or the acknowledgement by all of 'them' that they already understand by 'hierarchy of social prestige' exactly what the table about them reports. Since neither is the case, the sceptical reader is quite right to ask what purpose the tables are intended to serve. It is likely enough that they serve it well: the first may sustain a coherent evaluation of social relations in English factories as bad because snobbish and stigmatizing; the second may convey an authentic description of what it is like for the inhabitants of an Indian village to feel bound within a code of ritual pollution in almost every act of daily life; the third may yield a valid explanation of the way in which Americans, despite an overtly egalitarian ideology, betray an acknowledgement of differential status when confronted with the quasi-experimental possibility of intimate relationships with fellow-Americans who do different things for a living. But these are no more indisputably reports of the precise distribution of status in a 'hierarchy of social prestige' in the community studied than Stanford-Binet test scores are indisputably reports of the 'intelligence' of those tested. In none of them can 'social prestige' be construed as a theory-neutral term. The trouble is not technical. It is methodological. It arises because the point of reporting these observations was to find out about something of which they are an instance by a criterion not directly derivable from the intentions and beliefs of the agents about whose behaviour the report is made.

DEFINITION AND CLASSIFICATION

§ 18. The use of the term 'instance' in this context thus runs directly up against the problem of pre-emptive taxonomy which I have so far skated round. I have done so because the first test of the terms used to designate a social event, process or state of affairs is their acceptability in principle to those whose actions, and therefore intentions and (where relevant) beliefs, it designates. Accordingly, I have assumed that as long as the dictionary meaning is unproblematic, we are dealing with a matter of reportage alone: don't we and 'they' alike know well enough what they are doing when they do what we and they both call rain-dancing, marrying, rabbit-shooting, asserting a belief in God, advertising a panto-mime, fighting a battle (or even a civil war), or buying and selling persons as things and therefore 'owning slaves'? But as the examples of both 'magic' and 'feudalism' showed, it may be premature to assume that just because their usage can be shown to conform to a consistent dictionary meaning, any rival observer's reluctance to apply it can be treated as a boundary dispute of the innocuous kind. Suppose a reader explicitly requests (and why not?) a rigorous and exhaustive definition of the terms used for the reportage of 'their' institutions and practices. The reply must, as I have conceded, be grounded elsewhere than in the observations the reportage of which has prompted the request. So will it not depend on the further purpose which the researcher has in mind, no less in the case of what he takes to be a 'rain-dance' or a 'marriage' than in the case of what he takes to be an instance of 'intelligence' or of a 'hierarchy of social prestige'?

At the risk of repetition, let me insist that the problem is not that of reconciling the viewpoint of the observer with that of those whose behaviour he observes – the 'etic/emic' distinction, as one school of anthropologists calls it.* It is true that the relation between observers' and agents' categories is inherently problematic. But the problem will not be resolved by keeping them apart, since the necessary distinction between reportage of agents' behaviour on the one hand and its explanation, description and evaluation on the other depends from the outset on the inclusion in reportage of enough (but not too much) of what goes on 'inside the natives' heads'. Likewise, let me insist once again that the problem is not one of translation. It is true that it has to be demonstrated, not assumed, that the terms employed in different languages which appear to match the observer's are indeed equivalent to them. A Roman *patronus* may or may not be performing an equivalent role to an Italian *padrone*, a French *patron*, or an English patron, while the *babas* (literally, 'fathers') of the Oyo Empire of seventeenth-century West Africa† may be closer to the ideal type than any of them. Conversely, the *laboureurs* of eighteenth-century France were not, whatever else they may have been, 'labourers' in the English sense. But the challenge to produce a rigorous and exhaustive definition is neither more nor less formidable if the term in question has been chosen and applied across a linguistic frontier. The reason why I have now to confront the problem of taxonomy directly is that although I have claimed that the 'dictionary' meaning of 'marry' is adequate for the purpose of reportage, I have at the same time to concede that there are very different kinds of marriage. But if so, does not the reader have to be told what it is of which the marrying reported in any given instance is one or another kind? And

* See Marvin Harris, *The Nature of Cultural Things* (1964), and *Culture, Man and Nature* (1971).
† On whom see Robin Law, *The Oyo Empire* (1977).

without a rigorous and exhaustive definition, is not the status of 'marriage' as a term of reportage undermined? What difference is there, despite what I have said, between 'marriage' and 'magic' or 'feudalism'?

A reply along the lines that 'marriage' is defined by competent authorities as 'a union between a man and a woman such that children born to the woman are recognized legitimate offspring of both partners'* will be of no help at all. That definition notoriously fails to cover the whole range of cases reported across the historical and ethnographic record. What is the fieldworker who accepts it to do when confronted with the adelphic polyandry of the Iravas, among whom, after the bride has been fetched from her father's house by the eldest brother, 'marital' rights are all vested in the whole corporate group of brothers? or with the practice of the Nayars, among whom the woman has a single ritual husband but also a set of lovers *en titre* with recognized sexual access but no rights of paternity over the children whom they may have fathered? Armed with examples like these, sceptics of the possibility of a theory-neutral definition can mount a two-pronged attack from both the philosophical and the technical flanks. The moral which they can be claimed to point is not only that practising anthropologists are confronted with much more exacting problems of fieldwork than armchair theorists of kinship are aware, but also that the uniqueness of societies' institutions and therewith their members' conceptualizations of them make nonsense of the claim that the so-called 'dictionary' meaning can, or ever could, be applied across the board.

But the challenge can, all the same, be met. Nothing prevents the fieldworker who recognizes that a working definition with which he began is inadequate from extending or modifying it as may be necessary to accommodate the awkward case. Nor need he be pre-empting any subsequent explanation, description or evaluation in doing so: the statements just made about the Iravas and Nayars can still be construed as reports which the rival observer can go and check for himself. Just as 'ownership' can be used to cover a range of cases diverging increasingly from the ideal type first formulated by the Roman jurists, whether (as among the Siane of New Guinea) in terms of a distinction between the rights of appropriation which a man has over his goods and tools and the relationship in which he stands to the land and the sacred flutes of his people as a whole, or (as among the Nyanga of the Eastern Congo) in terms of a varying approximation to ownership *ex jure Quiritum* in the

---

* The definition is that of the Royal Anthropological Institute's *Notes and Queries on Anthropology* (1951).

rights to more or less accessible and abundant hunting and gathering territory, so can 'marriage' be used to cover a range of cases diverging increasingly from the Royal Anthropological Institute's ideal type. No doubt there may be discovered in the course of further research societies in which any conception of either legal or customary exclusiveness of sexual access, regularity of cohabitation, or parental or quasi-parental rights or duties shared between or on behalf of biological progenitors or their stand-ins are either so far attenuated or so thoroughly repudiated that a borderline has somewhere to be arbitrarily drawn. But that no more undermines the status of 'marriage' as a term of reportage than the Chinese *mui jai* undermine the status of 'slavery'. On the contrary: effective criticism of the previously accepted definition depends precisely on the possibility of reporting to the satisfaction of all rival observers where and to what extent the practice of the Iravas or the Nayars is incompatible with it.

However awkward for a hitherto standard definition the awkward cases may be, the moral to be drawn is not, therefore, that practising sociologists should be deterred from making and standing by reports that they have observed instances of marriages of one or another discrepant kinds. It is that once a researcher's purpose is to do more than to present his readers with the report for its own sake alone, he must at the same time be ready with an answer to the questioner who wants to know what he *wouldn't* have regarded as an instance. Just as no researcher reports a Stanford-Binet test score without some idea in his mind about how it relates to the theoretical concept of intelligence, or reports a pattern of differential modes of access in face-to-face interaction without some idea in his mind about how it relates to the theoretical concept of social prestige, so must any researcher reporting one or more cases of marriage be presumed to have some further purpose in mind which somehow relates to an explanatory, descriptive or evaluative theory of kinship. He does not need to have formulated a rigorous and exhaustive taxonomy before going out into the field at all. But when he relates his working definition to his theoretical purpose he will need to be prepared for it to come under scrutiny. It is then that no matter how modest the generalization or narrative or pattern which he ventures to report, or how cautious the explanation, description or evaluation of it which he advances, he will have to offer some further defence of the term by which he has chosen to designate the behaviour he has observed than merely to retort that his definition does not of itself commit him to any pre-emptively explanatory, descriptive or evaluative presuppositions.

§ 19. The lurking significance of an unstated taxonomy (or unstated assumption about the lack of a need for one) can most clearly be brought out where the researcher is claiming for his report the status of *discovery*. Such claims are a function at once of the existing state of knowledge in the field and of the purpose for which the research was carried out. But they do not assume either that what has been discovered is unique or that discoveries themselves are rare; they may, in a particularly fortunate state of the discipline concerned, be almost a matter of routine. On the other hand, only a minority of reports will qualify. No researcher will claim to have 'discovered' an instance of marriage, slavery or warfare, but only, say, of adelphic polyandry or slavery including the right of slaves to own other slaves, or warfare between fellow-nationals. There has, in other words, to be something special about it. Sometimes, this is no more than the correction of an entrenched misconception or the resolution of a contrived paradox: the discovery, for example, that the traditional Scottish clans were not clans at all means only that given the dictionary meaning of 'clan' as 'unilineal descent group' the Scottish clans fail to qualify, since they include all the cognatic descendants of an eponymous ancestor. But in the ordinary way, a sociologist who claims to have discovered an instance of X will have in mind both a latent taxonomy and a theoretical purpose.

By way of illustration, here are three examples from the ethnographic record where a claim of discovery is, to my mind, appropriate but the purpose is different in each case: explanatory in the first, descriptive in the second and evaluative in the third. The first is the account of the Turkana given by P. H. Gulliver in *The Central Nilo-Hamites* (1953), the second the account of the Nupe given by S. F. Nadel in *A Black Byzantium* (1942) and the third the account of the Ik given by Colin Turnbull in *The Mountain People* (1972).

Gulliver reports the Turkana as, among other things, an instance of a 'stateless society'. This is not, in the present state of knowledge, so remarkable as to count as a discovery in itself, even if there was a time when it would have been. There are numerous societies where there is no centralized coercive authority exercised by persons occupying specialized administrative roles. But the Turkana, together with a number of other Nilo-Hamitic peoples, are distinctive in that political authority resides in age-sets. Outside the family, order is maintained by the holders not of office, but of status deriving from age: in any group or gathering, the oldest men are accorded the highest ritual and therefore political status. What is more, all Turkana acknowledge an unambiguous tribal designation, so that the rival observer cannot claim that the boundary of their society is so fluid or indeterminate that the categorization of them as a 'stateless *society*' rests on a primary misunderstanding. Yet their 'statelessness' is not a property directly observed. A report of the workings of their age-set system and of the manner in which it restrains inter-local violence neither requires nor suggests any notion of 'the state' to which it stands in contrast by virtue of its absence. To report the Turkana as 'stateless', and to point the contrast between their way of doing without a state and that of others (such as segmentary lineage systems), is perfectly legitimate once given a definition of 'stateless' in accordance with its dictionary meaning and an adequate documentation of the exercise of social control by other means. But what is the purpose of doing so? It can only be because of a presupposition to the effect that the maintenance of social control by other means calls for special explanation. It is this which turns the report of Turkana age-sets into something, at least, of a claim to discovery and which gives the designation 'stateless', and therefore the reportage of its functional equivalent, its point.

In the case of the Nupe, the designation which immediately raises the question of the researcher's purpose is given in the chosen title. What, then, is 'Byzantine' about the Nupe? The claim to discovery here rests in part on a presumptive state of knowledge such that the reader is expected to be surprised to learn what a complex system of political, military and economic organization Nadel has found in the middle of Africa. But the presupposition which underlies the distinction between 'Byzantine' societies and others is only marginally explanatory, if at all. The resemblance to the historical Byzantium is too tenuous and the differences from it too marked for the workings of the two to be related except at the most general level (and, therefore, along with a host of others) within an explanatory theory of the workings of pre-industrial societies of a certain complexity and size: apart from anything else, the significance of the capital city of Bida is quite different from that of Byzantium itself, whatever the parallels between the relations of the bureaucracy to the ruling dynasty, or of the rural producers to the members of artisan guilds. Nadel can only be construed, therefore, as implying that Nupe society is *like* that of Byzantium for those who live in it, if only in the intricacy of its politics and in the tortuous palace intrigues which have come to give 'Byzantine' its dictionary meaning, and it is only by reference to some such descriptive presupposition that his claim to have discovered a black 'Byzantium' can be assessed.

In the case of the Ik, Turnbull is quite explicit about his claim to have discovered an instance of a 'non-moral' society, by which he makes it clear that he means that the Ik, who once upon a time held that theft,

incest, promise-breaking and refusal of help or compassion to the unfortunate were wrong, have ceased to do so. Now his evidence certainly
accords with his claim that the Ik consistently violate the conception of
right and wrong which they formerly had. Thus, he reports it as accepted
generally among them that a stronger person should literally take food
from the mouth of an older and weaker, or a spouse's death be concealed
so that the survivor should both procure food from Turnbull himself on
the spouse's behalf and avoid any pressure from other Ik to provide a
funeral feast. It follows, therefore, that on the definition of 'moral' as
unselfish and dutiful, Turnbull's designation of the Ik as 'non-moral' is
a matter of reportage which a rival observer with a different terminology
can transpose *salva veritate* into his own. But as soon as the reader asks
what is Turnbull's purpose in using 'moral' as he does, it becomes
apparent that he uses it, among other things, to rule out as 'moral' the
general avoidance by the Ik of murder. Although he reports, for
example, cases of deliberate neglect resulting in death, he also shows the
Ik as not wanting actively to kill each other, and he declines to attribute
this to moral restraint on the grounds that their avoidance is inspired
only by motives of personal advantage. But this not only goes beyond
what can be counted as reportage; it also betrays what one of his
commentators has called, in discussing this very point, a 'near-Kantian'
concern for other human beings and acceptance of a duty not to use them
as ends-in-themselves.* And it is this evaluative presupposition which
discloses the purpose of his claim to have discovered a 'non-moral'
society.

An unquestioning reliance on dictionary meanings will not, therefore,
always be enough to absolve the researcher from justifying the latent
taxonomy behind his designation of the events, processes and states of
affairs on which he has chosen to report. Indeed, the stronger his claim
that the report amounts to a discovery, the more important it is that he
should declare his purpose in making it. There is no need for him to
preface his report with a glossary containing all the terms denotative of
human behaviour which are going to be employed in it. But there *is* a
need for the reader to be able to tell which of the chosen terms *do* have
to be rigorously and exhaustively defined if the report, although not in
itself pre-emptive of explanation, description or evaluation, is not to be
used in covert support of a larger argument whose presuppositions rival
observers might rightly wish to reject.

§20. Once this is conceded – as it has to be – another complication

---

* Christine Battersby, 'Morality and the Ik', *Philosophy* LIII (1978), p. 212.

follows. If reportage was all that sociologists ever tried to do, dictionary meanings would be all that they needed. But once it isn't, then even where a report is innocent of any discernible trace of theoretical pre-emption its prospective use in support of an explanation, description or evaluation has implications for the treatment of borderline cases which, for that very reason, can no longer be settled by fiat.

Consider from this point of view the term 'peasant'. Its application depends, as all observers will agree, on some shared conception of what it is that a 'peasant' typically does. The trouble is not that the constitutive intentions and beliefs of what he does are problematic, as they are with the 'magician'. But the context in which peasants do what they do is problematic, and the differences between rival schools over the features of the context which should be built into the definition cannot be treated like the difference between fights and battles, houses and cottages, groups and crowds or pamphlets and books. All observers can agree that peasants are typically engaged, during their working hours, in cultivating the soil. But is it or isn't it the only thing they do in their working hours? Do they do it with the help only of members of their families or with that of other people? Do they own the land whose produce they are extracting, or do they not? Do they keep that produce for themselves and their families, or do they share it with, or sell it to, or surrender it into the hands of other people, and if so who? Are they free to bequeath or dispose of the land at will, or are they not? A common answer to these questions is to say that the notion of a peasantry should be interpreted as an ideal type not all of whose features need to be instantiated in any given instance for the designation to be applied. But this does not enable us to treat the borderline cases as methodologically innocuous. What marks the line between a peasant and a crofter, a rancher, a market-gardener or a farmer? If reportage alone were at issue, it might be enough to lay down the size of the holding, or the proportion of the crop sold outwith the village community, or the ratio of pasturage to arable, or the extent of legal restraints on alienability, and narrate the changes in the composition of the rural population in accordance with a convention based on these. But no such convention will be of any help in bringing sociologists, anthropologists and historians of rival schools into agreement with one another, for the disagreements between them are not over what the 'peasants' were doing but over why, or more importantly, why not. 'Peasant', in other words, is another of those standard sociological terms which can only be theory-neutrally construed if either so loosely or so restrictively defined as to defeat the purpose of introducing it in the first place. The question whether, for example, the English peasantry 'disappeared'* between the mid seventeenth and the mid nineteenth century is not one which the recording angel can settle. Under one definition the answer will be yes, but under another no, if only because under at least one possible definition England never had a peasantry at all, even in the Middle Ages.† If the disputes between rival observers are to be resolved, the defining characteristics of 'peasants' (and therefore the necessary and sufficient evidence of their 'disappearance') must be so chosen as to lend themselves to being better explained (and/or described and/or evaluated) by one than another substantive theory, and the relative emphasis on one rather than another constituent of the ideal type will need to be shifted as the success or failure of rival theories may require.

Whenever, therefore, two or more equally knowledgeable researchers are in dispute – as they all too often are – over the definition of a standard term which both agree to be useful, they owe it to their readers to make it clear whether the dispute is about its usefulness for reportage or about its usefulness in furthering the theoretical purpose to which reportage is to be put. Contrast, as an illustration, the two following dicta: (i) 'When ancient historians write "caste" they mean "order"' (M. I. Finley); (ii) 'Religion is a sixteenth-century word for nationalism' (Lewis Namier). In (i), the charge is being levelled against rival observers that by their use of 'caste' they misreport what the Romans were doing in treating persons of higher or lower status differently from each other. The treatment of groups or strata in Roman society – and particularly the society of the later Roman Empire from Diocletian onwards – which appear to fit the dictionary meaning of 'caste' is, so Finley claims, being misunderstood in the primary sense if they are so designated. Admittedly, the sources report to us the existence of closed, hereditary, endogamous, ranked occupational groups. But their treatment of each other was informed by different intentions and beliefs, and defined for the Romans themselves by reference to a different historical and cultural context, from those of a society like traditional India in which a ritual scale of purity and pollution is a guiding principle of the division of labour. In (ii), on the other hand, when Namier asks his readers to substitute 'nationalism' for 'religion', he is not charging rival observers with the attribution to sixteenth-century Europeans of beliefs or intentions which they didn't have. He is suggesting that their behaviour should be explained by reference to political interests and loyalties which

---

* See H. J. Habbakuk, 'La Disparition du Paysan Anglais', *Annales* xx (1965).
† See Alan Macfarlane, *The Origins of English Individualism* (1978).

influenced, and were influenced by, the emergence of nation-states whose significance contemporaries could not fully appreciate at the time. Both are polemical injunctions directed to fellow-researchers held to be making mistakes. But in the first, the mistake (if it is one) rests on a violation of theory-neutrality; in the second, it rests on a failure to perceive the kind of theory which is required.

§ 21. These same considerations apply whenever a sociologist, anthropologist or historian decides for reasons of his own to enlarge on or modify a dictionary meaning. Neither language nor the behaviour which it denotes are, after all, static. Whatever the terms applied by the members of any society to their own and others' behaviour, they must all at some time or another have been *neologisms*. By no means all neologisms are coined by professional social scientists. But where they are, there are four good reasons for their doing so: because 'they' have coined a term for an institution or practice which is new to themselves; because 'we' have detected an innovation for which a new term of ours would be acceptable in principle to 'them'; because there is a need to designate under a common heading behaviour which is not yet covered by any single term; or because the current dictionary meaning fails to make sufficient discrimination between forms of behaviour whose constitutive intentions and beliefs ought *not* to be understood in the primary sense as equivalent to one another. But it holds no less of new definitions than of old ones that a term which can be shown to be useful in making reportage more accurate, or at least more concise, is not always an improvement for the theoretical purpose which the report is to be used to serve.

Neologisms introduced for either of the first two reasons are commonplace even in the study of societies whose institutions and practices change so little and so slowly that the observer is hard put to it to find any behaviour which strikes either him or its members as new. Nowhere are roles so stereotyped and the hold of tradition so binding that people never behave in ways which call for designation in terms which modify previous usage. In complex and fluid industrial societies this is one of the tasks which falls explicitly on the census-takers, whose previous terminology is so regularly overtaken by further advances in the division and specialization of labour that comparison between the activities of the working population between one decade and the next may be made virtually impossible. But the difficulty facing the twentieth-century census-taker is the same as faced Tacitus when he had to decide on a term with which to designate the leading men of the Germanic tribes. There is always an attendant risk of misreportage, since whatever term is used to designate the role or behaviour regarded as novel will have antecedents and overtones of its own. The neologist, whether participant or observer, may be tempted to read into the behaviour which he designates by his chosen neologism intentions or beliefs which either 'they' or a rival observer might plausibly repudiate: thus, a number of authorities have accused Tacitus of assuming too readily that his German *'principes'* performed a role more nearly analogous to that of Roman aristocrats than a qualified and diligent fieldworker would have been prepared to confirm. But it is then for the rival observer, as always, to proffer an alternative designation supported by evidence to show that what the so-called German *principes* typically did has to be understood in the primary sense in some different way from that in which Tacitus has understood it.

The other two reasons, however, raise more acutely the problems both of possible misreportage and of possible conflict between reportage and its purposes. Consider, for example, the term 'burial-club' which must at some time (I do not know when) have been coined to designate the practice of pooling resources for funerary rituals in a society whose members had not been using either that or an exactly synonymous term. It has a readily justifiable use in the reportage of behaviour observed in societies as far apart in time and place as Tacitus's Rome and the Galla of the Western Shoa province of Ethiopia in the mid twentieth century.* What objection can the rival observer make to its application alike to the Roman *collegia* and the Shoa Galla *iddir*? There in the historical record the *collegia* are, taking monthly contributions from their members towards the cost of funerals, laying down the form of the ceremony thus provided for, and penalizing the disorderly or recalcitrant; and there the *iddir* are in the ethnographic record, taking grain and coffee-money from their members for memorial feasts, requiring those so enjoined to dig the grave and carry the coffin, and fining those who disobey the officers or default on their contributions. There can surely be no dispute that both do what falls properly within the dictionary meaning of 'burial-club' and that the term cannot possibly be claimed to involve any primary misunderstanding of what their members do. Yet the designation may not be quite so uncontroversial when it comes to the exposition and test of a theory about funerary rituals in general. For no set of practices like these can be identical in *all* respects, any more than can the roles of

* On whom see Herbert S. Lewis, 'Wealth, Influence and Prestige among the Shoa Galla', in Arthur Tuden and Leonard Plotnicov, eds., *Social Stratification in Africa* (1970).

Ahoka's *dhamma-mahāmāttas* and Charlemagne's *missi dominici*. This may not give the rival observer any scope for charges of misreportage. But it may still impede, or even preclude, the drawing of other similarities and differences on which more successful explanations, descriptions and/or evaluations of the same reported behaviour might be based.

Similarly, a neologism coined because a dictionary meaning turns out to be inadequate may in turn be less useful for the purposes which the report is to serve than the term which it has replaced. Suppose, for example, that a comparative sociologist discovers from his sources that a term with the dictionary meaning of 'non-human' is used by both third-century Greek-speaking Romans (the actual word is *ananthrōpos**) and seventeenth-century Japanese (the actual word is *hinin†*) to refer to persons of very low status. He will be right to regard the dictionary meaning as misleading because of the difference between, in the first case, a half-serious synonym for 'barbarian' and, in the second, a label denoting registered beggars whose place in a complex but recognized hierarchy is sanctioned both by law and by custom. But suppose he then tries to improve on 'non-human' by replacing it with 'outcaste' – outcastes being defined, like 'pariahs', as persons regarded by other members of their society as of the lowest category of ritual status recognized within the non-criminal adult population. So defined, it is a matter of reportage that there were Egyptians in the Roman Empire and Tokugawa Japanese who were regarded by their higher-ranking compatriots as 'outcastes'. But this only recreates the very confusion which the neologism was intended to cure. For Finley's objection to the use of 'caste' for the ancient world now re-enters with added force. Nobody in the Roman Empire was treated in a way which was constituted by intentions and beliefs like those characteristic of traditional India, and although this overtone can be stipulated out, so to speak, by definition, it does to some degree apply to Tokugawa Japan. There *is* a good theoretical reason for bracketing the *Hinin* with the Indian *Harijan* for the purposes of both explanation and description (and, many would say, of evaluation) which does not apply within the Roman Empire, and it makes no difference whatever that there happens to be a documentary source in which third-century Egyptians are referred to by a term with the dictionary meaning 'non-human'. Where, accordingly, the usefulness of a newly coined or borrowed term so clearly depends on the use to which it will be put, the

---

* The example is taken from Ramsay MacMullen, *Roman Social Relations 50 B.C. to A.D. 280* (1974), p. 56 n.55.

† See John Price, 'A History of the Outcaste: Untouchability in Japan', in George de Vos and Hiroshi Wagatusma, *Japan's Invisible Race* (1966), Ch. 1.

reader's insistence on a rigorous and exhaustive definition will be fully justified once again.

§ 22. Classification, therefore, should always be seen as serving some implicit or presumptive theoretical purpose. But is there no general methodological principle by which sociologists, anthropologists and historians should be guided in framing the taxonomy which suits their purposes best? Large as the literature is on the methodology of the social sciences, there is nowhere in it, so far as I have been able to find, a comprehensive and systematic treatment of classification in social theory. I shall not attempt to provide one. But this chapter must offer some sort of account of the criteria by which it may be possible to judge the success of a scheme of classification for a purpose which may, in the first instance, be reportage only, but cannot but carry implications for the subsequent explanation and/or description and/or evaluation of whatever it is of which the report has been made.

Any chosen taxonomy will have to be imposed by the researcher on his observations. It cannot but derive from presuppositions not given to him by them. Categories and kinds, whether of actions, practices, institutions or societies, are not natural entities waiting to be run into, and the construction of them is not a theory-neutral exercise. But nor, at the same time, is the observer free to invent them in any way he pleases. The hilarious taxonomy attributed by Jorge Luis Borges to a 'certain Chinese encyclopaedia' and taken as his starting-point by Michel Foucault in *Les Mots et les Choses*** is, admittedly, a salutary reminder of how little we can afford to take for granted what Foucault calls 'our age-old distinction between the Same and the Other': according to it, animals are divided into '(a) belonging to the Emperor, (b) embalmed, (c) tame, (d) sucking pigs, (e) sirens, (f) fabulous, (g) stray dogs, (h) included in the present classification, (i) frenzied, (j) innumerable, (k) drawn with a very fine camel-hair brush, (l) *et cetera*, (m) having just broken the water pitcher, (n) that from a long way off look like flies'. But by no stretch of fancy can these marvellously subversive distinctions be incorporated into a workable zoology. However much scientists in any field may need to be shaken out of the habits of thought of their period and milieu, the test of a taxonomy is, and can only be, its reliability and consistency when put to use; and this applies no less in the study of human societies than in the study of plant and animal species.

There is, however, a choice which confronts the sociological taxonomist at the outset. There are two possible ways of classifying the objects

* English translation as *The Order of Things* (1970), p. xv.

of a historical science – historical, that is, in the sense that sociology and biology are historical but physics and chemistry are not. The first may for convenience be called the Linnaean and the second the Darwinian. A 'Linnaean' classification is synchronic rather than diachronic, and it relates societies or species to one another by reference to similarities and differences in their observable workings and forms. A 'Darwinian' classification, by contrast, is diachronic rather than synchronic and draws its connections between societies or species on the basis of properties inherited (or not) from a presumptive common starting-point within an observable sequence. The two are, to be sure, complementary. Societies, no less than species, are best classified in a way which accommodates similarities of origin without denying independently-derived similarities of structure and function. The difference is between starting with a multidimensional grid into which societies are fitted according to their structural or functional resemblances and differences, and starting from a node from which societies with their various structural or functional resemblances and differences are seen as branching off along various paths. In practice, the outcome may be the same, however arrived at: a traditional pre-industrial African kingdom or a twentieth-century capitalist industrial liberal democracy may be classed relative to others like and unlike them in the same way whether a Linnaean or Darwinian principle of taxonomy was adopted in the first place. But it should always be possible for the reader to be told, if necessary, which and why.

At the same time, the analogy between societies and species should not be pressed too far. The misuse of it has by now a history of its own extending at least as far back as Balzac's Preface of 1842 to the *Comédie Humaine* and at least as far forward as Radcliffe-Brown's posthumously published *A Natural Science of Society* (1957). But just because the relation of individual lions or tigers to the species of which they are members is not the same as that of individual Frenchmen or Andaman Islanders to the society of which they are members, it does not follow that the principles of taxonomy successfully developed within biology have no application in sociology too. Indeed, the lesson to be learnt from them is twofold. Not only do they show how the need for clear demarcation by reference to similarities and differences of structure and function may be reconciled with the need to take account of the workings of a historical process of differentiation; they also show how the prodigious variety which has been generated by that process – more than ten million distinct plant and animal species – can still be reduced to manageable order. It may be that the concept of a society (which I shall not attempt to define until Volume II) is more problematic than that of a species. But there is no reason why forms of social organization should not lend themselves to categorization in such a way as to make it possible to build up a taxonomy of societies which has both a Linnaean and a Darwinian rationale.

The difficulty with a purely Linnaean taxonomy in sociology is that similarities and differences of structure and function by themselves will not yield clear-cut categories to which each different society can be separately assigned. The zoologist confronted with a specimen wants to be able to identify it – that is, to pick out those of its observable characteristics which will enable him to say that it is an instance of one of the Latin polynomials such as Linnaeus devised. He wants to be able to say 'this is the fern *Comptonia aspeniflora*', or 'this is the barnacle *Megalasma gracilis*'. But when Radcliffe-Brown is confronted with the Andaman Islanders, he cannot, even after he has ascertained their several roles in Andaman society, at once label them as members of a society with a Linnaean polynomial and a distinctive place in the sociological grid. True, if one Andaman Islander is, say, a chief, Radcliffe-Brown may safely categorize Andaman society as a chiefdom,* just as the zoologist whose barnacle has a carina projecting below the scutum with a basal margin as long as that of the scutum may safely categorize it as *Megalasma gracilis*. But chiefdoms are not like barnacles. There is no Linnaean key to the forms and varieties of chiefdoms on which anthropologists of rival schools could all agree, even for the purpose of reportage alone. Synchronic taxonomies by structure and function can certainly be constructed up to a certain point: the distinction between, say, monarchy, despotism and republic is no more a pure invention arbitrarily imposed à la Borges on the governments of Montesquieu's world than is the distinction in the inanimate world between solids, liquids and gases. Nor does the distinction presuppose an evaluation, even if 'despotism' as used by other sociologists (such as Herbert Spencer) is by definition 'evil': it is up to you whether a ruler who is *legibus solutus* is worse than one who is not. But nor can Montesquieu's distinction be fitted into a classification which is anywhere nearly exhaustive. The distinctions that can be drawn by synchronic diagnosis fall too far short of giving each society identifiable in time and place both a unique set of defining characteristics and a corresponding Linnaean label.

This being so, it might seem that a purely Darwinian approach to taxonomy would be more promising for sociological theory. The

---

* Which it is not, *pace* Capt. Archibald Blair who concluded from an exploration in the summer of 1789 that Andaman chiefs were 'generally painted red' (quoted by Morton H. Fried, *The Evolution of Political Society* (1967), p. 86).

thousands of societies in the ethnographic and historical record are, after all, to be found as they are because of the sequence in which they have followed their predecessors. But a purely historical typology will be no more workable than a purely structural and functional one. In sociology, unlike biology, not only convergence but regression is frequent. Societies not only imitate each other directly but also revert, whether by design or under compulsion, to forms of organization from which they had previously evolved. Social evolution cannot be represented like a genealogical tree starting from Adam and Eve and branching out from a central stem; and to the extent to which it can, it has still to be supplemented by a categorization in terms of structure and function which will cut across the lines, as it were, of genealogical cousinage.

Any sociological taxonomy, therefore, which hopes to be acceptable to all rival observers even for the purpose of reportage alone, will have to be based on some combination of both Linnaean and Darwinian principles; and there are, as it happens, two devices which lend themselves to either or both synchronic and diachronic application, and which can be so combined as to generate the kind of taxonomy which need not be pre-emptive of any particular explanatory, descriptive or evaluative theory. The first is to exhaust the logical possibilities; the second is to isolate the common constituents.

The first is most easily illustrated in the form of a 2 × 2 table, which can then be extended to any number of possible alternatives in any number of further dimensions. Consider, for example, the distinctions drawn by anthropologists between patrilineal and matrilineal societies on the one hand and patrilocal amd matrilocal societies on the other. They appear, at first sight, exhaustive and given sufficiently accurate reportage of the rules of residence and descent it should be possible to assign any chosen society to its appropriate box, as in the diagram below.

	patrilineal	matrilineal
patrilocal	Kachin Mara	Aluridja Ashanti
matrilocal	? Karadjeri	Bemba Nayar

I have included, but queried, the Karadjeri because although I have found them cited as matrilocal in an anthropological text,* this is an evident misunderstanding in the primary sense. Not only are the

* Maurice Godelier, *Perspectives in Marxist Anthropology* (Eng. trans., 1977), p. 106.

Karadjeri patrilocal, but a number of authorities have doubted whether any patrilineal and matrilocal societies have existed at all. But this increases rather than diminishes the theoretical interest of the taxonomy, for if one of the logically possible classes turns out to be null, the distribution of the total, whatever it is, is certainly not random. As it turns out, there are more complications to come, not just because at least two patrilineal societies are *uxori*local* but also because some matrilineal societies, such as Malinowski's Trobrianders, are *avuncu*local, while the practices reported of other societies are such that they have had to be labelled *ambi*patrilocal, patri-*viri*local, *bi*local, *neo*local and even 'miscellaneous' or 'mixed'. But the complexities involved in the detailed analysis of rules of residence and descent, and the controversies to which they have led, do not destroy the value of the taxonomy which has given rise to them. This is an aspect of social organization for which a logically exhaustive list of possible forms can in principle be constructed, and any society whose rules have been correctly understood in the primary sense can be assigned its proper place. It is true that the importance of such rules diminishes markedly as societies evolve towards a greater individual freedom and away from a systematic and collective organization of marriage, whether prescriptive or preferential. But the taxonomic table which accommodates the possible alternatives, however little it explains, describes or evaluates by itself, has both a Linnaean and a Darwinian rationale: it can be incorporated either within a wider set of structural and functional distinctions in which institutions of marriage and kinship can be seen to be related in different ways to other aspects of social organization, or within a longer sequence of societal forms in which different rules of residence, marriage and descent can be seen to follow from specified antecedent cultural and/or ecological conditions.

The second device, by contrast, starts by viewing such things as rules of preferential cross-cousin marriage not as one of a range of logical possibilities but as an ingredient which may be combined with others in a range of different mixtures. It too presupposes, whether implicitly or explicitly, a contrast between the form of the particular role, or relationship, taken as fundamental and some other form which is found at other places and times. For example, a taxonomy which isolates societies whose politics are of the 'patron–client' type and then arranges them by reference to the economic or other characteristics which permit, require

---

* They are the Agbo villagers of Adadama in West Africa as reported by Rosemary Harris in Mary Douglas and Phyllis M. Kaberry, eds., *Man in Africa* (1969), and the Mundurucú Indians as reported by Robert F. Murphy in his *Headhunter's Heritage* (1960). I owe these references to Professor J. A. Barnes.

or inhibit the dominance of patron–client relationships presupposes a contrast at once synchronic and diachronic between 'clientelism' and, on the one hand, a 'primitive' politics based purely on kinship, residence or age-grades and, on the other hand, an 'advanced' politics based on horizontal loyalties and mass parties.* But the taxonomy rests on the compilation, as it were, of a recipe-book. The ingredients available cover every aspect of social organization from the purely technological to the purely ideological: the taxonomist may want to pick out anything from iron-tipped weapons or steam-mills to age-sets or parliaments to witch-doctoring or Roman Catholicism. But just as some of the logical possi-bilities turn out to be a null class, so do some of the recipes turn out to be impossible: it would be at least as startling to find slash-and-burn cultivation in combination with a hereditary court aristocracy as it would to find a patrilineal-matrilocal kinship system. The resulting table thus has likewise both a Linnaean and a Darwinian rationale: the recipe-book can equally well be construed as a guide to the labelling of interrelated sets of combinations known to be possible and as a list of combinations whose ingredients can be given a place in a historical sequence.

The test of the argument put forward in this section will come only in Volume II when I advance some rudimentary classifications of my own. But the methodological point is that any terms of reportage in which different societies are distinguished from each other, however un-systematically, beyond time and place alone already appeal to a presump-tive taxonomy of some kind. To speak only of 'the traditional pre-industrial African kingdom of Oyo' or of 'twentieth-century capitalist-industrial liberal-democratic Britain' is already to use a kind of Linnaean polynomial with some Darwinian implications. It is still true that to make such a differentiation the basis of a report may not in itself pre-empt any explanatory, descriptive or evaluative theory. But it raises the very same issue as does the presentation of reported observations in such a way as to impose, or create, a pattern. The reader is always entitled to ask the purpose for which one differentiation is highlighted instead of another; and the answer may well be open to further question by those with other presuppositions and purposes in mind.

INFERENCE WITHIN REPORTAGE

§23. This chapter has so far been almost exclusively concerned with the delineation of the all-important frontier between the theory-neutral (but

---

* For examples, see the copious references cited, e.g., in S. N. Eisenstadt and Louis Roniger, 'Patron–Client Relations as a Model of Structuring Social Exchange', *Comparative Studies in Society and History* XXII (1980).

not presuppositionless) reportage of an event, process or state of affairs on the one side and its explanation, description or evaluation on the other, and thus with the danger that a report, or set of them, may be so framed as to pre-empt the explanation, description or evaluation to which the author's theoretical presuppositions have already committed him. But suppose that what is pre-empted is not an explanation, description or evaluation but a further report. Is that something to which a rival observer can object?

Where the link between the two is by way of a deductive mode of reasoning, there will obviously be nothing more to be said. The conclusions of logic and arithmetic are as inescapable in sociology as anywhere else. They may not be easy to arrive at: a considerable degree of technical skill may be required, for example, to embody a set of observational data in rows and columns and to extract from it, by way of the appropriate operations of matrix algebra, information which would not have been obvious from the reportage of the data in their original form. But no methodological commentary is called for. The mode of reasoning is problematic only where the inference is either semi- or quasi-deductive.

A *semi-deductive* inference is one which, although not as strong as logical entailment, rests on a subsumed premise so little open to question that no rival observer could in practice undermine the resulting syllogism. Suppose, for example, that a sociologist studying the population of Liberia in the 1960s wants to be able to say how many of its citizens are descended from the American settlers who founded it.* The question is not directly answered by the 1962 Census which he has before him. But he notices that there are 6,452 citizens enumerated in it who claim no tribal affiliation. It occurs to him that the people without a tribal affiliation can only be those of American descent, and he is therefore in a position to answer his original question as follows: 6,452 Liberians claim no tribal affiliation; any Liberian claiming no tribal affiliation is of American descent; therefore there are (in 1962) 6,452 Liberians of American descent. Admittedly, this conclusion is almost certainly false, since it is most unlikely that the recording angel would confirm the Liberian census to be accurate. But the inference is sound. No rival observer could undermine it except by a demonstration that 'their' behaviour has been misunderstood in the primary sense – those who didn't give a tribal affiliation were joking, or deliberately misleading the

* This example is taken from Christopher Clapham, 'Liberia', in John Dunn, ed., *West African States: Failure and Promise* (1978), p. 120.

census-takers, or didn't themselves understand the question being put
to them. Semi-deductive inferences can, of course, be mistakenly drawn,
just as deductive ones can. But if so, it is because of a flaw in the
intermediate link which further research will disclose. When Halévy, for
example, discusses the second General Election held in the year 1910,*
he reasons like this: an appreciably smaller proportion of a fractionally
larger electorate turned out to vote than had done so earlier in the year;
anyone who voted in January but didn't bother to vote in December must
have been more indifferent to the issues on which the election was fought
than the time before; therefore the electorate as a whole was appreciably
more indifferent to the issues in December than in January. The trouble
with this syllogism is not that it begs a theoretically pre-emptive definition of electoral indifference or that it discounts the possibility that those
who *did* vote both times were more worked up about the issues in
December than they had been in January. In the context of Halévy's
argument, a lower turnout could be accepted by rival observers as
indicating a failure by the party stalwarts to keep the electoral temperature as high as it was. But the inference collapses as soon as it is observed
that the number of uncontested seats rose from 75 in January to 163 in
December.

A *quasi-deductive* inference, on the other hand, is one whose minor
premise presupposes some further battery of ancillary reports which are
not directly given. Inferences of this kind are commonplace in works of
sociology, anthropology and history, and they may be signalled by a
variety of phrases all the way from 'serves to suggest ...', to '... tantamount to proof'. But the rival observer is always entitled to query the
presuppositions on which they depend, and the strength of the inference
has to be measured by reference to the plausibility of the reply.

As an example, consider the following: 'The heavy sales of wheat
recorded in the bailiffs' accounts of manors in corn-producing areas are
proof enough of the cash crop basis of a good deal of manorial economy,
even if it could not be inferred indirectly from the existence of towns.'†
Notice first, that the sales in the bailiffs' accounts are claimed to be 'proof
enough' of the cash crop basis; and second, that the inference from the
existence of towns is said, by contrast, to be indirect. In other words, the
syllogism 'towns existed in mediaeval England; towns could not exist in
mediaeval England unless the manors in the corn-producing areas were

---

*Elie Halévy, *A History of the English People in the Nineteenth Century* VI: *The Rule of
Democracy (1905–1914)* (Eng. trans., 1934), p. 342. I owe this reference to Mr John
Grigg.
† Eileen Power, *The Wool Trade in English Medieval History* (1941), p. 3.

to a considerable degree on a cash crop basis; therefore a good deal of manorial economy was on a cash crop basis' presupposes more which the rival observer might query than does 'heavy sales of wheat are recorded in the bailiffs' accounts of mediaeval English manors in corn producing areas; any manorial lord who sold substantial quantities of wheat must have planned for, and depended on, a substantial annual cash income; therefore a good deal of manorial economy was on a cash crop basis.' Perhaps it is conceivable that, say, largely autarkic manors with different crop mixes and storage capacities sold their surpluses to each other and that the cash receipts, instead of being used to buy in goods which the manors could not produce for themselves, were simply hoarded, like the tripods and cauldrons of the Homeric heroes or the aragonite stones of the Yap Islanders; and in that case, it would be palpable misreportage to speak of a 'cash crop basis'. But what serious historian of mediaeval England has, or ever will, put forward an argument to this effect? 'Proof enough' can be acknowledged to have been given within the frontiers of theory-neutrality because of the uncontentiousness of the additional reports which could have been given if required.

Now, however, compare that example with this one:

'In the general election of 1705, twenty-six out of forty English counties were contested, a record for the century, although that of 1710 came close when twenty-three went to the polls. As late as 1722 there were seventeen county contests. Thereafter the total drops dramatically, down to four in 1741, three in 1747, five in 1754 and four again in 1761.
    This is the most compelling evidence that the political elites of England fused into a homogeneous ruling class in the central decades of the eighteenth century.'*

This time, rival observers will find the inference very much easier to resist. Starting from the reported decline in contested constituencies, and assuming that this denotes, in the absence of special explanation, an abatement of partisan animosity, the author concludes that the warring factions of Whig and Tory had therefore fused into a 'homogeneous ruling class'. But this is both questionable and pre-emptive. 'General election' is a theory-neutral term, but 'ruling class' is not; and it is perfectly possible that factional conflict had simply been transferred into other institutional spheres, if only because the costs of contested elections were rising so high and fast. Even if we assume that 'ruling class' could have been theory-neutrally defined, 'homogeneous' still here pre-supposes that there were no continuing differences over the use of

* W. A. Speck, *Stability and Strife: England 1714–1760* (1977), pp. 163–4.

patronage, the role of the Crown, the doctrines and functions of the Established Church and matters of fiscal, commercial and diplomatic policy. Perhaps there weren't. But a solid battery of further reports is necessary to demonstrate it.

Both semi- and quasi-deductive inferences, whether correct or mistaken, can always be rephrased as answers to the question 'Why ...?' 6,452 Liberians gave no tribal affiliation to the census-takers of 1962 because they were of American descent; Halévy failed to see that the turnout in the second British General Election of 1910 was lower than the first because of the increase in the number of uncontested seats; heavy sales of wheat are recorded in the bailiffs' accounts of the manors in the corn-producing areas of mediaeval England because much of the economy was by then on a cash crop basis; the number of English counties contested in general elections between 1705 and 1760 fell dramatically because the intensity of party conflict had waned. But this does not mean that these inferences lead the reader across the frontier between reportage and explanation as here defined. All reports of behaviour can, as I have acknowledged already, be rephrased as explanations at a different level. But to assimilate those questions to questions about what caused the events, processes or states of affairs constituted by the reported behaviour would be to blur the very distinction between the presuppositions underlying primary understanding alone and those underlying an explanatory (or descriptive or evaluative) theory on which diagnosis of the disputes between rival schools depends.

§ 24. There only remains to be elucidated one final distinction before the frontier between reportage and explanation can be crossed – that between the drawing of an inference, whether semi- or quasi-deductive, from one report to another and the choosing of an *indicator* in terms of which a report is to be framed.

Suppose, for example, that an economic historian wishes to report to his readers the distribution of personal wealth in mid nineteenth-century England. There is no particular difficulty about a theory-neutral definition of 'wealth' in terms of the net total cash and other assets at market value held by each person at a given date: although the market value becomes progressively more difficult to arrive at the less of a market there is for the type of asset in question, this is a purely technical problem which gives no support to the rival observer who requests an exhaustive definition of 'wealth' in the hope of finding grounds for a charge of misunderstanding in the primary sense. But we do not have copies of the bank statements, balance sheets, inventories, stockbrokers' and land agents' valuations and suchlike from which we could calculate the totals we need, and it is only the recording angel who could provide us with them. What then does the economic historian do? He falls back on the source which *is* available to him in the form of probate records, and uses these to estimate the figures.* He is not, in so doing, giving a pre-emptive definition of 'wealth' as whatever it is that the probate records record, like the psychologist who defines 'intelligence' as whatever it is that Stanford-Binet tests test. Nor is he inferring from the probate records anything more than they are evidently telling him. He is merely observing, so to speak, by indirection what he cannot observe and report directly.

There is a large literature on the construction and selection of indicators in the various branches of social science, and where the questions raised are no more than technical then it is only the accuracy of the report based on one indicator rather than another which is a matter of concern. But there are still the two familiar dangers: first, that a chosen indicator rests on a misunderstanding in the primary sense; second, that it embodies an inference which can be shown to be theoretically pre-emptive even where it does not embody a definition which is pre-emptive in itself.

As an example of the first, consider Matthew Arnold's remark in his essay on Marcus Aurelius in *Essays in Criticism* (1865) that the busts of the Emperor found in the homes of Roman Gaul, Italy and Britain 'bore witness', as he put it, 'not to the inmates' frivolous curiosity about princes and palaces, but to their reverential memory of the passage of a great man upon the earth'. This is not an inference from one reported state of affairs to another; it is the use of one available kind of evidence as an indicator of sentiments which cannot be observed and reported directly. But can we be sure that Arnold is right? How do we know that what 'they' were doing in keeping the busts in their homes was a case of 'reverentially commemorating' and not merely of hoarding a curio or displaying an heirloom? Might this not be a primary misunderstanding of the very same kind as to mistake a cosmetic implement for a weapon of war?

But then contrast with this the example of an archaeologist of early Sparta who discovers a sudden increase in the number of lead figurines of hoplites which are to be found in the graves of the mid seventh century B.C., and concludes from this that the emergence of the Spartan hoplite class can be dated to those years.† There is no risk of primary misunderstanding unless the figurines are not after all, of hoplites; and if we may

---

* See W. D. Rubinstein, *Men of Property* (1981), Ch. 1.
† This example is taken from A. M. Snodgrass, 'The Hoplite Reform and History', *Journal of Hellenic Studies* LXXXV (1974).

assume that they are, then it might seem plausible to argue that the archaeologist is using them as indicators of a process which he cannot report directly. But this would be to stretch the term too far in the other direction: lead figurines in graves are not *indicators* of the emergence of a social class in the way, say, gold ones might be an indicator of the social class of the persons whose graves they are. This is another case of semi-deductive inference from one report to another. Once given the pre-supposition that nobody who was not a hoplite in his lifetime has a figurine of a hoplite buried with him in his grave, the conclusion that the number of hoplites rose so far in the given period as to amount to the emergence of a class – in the numerical sense, at least – of hoplites follows in just the same way that the number of Liberians of American descent follows from the premise that no Liberian who is not of American descent lacks a tribal affiliation.

A more persuasive example of the choice of an indicator might be the use by a mediaeval historian of evidence for the number of communion wafers sold in a given diocese over a given period to estimate the increase (or decrease) of religious observance. But this too goes beyond indication into what is this time a case of quasi-deduction. Communion wafer sales are not *indicators* of the number of regular communicants per diocese in the way, that, say, the number of communicants might be an indicator of the prevalence of what came in a later period to be called 'high' doctrines and the rituals accompanying them rather than 'low'. The historian is not measuring indirectly what he can't observe and report directly. He is measuring something else from which he can then deduce it. His inference from rising sales of what communicants consume to rising numbers of regular communicants depends, like the inference from sales of wheat to the cash crop basis of much of manorial economy, on the accuracy of a battery of ancillary reports about the inhabitants of the diocese and their behaviour which might, however plausible it may seem to take them for granted, turn out to be ill founded after all.

It may seem unnecessary to elaborate these distinctions when all that matters, on my own argument, to the practising sociologist, anthropologist or historian is that what he presents to his readers as reports should be defensible as such against rival observers. But the pre-emption of a covert explanation, description or evaluation may be hardest of all to diagnose at the very point mid-way, so to speak, between cases where primary misunderstanding has arisen despite a clear-cut dictionary meaning and cases where it is the definition of the seemingly obvious term for what 'they' are doing which the rival observer can show to be theoretically pre-emptive. Nowhere in social theory is this more clearly illustrated than in the study of 'social class' itself, with which much of Volume II will be directly concerned. However wide the differences between sociologists, anthropologists and historians of rival theoretical schools over the proper definition of it, they are at least agreed that it is to do with a ranking of groups or categories of persons relative to each other in terms of powers and privileges institutionally allocated within the society to which they belong. But they have also to agree that it is not, even in principle, something which can be measured directly. It is true that some of its constituents can in principle be measured in at least some societies: have I not myself just used the example of personal wealth in nineteenth-century England? But 'social class' is no more a theory-neutral term than 'magic' or 'peasantry' or 'intelligence' or 'feudalism'. The indicators of it used by different authors for their different purposes are not, strictly, indicators of it unless made so by pre-emptive definition. They are indicators only of something to do with it, and it is more than a matter of reportage what exactly it is to be taken to be.

The difficulty here is not, although it is sometimes so presented, that there is a 'subjective' element which is not measurable in terms of any 'objective' indicator. As I remarked in Section 18, the so-called 'etic/emic distinction' does not at all correspond to the distinction between those observations of behaviour which are matters of reportage and those which are not. It is not, for example, less 'theoretical' to use as an indicator of that aspect of social class usually designated as 'status' information on the observed consumption patterns of different people as opposed to the estimates of their rank assigned to them by fellow-members of their community in answer to a questionnaire. Nothing more than reportage is at issue until the point at which the reader asks to be told why these, and not other, observations and measurements are taken as indicators of what is defined for the researcher's purpose as 'status'. Then, as with the three tables set out in Section 17, theoretical pre-suppositions will have to be invoked which the rival observer may well call into question. But this is not because we are being taken further inside the natives' heads. It is because the purpose of defining that of which either consumption patterns, or reputations, or both are thereby made indicators depends on a theory of 'social class'.

That a technically skilful design and use of indicators can not only enlarge the sum of reports acceptable to all rival observers but also generate more valid explanations, more authentic descriptions and more coherent evaluations is not a claim which any practising sociologist is likely to dispute. The temptation which they carry, however, is that they can be used to disguise a pre-emption which would have been easier for the reader to detect, and the rival observer to criticize, if the reports had been of observations directly made. Inferences too, whether semi- or quasi-deductive, can be so framed as to serve an explanatory, descriptive or evaluative purpose which may not have been overtly declared. But indicators, if either carelessly or disingenuously selected or constructed, may combine the indirection of inference with the pre-emptiveness of stipulative definition. Reportage can and should be extended as far as possible beyond the direct observations by which the interest of the sociologist, anthropologist or historian was first aroused. But if its frontiers are obscured in the process, more will have been lost than gained.

CONCLUSION

§ 25. Some readers may, by this point, have begun to feel that the analysis of reportage which I have given smacks of an attempt to have it both ways. I began by conceding that no practising sociologist, however open-minded, brings to his researches the *tabula rasa* of old-fashioned empiricism; but in then defending his reports against the strictures of the hypothetical rival observer, have I not ended by recreating the very illusion of a presuppositionless innocence which I claimed to have been dispelled by twentieth-century history and philosophy of science?

But innocence (if that is the right word) is relative to the kind of presupposition of which it is claimed; and the benefit of a successful demarcation of the territory of reportage is precisely to enable the practising sociologist to reconcile his recognition that to say what is/was going on is not a matter of 'pure' observation with his conviction that he can, nonetheless, say so in such a way that any rival observer will be bound to agree, however much the two of them may differ over the further presuppositions which underlie, or even dictate, their subsequent explanations, descriptions or evaluations. There have always been, and no doubt always will be, philosophers determined to persuade social scientists that their enterprise is inherently misconceived, just as there have always been, and no doubt always will be, social scientists determined to persuade each other that philosophers have nothing to tell them about the conduct of their research. But both are wrong. Social scientists are confronted with problems of method which are not purely technical and which if ignored or mishandled will weaken and may even destroy their claims to have discovered how human societies work; yet having come to terms with those problems they can proceed – and should –

without worrying whether or not they can provide a rationale for what they do which is adequate to satisfy philosophers of science.

Notice, finally, that I have spoken of the criteria which are to *govern* research, not merely to permit it. I have not, in this chapter, sought to deny – how could I? – that certain conditions must be fulfilled for it to be possible to claim of an observation of human behaviour that it conveys a fact about the world in which it has taken place, or that the formulation of these conditions is a proper task for the philosopher of science. But the methodological problem of the practising sociologist is not to justify a claim that *anything* he wishes to report to his readers as a 'social fact' is true. It is to avoid a claim that his report of it is theory-neutral when it is not. He does not need by now (if he ever did) to be reminded that his observations do not in themselves constitute 'raw' data or 'brute' facts to be accepted unquestioningly as given. But nor does he need any longer to defend himself against the charge that to report anything about human institutions or practices as a matter of fact is to presume an objectivity only attainable in the sciences of nature. What he needs is an awareness of the point beyond which a claim to be reporting a social fact does indeed presuppose more than reportage alone, whether because it cannot be reconciled with the agents' own account in those aspects where their account is privileged, or because it pre-empts an explanation, description or evaluation. Without such an awareness, he will continue to be vulnerable to methodological as well as to substantive arguments by which he may find his reports of observed social facts undermined. But with it, he can be confident of steering a safely manageable course between the Scylla of positivistic empiricism and the Charybdis of phenomenological hermeneutics.

3

Explanation in social theory

§ 1. The practising sociologist's task (I have said) may be taken to begin
with the reportage of the event, process or state of affairs which he then
proposes to explain. But this straightforward-looking formulation con-
ceals not only the diversity of possible explananda but also the diversity
of possible types of explanation which different explananda may turn out
to require. The possible explananda cover, in principle, the whole range
of events, processes and states of affairs reported across the whole range
of human societies, and the types of explanation which they may require
will vary not only in accordance with the institutions or practices chosen
for study and the location of whatever is reported about them along the
axes of time, place and generality, but also with the nature of the
particular contrasts which the particular sociologist is concerned to draw.
Here is a short list of examples culled from the books or articles in sight
on my shelves: why didn't French musicians of the nineteenth century
compose more symphonies? how far is the dominant position of Seville
to be attributed to the consequences of the successful bringing under
cultivation of the Andalusian plain? how is it that 'primitive' men could
be apparently indifferent to logical contradictions? why do English girls
cluster closer, but to a higher average, of reading ability than English
boys? is a traditional world-view containing the promise of a future age
of bliss a necessary precondition of the emergence of millenarian political
movements? what made it impossible for British governments of the
nineteenth century to continue to rely upon influence to protect traditional British interests in Africa? why are rates of social mobility among
industrial societies relatively invariant even under the impact of educa-
tional policies intended to raise them? why was there a recrudescence of
interest in the 'art of memory' when the invention of printing had
rendered the great Gothic artificial memories of the Middle Ages redun-

dant? is there a particular kind of upbringing which justifies the labelling of certain families as schizophrenogenic? how important is the role of government in influencing rates of white-collar unionization in a mixed industrial economy? do arms races increase the likelihood of war?

The point of a list such as this one is not that the questions in it are impossibly difficult ones. Still less is it that they are 'ideological' in some sense that natural-scientific questions are not. The authors who have raised them have all gone on to offer answers to them, and in several cases (although by no means all) their answers appear to command fairly wide assent among fellow-specialists in the relevant field. The point is that the forms of answer which they invite are so diverse as to frustrate any attempt to classify and analyse sociological explanation under a comprehensive list of mutually exclusive headings. In this chapter, I make no attempt to offer a list of this kind, and although I shall have to say something about the peculiarities of teleological explanations in particular, I shall not offer any general account of scientific explanation as such. Instead, I shall try to answer four connected questions of a different kind: first, how do the various kinds of explanation offered by sociologists, anthropologists or historians relate to the presuppositions which underlie them? second, what kinds of contrast do they draw between what has actually happened and what otherwise would or might have? third, where do their provisionally plausible explanations find adequate theoretical grounding? and fourth, is there a particular form of explanation appropriate to, and characteristic of, human history itself?

One possible objection to this way of looking at sociological explanation is that the answers to all four questions are predetermined alike by the avowedly untestable presuppositions which researchers of different theoretical schools bring to their task. To the ethological sociologist, all interaction is to be understood (in the secondary sense) as an expression of instinctual propensities already present in, and now inherited from, the higher primates; to the psychoanalytic sociologist, all interaction is to be understood as an expression of libidinal drives mediated by the successive constraints on their expression imposed over the course of life from the moment of birth by the familial, institutional and cultural environment; to the historical-materialist sociologist, all interaction is to be understood as an expression of social relationships ultimately determined by the forces of production. Yet even so, it is all the more important to see just how strictly the presuppositions of these rival schools do in fact dictate the range of the hypothetical contrasts admitted by the form of explanation offered and the nature of their relation to their presumed theoretical grounding. *Does* a presupposition which requires that interaction be understood as the expression of a propensity to bonding or aggression and that the grounding of explanations of it be therefore sought in the extension of Darwinian biology to encompass the natural selection of intra-specific behaviour-organs necessarily exclude explanatory reference to the plans and strategies of self-conscious agents who are capable of monitoring their own instinctual responses to external stimuli? *Does* a presupposition which requires that interaction be understood as the expression of libidinal impulses and that the grounding of explanations of it be therefore sought in a model of the personality such as was adumbrated by Freud necessarily exclude explanatory reference to the conscious pursuit of institutional goals or conformity to institutional standards? *Does* a presupposition which requires that interaction be understood as the expression of solidarities or antagonisms of class and that the grounding of explanations of it be therefore sought in what Marx called the 'economic structure of society – the real foundation' necessarily exclude explanatory reference to ideas as independent causes of the changes leading from one mode of production to the next? All these questions can be, and have been, answered in the negative with quite enough plausibility to demonstrate that the connection between a given type of explanation and the presuppositions behind it has itself to be examined as part of the assessment of the actual explanation advanced, not simply dismissed as a philosophical issue lying beyond the effective range of methodological concern.

A different objection, coming as it were from the plain man's end of the methodological spectrum, is that the four questions to which this chapter is addressed are unilluminating, not because the answer to them is already dictated by untestable presuppositions, but because adequate explanations can be arrived at and defended without bothering about them at all. On this view, explanations which appeal to the sort of theoretical constructions elaborated by ethology, psychoanalysis or historical materialism are not so much mistaken (although no doubt they often are) as redundant, since explanations of human behaviour which are valid in common-sense terms are not made any more or less convincing by the invocation of them. Where, or if, it *can* be shown that an item or sequence of human behaviour has been caused by an instinctual impulse of aggression or a neurotic anxiety symptomatic of sexual repression or a recognition of common interest among persons similarly located in the social relations of production, the explanation stands by virtue of its demonstrable concordance with the evidence, and nothing is added to it by methodological discussion of the kind of which this chapter is to consist. Objection along these lines does not – or at any rate, need not – imply a denial that successful sociological explanation requires not only patient observation and intelligent insight but also some familiarity with statistical or other appropriate techniques. But it does imply that the skill of the practising sociologist resides more in a capacity to perceive which of a range of familiar influences or motives is at work in the event, process or state of affairs observed than in a capacity to relate the observations made to some would-be general theory. There are no doubt some generalizations which can legitimately be invoked in proffering an explanation. But the useful ones will, on this view, be more like those to be found in the *Essays* of Bacon than in textbooks of social psychology. When, for example, Bacon in the essay 'On Envy' reports the observation that 'near kinsfolks, and fellows in office, and those that have been bred together, are more apt to envy their equals when they are raised' and explains it by saying that 'it doth upbraid unto them their own fortunes, and pointeth at them, and cometh oftener into their remembrance, and incurreth likewise more into the note of others; and envy ever redoubleth from speech and fame', what more needs to be said? This is not a 'common-sense' explanation in the sense that everyone knew it perfectly well already. But it is in the sense that it appeals to no theoretical concepts not already in use among non-academic, unreflective people, and draws its persuasiveness from the fact that it can be tested by such people against their own experience. It is not, to be sure, very precise: Bacon's use of such terms as 'oftener', 'more', 'never' and 'redoubleth' is not quantification of the kind which twentieth-century readers may have come to expect from works which lay claim to the title of 'science'. But would the explanation be any more illuminating if it were?

To this sort of objection, the answer is twofold. In certain contexts and for certain purposes, common-sense explanation will do perfectly well. But in the first place, there are other purposes which need to be fulfilled before a substantive theory extending across a defined range of ostensibly dissimilar explananda can be formulated; and in the second, it is only with the aid of such a theory that it is possible to answer the question why the *ad hoc* explanations of common sense hold good as and when they do. Consider a simple example from physical science. Confronted with the boiling of water, the common-sense observer can say with indisputable validity that it is caused by heat – and the greater the heat applied, the sooner the water comes to the boil. For the purpose of cooking an egg he need have no more of a conception of atmospheric pressure than the eighteenth-century wage-earner of Section 4 of Chapter 1 had of multipliers, indifference curves or liquidity ratios. But he will be able neither to account for the variation in boiling-point with altitude which will be perceptible the minute that he carries a kettle up the Mont Ventoux for a picnic nor to explain why it is that boiling results from the application of heat in the first place. In the same way, it is no doubt valid to explain many observed instances of the envy of near kinsmen and fellows in office of each other by invoking one or more of the causes which Bacon lists; but this is not enough to tell us either why they don't when they don't or do when they do. It is not just a matter of more accurate reportage. It makes no difference what figures might be assigned to 'oftener' and 'more' or whether 'ever redoubleth' is to be taken literally. It is a matter of theoretical level – that is, of arriving at the formulation of an underlying theoretical concept of equivalent explanatory power to atmospheric pressure in the example of boiling which will tell us why proximity, both social and physical, generates envy as it does.

I shall accordingly assume without further argument that one of the objectives of social-scientific research is, among others, the formulation of theories which will help to explain different categories of events, processes or states of affairs and that this cannot be done without on the one hand transcending the limits of common-sense attribution of causes to effects, or on the other subscribing to one or another set of presuppositions which are not directly testable but which to some degree predetermine the form of explanation sought. The four questions which I have set out have all to be confronted by practising sociologists, anthropologists and historians, whether explicitly or not, if they are to be able to assess and defend the validity of the explanations which they put forward against those of rival schools. They do not have to be able to say what an explanation *is*; that is the task of the philosopher. Nor do they have to be able to say how best to construct and test one; that is the task of the technician. But they do have to be able to say what is in practice to count as one.

§2. Where, then, once the line has been drawn between reportage and explanation, is the line to be drawn between an explanatory presupposition and an explanatory theory? Which is which cannot be decided simply by grammatical or syntactical analysis of explanatory-looking propositions as set out on the printed page. Just as the same statement may function, according to context, as an explanation, a description or an evaluation, so may the same ostensibly explanatory statement express a testable or an untestable proposition according to the context in which it is advanced. Moreover, it may or may not be a damaging objection to it to point out that it can be construed as true by definition, like Malthus's 'population increases unless checked', or the neoclassical economists' 'all factors will receive a payment equal to the value of their marginal product' (or, for that matter, Newton's First Law of Motion).

A standard definition of a 'theory' is 'a set of deductively connected, empirically disconfirmable laws'; and a standard example is classical thermodynamics, in which the lawlike regularities between the pressure, volume and temperature of gases are explained at the more fundamental level by reference to the kinetics of molecules. But this definition, appropriate as it may be to classical physics, is inappropriate to sociology if only because of the different role of laws in it. It is not that laws play no role in it, but that those which do are not laws *of* it; as I said in Section 9 of Chapter 1, sociology is not a producer but a consumer of laws. What is needed, therefore, is a working definition of 'theory' which preserves the requirement that it involves a deeper level of reference than the mere identification of a more or less constant conjunction but discards the requirement that it should be a law which is referred to. Such a definition does not need to be all that precise. Indeed, it may even be more useful if it is not. In what follows, I shall take it to stand for a body of ideas, rather than a set of laws, within which an explanatory hypothesis which is demonstrably in accordance with the evidence is itself provisionally explicable. In the social sciences, this explanation is typically by reference to psychological dispositions. Thus, Keynes's theory of employment, interest and money explicitly rests on propositions concerning the motives of savers,* just as Maurice Duverger's formula that the simple majority, single-ballot system favours the two-party system explicitly rests on propositions concerning the motives of electors.† But this is not to be assumed in advance as a methodological rule.

Even under this relaxed definition, however, a theory must still be held to be testable in principle: a researcher who claims to have discovered one, or to have found an explanation of his chosen explanandum which is grounded in one, must be able to specify an observation or set of observations which would disconfirm it. It is most unlikely that in practice a single observation will do so. Crucial experiments are elusive enough even in the most exact of the natural sciences. In the social sciences they are more elusive still, not only because of the technical

---

* J. M. Keynes, *The General Theory of Employment, Interest and Money* (1936), Ch. 9 ('The Propensity to Consume: II. The Subjective Factors').

† Maurice Duverger, *Political Parties*² (Eng. trans., 1954), Bk II Ch. 1 ('The Number of Parties').

difficulty of securing adequate controls but also because of the problems of replicability which derive from the need for the explananda chosen to have been correctly understood in the primary sense. Nevertheless, it should generally be possible to give grounds for discarding a theory along the lines of 'if *this* behaviour is what we observe despite such-and-such conditions in cases ranging from *here* to *there*, it is difficult if not impossible to see how the well-attested, presumptively causal connection between A and B can be accounted for by invoking *that*'. For example: if behaviour independently diagnosed by rival observers as 'schizo-phrenic' is observed at a rate *many* times higher than the general popula-tion in *both* identical twins born of schizophrenic parents *even* when one of them has been fostered away from home in cases ranging across *numerous* environments, then the well-attested, presumptively causal connection between schizophrenia in the parent and the child cannot plausibly be accounted for by invoking the psychological, as opposed to genetic, influence of the family. I have reverted to this example, on a topic which is still a matter of debate, without seeking to suggest that this is an accurate summary of the present state of research: schizo-phrenia is not, or not yet, like porphyria, which I cited in Section 3 of Chapter 1 as furnishing an example of behaviour whose explanation by reference to a dominant autosomal gene is now established. But for methodological purposes, it illustrates very well the way in which two rival theories can in principle be tested against each other given the appropriate set of observations. Notice too that those who presupposed that the behaviour in question was to be explained without reference to genetics as a psychological response to the stresses of family life would still be entitled to maintain a *description* of it, and perhaps an evaluation too, as (in the words of one theorist of this school, R. D. Laing), 'a special strategy that a person invents in order to live in an unlivable situation';* but as an explanation this could no longer hold without the radical qualification that what drives such a person to invent such a strategy is not the 'unlivable' situation in itself but its conjunction with an innate disposition genetically caused.

A proffered explanatory theory which turns out not to be testable against any set of observations can, accordingly, only be rescued if at all by being reinterpreted as a theoretical presupposition. But it is not on that account vacuous; and it may even be a useful tactic deliberately to

* It is worth noting that Laing himself can be construed as using both 'describe' and 'understand' in this way; see *The Divided Self* (1954), p. 77: 'We suggest, therefore, that the schizoid state we are describing can be understood as an attempt to preserve a being that is precariously structured.'

immunize a theory against disconfirmation by doing so. It is a criticism which has often been levelled against Darwinian, Marxist and Freudian sociologists alike that when one of their ostensibly causal hypotheses is disconfirmed by empirical observation they redefine the underlying concepts from which it appeared to derive in such a way as to fit both the hypothesized and the actual observation. But there is no rule of method which forbids social scientists to *reculer pour mieux sauter*. It becomes difficult, after a time, to justify the abandonment of each of a continuing series of would-be explanations as merely another tactical retreat. Indeed, the weight of uncomfortable evidence which has by now accumulated has become, by almost universal consent, too great for the claims of ethology, Marxism or psychoanalysis as general explanatory theories of human behaviour in all its aspects to be tenable even after radical modification of the doctrines originally set down by their founders. But it has taken very much more than the disconfirmation of a single hypothesis, however ambitious, to undermine them. It has time and again been shown possible to reconstruct from the wreckage another would-be theory, still recognizably Darwinian, Marxian or Freudian, in which at least some provisionally confirmed hypotheses would appear to be grounded. The obstinate survival of theories of a 'territorial imperative' or of the impending collapse of 'bourgeois' capitalism or of collective 'neurosis' as the price to be paid for a civilized social order is not necessarily to be interpreted as a symptom of their inherently unscientific status. Let us by all means discriminate between those parts which are testable and those which are not; but let us at the same time beware of dismissing those which are not as incapable of contributing in any way at all to the explanation of human behaviour.

The same holds, indeed, for the now thoroughly discredited kind of 'functionalism' at one time put forward as a would-be general theory by Malinowski,* according to which the explanation of behaviour and ideas alike is to be sought in the contribution which they make to the maintenance of the society within which they have been observed. Malinowski has been much criticized for this doctrine on the grounds that it is either trivial or false. But to criticize it on these grounds is not necessarily to undermine its value as a presupposition to the effect that all societies tend, in the absence of exogenous disturbance, towards an equilibrium between their component institutions even without conscious effort on their members' part. No more than Marx's or Freud's or the ethologists' have Malinowski's presuppositions lost all relevance for the practising

---

* See in particular his article on 'Anthropology' in the 1926 *Encyclopaedia Britannica*.

sociologist. They may not be directly testable. But there is much to be learnt in seeing how far they have come in the course of continuing research to seem either more or less persuasive when viewed against an accumulated body of provisionally validated hypotheses and the theories in which these hypotheses are claimed to be grounded; and there may always remain a limited subset of confirmed explanations which conform to them even after the would-be general theory derived from them has been overtaken by a better one.

The range of presuppositions from which would-be general socio-logical theories have been derived over the course of the history of the social sciences extends a great deal more widely than those of Marx, Freud, Malinowski or the ethologists. There have been theological theories presupposing the willingness of God to intervene in human affairs, quasi-organic theories presupposing the inevitability of cycles of growth and decline, psycho-physiological theories presupposing the fundamental influence of stereotypical character and temperament, teleological theories presupposing the inexorability of some ultimate future condition of mankind, and many more besides. Some of them are dead and buried beyond hope of exhumation. But what has killed them is neither a single crippling observation nor a single knock-down argu-ment but rather a mounting unease in the face of the consequences of reworking them in order to assimilate increasingly awkward-looking counter-examples. Implausible and even bizarre as they may seem to later generations of researchers, they are not just random or whimsical constructions of their author's fantasy. They are developed, whether articulately or not, out of a dialectic between *a priori* reasoning and at least some empirical observation of human institutions and practices. Theory-making is not just word-play, and the presuppositions behind it are not just myths.

Nor need these presuppositions imply – or secrete – latent value-judgements any more than do the theories derived from them. No doubt there are contingent connections of the kind discussed already in Chapter 1 between the presuppositions underlying the would-be general explana-tory theories of Marx, Freud, Malinowski or the ethologists and their views about the forms of social organization which they hold to be desirable. But their theories are neither more nor less likely to be valid, or the presuppositions behind them to be tenable, on that account. Of all the 'classical' sociologists, I can think of none whose explanatory presuppositions and theories were more blatantly connected with his political values than Herbert Spencer. But later researchers are perfectly free to subscribe to his theory of social evolution as the 'survival of the fittest' while at the same time repudiating every one of his strictures against import duties, poor laws, housing regulations, registration of medical practitioners, free public libraries and 'injudicious charity' in general. To argue that untestable presuppositons are not on that account vacuous is not to concede that they must therefore be construed as a covert plea for the researcher's own moral or political ideals.

The relation between explanatory theories and the presuppositions underlying them can, perhaps, be analysed formally by treating the presuppositions as axioms and the theories as theorems derived from them by way of transformation rules. But the methodological benefit will be limited even if the philosophical exercise is successful. In the first place, even the well-validated theories of the exact sciences seldom lend themselves to such treatment rigorously and in detail; and in the second, the terms in which the presuppositions underlying sociological theories are couched neither can nor need to be taken as logically primitive. Just as it is more useful to relax the definition of 'theory' to cover more than sets of deductively related (albeit empirically testable) laws, so is it likewise more useful to relax the definition of whatever further body of ideas it may be which underlies a given theory but is not susceptible to invalidation itself. It is true to say that the implications of many of the presuppositions underlying would-be explanatory theories can be analysed without fear of controversy: no researcher will in practice hesitate to commit himself to the claim that, for example, the presumptively causal connection reported by successive political scientists between age and conservatism can only run one way.* But this is not the kind of problem which will either promote or retard the quest for as wide-ranging and powerful theories as can be found. What matters in practice is that researchers should not be discouraged from pursuing their quest by being told that they cannot either formulate rigorously or test empirically the vague, unexamined and even inchoate convictions which may have dictated their plan of research. The justification for methodological discussion of them, as of the theories derived from them, is that it can lead to better explanations of the reported events, processes or states of affairs in the historical and ethnographic record, and too much logic can have just as unhelpful an influence as too little. In terms of the distinction which I have drawn, therefore, a sociological explanation involves a twofold claim: first, that a reported event, process or state of affairs has taken place, or been the case, because and only because some

---

* On which see Herbert A. Simon, *Models of Man* (1957), Ch. 2 ('Spurious Correlation: a Causal Interpretation').

other specified event, process or state of affairs took place or was the case beforehand; and second, that this connection holds for some more general underlying reason whose conceptualization derives in turn from some set of presuppositions to which the researcher is willing to subscribe but which he cannot directly test. This formulation may not by itself be of any help in directing practising sociologists, anthropologists or historians to the best explanations. But it does provide the framework within which their choice between alternative hypotheses and the grounding of their chosen hypothesis in a prospective theory can be analysed in more detail.

§ 3.   Some readers may wish to protest that 'because and only because' is a phrase which already presupposes some notion of counterfactual conditionals, about which there is an extensive and still. controversial literature in the philosophy of science. But as I remarked in the very first section of Chapter 1, the difficulties which surround the notion of causality have not prevented the emergence of well-tested, strongly-grounded and wide-ranging explanations in biology, chemistry and physics. The longstanding inability of philosophers of science to produce a wholly satisfactory analysis of 'because' in terms of necessary and/or sufficient conditions is not a reason to suppose that social-scientific explanation is any more inherently problematic than natural-scientific. It is, rather, a reason for social scientists to be careful to specify the counterfactual conditional(s) whose validity their explanations imply and for methodologists of social science to allow them, as with 'theory' and 'presupposition', as relaxed as possible a definition of 'cause'. To say that an event, process or state of affairs, or part or aspect of one of these, is or was as observed and reported because and only because of X is to identify X as something but for which that event, etc. would be other than it is or was, and it is on the particular contrast drawn and the particular initial conditions assumed already to hold that the rival observer's assent will depend, not the logical analysis of conditionality to which the explanation may subsequently be shown to conform.

A more awkward difficulty, perhaps, is that there are many counter-factual conditionals relevant to a proffered explanation which stretch the use of 'because' beyond what seems natural in ordinary speech. Thus, if Queen Victoria had not been born in 1819 she would not have ascended the throne at the early age of eighteen. But it would be odd for a historian to tell his readers that she ascended the throne at the early age of eighteen because and only because, given the other relevant initial conditions, she was born in 1819 (and odder still to tell them that her birth in 1819 caused her to ascend the throne at the early age of eighteen). Similarly, in a social mobility matrix connecting the occupation of sons to that of their fathers, it will be true to say that if the marginal totals – i.e., the sums of the rows and columns – were other than they are, the rate of occupational mobility in the sons' generation would be different. But it would be odd for a sociologist to tell his readers that it is because and only because, given the other relevant initial conditions, the occupational distribution of the fathers in the sample is as it is that the sons' mobility rate is what it is (and odder still to tell them that the occupational mobility rate among the members of a chosen age cohort is caused by what their fathers' occupations happened to be).

But this difficulty can be resolved by distinguishing between 'because' where used to point to what it does seem natural in ordinary speech to label a 'cause' and 'because' where used to invoke what can better be labelled a 'constraint'. Causes, broadly speaking, are the contingent antecedent conditions, both immediate (or 'proximate') and background (or 'ultimate'), by which outcomes are determined; constraints are, rather, necessary limitations on the outcomes which any combination of causes is able to effect. The distinction may not be sufficiently precise to dispose of all possible doubt over which, in a given context, is to be construed as which. But it does dispose of the objection that 'because' is itself so ambiguous a term that its use risks begging a distinction which does unquestionably need to be drawn. There still remain the two further problems that first, outcomes may be *over*-determined, so that the use of 'only because' may have to be qualified accordingly; and second, the choice of what is to count as a cause and what as a constraint may itself be a function of the type of theory in which the attempted explanation is grounded. But neither of these problems is peculiar to the sciences of man; and in neither case is it any less essential to the success of the explanation offered that the range of relevant conditions, constraints and/or causes should first have been sufficiently narrowed for a clear-cut contrast to be drawn in terms of which 'but for . . .' and 'only because . . .' can be so completed as to enable rival observers to see for themselves what degree of support the reported evidence supplies.

In practice, this is no more than is done already by practising sociologists, anthropologists and historians of widely different presuppositions and purposes, however little they may be interested in methodology for its own sake. It is not, after all, as if even the most empirically-minded just hold up before themselves whatever event, process or state of affairs has caught their attention and then say to themselves 'explain it!'. It all depends what it is about it that is taken to need explaining. The observer of, say, the dances of the Zande witch-doctors presumably goes on to frame an explanation of them which can be tested against his observations together with any relevant evidence reported from other sources. But an explanation in terms of what? of the foreign or indigenous influences behind the dances? of the emotions which are given outlet in them? of their performance on some occasions rather than others? of their public but not private performance? of the symbolism of the gestures of which they consist? or what? The same question has equally to be answered when the explanandum is as vast as, say, the decline and fall of the Roman Empire in the West. Even if it is answered in the grand Gibbonian manner by saying that 'the story of its ruin is simple and obvious' since 'as soon as time or accident had removed the artificial supports, the stupendous fabric yielded to the pressure of its own weight', this at once invites the supplementary questions: which accidents? in what sequence? which artificial supports? and which exactly were the institutions and practices which constituted the 'weight'? The contrast, or the several contrasts, within the causal field on which a given explanation rests may be of a very, very wide variety of kinds. Indeed, the list of questions with which I began this chapter was already enough to suggest the range of possible contrasts and thus of possible explanations among which practising sociologists, anthropologists and historians will have to pick their way in pursuit of secondary understanding. Those examples, however, were chosen because the answers to them are, although not impossible, still difficult to establish to the satisfaction of all rival observers. To meet the objection that a too easygoing interpretation of 'because' will leave explanations of human behaviour too vague or inconclusive to warrant a claim to science, here is a further list of six examples as different from one another as I can find where the explanations given, although at least as diverse as are called for by the questions in the previous list, are all of overwhelming validity. By this I do not mean either that they have the force of logical deduction or that they can be assigned a probability of 1.0. It would be possible for the sake of argument to conceive of circumstances, however unlikely, which if discovered would undermine all of them. But they exemplify the degree of validity to which practising sociologists, anthropologists or historians can realistically aspire. To ask for more would be as pedantic as to cavil at the insignificant inaccuracies of reportage of which I gave some examples in Section 9 of Chapter 2; to settle for less would be to give in to the lecture-room sceptics who seek to maintain that human behaviour is inaccessible to scientific explanation at all.

1. The hypothesis that one rather than another proposed alternative to the extant manuscript reading in a classical text is the correct one

cannot be conclusively tested: the author isn't available to tell us, and although the recording angel knows what he wrote down it cannot be a matter of mere reportage for 'us'. We have to explain why and how a copyist's error should have crept in. But sometimes there is really no doubt about it. When Scaliger, in 1579, corrected the *timidiquoque* of line 422 of the first book of Manilius's *Astronomicon* to *tumdiquoque*, it was (says A. E. Housman) 'a feat of easy brilliancy, and such corrections do less of an honour to Scaliger than a shame to his predecessors'. But this verdict testifies all the more strongly to the overwhelming plausibility of the emendation. Not only does *tum di quoque magnos Quaesivere deos* ('then [when all sorts of fearsome portents were seen] gods too sought great gods') read far more convincingly than *timidi quoque* ... ('timorous men too sought great gods', which makes the 'too' almost nonsensical), but the copyist's slip involved is one of the easiest kind to make. So even without the testimony of the recording angel, or Manilius himself, the hypothesis can in practice be accepted as proven and the explanandum accounted for to the exclusion of any alternative suggestion about what might have occurred.

2. The Hanunoo of the Philippines have a language whose personal pronouns* include not merely a first, second and third person singular but four others: *mih* ('we'), *tah* ('we two'), *tam* ('we all'), *yuh* ('you all'), and *dah* ('they'). Why? Historically, the answer is irrecoverable and in any case of little linguistic interest. But analytically, the answer is that they enshrine a threefold distinction – obvious only when pointed out – along the axes of (i) minimal *vs* non-minimal membership, (ii) inclusion *vs* exclusion of the speaker and (iii) inclusion *vs* exclusion of the listener. It is one out of the range of possible schemata for the construction of an actual system of personal pronouns; and an ethnographer who had not happened to hear, say, *tam* used could nevertheless predict its existence with the same confidence as Scaliger emending the text of Manilius.

3. Ivan the Terrible only succeeded in reducing the Crimean town of Kazan, after several attempts, in October of 1552 by the use of mines and artillery. It is true that by then the Crimean Tartars were not as powerful as they had been: they were weakened by internal dissension as well as by the increasing military pressure from Moscow, and it was in all probability only a matter of time before the whole of the Lower Volga region would fall under Russian control. But equally, there can be no doubt at all that without the application of the appropriate military technology Kazan would not have fallen to the Russians when it did.

4. In an experiment designed to test the influence of considerations of prestige on judgements of literary value, a social psychologist gives groups of college students to read a set of short prose passages each of which is attributed to one of a set of well-known authors whom the

* On which see Nicolas Ruwet, 'La Linguistique Générale Aujourd'hui', *Archives Européennes de Sociologie* V (1964), pp. 306–7.

same students have already ranked in order of merit. Unbeknownst to them, the attributions are false: all the passages are by the same author, Robert Louis Stevenson, and they have been chosen by the experimenter to be as similar as possible to each other in presumptive literary merit. As expected, the judgements which the students make turn out to be influenced by the false attributions. The average correlation between the rank order assigned to the authors and the passages ranges from 0.3 to 0.53. There is admittedly no way of being able to predict in advance what the correlation was going to be, let alone which individual student would rank the passages more or less closely in accordance with his or her previous ranking of the authors. But could anyone seriously dispute that the ranking of the passages would have been the same if they had all been overtly credited to their actual author?

5. Catalonia was contributing nothing to the struggle of Spain against France in the Thirty Years' War, and as the need for its involvement became increasingly pressing Olivares decided that the only hope of achieving it lay in an invasion of France across the Catalan frontier. But the outcome was disastrous. Far from involving the Catalans against the French it turned them against the Habsburgs, and after a violent uprising involving peasantry, clergy and the urban poor alike the Catalan nobility invited the French to take over Catalonia as a protectorate. Olivares's miscalculation had brought about the very opposite of what he had hoped to achieve. He knew from the outset that the risks attendant on his chosen policy were high; and when it failed, neither he nor anyone else was in doubt that it was a direct result of his own miscalculation.

6. A painting by Piero di Cosimo now hanging in the National Gallery of Canada depicts Vulcan, the arch-craftsman and blacksmith of the gods, in his mythological role as the first teacher of human civilization: he sits, instantly recognizable, in the left foreground, making a horseshoe at his anvil, while behind him to the right four sturdy labourers are erecting the frame of a primitive house just as recounted by Vitruvius in his references to the earliest phase of civilization. But also crouching behind the fire is an old man holding two leather bags in his hands – Aeolus, the god of the winds. But why should Piero di Cosimo put Aeolus into a picture about Vulcan? The answer is that Virgil, in the *Aeneid*, places Vulcan's workshop on one of the islands between Lipari and the Sicilian coast where Aeolus reigned, and in consequence later mythographers enshrined in the Renaissance tradition a close association between them, almost amounting (according to Panofsky)* to a 'sort of business partnership'. Without the authority of Virgil's text, there would have been no reason for Aeolus to be included in the picture, but with it, his presence is satisfactorily explained.

Now there evidently lies behind each of these examples a multitude of unquestioned presuppositions and a whole set of initial conditions and

* See Erwin Panofsky, 'The Early History of Man in Two Cycles of Painting by Piero di Cosimo', in *Studies in Iconology* (1939).

constraints taken for granted. Their persuasiveness depends on an arbitrary exclusion of other relevant contrasts and a presentation deliberately tailored to fit it. They could be so dissected as to pose any number of difficulties about the relation of necessary to sufficient conditions. But the point is that the explanations proffered are all, for practical purposes, cast-iron. What rival observer from what conceivable theoretical school is seriously going to question that line 422 of Manilius's *Astronomicon* has *timidiquoque* because and only because a copyist mistranscribed *tumdiquoque?* or that the Hanunoo have a pronoun for 'we all' because and only because their language has so evolved as to categorize designated but unnamed persons in terms of the three axes of minimal *vs* non-minimal membership, inclusion *vs* exclusion of the speaker and inclusion *vs* exclusion of the listener? or that Kazan fell in October 1552 because and only because of the use of mines and artillery against it? or that the college students' rankings of the passages shown to them came out as they did because and only because false attributions were attached to them? or that the Catalans turned against the Habsburgs when they did because and only because of Olivares's miscalculation of the consequence of an invasion of France across their frontier? or that Piero di Cosimo put a representation of Aeolus into his picture of Vulcan because and only because of a mythographic tradition based on the *Aeneid?*

I dare say that none of these examples would be of the least help to a philosopher of science trying to construct a theory of explanation. Indeed, for the very reason that something *could* be the case which would invalidate them, they might well be used to tell against the attempted theory: what happens to 'because and only because' if, say, there is another possible pronominal schema which would require the Hanunoo to coin *tam* or its equivalent, or if there was a serious likelihood that Kazan would have fallen anyway in October of 1552 because of incipient treachery within the Tartar garrison? But it is just because there are possible alternatives that these explanations are genuine – that is, neither vacuous nor circular; and it is just because the alternatives are so very highly improbable that I have ventured to call them, from the practising sociologist's as opposed to the philosopher's point of view, 'cast-iron'. There is nothing of which to be suspicious in the implicit presuppositions underlying them; the initial conditions have been so specified as manageably to narrow the causal field; the contrast between what happened and might have but didn't can be clearly defined; the resulting hypothesis accords with the reported evidence; and there is no other hypothesis in the offing which offers remotely as plausible an answer given the contrast drawn.

Notice too that secondary understanding is not necessarily harder to come by at a macro- than a micro-sociological level. Olivares's miscalculation turned the Catalans against the Habsburgs just as surely as a copyist's error presented Housman with a line which Manilius never wrote. What matters is that enough of the initial conditions can be taken for granted by all rival observers. It may turn out to be just as difficult to defend the hypothesis, plausible though it is, that the Crimean War would not have happened if Lord John Russell had not been in office in London and Metternich out of it in Vienna than the vastly more sweeping hypothesis that no revolution has ever succeeded without the intervention of a foreign power.* There is no formula which will tell practising sociologists how best to deal with their chosen explananda, large or small. But if they are to be able to deal with them at all they will have first to have narrowed their options within the causal field, and this may be no more difficult in practice in dealing with the fall of the Roman Empire in the West than with Mr Morley's rain-dance in the outskirts of Bournemouth in the summer of 1976.

THE GROUNDING OF HYPOTHESES

§4. Yet however successfully it has been done, and however plausible the hypothesis, or set of them, then offered to explain a reported event, process or state of affairs, the request for its theoretical grounding has still to be capable of being met. The question which next requires an answer, therefore, is how firm a grounding is needed in practice for an explanation to be accepted as uncontroversial even by theorists from rival schools. If 'theory' and 'cause' are best analysed in terms of as relaxed a definition as possible, might it not follow that 'grounding' need not be quite as strictly construed as in textbook examples from the enchanted garden of natural science?

There is no disagreement among the disputants in the voluminous philosophical literature on the role of laws in scientific explanation that where, in practice, a well-tested law *can* be invoked to link an explanans to an explanandum, the hypothesis 'X because Y' will be a strong one; and where the law is in turn derivable from others of greater generality, the explanation in question will be as well grounded as any researcher could ask. It is notoriously difficult to find examples in the sciences of man as convincing as those given in the standard texts from such sciences as optics, thermodynamics, electromagnetism or celestial mechanics. But

---

* These examples are borrowed from L. C. B. Seaman, *From Vienna to Versailles* (1955).

suppose, for the sake of illustration, that the observed difference in reading ability between girls and boys which I cited in Section 1 did turn out to be genetically caused: the otherwise inexplicable proportion of the variance would then be linked to the known mechanisms of genetic transmission and the regularities generated by them, so that an unquestionably solid grounding for the confirmed hypothesis would be to hand. Plausible or not, the example at any rate serves to show the kind of conviction carried by explanations with access, as it were, to the uniformities and predictabilities of the enchanted garden. Yet this, although an enviable condition, is not an essential one. The continuing dispute about the possibility of non-trivial general laws of human behaviour has significant implications for practising sociologists, anthropologists and historians not so much because they need to know what laws can do for them if there are any as because they need to know whether, if they have to go without them, their would-be explanatory hypotheses can still claim adequate theoretical grounding.

There is already some reassurance to be found in the fact that even in the physical sciences there are any number of successful explanations which invoke no laws at all.* The geologists who for a long time were puzzled by the formation of the Carmarthenshire plateaux resolved their puzzlement by the discovery that their formation could only be the result of prolonged subaerial denudation down to a sea level 400 feet above that of the present day; but they neither cited nor discovered a geological law. Even in classical physics, which unlike geology is an ahistorical science, the discovery that cathode rays are charges of negative electricity carried by particles of matter rather than waves emanating from the cathodes involved neither the citation nor the discovery of a law. The once fashionable view that the human sciences are 'idiographic' but the natural sciences 'nomothetic' can be discarded without further discussion, and with it the claim that requests for an explanation of the form 'how possibly?' are peculiar to the human, and of the form 'why necessarily?' to the natural, sciences. No doubt there are laws of matter but for which the explanation of the Carmarthenshire plateaux and of cathode rays would fail to hold. But without underlying regularities of some kind or other no explanation of anything would be possible at all. Explanations of behaviour similarly rest on a presupposition of psychological and/or physiological uniformities between one human being and the next. But their relative strength or weakness does not depend on whether, or how nearly, they conform to the pattern of 'because it invariably does' rather

* The two following examples are borrowed from C. F. A. Pantin, *The Relations between the Sciences* (1968), Ch. 1, and Peter Achinstein, *Law and Explanation* (1971), Ch. 5.

than of 'because it can and in this case did'. Either way, if it is claimed that – given specified initial conditions and constraints – the aspect or feature of the event, process or state of affairs taken as the explanandum is as it has been observed to be because and only because of X, the claim has to be supported by an argument showing why, or how, X was capable of producing the observed effect. The sceptic who queries the explanation of a puzzling figure in Piero di Cosimo's painting of Vulcan by reference to a Virgilian quotation about Aeolus is as effectively answered by the invocation of a well-documented history of Renaissance mythography as is the sceptic who queries the explanation of a puzzling wetness on the outside of a glass of water by reference to the weather by the invocation of a well-tested law about temperature difference and atmospheric condensation.

It is not surprising, therefore, that in practice explanations of human behaviour are sometimes weaker and sometimes stronger than the theories in which they are claimed to be grounded. Bacon's remarks about envy, which I quoted in Section 1 to illustrate the difference between common-sense induction and a fully-fledged scientific theory, may nevertheless be perfectly adequate to explain what would otherwise be puzzling in a particular case: the resentful or treacherous actions of the illegitimate half-brother, or the less successful of two coeval *associés-rivaux*, or Byron's 'hoary cripple with malicious eye' may well be rendered understandable in the secondary sense, given the initial conditions, by a hypothesis of envy even in the absence of anything approaching a theory capable of predicting its incidence in advance. The hypothesis owes its plausibility not to the grounding which a more advanced psychology may or may not one day provide but to the implausibility of any and all other hypotheses capable of fitting the observations made. Explanations of this deliberately *ad hoc* character are common in history and by no means unusual in anthropology and sociology, and there is nothing spurious about them. Indeed, it may be at the other extreme, as in some areas of economics, where the theory is much better developed but the behaviour which constitutes the explanandum much more susceptible to exogenous disturbances, that the researcher will turn out to have more serious grounds for suspecting that the fit between his hypothesis and his observations is spurious. The theory says that given the initial conditions an increase in supply should have been followed by a fall in price – and so it was; but can we be sure that the predicted movements in the indices are the result of market behaviour which is 'rational' in the sense demanded by the theory and not of a conjunction of individual decisions many or all of which were prompted by motives and circumstances about which the theory has nothing to say?

§5. One possible tactic is to try to frame the connection between the particular explanation and the supporting theory in terms of a weakly lawlike *ceteris paribus* generalization. For if the explanation is, indeed, valid there can be no questioning the inference that if all the same circumstances were to repeat themselves the chosen cause would again produce the observed effect, irrespective of whether the hypothesis to which the options have been narrowed is idiographic or nomothetic in form. But what is achieved by saying so? *Ceteris paribus*, any necessary or sufficient condition can be claimed to stand in a replicable causal relation to the chosen explanandum: if other things *are* equal, then not only are Bacon's maxims laws of psychology after all but the cession of Corsica to France was the cause of the Battle of Waterloo. This is no help whatever to the practising sociologist, anthropologist or historian, whose need is for priorities which will dictate the choice of one rather than another presumptive cause in the light of the reciprocal implications between his chosen hypothesis and its theoretical grounding.

Consider the following example taken from the field of industrial sociology, where there is a substantial literature directed to establishing the influence – *ceteris paribus* – of technology on social integration. The rationale for an attempted causal generalization is clear enough: there is a long tradition which holds that the nature and organization of work within the industrial enterprise, as dictated by the technology employed, dictates in its turn the degree to which the workforce identifies its objectives with those of management. Under mass-production, it was (so it is argued) inevitable that the aims and tactics of the old craft unions should give way to fewer and larger national unions concerned to secure for their members a guaranteed minimum rate for unskilled work and to resist the attempts of management to raise production per man by heightening the pace of assembly-line throughput. But when mass-production technology is replaced by capital-intensive continuous-process technology, the nature and organization of work is transformed: it is made more interesting (or less boring), more remunerative, more responsible and more secure. What, therefore, is the effect on social integration? According to one school, it promotes it by rewarding skill in a manner more readily seen to be fair, narrowing the distinction between manual and non-manual status, promoting solidarity within the work team, diminishing the sense of anonymity and impersonality and at the same time enabling management to be more generous in matters of welfare. But according to a rival school, it undermines it by shifting the aspirations of workers from economic to political goals, alerting them to the contradictions inherent in the system which governs their lives, exacerbating their resentment at their continuing subordination and encouraging them to demand a direct involvement in the decisions which are traditionally the prerogative of management. Both hypotheses, or sets of hypotheses, have some evidence to support them and some semblance of grounding in a presumptive theory: which, therefore, is – *ceteris paribus* – valid? The likely answer, as it turns out, is for practical purposes neither. A comparative study of British and French refinery workers at four different sites carried out in the early 1970s* showed convincingly that national differences in politics, ideology and union and management organization and strategy can override whatever differences process technology makes. No one such study can be conclusive by itself, and it remains the case that technology can and sometimes does – *ceteris paribus* – make *a* difference. But what is achieved by framing a lawlike-looking generalization in these terms if its explanatory potential is so limited? And are such generalizations not bound to be thus limited, given the range and diversity of the other relevant influences with which researchers will in practice always have to contend?

Where reportage alone is at issue, then (as we saw in Chapter 2) recourse to a *ceteris paribus* clause may yield a generalization which, however trivial it may seem, is at any rate accurate. But where explanation is at issue, triviality is fatal. Nothing is gained by trying to give a nomothetic air to an explanation whose success or failure depends not on how closely it approximates to that form but on the strength of the justification which can be given for linking the particular explanans to the particular explanandum. Lawfulness should be regarded as relative – which it is in natural no less than in social science. Despite what I earlier said about the regularities generated by the known mechanisms of genetic transmission, it is a view strongly held by some philosophers of science that there are no laws of biology as such – laws, that is, which like those of physics and chemistry display the invariances deserving of the title. It is true that this view is rejected by other philosophers,† in whose eyes it hinges on a purely verbal trick of definition: why shouldn't the Hardy-Weinberg Law about the constancy of gene ratios over successive generations in a population of sexual organisms not acted on by external forces

---

* Duncan Gallie, *In Search of the New Working Class: Automation and Social Integration within the Capitalist Enterprise* (1978).
† See M. E. Ruse, 'Are there Laws in Biology?', *Australasian Journal of Philosophy* XLVIII (1970).

be called a 'law'? Why does it matter that there are exceptions due to extra-chromosomal genes any more than that there are exceptions to Galileo's Law about falling bodies at distances not negligible by comparison with the radius of the earth? This, however, is another dispute which the practising sociologist, anthropologist or historian can safely bypass. For his purposes, the moral to be drawn from it is that he need not set himself in quest of strict invariances, but only of qualified regularities adequate to vindicate whatever contrast he has drawn between what has happened and what might have but didn't. They do not have to be more than relatively lawlike, and he does not need to have access to them directly: reductionist explanations, impressive as they may be, are neither the only ones nor the best. Nor does he always need to be able to spell them out. It may sometimes be enough for him to say that his chosen hypothesis is grounded in whatever it is that makes people behave, or react, in a sufficiently predictable and uniform manner under specified conditions. He may draw them from any field of science, whether natural or social, on which his explanation implicitly or explicitly depends. All he can be sure of in advance is that they will not be laws of sociology itself except on so generous a definition of 'law' that any *ceteris paribus* generalization will count as one. Every science depends for its grounding on the stricter regularities disclosed at some relatively more fundamental level, and sociology, which is not merely historically but analytically the last of the sciences, cannot but be the least autonomous in this respect. But it is not the less scientific for that. There is no denying that there must be laws at some level or other if sociological or any other causes are to be causes of social or any other events, processes or states of affairs. But there is no need whatever for them to be related to the explanandum and each other as they are in so atypical a science as Newtonian mechanics, with its closed systems, time-reversible regularities and interlocking differential equations.

Once it is realized that the requirement for theoretical grounding can be so indirectly and inexplicitly met, it becomes possible to bypass also the long and largely fruitless debate over historical inevitability. It may still be argued, and irrefutably so, that anything that is explicable must in principle have been inevitable: if E because X, then given X, E was bound to follow. But the force of 'bound' is very different as between that inherent in the claim that Halley's comet was bound, given the initial conditions, to reappear in the year 1758 and that inherent in the claim that Piero di Cosimo was bound, given the initial conditions, to put a representation of Aeolus into his picture of Vulcan. For Halley's comet, there is predictability in the Laplacean sense: Laplace's Demon, equipped with a knowledge both of the initial state of the system and of the classical dynamical laws, complete with Newtonian axioms and derivations, is able to calculate all past and/or future states of the system. But a Laplacean mode of reasoning is not merely inapplicable in, but irrelevant to, the open systems studied by biological, and *a fortiori* social, science. The laws to which they appeal are not laws of a Laplacean kind and do not need to be. To abandon the hope of a theory which would enable the sociologist equipped with an adequate knowledge of the initial state of social systems to predict the lawlike sequence of stages through which they must henceforward proceed is not to have made sociology any less scientific than the Encyclopaedists or Saint-Simon or Comte or Marx or Spencer or the members of the Anthropological Society* wanted to make it.

Emancipation from methodological bondage to Laplacean laws does not, however, diminish the risk of spurious theorizing. If anything, it heightens it. The regularities in which explanations of behaviour are grounded may not need to be understood in the secondary sense as the relations of mass, volume and temperature of gases are understood, and they may not need to be strictly deducible in their turn from any more general law or laws. But they must still be capable of supporting the hypothesized causal connections which make up the explanation against its competitors, and there is a risk that the illusion of support can more plausibly be sustained where the theory providing it has been exempted from the requirement that it should do so in a deductive-nomological way. In sociology, moreover, this risk is compounded by the ever-present possibility of an intrusion of moral and political value-judgements which, logically independent as they may be, can still tempt researchers who subscribe to one or another untestable evaluative presupposition into substituting a high-sounding redefinition for a genuinely explanatory theory. Not that examples of spurious theorizing are peculiar to sociology; examples can as readily be cited from the writings of biologists and psychologists as of sociologists, anthropologists or historians. But it is only to be expected that a prior attachment to the conception of one or another form of social organization as good or bad should, for example, encourage some 'right-wing' sociologists of the structural-functional school to try to justify their preferred hypotheses by phrasing them in a language of 'feedback' and 'pattern-maintenance' and some 'left-wing' sociologists of the historical-materialist school to try to justify theirs by phrasing them in a language of 'crisis' and 'contradiction'. Nothing, to

* Of 1863 – *not* the one of 1837–42 which merged with the Christian Phrenological Society (J. W. Burrow, *Evolution and Society* (1966), p. 120 n. 1).

be sure, prevents language of either kind from being used in the framing of a theory which does provide adequate grounding for the initial hypothesis of the cause of the reported change, or lack of it, in the institutions and practices of the society under study. But it has to be shown to do so by the strength of its resistance to attempted invalidation. Sociological theories may not have to consist of deductively connected sets of laws. But they do still have to be capable of persuading readers of any and all persuasions not only that, but why, the causal hypotheses derived from them are valid.

§6. If the range of explananda with which sociologists, anthropologists and historians are concerned is as broad as I said at the beginning, and if in addition the ways in which their explanations are grounded can be as inexplicit and indirect as I have been suggesting just now, it might seem that there can be no methodological directives of any practical value to be laid down in advance of direct confrontation with a reported event, process or state of affairs of which secondary understanding is called for. But it follows from the account which I have given so far that the mode of reasoning most appropriate to sociological explanation is neither deductive-nomological nor inductive-statistical but quasi-experimental; and if, accordingly, there is a directive to be framed it is to the effect that practising sociologists should normally be looking neither for regularities nor for probabilities but for suggestive contrasts – suggestive, that is, in that they may either test or extend a theory which has application over as much as possible of the range of events, processes or states of affairs which have been chosen for study.

This is not to deny that experimentation in sociology is often inappropriate or impracticable, whether because the result will at best be trivial or because the control group can never be fully controlled. There is nothing more intrinsically scientific about an experiment than a piece of fieldwork or a study of documentary archives, and many of the meticulous and thoroughgoing laboratory experiments conducted in social psychology (and, for that matter, the study of animal behaviour) have added nothing of value to the resolution of the wider problems to which they were ostensibly addressed. But just as a quasi-deductive inference of the kind discussed in Section 23 of Chapter 2 may, in practice, be virtually as compelling as a deductive one, so may a quasi-experiment be virtually as compelling, in practice, as a real one. Just because we shall never be able to answer such questions as whether France would have evolved the institutions of liberal parliamentary democracy without the French Revolution, it does not follow that we cannot hope to answer such questions as whether rural social relations in France, as contrasted with those in England, in the century before the Revolution were such as to prevent the increasing commercialization of agriculture which occurred in both countries from altering those relations in the direction which they took in the English case.

It is therefore likely to be more rewarding to look for hypotheses of which history has happened to furnish a chance of quasi-experimental test than for hypotheses which, however significant their theoretical implications, history has not furnished the means of testing even with the help of the most ingenious statistical or other techniques. If you are interested in what will turn a patrilocal into a matrilocal society, follow the Shoshone Indians who moved South from the Nevada/Utah desert plateau into an ecological zone suitable for small-scale agriculture.* If you are interested in testing the strength of a traditional political allegiance which rests on a supernatural belief, analyse the failure of the previously all-powerful Paduka Raja Tun Abdul Jamil of Johor in 1688 to purchase the allegiance of the 'sea people' (*Orang Laut*)† against an abducted child leader, the founder of whose dynasty had undergone a special rite of consecration nearly three hundred years before. If you are interested in whether ties of vassalage displace ties of kinship in a feudalized clan society, study what happened on the edge of the Scottish Highlands in 1562 when Mackintosh tenants of the Earl of Huntly, who as their feudal lord had called them out to fight against Mary Queen of Scots, were called out on their way by the head of Clan Mackintosh to fight against Huntly.‡ In none of these examples can hypotheses be framed for which, if the evidence supports them, the validity of a strictly controlled experiment can be claimed. But in all of them there is at least the possibility of framing a hypothesis which the available evidence can provisionally confirm and which can be supported by, and give support to, a more general body of ideas.

This bias, if such it seems, against attempted generalization is not argued on epistemological but only on practical grounds: every explanatory hypothesis still implies some sort of causal generalization and vice versa. But in sociology, attempts to generalize across a sufficient range of events, processes or states of affairs as thereby to extend or test a provisional theory are time and again frustrated by the imposition of qualifications which progressively diminish the scope and interest of the presumptively causal connection. It is not a matter of the complexity so

* Cf. Godelier, *Perspectives in Marxist Anthropology*, pp. 106–7.
† On whom see L. Y. Andaya, *The Kingdom of Johor 1641–1728* (1975).
‡ See T. C. Smout, *A History of the Scottish People 1560–1830* (1969), p. 42.

much as the diversity of influences on which the variations in human institutions and practices depend. Nor is it only the large generalizations of comparative sociology which gain their scope only at the cost of their theoretical potential: even the cautious conjectures of anthropologists or historians who limit themselves to a single topic, region or period are vulnerable to it. How often do we not read that, for example, peoples with a strong military tradition make inefficient tillers of the soil only to be confronted with the Jats of the Punjab? or that a sense of national identity is a function of a common language only to be confronted by the ancient Greeks whose pervasive consciousness of 'Hellenism' was combined with an ineradicable self-differentiation among rival *poleis*? or that the failure of Habsburg imperialism caused the independent power of towns in Europe to decline at the expense of national nobilities only to be confronted with counter-examples from Switzerland? or that political organization in 'primitive' societies is based on kinship only to be confronted, even at the level of hunter-gatherers, with the Andaman Islanders among whom not all the members of distinguishable communities claim to be related to one another? The exceptions to such presumptively causal generalizations do not deprive of their potential theoretical interest reports which, as far as they go, sustain a claim of multiple occurrence or conjunction. Not only may a high empirical correlation over a large number of cases be sometimes as suggestive as a single startling contrast, but even some ostensibly suspect generalizations can be shown to be stronger than they look: the generalization that the ineradicably self-differentiated Greek *poleis* were always in conflict with each other, to which those of the Asia Minor coast might appear to offer a damaging exception, is effectively redeemed by a reminder of the inhibiting proximity of the 'Great King' of Persia. But even at their most nearly universal, such generalizations are not to be construed as explanations in themselves so much as reports implicitly suggestive of causal hypotheses which may be expected in due course to be derivable from a common theory.

In sociology, persistent correlations and striking parallels, whether within societies or between them, kindle the expectation of a significant advance in secondary understanding not because of the number of instances accumulated in the historical and ethnographic record but because of the likelihood that there is a theory at a more fundamental level in which the presumptively causal connection can be grounded. The researcher who is reminded by the Dinka sacrificial ritual in which raw meat is eaten before sunrise of the same practice as reported for the Saracens, or by the involvement of a minority of aristocrats in trade and commerce in Archaic Greece of a similar involvement of a minority of the Portuguese nobility in the first phase of colonial expansion, or by the eschatological myths of the Mbaya shamans of eastern Paraguay of those of the Old Testament prophets, or by the *Insten* system of rural labour relations in East Elbian Germany in the late eighteenth century of the '*izbah* system in Egypt in the late nineteenth, will no doubt do his best to specify just what the two (or more) reported events, processes or states of affairs have in common. But if this is done for the purposes of linking them in a would-be general law, it will only invite counter-examples from other societies which will be all too ready to hand. They may well turn out to share one or more common antecedent conditions. But these will be contingently sufficient only given a further set of similar (but not identical) constraints and causes whose effect in making them so has itself to be explained at another level.

Emphasis on the value of a quasi-experimental mode of reasoning in sociological explanation does not diminish the value of techniques designed to sift out the relative causal importance of different antecedent variables. Often, the problem which the practising sociologist, anthropologist or historian needs to resolve is not the identification of any one contingently sufficient condition at all but the analysis of the causal interrelation between a set of variables all of which are known to be contingently sufficient if the others are held constant. This, however, is a technical problem which does not require any modification of the methodological argument. It may involve, in a way that the examples which I have thus far given do not, the calculation of sets of product-moment or other correlation coefficients, or the isolation through factor analysis of the smallest set of causal candidates which account for the largest proportion of the observed variance, or the mapping of path diagrams showing the strength of the association between different presumptive causes as well as between the presumptive causes and the explanandum. But it is the same purpose which is being served – that is, the approximation to experimental controls whereby hypothesized causes can conclusively be shown to be so; and it is the same methodological moral which is all the more forcibly pointed – that is, the lack of explanatory power in the generalization *ceteris paribus* of singular causal connections. The resulting model of what may be a complicated social process will not by itself furnish an adequate grounding for the interrelated hypotheses which it embodies. Indeed it may, in practice, suggest a still wider range of possible theories which will need somehow to be tested against each other. But there is still no special problem of explanation in sociology, however difficult it may be on any given topic to relate causal hypotheses at the sociological level to underlying regularities as accessible and as reliable as those of natural science.

§7. To illustrate the operation of the mode of reasoning which I am concerned to recommend, I have chosen two examples which fulfil the conditions that (i) the explanations given are, as far as I am able to judge, valid, (ii) the reportage of the explananda is uncontroversial between rival observers, (iii) there is an immediately obvious candidate for 'the' presumptive cause, and (iv) the first appears, at first sight, to have an idiographic rather than a nomothetic grounding and the second a nomothetic rather than an idiographic.

The first is taken from the nineteenth-century history of a geographically isolated and culturally homogeneous area: the central plateau of the island of Madagascar. Originally the area was divided politically among a large number of small, mutually hostile and often impermanent kingdoms based in fortified mountain-top villages and supported by levies of produce imposed on the inhabitants of the valleys immediately surrounding them. But by the early years of the nineteenth century several of them had succeeded in expanding to an altogether greater size by extracting corvée labour instead of produce from the inhabitants of the valleys and employing that labour to build and maintain the earthworks necessary to turn the permanent marshland of the valleys into highly productive labour-intensive ricefields. This in turn required both the creation of a supervisory bureaucracy and the procurement of slaves to supplement the indigenous corvées; and the procurement of slaves on a sufficient scale could only be done through war. The previous equilibrium between small kingdoms, none of which had the necessary means of extending their domination beyond the irrigated valleys a few miles round them, was thus replaced by an equilibrium between relatively large ones capable of conquering those in their neighbourhood which had remained at the previous stage of development, but lacking the necessary means of conquering the rest of each other. In the course of the nineteenth century, however, one of them succeeded – the Merina kingdom based on Tananarive which, under its king Radama, captured sufficient numbers of slaves not merely to exploit to the full the ricefields of the Betsimitatra marsh but to be exchanged for the then available European weapons with which fresh conquests and the capture of yet more slaves might be achieved. Radama, as he is depicted in the *History of Madagascar* by the Rev. William Ellis published in 1838, was a ruthless, intelligent and energetic ruler well capable of dealing with Europeans to his own best advantage, and it is no doubt the case that had he not been, or had his kingdom been riven with dynastic and factional conflicts to the degree that some others were, the expansion which by 1890 found the Merina kingdom in possession of the whole of Madagascar would have been curtailed. But once given the initial conditions, Radama's access to European weapons on the one hand and slave-markets on the other enabled him to maintain the momentum of conquest in a way that his rivals could not. In the words of the twentieth-century anthropologist on whose account I have principally relied, 'The combination of the availability of efficient weapons and the fact that at the time when they were beginning to circulate the Merina kingdom was in its expansionist take-off stage, meant that trade in weapons, like other trade, was *inevitably* [my italics] channelled towards Tananarive.'* An explanation can therefore be given in quasi-experimental terms whereby it can convincingly be argued that because and only because of the introduction of rifles and cannon into Central Madagascar at the time and in the quantity that took place, there came about – which there otherwise would not have done – the decisive expansion of the Merina kingdom.

The second example is taken from the electoral geography of pro-vincial France. It has long been noticed that following the introduction of adult male suffrage there has been a remarkable consistency in the pattern of votes cast for left-wing or right-wing parties in different Departments, and that their patterns can be related to specific ecological and sociological characteristics of the regions concerned. Thus, there is a demonstrable tendency for regions where the Church is strong to vote Right and regions of high population density to vote Left, for regions with large resident landlords to vote Right and regions of single-crop commercial farming to vote Left, for regions less economically developed and with a higher proportion of subsistence farmers to vote Right and regions more economically developed and with a higher proportion of artisans to vote Left. Moreover, many correlations of this kind, including some very specific ones, can be paralleled from elsewhere: the radicalism of fishermen, first pointed out by André Siegfried for France in 1913, has been observed also from Iceland and Norway to the West Coast of Canada and the United States. There are thus sufficient data available in which consistent correlations can be found to suggest explanations of voting by region which can be supported both by precise empirical generalizations and by presumptive connections (now supported by the

* Maurice Bloch, 'The Disconnection between Power and Rank as a Process: An Outline of the Development of Kingdoms in Central Madagascar', *Archives Européennes de Sociologie* XVIII (1977), p. 119.

evidence of opinion polls) between the ecological and sociological context and perceived political interest. If, therefore, we take as an example the Department of Sarthe, whose Western half has voted for the Right and its Eastern half for the Left for more than a century, it is only to be expected that a detailed analysis of its ecology and sociology will confirm that this is by no means random. The Department as a whole is agricultural; but the peasants of the West have always been richer – to the point, indeed, of being able to survive bad harvests – less exposed to the influences of the towns and more closely involved with the Church. The peasants of the East, by contrast, have not only been poorer but have had to supplement their income by weaving; this has at the same time brought them into closer contact with the towns and made them dependent on fluctuating prices for their cloths out of which they have to pay cash for their food which, in the bad years from which the Western peasants profit, becomes too expensive for them. These differences have been consistent ever since the French Revolution, and the equally consistent pattern of voting behaviour is, accordingly, convincingly explained by reference to them.*

Notice first how much is left unsaid in both of these explanations. It is not only that they involve none of the risks of misunderstanding in the primary sense which attend the secondary understanding of behaviour informed by arcane beliefs or constituted by intentions whose meaning is ambiguous or obscure. It is also that the contrast between what happened and what might have but didn't has been so defined that the explanations offered are independent of answers to detailed questions about the precise motives of King Radama in the first case and of the individual Frenchmen comprising the electorate of the Sarthe in the second. The student of nineteenth-century Madagascar who wants an explanation of Radama's wars of conquest may be treating the flow of European firearms to Tananarive as an initial condition and asking why Radama decided to ignore the pleas of the missionaries who hoped, at one time with some apparent reason, to persuade him to abolish the slave trade; the student of nineteenth-century France who wants an explanation of the behaviour of the electorate of the Sarthe may be assuming already that the peasants of the East will incline to radicalism on economic grounds and asking why a continuing allegiance to the Church among the peasants of the West should necessarily have disposed them against the parties of the Left and not towards the kind of *Démocratie*

* Theodore Zeldin, *France 1848–1945* I (1973), pp. 374ff., drawing on Paul Bois, *Paysans de l'Ouest, Des structures économiques et sociales aux options politiques depuis l'époque révolutionnaire dans la Sarthe* (1960).

Chrétienne later preached by the Abbé Trochu of Rennes. But these different questions do not need to be answered before it can be claimed that given the state of politics in nineteenth-century Madagascar Radama's kingdom was able to expand as it did because and only because of the introduction of European firearms on a substantial scale, or that given the state of politics in nineteenth-century France the dependence of the peasantry of the Eastern Sarthe on weaving to supplement their incomes was decisive for the persistent difference in voting behaviour between East and West. Once the contrast between the chosen explanandum and what would, in the absence of the hypothesized cause, have been the case has been sufficiently tightly drawn, there is no need for the researcher to be able to say exactly what motivated the agents concerned before he offers his chosen quasi-experimental explanation, any more than a biologist has to be able to say exactly what neurophysiological changes took place among the individual members of a primate species before he offers his quasi-experimental explanation of the evolution of its social organization in one direction rather than another. Nor does the one explanation appeal any more directly to a presumptive law than the other: the fortuitousness of Radama's access to European firearms does not make the expansion of his kingdom any less inevitable, and the consistency of the correlation between peasant prosperity and electoral support for parties of the Right does not obviate the need for an account of the politics of the Sarthe to include reference to the influence of weaving, agriculture, towns and the Church.

These two explanations, therefore, different as they are, are both good explanations for the same two reasons: first, they specify an antecedent which, given a set of initial conditions and constraints which rival observers can check for themselves, can be claimed to have made the decisive difference; and second, they furnish a plausible answer to the question why the chosen antecedent should have the capacity to be decisive in the first place. Radama waged a series of wars of conquest which, thanks to his privileged access to European firearms, were a success neither because all known kings with access to more effective weapons than their rivals wage wars of conquest nor because he was driven by an ineluctable impulse to territorial aggression which is latent in us all, but because the political circumstances of nineteenth-century Madagascar were such that if he hadn't conquered his rivals one or other of his rivals would have conquered him. The peasants of the Eastern Sarthe tended, thanks to their involvement in the weaving trade, to vote for parties of the Left neither because all known peasant communities involved in weaving have more left-wing than right-wing electors nor because they were, like us all, maximizing their perceived cost-benefit ratios in doing so, but because the political circumstances of their particular Department were such that the parties of the Left were their natural allies against the richer peasants of the West. To the sceptic who objects that these explanations which I have offered as 'good' invoke no concept as subtle or fundamental as those of molecular excitation or atmospheric pressure, the answer is: no, but that doesn't make them either invalid or uninteresting. To the sceptic who objects that they have been constructed *ad hoc* and *faute de mieux*, the answer is: yes, but that doesn't make them either obvious or trivial.

§ 8. These two examples serve also to illustrate the way in which processes integral to the connection between the explanandum and the hypothesized cause can – up to a point – be taken for granted. I remarked in Section 14 of Chapter 2 that there is, strictly speaking, no such thing as a synchronic report: events and states of affairs, whether featuring as explananda or explanantia, are themselves all processes of a kind. But to say that all sociological explanations can and must take for granted the workings of processes not themselves explained in the course of them is not to say that it is always as safe to do so as in the examples of the expansion of the Merina kingdom and the electoral geography of the Sarthe.

Behaviorist psychology, to which I referred in passing in Section 7 of Chapter 1, affords one good example of the danger. It may well be that for some areas of human as well as animal behaviour, the technique of operant conditioning can be shown to make possible both prediction and control. If the responses of experimental subjects can be seen to vary in precise accordance with stipulated difference equations as a schedule of reinforcing stimuli is administered, the experimenter can quite well afford to remain ignorant of the internal process by which the subjects are enabled to respond. It need make no more difference to the validity of the explanation given than ignorance of the physiology of locomotion to a military historian's explanation of the retreat of the French infantry to the Marne in 1914 in the face of the German conquest of Belgium. But the danger lies in the possibility that the internal mechanism may be such as not only to provide the link between these responses and the stimuli which have caused them but also to provide or, on the contrary, fail to provide links between other kinds of stimulus and other kinds of response and thereby to force a radical modification of the presumptive theory which appeared to furnish the original experimental results with an adequate grounding. In the case of Skinner's own theory of stimulation and reinforcement, this neglect of what might be happening internally has proved fatal to the attempted extension of the theory to cover the learning of language. Not only does it render the connection between any particular pair of stimulus and response untestable against alternative hypotheses; it also rules pre-emptively out of account the possibility that innate capacities and dispositions may be of equal or greater importance.* It does not follow that all explanations of behaviour in terms of stimulus and response are misconceived. But it does follow that where they are valid they are valid in the way that common-sense explanations of the boiling of water by reference to the application of heat are valid: there is a theoretical lacuna analogous to the lack of the concept of atmospheric pressure which cannot safely be ignored if further progress in secondary understanding is to be made.

The danger equally attends explanations of the outcome of singular narrative sequences which correctly assume the efficacy of an unanalysed interaction between initial conditions in converting, so to speak, the necessary into the sufficient. Consider for example the outbreak of the French Revolution. For all the disputes which continue over its explanation,† let me assume for methodology's sake that all rival observers agree that given the previous political and economic history of eighteenth-century France, the conjunction in 1788–89 of a serious harvest failure, the collapse of the government's finances and the calling of the Estates-General so far undermined the authority of the monarchy as to make it possible in a way that it had not hitherto been for the *ancien régime* to be overthrown. But it is not enough just to say, true as it may be, that the conjunction of these was contingently sufficient – given the other initial conditions – because there was a reciprocal feedback between manifestations of rural discontent and loss of repressive capability by the army and therefore the king. The hypothesis of causal interdependence needs to be grounded itself in some further underlying account of why this particular conjunction should have induced in the delegates to the Constituent Assembly a concessionary rather than a reactionary response. Until there can be established to the satisfaction of rival observers the pattern of causal interdependence between the actions not merely of the peasantry and the central government but of the royal family, the provincial nobility, the *parlements*, the militia, the Parisian mob and all the other agents involved in the unfolding sequence of events, the invocation

* See the review of Skinner's *Verbal Behaviour* (1957) by N. Chomsky in *Language* xxxv (1959).
† See William Doyle, *Origins of the French Revolution* (1980), esp. Part I ('A Consensus and its Collapse: Writings on Revolutionary Origins since 1939').

of reciprocal feedback is as limited in explanatory potential as the invocation of stimulus and response.

This example might seem to suggest that the theoretical lacuna could adequately be filled by extending the hypothesis of causal interdependence against a background of initial conditions to a flow-chart linking the initial conditions both to the interdependent and therefore contingently sufficient conditions and to each other. But even this will not necessarily be enough. Here, for example, is a flow-chart labelled by its author 'The growth of slavery in Roman Italy – a scheme of interdependence'* in which each of the arrows denotes a causal relation which may again, for methodology's sake, be assumed to be validated by

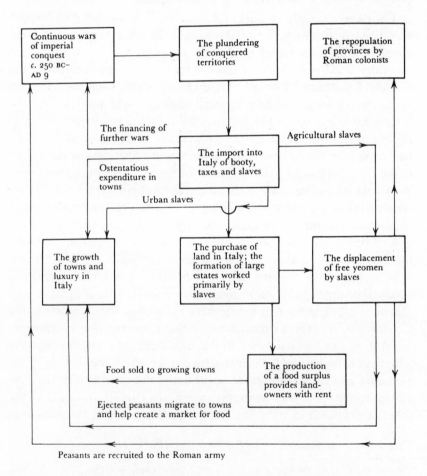

*Keith Hopkins, *Conquerors and Slaves* (1978), Fig. 1.1.

the sources to the satisfaction of all rival observers. There is perhaps a technical objection to be made in that a flow-chart of this kind ought to specify temporal as well as causal relationships. But even if this were to be remedied, the flow-chart could not be claimed (and is not claimed by its author) to have explained the growth of slavery in Roman Italy in the way that the account summarized in Section 7 can be claimed to have explained the expansion of the Merina kingdom. For just as a mere invocation of reciprocal feedback between the several influences which undermined the government's authority is not enough to justify the claim that the French Revolution happened because and only because of it, so the mere invocation of a causal connection between wars of conquest, plundering of conquered territories, import of booty, taxes and slaves and the purchase of large estates to be worked primarily by slaves is not enough to justify the claim that because and only because of the inter-dependences set out in the flow-chart Roman Italy came by A.D.9 or before to be characterized by large slave-worked estates. For why did the Romans *have* to respond to the opportunities opened up to them by their successive wars of conquest by introducing slaves on to the large estates formed in Roman Italy any more than the Constituent Assembly *had* to respond to the government's weakness by voting away feudal privileges on the evening of August 4, 1789? There are other ways of exploiting conquered territories and extracting a maximum surplus from cultivable land, and a proper understanding (in the secondary sense) of the growth of slavery in Roman Italy requires in addition to the causal hypotheses of the flow-chart an underlying account of what led the Romans to adopt this one.

Unexplained processes, accordingly, can be taken for granted when but only when it can safely be assumed not merely that the process does link the explanandum to the hypothesized cause but also that it does not do so in a way which would undermine the causal hypothesis's presumptive theoretical grounding. Certainty, of course, will never be attainable: something always might turn out to be the case which would, after all, force an unwelcome revision. But if (and only if) in a given state of knowledge it is equally implausible from the standpoint of the partisans of all theoretical schools that it will, then even complex and mysterious processes can sometimes be left imperfectly explained without the explanation which takes them for granted being compromised.

INTERPRETING WEAK BUT ADEQUATE THEORIES

§9. The goal of the practising sociologist is still the grounding of precise and plausible hypotheses in strong and surprising theories. But in default of such theories, the value to him of methodological discussion about theory-construction is that it can tell him not only what he lacks but how serious, or not, it is for him that he lacks it. Much of the technical literature on explanation in sociology takes it as axiomatic not only that explanations should be based on precisely measurable differences between observed and alternative possible outcomes but also that they should be related to their presumptive grounding by an unbroken sequence of deductive, or at any rate semi- or quasi-deductive, steps. One favourite paradigm of bad explanation is Molière's foolish bachelor of medicine who proclaimed that opium puts people to sleep because of its possession of 'dormitive power' – an explanation which is evidently both vacuous and circular. But wait. Even the feeblest-looking explanations are by no means always quite as feeble as they may, appear. It may, depending on the state of current theory, have been a significant discovery that whatever it is that puts people to sleep after the ingestion of opium is indeed an inherent property of opium, even if its precise pharmacological analysis was beyond the skills of seventeenth-century practitioners of investigative medicine. When, for example, Montesquieu in Book x of *L'Esprit des Lois* attributes the failure of the Persian invasions of Greece to the Greeks' 'superiority in their manner of fighting', he is saying more than that the Greeks won the battles because they were better at winning battles. There is a quasi-experimental contrast implied between the tactics, training and morale of the Greeks which, despite the superiority of the Persians in numbers and resources, is hypothesized to have been decisive, and the refusal of the Persians, which Montesquieu attributes to pride, to learn from the Greeks' example. His account is, admittedly, not very much nearer to a strong grounding in the theories of political science than Molière's *bachelier*'s invocation of *virtus dormitiva* to a strong grounding in the theories of chemistry. But it presumes, and fairly so, the possibility of a grounding in the secondary understanding which we might one day arrive at of the causes which, in a given state of technology, make one army more effective than another. However far the documentary sources on the Persian Wars available either to Montesquieu or to ourselves may fall short of the contents of the recording angel's archives, it would be rash to insist that Montesquieu's explanation could never be shown to be valid.

This licence to the practising sociologist to rely for the grounding of his hypotheses on theories which he doesn't yet have must, like the licence to take unexplained processes for granted, be sparingly used. For him to tell his readers that he has a valid explanation of the decline and fall of the Roman Empire in the West in which the hypothesis that it was a military weakness which left the frontiers inadequately defended is grounded in whatever the reasons may be which weaken once military powerful empires will be to tell them as little as in giving them the report that 'It is an advertisement for whatever "All Races" took "Humpty Dumpty on Ice" to be', or 'They are doing whatever it is that is called "marrying" in their culture.' But suppose instead that the military weakness is specifically attributed to the debilitating frequency of the disputed successions to the imperial title which are fully reported in the sources. There can then be drawn a two-fold quasi-experimental contrast: first, between the relative stability of the period of the earlier emperors and the instability which followed it; second, between the instability of the Western and the relative stability of the Eastern Empire after the separation of the two. What is more, there is to hand a theory to the effect that a necessary condition of stability is a tradition of obedience to, and veneration for, an established monarchy. From this theory, there can be derived the plausible hypotheses first, that the Eastern emperors were the beneficiaries of the monarchical tradition of the Hellenistic states but for which local magnates would have been much readier to try to usurp the imperial title by force of arms; and second, that it was the extinction of successive dynastic lines of Western emperors which offered successive precedents for usurpation, each of which increased the likelihood of another civil war whenever the problem of succession next arose.

The rival observer may still object that there remains to be answered the question why the armies attached such importance to hereditary succession: why should they be loyal even to an adoptive or fictive Caesar who might well be less congenial to them than one of their own commanders both in his person and in his likely policies in the matters most directly affecting themselves? To this, there may be no more convincing answer to be offered than that a hereditary allegiance did clearly seem natural to the rank and file and indeed to the mass of the population generally, even if not to the senatorial aristocracy. But does the lack of any stronger grounding than this weaken the quasi-experimental hypothesis claimed to offer an explanation? Surely not. The hypothesis asserts that given the initial conditions, which the rival observer can check for himself in the sources, there would have been significantly fewer civil wars on the death of each emperor if there had been a single heir legitimized by descent, whether actual, adoptive or even fictive. There might still have been as many plots and assassinations within the imperial household, just as there might still have been as many mutinies and rebellions in the provinces. But there would not have been the destructive free-for-alls which time and again diverted the armies from the defence of the frontiers to internecine battles on behalf of a favoured pretender. To the question why this hypothesis should be thought to hold, the theory need claim no more than that dynastic loyalty tends, once established in a society already permeated by patronage and paternalism, to be self-perpetuating. It does not need to be capable – much as we might like it to be – of generating hypotheses which would tell us whether the stability re-established under the Antonines would have lasted if Marcus Aurelius's son had been more like himself. Nor does it need to be derivable in turn from a still more general theory – much as we might like to have one. Not only does the request for another theory to ground the theory in which the initial causal hypothesis has been grounded merely lead to an infinite regress; in addition, the plausibility of the initial hypothesis rests on the adequacy of the theory in which it is grounded to meet the conventional objection that correlation is no proof of causation, rather than to specify the precise conditions – much as we might like to know them – under which the causal connection would or wouldn't hold.

This kind of weak but adequate grounding, dangerous as it may be to rely on too heavily, underlies many thoroughly convincing explanations of the type which links Piero di Cosimo's inclusion of Aeolus in a picture about Vulcan to the mythographic tradition within which the picture was painted. To the question 'What is it about the *Aeneid* which makes it the cause of the inclusion of the old man with two leather bags in the left foreground?', the answer 'Book VIII, ll. 416–17' can be very adequately grounded (as I suggested in Section 4) in a documented historical account of Renaissance mythography. It may be that to the objection that this does not explain why Piero di Cosimo chose – which he might not have done – to follow the mythographic tradition, there is nothing more to be said than that he evidently *did* choose to. Yet does it matter that we lack a secondary understanding of precisely what causes individual painters to follow or discard a mythographic tradition any more than that we lack a secondary understanding of precisely what causes individual soldiers to be loyal or disloyal to an imperial dynasty? No explanation can be expected to encompass every aspect of the event, process or state of affairs of which a chosen antecedent, or set of them, is hypothesized to have been the cause; and no theory can be expected to encompass every one of the antecedent conditions whose joint occurrence so far narrows the range of alternatives that the hypothesized cause can be shown to have been contingently sufficient. No doubt it is possible to envisage in principle a general explanatory theory of art within which the motives of artists and the influences acting on them are so thoroughly understood in the secondary sense that Piero di Cosimo's decision to paint precisely this picture in all its details could, after all, have been as safely predicted as the reappearance of Halley's comet. But the force of 'in principle' here is that no incantation of the ultimate presupposition of all science – that everything is, indeed, explicable – is ever going to bring every brushstroke of Piero di Cosimo's, every note of *The Art of Fugue* and every line of *Hamlet* into a precise and plausible quasi-experimental hypothesis grounded in a strong and surprising theory. Protestations of faith in the presupposition of metaphysical determinism have never brought a practising sociologist a single step nearer a valid explanation of anything, any more than protestations of faith in the presupposition of freedom of the will have ever brought a lecture-room sceptic a single step nearer the invalidation of a sociological explanation which has been successfully arrived at.

§ 10. The explanation of things like pictures and poems is sometimes held to be of quite a different order from the explanation of things like wars and revolutions, and the evident hopelessness of a quest for strong grounding in relatively lawlike regularities attributed to the difference between 'causal' explanation on the one hand and 'hermeneutic' or perhaps 'structuralist' explanation on the other. But the relation between reportage and explanation is the same across the whole range of human institutions and practices: the difference lies only in the nature of the difficulties which there may be in the primary understanding of the intentions and beliefs constitutive of what has then to be assigned a cause which can be vindicated as such by a theory. The primary understanding can itself, as always, be construed as an explanation at another level: 'He was depicting Aeolus' answers 'Why did Piero di Cosimo put those lines and colours on to that part of the canvas?', just as 'He is doing a rain-dance' answers 'Why is Mr Morley stamping about in the outskirts of Bournemouth with feathers on his head?' But a connection between the explanandum thus constituted and a presumptively causal antecedent has still to be made, whatever the field of activity may be. Even if both the primary and the secondary understanding of it are more difficult in the case of works of art than of explananda of other kinds, the methodology of explanation remains unaffected. The questions 'What exactly are they doing in performing *Humpty Dumpty* on ice?' or 'What exactly is he doing in depicting Aeolus and Vulcan on canvas?' are, arguably, different from the question 'What exactly are they doing in storming the Bastille?' in that the risk of primary misunderstanding is higher, and the need for tertiary understanding greater. But once an answer has been given whose accuracy as a report could be confirmed by the recording angel, explanation proceeds in accordance with the same criteria of validity. Lévi-Strauss's hypothesis that the story of Asdiwal has been composed and transmitted as we observe it to have been because it is an expression of the strain inherent in a system of patrilocal but matrilateral cross-cousin marriage stands or falls by the same criteria as Tocqueville's hypothesis that the storming of the Bastille gave expression to a resentment of the institutions of the *ancien régime* which came to seem progressively less tolerable as the possibility of removing them came to seem progressively more feasible. If plausible, albeit weakly grounded, explanations look different when the question asked is of a form to which iconographical analysis of a school of painting rather than a narrative chain of actions and reactions provides the answer, this is neither because 'explain' is being taken in a different sense nor because the attribution of motives to the agents performs a different explanatory role.

'But this assertion merely begs the whole question of the nature of the difference between causes and meanings.' No – not once the distinction between primary, secondary and tertiary understanding has been drawn. In the writings of sociologists, anthropologists and historians, meanings will feature both as constitutive of actions and as causes of actions. Whatever the difficulties which stand in the way of a philosophical theory of meaning, their need is not for a formula which will account for the different uses which they make of the concept of it but only for a criterion which will enable them and their readers to tell whether the particular use which they make of it has succeeded in serving the purpose for which it was made. Both for Piero di Cosimo's painting and for the storming of the Bastille, there are any number of answers which can be given both to the question 'what?' and to the question 'why?', and meanings may feature in both of them. There is no methodological impropriety in saying of the painting of Aeolus both that the meaning of the leather bags in the old man's hands is constitutive of what the painter was doing in painting him and that the meaning of lines 416–17 of Book VIII of Virgil's *Aeneid* is a – or, depending how the initial conditions are defined, the – cause of his doing so, any more than in saying both that the meaning of 'storm' is constitutive of what 'they' were doing in their manner of seeking to enter the Bastille and that the Bastille's meaning to the people of France as a symbol of monarchical oppression was a (or the) cause of their doing so. There is an impropriety only if the first is taken to substitute for the second: to 'explain' a piece of music in the sense of showing that it is a fugue is not to tell the reader either why Bach wrote it or why his predecessors didn't.

Whether, in context, plausible explanations in which meanings feature as causes are more strongly or weakly grounded than those in which they do not is not, therefore, a matter to be decided *a priori*. It is true that their plausibility often rests on the uncontroversial nature of the agents' presumptive motives. Where a connection is convincingly drawn between the content of a work of art and the fears or fantasies of the author's which it appears to express in symbolic form, the author's motives in composing it at all may be taken for granted, whereas the lack of agreement among historians of the French Revolution about what set it off is in part a lack of agreement about the causal relation between the political and economic conditions of the time on the one hand and the strength of the urge to violent protest against them on the other. But the difference is a function of the difference in the context in which the search for an explanation takes place. It is not a function of the difference in the nature of the subject-matter. It depends, as always, on how the causal field is defined, what are the antecedent conditions taken for granted, and what is the quasi-experimental contrast drawn. If, in the event, the explanation given appears not to need to be grounded directly in lawlike regularities but only in some other underlying explanation which is itself idiographic in form, this is not because there are separate 'scientific' and 'hermeneutic' modes of reasoning in sociological explanation. Explanations are more likely to be valid, and their grounding adequate, not because the explanandum is 'hard' but because (to switch to yet another favourite metaphor of philosophers of science) the quasi-experimental contrast is 'clean' and its own explanation at another level neither vacuous nor circular.

It could still be objected that in the absence – for the time being, at least – of a comprehensive and well-tested psychology, all explanations of explanations in the social sciences are merely speculative and provisional. Only when there is adequate knowledge of the human mind at the neuronal level will the behavioural repertoire of the species be fully explicable, and by that standard none of the theories yet framed by social scientists can be more than marginally better-grounded than the example which I took in Section 1 from Bacon's essay on envy. But the practising sociologist can quite well accept this without being disheartened by it. Darwin, after all, was broadly right about natural selection although wrong about genetics, and however important the discoveries which psychologists may make in the course of the next few hundred years sociologists do not need to wait for them before formulating explanations of human institutions and practices which can be shown to be valid for reasons which rival observers who dispute them can go out and test for themselves.

§ 11. More does still need to be said, however, about the relation between explanations and their grounding. A quasi-experimental hypothesis (I have argued) needs the support of a theory which it at the same time tests and extends, and it is the testability of the theory which distinguishes it from a presupposition. But how can the reader be sure that the theory really *is* being tested and that the initial hypothesis, if valid, is not valid for some other reason than the theory claims?

To answer this question, it is necessary to reintroduce from Section 6 the concept of a *model*. This is yet another term on which there is a large philosophical as well as technical literature and which is used by different authors in a wide variety of different senses. But just as a cause is, for practical purposes, best defined as whatever it is but for which the explanandum would not be as it is in whatever respect the researcher finds puzzling, and a theory is best defined as whatever it is which makes the cause a cause, so is a model best defined as whatever interpretation of the theory makes the initial, presumptively causal, hypothesis a test of it. If, in the language of one influential school in the philosophy of science, the untestable presuppositions are the 'hard core of the research programme' within which the initial hypothesis was framed and tested, then the theory is the so-called ' "refutable" protective belt'.* The reader who is presented with an explanation which is consistent with the reported evidence and a theoretical grounding claimed to underlie it must be told not only what sort of evidence might have invalidated the initial hypothesis but also what sort of evidence might show that the cause was not a cause for the reason claimed – in which case either the theory is the wrong one or the ' "refutable" protective belt' has indeed been refuted.

The examples chosen for discussion in the philosophical literature on refutability are generally drawn from areas of the natural sciences where there are lawlike regularities to hand. But the problems are the same whether the theory to be interpreted is idiographic or nomothetic in form. Where there is a dispute between rival schools over the grounding

---

* Imre Lakatos, 'Falsification and the Methodology of Scientific Research Programmes', in Lakatos and A. Musgrave, eds., *Criticism and the Growth of Knowledge* (1970), p. 135.

of a presumptively causal hypothesis which both sides accept as at least provisionally confirmed, it may arise from a difference in the interpretation of a theory accepted as adequate, or from a difference between rival theories which derive from a common presupposition or from a difference between rival presuppositions both of which generate a theory and an interpretation to go with it. If the initial causal hypothesis is symbolized as $h(c \rightarrow e)$, then these three possibilities can be represented diagrammatically as below:

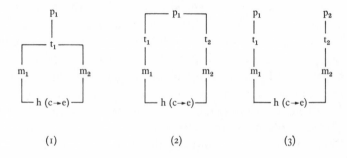

These diagrams are themselves, in one of the senses of the term, models of the theory of sociological explanation which this chapter seeks to expound. As such, their function is not to stipulate how particular explanations are to be set out and defended but only to illustrate where and how differences may arise between rival theoretical schools. Still less is it their function to impose a terminology. On the contrary: the relaxed definitions of 'cause', 'theory' and 'model' are intended to allow for the widest possible tolerance of differing usages. A 'model' like the 'learned deep structure model' in psycholinguistics may be used to function as an untestable presupposition; a 'law' like the 'rank-size law' in economic geography may be used to function as the model of a theory about the location of centres of manufacture and/or commerce; a 'theory' like the 'wage-pull theory of inflation' in neo-classical economics may function as a model interpreting a more general theory about the workings of a market economy. There is no point in trying to impose a restriction on any usage or any technique which will yield a stronger explanation of some aspect of human behaviour than its predecessors. But where even the strongest-looking explanations are still not grounded in lawlike regularities at a deeper level, it is important to be able to analyse the relation between a presumptively valid explanation and its presumptively adequate grounding in such a way as will make clear just how strictly tested the explanation has been.

Let me therefore illustrate the three alternatives set out in the diagrams by reference to the same long-standing example which I have used already – the fall of the Roman Empire in the West. The difficulty is not just that a hypothesis to the effect that the frontiers ceased to be defensible by the forces available to man them may not be genuinely explanatory: as we have seen, it can already be made so, at least to some degree, by pointing to the frequency of disputed successions to the imperial title. But this will not by itself satisfy rival observers of all theoretical schools. How (they will ask) can we be *sure* that this was enough to cause the Western armies to be so far weakened that the Western Empire should collapse in the second half of the fifth century when it seemed only a short time before to have re-established itself? Let me assume, for methodology's sake, that there is no dispute that the evidence reported to us supports the causal hypothesis that if substantially larger armies could have been deployed along the frontiers, the barbarians would not have been able to penetrate into Gaul, Spain and Italy. But until there is a theory in which the hypothesis can be grounded by way of a model which excludes rival theories, there must remain the risk that what passes for grounding is no more than the invocation of a proposition at another level sufficiently general to be consistent with a number of other hypotheses with which the reports accepted as accurate by all rival observers are consistent too.

Suppose, therefore, that the theory claimed to provide adequate grounding is a so-called 'theory of imperial involution' according to which expansionist military regimes are driven to continue their annexation of territory until the point at which the costs of maintaining control throughout the territory annexed outrun the capacities of the central government. This proposition is, as it is bound to be, underlain in its turn by an untestable presupposition – in this case, something to the effect that 'power abhors a vacuum'. But there is nothing which can be shown to be mistaken *a priori* about the explanation of the weakness of the Western Empire's frontiers by reference to a momentum of expansion which carried it to the point where it had not only twice as long a frontier to guard as the Eastern Empire did, but an army progressively weakened by internal dissensions with which to guard it. The problem is to show that, and how, the theory really *does* ground the chosen hypothesis. It can do so if, but only if, it can be interpreted to show what it was that made the expansion to the Western frontiers an overexpansion relative to the resources available; and this question will have to be answered in a way which is not merely consistent with the evidence but consistent to a degree that the most plausible alternative is not.

The example is one which might appear to have been chosen to show that 'clean' qualitative contrasts are the stuff of macro-sociological explanation, not statistical manipulations designed to isolate measurable proportions of observed variance. But there is, as it happens, a quantitative model ready to hand in the literature of political – or rather, 'geopolitical' – science.* Assume for methodology's sake that the resources in either cash or kind available to support the armies are directly proportional to the taxable agricultural surplus of each province, that this surplus increases with density of population and that recruits are available in sufficient numbers for the size of the armies to be increased as resources permit without the total surplus being reduced in consequence. If p_i is the population of province I and s is the taxable surplus per capita, then the total military capacity of the Empire is $\sum_i ksp_i$, k being a constant of proportionality related to the effectiveness of the current military technology. But the larger the number of provinces, the greater the length of frontier to defend, and the effectiveness of this capacity depends on the costs of transporting the necessary military resources to the points at which barbarian pressure has to be met. Assume further, therefore, that its effectiveness declines with the cost of each mile that has to be moved, and that the proportion of military resources consumed per mile moved is c. If all the resources available are to be concentrated at a given point of barbarian pressure, and if d_i is the distance from each province to that point, then the amount of military resources which can be concentrated by the imperial government at the point of pressure is given by the expression $\sum_i (1 - cd_i)ksp_i$. Unhappily for the Romans, the value of k is low since military capacity depends on the continued maintenance of the largest possible number of men and horses whose average cost is constant, whereas c is high relative to nomadic opponents who are able to strike at will anywhere along the frontier; and if the expression $\sum_i (1 - cd_i)ksp_i$ is mapped onto the territory of the Western Empire, then it will be clear at once from the distribution of the taxable surplus in the various provinces and their distance from the points of barbarian pressure that the vulnerability of the frontier was such that it was only a matter of time before there would be a barbarian incursion which Rome would be unable to resist.

In the actual case, this way of putting it, plausible within limits as it is, does not constitute any more precisely testable an interpretation of the

* See Arthur L. Stinchcombe, *Constructing Social Theories* (1968), Ch. 5, Section 5.

theory than could be arrived at in less ostensibly rigorous language. This model merely claims, in effect, that the vulnerability of the frontiers was a function of the costs of maintaining and transporting sufficient legions to wherever they might be needed. But the methodological moral is the same. The model's claim needs to be tested against the obvious rival interpretation of the same theory according to which it was precisely the costs per soldier – or rather, per *reliable* soldier – which were too high because the taxable capacity of the empire was too low. It is not in dispute, on this view, that if the appropriate measurements could be made and numerical values assigned to the constants k and c the geopolitical model would support the claim that the Western frontiers would be difficult to defend when under pressure from barbarian tribes themselves under pressure from the East. But why should the reason for the costs of its defence to outrun the capacity of the central government not lie in the government's inability to raise the revenue to cover those costs, rather than in its inability to translate its revenues into a sufficient defensive capability at the points of pressure? And until that question has been answered, how can it be claimed that the initial hypothesis that the collapse was a military one be claimed to have adequate grounding in the mere invocation of the concept of 'imperial involution'? There is a rival model with much evidence to support it according to which, once given the dependence of the Roman economy on a technologically static agriculture, the combined effects of monetary inflation, decline in productive manpower and superexploitative tax-farming made it impossible to continue to maintain an army of the size to which Diocletian enlarged it. This is still an explanation grounded in the same underlying theoretical concept. But the theory is now being given an economic rather than a military interpretation.

It may well turn out in practice that the most plausible interpretation of the theory is a model in which the relative influence of both military and economic variables can be estimated and their interaction quasi-experimentally manipulated. But to say this is still only to reaffirm the methodological point that *a* model is necessary to relate the hypothesis singled out to the underlying reason for which it is held to be valid; and not even this is enough by itself. For the problem which remains is that even if there is a plausibly-grounded hypothesis which has convincingly defeated its immediate competitors, the researcher of a rival school is still free to dispute the theory of imperial involution itself. He may not dissent from the presupposition that power abhors a vacuum. But he may hold that the reason for which the hypothesis of military weakness at the frontiers holds good is simply that the quality of both government and generalship had declined, and that this, coupled with the unfortunate lack of a stable dynasty, is sufficient to account for Rome's inability to deal with invaders whose actual numbers were never as large as contemporaries liked to pretend and whose defeat would have been child's play to the legions which defeated Hannibal. On this view, the theory of imperial involution is invalidated by the simple observation that the Western frontiers *were* defensible – an observation supported by the incontrovertible evidence of the success of the Roman armies when well led. A 'bad generalship' theory does not imply a presupposition that Rome was impregnable or that its empire could last for ever. But it does imply a testable contrast with the Eastern Empire, which did survive and whose rulers did display a degree of military and diplomatic skill which their Western counterparts visibly lacked. Diocletian's reforms, after all, were very successful, and they were successful precisely because he recognized and responded to both the military and the economic burdens which a defence of the imperial frontiers required. By sending his Caesar Galerius on a second invasion of Persia in 298, this time with adequate reinforcements from the Danubian legions, did he not secure a more defensible frontier as well as a thirty-year peace? By developing an effective system of taxation in kind, did he not make it possible for a much enlarged army to be given the necessary logistic support on the basis, for the first time, of an annual budget? By his creation of a tetrarchy, although he failed to solve the problem of a peaceful succession, did he not succeed in remaining securely in power until he chose to abdicate and in defeating the two rebellions mounted against him? By refortifying a perimeter whose reduction in the Rhine/Danube area and also in Africa he did not seek to reverse, did he not make possible a system of flexible defence whereby barbarian incursions could be contained by the frontier troops until such time as the mobile reserves could be deployed against them? Even the most plausible model linking economic-cum-military weaknesses to the final irruption of invaders who could be neither placated by tribute nor expelled by force of arms is, therefore, inconclusive in the face of an alternative theory whereby given the initial conditions the Western Empire was as defensible in 400 as 300 if the emperor and his generals were up to the task.

Yet now suppose that the evidence is such that all rival observers are, after all, satisfied that the theory of 'imperial involution' modelled in terms of a cumulative interaction between economic and political variables is demonstrably superior to the 'bad generalship' theory. It still cannot be claimed that the theory of imperial involution has been conclusively vindicated. For the adherents of a rival school can still argue that the presupposition underlying the theory has simply ruled out of court what they regard as the right one – a theory deriving from the presupposition of economic determinism whereby the eventual indefensibility of the Western frontier was not due to a lack of either military or fiscal resources as such, and still less to a lack of the necessary personal qualities in its generals and emperors, but to its dependence on slavery. A model of this theory can be elaborated which not only connects the initial cycle of conquest in the West to the use of slave labour but attributes its decline to an eventual shortage of supply which could not be met by domestic breeding or purchase across the frontiers; and the model is testable by its own quasi-experimental contrast with the Eastern Empire, whose peasant smallholders and prosperous municipalities gave it not only a higher agricultural productivity but a more amenable political structure. On this view, the initial hypothesis is still incontrovertible: the Western Empire fell because even an army of half a million men was not enough to hold the frontier against the by then increased barbarian pressure. It did not fall because of plague, homosexuality, moral decline or the conversion of the emperors to Christianity, all of which have been hypothesized at one time or another. But the explanation of the explanation on which the test of its validity depends now invokes a further series of related comparisons which can be fitted into a model deriving from the theory of imperial involution only if the implications of that theory are so radically revised as to reverse the emphasis on purely military and logistic variables which gave it its earlier point.

At this stage of the argument, therefore, we have arrived at a disagreement between observers of rival schools of the third kind; and the only hope of resolving it will be to find some yet other quasi-experimental contrast by which the influence of slavery can be put to the test. The contrast between the Western and Eastern Empires is not enough by itself, since it may very well be that the Eastern Empire's shorter frontiers, stronger logistic base and more loyal and skilful administrators and diplomats are already more than sufficient explanation by themselves. What is needed is a report of the fate of some other overexpanded empire at a similar technological level which also succumbed to barbarian pressure on its frontiers but whose workforce was only negligibly servile. It is a fortunate accident of history, therefore, that there is one to hand in the instance of the later Han Empire in China, of whose agricultural population only a few per cent, at most, were slaves but which progressively succumbed to barbarian pressure from the North, culminating in the sack of Lo-Yang in 311, after which the central government fled

South, and North China, like the Western Roman Empire, was completely overrun. Striking as the parallels are between the two, including
both a mounting dependence on federated barbarian auxiliaries and an
increasing pressure on the peasantry to accept a form of dependent
tenancy in return for the protection of powerful semi-autonomous landlords, they are of course far from furnishing a strictly controlled comparison. But this is the level at which arguments between rival schools
require to be conducted when, as so often in sociology, anthropology and
history, there is room for dispute over models, theories and presuppositions alike.

Sceptical readers may, perhaps, wish to point the moral not merely
that the three separate levels need to be distinguished but that in the
particular example which I have chosen the conditions which need to be
met before rival schools will come to agree are insurmountably difficult.
Do I really believe that there will ever be an explanation of the fall of
the Roman Empire in the West as uncontroversial as the now accepted
explanation of the formation of the Carmarthenshire plateaux? But this
question, whatever the proper answer to it, is irrelevant to the methodological issue. If some things, both human and natural, are too inaccessible to quasi-experimental contrast over a sufficient range for rival
explanatory theories to be tested conclusively against each other, that
does not alter the conditions which any proffered explanation has still
to meet if it *is* to succeed.

VARIETIES OF CAUSES

§ 12. Within this framework, moreover, it becomes possible to construe
and assess claims to have established 'the' explanation of a chosen event,
process or state of affairs in such a way as to make clear where exactly
it is that the differences arise between rival schools. There will be no
disagreement that such claims have always to be taken in their context:
even where the hypothesis put forward can be subjected to direct, and
not quasi-, experimental test, the antecedent condition isolated as the
experimental variable is 'the' cause of the explanandum only in a sense
defined by a chosen set of initial conditions and constraints. What is
more, even if it is correct to say that all of the multifarious forms and
kinds of sociological explanation can be accommodated within a common
mode of reasoning, they are far from conforming directly to the
procedure implied by my analysis of it. It is not just that reportage and
explanation do not proceed independently of each other and that practising sociologists, anthropologists and historians seldom, if ever, complete

the assemblage of the reports which they hold to be relevant to their chosen topic before setting out to frame the explanations appropriate to them. They may even reverse the sequence altogether, and only assemble their reports when they have chosen a presumptive cause of which they then seek some observed effects: a historian may decide to specialize in the study of the influence of syphilis, the potato, Manichaeism or the stern-post rudder, just as a physiologist may decide to specialize in the study of pathogens. Or they may start by tracing the presumptively causal interconnections between different institutions and practices within the same society in such a way as to show what changes in one or another of them will tend to maintain or disrupt its equilibrium. Or they may frame a model, whether mathematical or not, of a chosen process such as the diffusion of agriculture or the redistribution of income and look for patterns of reported observations which can be fitted to it. Yet whatever the technique by which the constituent parts of an explanation are pieced together, the test of any claim that it is 'the' explanation can only lie in the answer to the question what difference it would make if it were to be shown to be invalid. Would it compel its proponents to abandon their presuppositions, their theories, their models, their hypotheses, or all of them?

Given not only the variety of forms which sociological explanations can take but the imprecision with which they are often set out, this question is not always as easy to answer as it should be from the standpoint of methodology alone. But there is sometimes a clue to be found in the metaphors in which researchers present 'the' explanation to their readers as decisive. Thus, a 'trigger' or 'catalyst' is likely to be 'the' proximate cause which, given the initial conditions, brings the explanandum immediately about. But talk of 'links' or 'networks' is more suggestive of an interpretation whereby the chosen set of interrelated conditions singled out can be shown to be 'the' decisive model of an accepted theory. Where, by contrast, it is the theory itself whose invocation is claimed to furnish 'the' explanation required, the metaphors used are typically those cognate to the notion of 'grounding': the explanation whose rationale the chosen theory provides will be claimed as 'basic' or 'fundamental', with the tacit (or sometimes overt) implication that those of the rival school are superficial if not downright invalid. Finally, where the difference is at the level of the presuppositions behind the theory, the argument between rival schools is likely to be couched in metaphors which distinguish kinds of explanation as such: terms like 'global' or 'piecemeal' or 'structural' or 'materialist' or even, sometimes, 'sociological' itself typically signal claims for the superiority not of one theory over another so much as one presupposition which, although untestable in itself, is presumed to generate theories which can be so interpreted as to provide more convincing and economical explanations of a wider range of explananda to which causes, constraints and initial conditions have been assigned. The methodological problem, in these contexts, is neither to devise the technical means by which quasi-experimental controls can best be simulated nor to vindicate a philosophical criterion of validation. Differences over these may, it is true, further compound the differences between rival schools. But where the argument is over whether 'the' decisive antecedent condition is, as it might be, demographic pressure rather than class conflict, or diffusion of technology rather than autonomous economic development, or geographical and climatic constraints rather than ideological conservatism, or a strategic extension of vulnerable frontiers rather than a commercially-inspired expansion in pursuit of new markets, the methodologist's task is simply to prevent the disputants from continuing to talk past each other in defiance of any evidence whatever which either has been or might be put before them.

Daunting as it may be, this task is helped by the recognition that the mode of reasoning appropriate to sociological explanation generally is quasi-experimental, since it follows that rival explanations can all be assessed and compared for the purpose by reference to the methods of similarity and difference classically expounded by J. S. Mill in Book VI of his *System of Logic*. If, in Mill's terms, an explanation is to carry overwhelming conviction against the preferred alternatives of theorists of any and all rival schools, it will have to have the support of both: 'the' decisive antecedent condition will need not merely, as the 'Method of Difference' requires, to be seen to cause the explanandum in the experimental or quasi-experimental case but also, as the 'Method of Agreement' requires, to be seen to be capable of causing it even when the initial conditions are varied. The complexity of human history being what it is, the controlled comparisons necessary for the purpose are seldom if ever available. But this does not mean that without them the theorists of rival schools have no choice but to persist in talking past each other in accordance with the untestable presuppositions to which they are committed in advance. In the first place, once it is clear what further comparisons *would* satisfy Mill's requirements, the difference between them can be assigned to the proper level as between presupposition, theory, model and hypothesis. In the second place, once this has been done it can be seen to what extent the rival theorists are in irreconcilable disagreement and to what extent their separate categorization of antecedents as causes, constraints or initial conditions can after all be construed as different but compatible models of a more general but still testable common theory.

We are still, no doubt, as far as ever from 'the' explanation of the Fall of the Roman Empire in the West on which theorists of rival schools can all be brought to agree. But it remains worth asking how many of the differences between them are not simply a function of ignorance. Once a range of initial conditions and constraints is accepted as given, contrasts can be defined in terms of an identified subset of conditions antecedent to a subsequent event, process or state of affairs on whose reportage rival observers are not in dispute; and the claim that any one condition or constraint, or subset of them, is of such importance as to constitute 'the' cause can then be construed in relation to that part of the whole long story of the decline and fall of the Western Empire against which it has been agreed in advance to test it. Its 'decisiveness' is a matter both of how *much* difference would have been made to the subsequent events, processes or states of affairs if it had *not* occurred or been the case and of how *little* difference would have been made if it *had* occurred even under different initial conditions. Rival theories can be tested against each other in this way without the disputants having either to agree on whether Mill's logic furnishes an adequate philosophy of social science in general or to share a common technical assessment of the capacity of the sources to be so exploited as to yield quasi-experimental comparisons across a wider range.

What is more, disputes between rival schools over 'the' explanation of an event, process or state of affairs which both sides agree to have been accurately reported are sometimes capable of resolution by simple appeal to the accuracy of the reportage of the antecedent condition invoked. Thus, a mediaevalist for whom 'the' explanation of the origins of manorialism in England is to be sought in the conjunction of a Teutonic social order which included servile or dependent cultivators with the presence of large estates deriving from the *villae* of the Roman occupation may find his explanation disputed on the simple ground that there weren't any large estates still recognizable as such by the time of the Anglo-Saxon invasions.* There need be no disagreement over the plausibility of a model linking the creation of large estates to the creation of a class of unfree cultivators to work them. But it is obvious that an explanation which takes non-existent estates as an initial condition has no more hope of being valid, however adequately it may appear to be grounded, than an explanation of the explosion of a powder-keg by

---

* Cf. H. R. Loyn, *Anglo-Saxon England and the Norman Conquest* (1962), p. 16.

reference to the lighted match applied to it if it turns out that there wasn't any powder in the keg. Only, therefore, when the adherents of the rival schools can both check the continued presence of large estates against the recording angel's archives – or a sufficiently detailed archaeological record for both to accept it as a substitute – can the cause which one side regards as decisive be accepted as a serious explanans at all. Yet this does not alter the relation between the different levels at which rival claims to decisiveness may arise. Nor is the position of the mediaevalist any different, from the methodological point of view, from that of the palaeontologist groping among the tide-pools of the pre-Cambrian era for evidence in the fossil record which will tell him whether his hypothesis about 'the' decisive step in the evolution of more complex organisms stands any chance of being confirmed as valid.

Nor are the methodological issues any different when the dispute is between applied sociologists seeking alternative remedies for an immediately topical problem of social policy. Consider, for example, how intractable are the divisions between rival schools over 'the' cause of what all of them agree to be the 'decline' of the inner areas of the industrial cities of Britain (and not Britain alone) in the third quarter of the twentieth century. These divisions are compounded on the one hand by a complexity of interacting variables not susceptible by any available technique to quasi-experimental manipulation and on the other hand by an urgency of practical concern. But the logic of explanation is no different for the decline of Liverpool or Manchester after the Second World War than for the decline of Rome after the reign of Diocletian. There is no disagreement about the reported loss of housing, fall in available manufacturing and distributive jobs, increasingly polarized occupational composition of the remaining residents, and persistence of pockets of multiple economic and social deprivation as measured by a variety of accepted indicators. But for one school, 'the' explanation lies in the effect of self-defeating government intervention in the mechanisms of the market; for another it lies, on the contrary, in the workings of the market which government intervention is powerless to deflect; while for yet a third, it is seen as part of an inevitable long-term change in residential and occupational patterns which would not be significantly affected if the extent of government intervention was either greater or less. No conclusive test is possible, and the topic is one which rouses sufficiently strong feelings for the choice of answers to be contingently influenced by value-judgements in many or even all of the ways which I listed in Section 2 of Chapter 1.

But if the adherents of the rival schools are indeed proffering rival explanations, they are proffering explanations which can be not only differentiated from each other in accordance with the same distinction between hypothesis, model, theory and presupposition, but compared by reference to Mill's same methods of similarity and difference. If the dispute is at the level of one (or more) initial causal hypotheses, then it must be possible for their proponents to specify what difference has been made by 'the' government policy or decision (or lack of one). If it is at the level of a model of the process of decline which links one or more of the reported symptoms of it to a presumptive grounding, it must be possible to specify what it is that it makes this process rather than another 'the' link between government intervention, or the lack of it, and the acceleration of decline. If it is at the level of rival theories of the general influence exercised by government on the workings of the house and job markets, it must be possible to specify why the conflicting or complementary motives and goals of agents in government on the one hand and in the market-place on the other are bound to generate a process which defeats the government's ostensible objective. And if, finally, it is at the level of rival presuppositions about the inevitability of a 'structural crisis' of late capitalism on the one hand or the outcome of the workings of an 'invisible hand' on the other, it must at least be possible to specify what evidence, if any, would have to be forthcoming to make the dispute amenable even in principle to quasi-experimental resolution at the theoretical level. It is quite possible that the disputants themselves will not conceive of their differences in terms of this distinction of levels and will protest that it is a methodological construction imposed on them from outside. So it is. But the justification for its imposition is that only by drawing these distinctions can any one recital of antecedent causes, conditions and constraints which the reader is being asked to accept as 'the' explanation be distinguished not only from reportage, description and evaluation but from its explanatory rivals.

§13. 'But what if a chosen explanandum, whatever its form, has *no* cause? Are there not many events, processes and states of affairs in the social as well as the natural world whose secondary understanding depends on a recognition that they are not merely unpredictable but fortuitous?'

These questions bring us once again to the brink of topics about which philosophers are by no means in agreement. But however intractable may be the controversies surrounding the concepts of probability and randomness, the practising sociologist, anthropologist or historian can safely disregard the suggestion that any behaviour which he has observed, or has been reported to him, is beyond the reach of causal explanation altogether. This is not merely because the suggestion undermines the point of his engaging in research at all; it is also because there is no convincing, let alone conclusive, argument for the claim that there is anywhere in the world an event, process or state of affairs such that its occurrence as observed or reported does not depend on any antecedent condition at all holding true. The concept of 'chance' occurrence should therefore be treated, like the concept of 'law', as relative, not absolute. That it has a role in the explanation of human behaviour no practising sociologist, anthropologist or historian is likely to deny. But its importance to the construction of a substantive social theory is not that it renders the reports on which it rests inexplicable. It is that it opens the possibility that they should not be so much explained as explained away.

When *The Times*, on the morning of October 10, 1940, told its readers that 'no more unlikely pattern of events could have been predicted' than that which brought Winston Churchill to the leadership of the Conservative party, it was not suggesting to its readers that the normal sequence of causes and effects in human affairs had been interrupted by an Act of God. 'Acts of God', in sociology as in commercial contracts, are merely events proceeding in a sequence of cause and effect independent of the sequence which has otherwise been provided for. The interaction of the two is taken to be so improbable that if it does happen – which it always may – and thereby modifies the outcome which would otherwise have been observed, the explanation forced on the researcher is to that extent of a special kind. If it is true that Harold would have won the Battle of Hastings if he had not been hit by an arrow in the eye, then that highly improbable event has to be introduced into the history of England as an accident by which everything subsequent to the battle was changed. This improbability too is a relative matter, since it can hardly be claimed that the two causal sequences were *wholly* independent: it was, as the saying goes, 'no accident' that the Norman archer who fired the fatal shot was where he was at the time and shooting, however absent-mindedly, in the direction of the Saxon host. But no participant or observer would ever have hypothesized before it happened that it was on this one shot that the whole future course of English history was to depend. Only if, say, later research were to reveal that it was a part of William's plan of battle that his archers should aim all their shots in the direction of Harold's unprotected eyes would it become inappropriate to speak of it as 'accidental'.

It is, therefore, both legitimate and apposite for the practising sociologist, anthropologist or historian who narrates an episode of this kind to make use of such phrases as 'quite by chance', 'it just so happened ...', 'by a curious mishap ...', 'fortuitously ...', 'as if from nowhere ...', 'but for the random intervention of ...' or 'more by accident than design ...'. But this does not force the methodologist of social theory to admit an exception to the standard mode of reasoning in the explanation of human behaviour. It merely forces him to recognize the possibility of intrusions into the causal field by unexpected explanantia exogenous to the set of variables by reference to which the initial conditions and constraints and the contrast class would otherwise have been specified. It may imply, to that extent, a belittlement of the elaborate apparatus of hypothesis, model, theory and presupposition. But if it is indeed the case that a bow drawn at a venture makes a difference to the subsequent course of the events for which an explanation is being sought, then the alternative hypotheses will have to be modified or discarded accordingly. There is, indeed, a sub-set of cases where the idea of chance enters in, so to speak, twice over, for it is always possible that an agent whose behaviour is decisive to the explanation sought may deliberately have introduced a random event into the sequence of which his actions are a part. The general who decides his strategy by haruspication, or *sors biblica*, or the toss of a coin is making into a matter of chance something which would otherwise not have been. But he is not making it from something caused into something uncaused but into something caused differently. The hypotheses which the military historians of the future might otherwise have framed in terms of tactics or logistical support and which might have enabled them to test or extend their rival theories about 'the' determinants of victory or defeat cannot now be brought to bear – or not directly. But the outcome of the battle may now be more, not less, easily understandable in the secondary sense. Indeed, it may even turn out to lend indirect support to one or other rival theory by displaying the folly of the 'chance' decision given initial conditions and constraints which would otherwise have ensured the opposite outcome.

The methodological issue is the same where a 'chance' conjunction generates a causal-looking pattern which then turns out to be spurious. Most sociologists reading this will have had dinned into them at some stage of their training the maxim that correlation is no proof of causation and will be well aware that even where the joint variation in the values of two independent variables is shown by a chi-square test to be statistically significant at a level of $p \leqslant 0.001$ there will in principle be one case in a thousand where the inference that the relation between them is in some way causal will be mistaken nonetheless. But this is no more an argument for saying that the behaviour under study is uncaused than the fact that a Norman archer happened to fire an arrow which happened to hit Harold in the eye is an argument for saying that the outcome of the Battle of Hastings was uncaused. It is only an argument for saying that causes may be other than they seem. Likewise, when a sociologist who inclines to the view that social mobility in the society which he is studying can be fitted to a matrix of transition probabilities generated by a random number table finds that the movements of children relative to their parents over successive generations between, say, three alternative states, or 'classes', fits it as exactly as he could wish, he is thereby entitled to offer 'the' explanation of the process by reference to the Markovian properties of his matrix. But his hypothesis, no less than those which it displaces, has to be defended by reference to a theory which will tell his readers why the reported pattern of social mobility *does* fit the matrix. The distribution of the population may be shown to approximate to a steady state whose equilibrial values he has computed. But he will not argue from this that the movements of the individual children of differently-placed parents between his three classes are unmotivated. He will argue that however strong their motivations, there are constraints acting on the system as a whole which channel their movements between one class and another in the direction of a steady state.*

The one other sense in which it is sometimes claimed that human behaviour is inexplicable because uncaused is that in which the operation of the distinctively human faculty of decision is regarded as immune from any lawlike relation of cause and effect. On this view, it is argued that behaviour which results (however 'results' is to be construed) from an act (if it is an 'act') of decision would not necessarily be repeated even if all the initial conditions were to be repeated on some other occasion; to say of someone that he decided to do something is to say that he could have decided to do something else, and to say that the initial conditions were such that he could not help deciding as he did is a contradiction in terms. But arguments of this kind, which lead all too easily into old debates about the freedom of the will which have never been resolved to the satisfaction of rival philosophical schools, should be sidestepped by the practising sociologist, anthropologist or historian with all possible speed. He may have to concede, if pressed, that his own presupposition that decisions *are* explicable and not merely justifiable is not susceptible of conclusive demonstration either. But he is not therefore required to agree that the quest for causes of decisions, and therewith their outcome

* For an illuminating example of this kind, see Raymond Boudon, *Education, Opportunity and Social Mobility* (Eng. trans., 1974).

in observed behaviour, is fruitless. Even where the agent whom he is studying says, as might the general who chose his strategy by the toss of a coin, 'Nothing made me decide to do it – I just did', this does not require him to treat it as uncaused. Nothing prevents him from asking what contingently sufficient condition, or set of them, brought about the decision and its outcome and why it should have done so; and however difficult it may sometimes be to find out, there are any number of instances in which sociologists, anthropologists and historians advance hypotheses to this effect which stand up to attempted invalidation perfectly well.

§ 14. Mention of *decision* does, however, take us the penultimate step to the last of the four questions to which this chapter is addressed, for even those practising sociologists most resistant to the suggestion that there is any difference of kind between the sciences of man and of nature are bound to concede that explanations which invoke self-conscious plans and stratagems are appealing to presumptive causes of a kind unique to human behaviour. It follows from the demarcation of the boundary between reportage and explanation that those aspects of self-consciousness which are constitutive of action cannot be candidates for the causal explanation of it even under the most relaxed interpretation of 'cause'. But there remains the question whether those that *can* be candidates have to be construed as causal in some special sense which might modify my denial that the sciences of man are confronted with any special methodological, as opposed to technical, problem of explanation.

It is a difficult question to answer conclusively, not merely because it is a matter of philosophical controversy but because of the lack of knowledge about the workings of the human mind – or brain – which might show to what extent it is a matter for philosophy rather than science. But if my argument thus far is sound, I have only to show first, that the distinctive aspects of human behaviour which are bound up with decision can be consistently accommodated within the methodology which I have put forward, and second, that practising sociologists, anthropologists or historians need not thereafter be concerned with the unresolved controversies either among or between either philosophers or psychologists of rival schools. One of the purely methodological issues which the topic raises is the logic of teleological explanation, since it can hardly be denied that the explanations in terms of plans and stratagems involve reference to the future in a way that standard causal explanations *a tergo* do not. But before the distinctive features of teleological explanation, whether purposive or functional, can be analysed, there has first to be settled the question whether plans and stratagems can indeed be construed as causes.

It is a common, even everyday, experience of practising sociologists, anthropologists and historians when at a loss for an explanation of an observed or reported event, process or state of affairs to feel that the agents in question must have had, so to speak, 'something in mind' which if ascertained would make their behaviour more readily understandable in both the secondary and, probably, the tertiary sense. There need be nothing problematic about the reports of the behaviour which constitutes the explanandum: their accuracy is accepted by all rival observers, and there is no difficulty in the primary understanding of what the agents did. But the puzzle is to answer the question: 'what on earth made him/her/ them do it?'. The answer will not always be in terms of plans, stratagems or even choices of any kind. If the army turned and fled despite its overwhelming superiority in numbers, it may turn out that it was because and only because of the panic caused by wounded elephants turning on their own supporting infantry; or if the garrison commander turned down an advantageous offer of a truce and the inhabitants were therefore starved into submission, it may turn out that it was because and only because of a sudden fit of rage which, given his exhausted state, made him insult the besieger's envoy. But often it is not an impulse but a process of reasoning or, as it is sometimes called, a 'decision-scheme' which furnishes the explanation. Both eyewitnesses and later historians were for long at a loss to explain the order to the Mediterranean Fleet signalled by the experienced and capable Admiral Tryon on June 22, 1893, which resulted in a disastrous collision between his own battleship and that of his second-in-command.* As it turns out, he had not taken leave of his senses, but had devised a testing manoeuvre which his subordinates misunderstood and were too much in awe of him to make clear that they had misunderstood: what he had in mind was that his order to the two parallel columns of the fleet to reverse course by turning inwards a mere six cables apart be taken in conjunction with a Queen's Regulation then in force enjoining that in these circumstances the normal rule of the road should be overridden – in which case his second-in-command would have given way and no collision have occurred. The hypothesis that this was what Tryon had in mind fits all the reported facts, and the collision is no longer baffling. What, therefore, is the objection to treating it as a causal hypothesis like any other which, in its

---

* The example is taken from John Watkins, 'Imperfect Rationality', in Robert Borger and Frank Cioffi, eds., *Explanation in the Behavioural Sciences* (1970).

context, furnishes 'the' explanation – an explanation, moreover, as securely grounded in the traditions of the British navy and the content of the Queen's Regulations as the explanation of Piero di Cosimo's decision to include Aeolus in his picture of Vulcan in the traditions of Renaissance mythography and the content of Virgil's *Aeneid*? It is irrelevant, although correct, to point out that Admiral Tryon's behaviour is *excused* by the hypothesis put forward, even if that was the purpose of Sir William Laird Clowes, its original proponent. An argument that his behaviour is not at the same time *explained* can only rest on one of two grounds: either that plans, stratagems or 'decision-schemes' like the one hypothesized here are constitutive rather than causal of the behaviour issuing from them, or that, although independent, they are correlated with but not causal of the behaviour.

The argument that plans have to be treated, like intentions, as constitutive of actions rests on the alleged dilemma that to plan something is either merely to envisage it (in which case it will only occur if something else happens as well) or else to be determined to do it unless prevented (in which case the determination cannot be its cause). The proper question to ask, on this view, is not 'what decision-scheme was the cause of Admiral Tryon's giving the order?' but 'what caused Admiral Tryon to decide to give the order that he had planned to give and therefore gave?'. Now there is a large philosophical literature on this topic, which has shown if nothing else how many pitfalls await those who rely too unthinkingly on the ostensible implications of ordinary speech. But for the practising sociologist, all that matters is whether his hypothesis, if framed as he chooses to frame it, is thereby rendered either vacuous or incapable of validation. Suppose he concedes that plans and stratagems should be assimilated to intentions proper to the extent that Admiral Tryon's decision-scheme should not, therefore, be spoken of as having made him give, or been the cause of his giving, the order which he gave. What follows? The explanation remains the same one as before and its validity as incontestable. The only difference is that it has now to be rephrased in such a way that what causes Admiral Tryon to plan to give his order (and therefore give it) is not the plan as such but his prior determination to put his subordinates to this particular test: given the initial conditions that the fleet had somehow to reverse course if it was not to run aground on the shallows off Tripoli and that Tryon was more familiar than his subordinates with the Queen's Regulation which lays down that if two ships under steam are crossing so as to involve risk of collision the ship which has the other on her starboard side shall keep out of the way of the other, he *implemented* his plan to put his subordinates to the test *by means of* an order to the two divisions of the fleet to turn inward in succession. But this is a difference in the way the explanation is phrased which can safely be treated as innocuously verbal. No doubt the language which I have used is far from precise and raises a number of further possible objections which might be debated by philosophers in their turn. But these should not be allowed to divert the methodologist from his claim that we do have an overwhelmingly convincing hypothesis whereby to explain Tryon's behaviour. Provided that the language in which it is couched preserves the minimally necessary distinction between the motives and dispositions which are constitutive of the agent's anterior state on the one hand and the intentions and beliefs which are constitutive of his subsequent behaviour on the other, the remaining imprecisions in the definition and use of these terms can be left unresolved without impairing the explanation's validity.

This still leaves to be considered the alternative possibility that the aspect of the agent's prior state hypothesized as the cause of his subsequent behaviour is no more than spuriously correlated with it. But that raises no special problem in the logic of explanation: it has simply to be tested so far as the available evidence and techniques for analysing it permit. It is difficult to construct a plausible supposition of this kind for the case of Admiral Tryon. But there are many standard cases of over-determination where a contingently sufficient condition is overtaken, as it were, by events, as when the chosen victim's inevitable death from the assassin's bullet is anticipated by a heart attack or the impending surrender of the Tartar garrison is overtaken by the use of mines and artillery against the fortifications of Kazan; and there are likewise standard cases where it is something in the mind of one of the agents whose behaviour is under study which renders an otherwise convincing causal hypothesis invalid. For example: the explanation of a particular marriage observed in a male-dominated bourgeois society in which there is free choice of partners might be offered in which it is claimed that John was 'trapped into it' by Jane. This is another hypothesis which cites a plan or stratagem as the decisive antecedent condition but for which Jane would not have behaved as she did and John reacted to that behaviour by an eventual proposal of marriage, and there may be even less doubt about what was in Jane's mind than about what was in Admiral Tryon's. But now suppose, for methodology's sake, that subsequent research discloses that John in fact wanted to marry Jane, but only for her money; his stratagem, accordingly, was to disguise his interest in her money and encourage, by studied indifference, her interest in his person, and although it is true that she was doing her best to trap him into marriage, she only succeeded – or appeared to succeed – because of *his* success in trapping *her*. The initial hypothesis therefore fails, not because Jane's stratagem was not a proper candidate for causal status but because the correlation between her avowed stratagem and John's proposal of marriage turns out to have been spurious in this particular case. In this, however, there is no difference from similarly plausible but deceptive correlations in the sciences of nature. The example shows not that plans, stratagems or decision-schemes cannot be causes of behaviour which the observer had initially found puzzling, but that even where one of them seems so plausibly connected with its outcome as to support the argument that the two are insufficiently independent to stand in a relation of cause to effect, it may in fact be so far independent as to have no explanatory function to perform at all.

It is not in dispute that plans, stratagems and decision-schemes, like ideas generally, are an odd kind of cause to which nothing corresponds in the sciences of nature. But this is an objection to the claim that the logic of explanation is the same only if their oddity debars them from performing the same explanatory role within the framework of hypothesis, model, theory and presupposition; and it will only do so if they are ruled out of court by a pre-emptive definition of 'cause'. For what is odd about them? They are not assimilable to the purposes (or if you insist 'purposes') programmed into electronic homing devices or mechanical tortoises like the so-called *Machina speculatrix* for the incontestable reason that they are differentiated by self-consciousness, and however much dispute there may be between rival schools about the nature of that difference, the fact of it is no more denied by programmers than by poets.* But it does not follow from it that Admiral Tryon's order has been 'explained' in some quite different sense from that in which a sudden movement in a *Machina speculatrix* in an unexpected direction is explained by the connections between photo-cell, amplifier and motors, which have been so designed as to cause it to check its exploratory behaviour on detecting a light of moderate intensity and move instead towards the light. In both cases, knowledge of the initial conditions, including the repertory and dispositions of the person, organism or machine, together with the invocation of one or more presumptive generalizations linking stimulus to response, are enough to yield a validated hypothesis. The hypothesis may be said to be more firmly grounded in the case of *Machina speculatrix* than the case of Admiral

---

* Erich Fried: 'A dog that dies, And knows that it dies, And knows that it knows that it dies, Is a man.'

Tryon because the theory which furnishes the grounding is stronger. But that is to say no more than that we know more about control engineering than we do about human psychology. As we have seen already, weak but adequate grounding is as much as we can, for the time being, aspire to in the sciences of man except in a very few restricted areas of behaviour. But adequacy is, so to speak, enough. The lack of better carries no implications of an inexplicability in principle of puzzling decisions and their outcome. A rival observer, or reader, who still wants to be awkward can voice an unsatisfied curiosity about the undisclosed mysteries of circuitry or the history of research into scanning mechanisms no less than into the undisclosed mysteries of the British naval tradition and the history of Admiral Tryon's upbringing and training.

These considerations apply with equal force in grand macro-sociological contexts and in individual decisions at the parochial level, and they apply in the same way when the hypothesized cause is not a plan, stratagem or decision-scheme but an opinion, prejudice or belief. The question 'why did they do what they did?' can properly be answered by hypothesizing a causal connection to any of these provided that their logical independence is clear. The fact that they can feature in the reportage of behaviour as constituent of it does not entail that they cannot feature in its explanation. The easiest practical test is simply to ask what difference, if any, is made to the reported explanandum if the anterior plan, stratagem, decision-scheme, opinion, prejudice or belief is removed. Without the priest's belief in God he cannot be 'really' praying to Him; from which it must follow that his mouthing the words of the prayer is not to be understood as caused by his belief. But when Firth, after many years' study of Tikopia society, asks himself why Tikopia chiefs should remain *tapu* to their people after the suppression of the traditional belief that after death their spirits were assimilated to the gods, he is searching for a causal hypothesis with which to replace his previous one; whatever the right answer may turn out to be, his observations, if accurately reported, compel the inference that either (i) the traditional belief did at one time cause the chiefs to be treated as *tapu* but their continuing to be so treated has to be explained by reference to other causes, or (ii) the initial explanation of their treatment by reference to the traditional belief was invalid and the correlation spurious. Either way, the belief is confirmed as a legitimate candidate for causal status in the context of the particular contrast which Firth has drawn.*

* Raymond Firth, 'The Sacredness of Tikopia Chiefs', in William A. Shack and Percy
   S. Cohen, eds., *Politics in Leadership: a Comparative Perspective* (1979).

GOALS, FUNCTIONS AND EVOLUTION

§15. There do, however, remain some particular difficulties associated with teleological explanations which cannot be ignored even by the least methodologically-minded sociologists, anthropologists or historians, all of whom have recourse to them at one time or another. But this is at the same time another of the topics on which philosophical discussion is of only limited methodological help. Just as the researcher's need is to know not what explanation is but only what is in practice to count as one, so his need is not to know what teleological explanation is but only what difference, if any, reference to goals or functions* makes to the construction and test of a would-be explanatory hypothesis about human institutions and practices.

Common to both kinds of teleological explanation – the purposive and the functional – is the invocation of some future state of the system under study as explanatory of its present workings. Future states cannot in themselves be causes even on the most generous definition of 'cause'. But where the explanation is purposive, this apparent anomaly is methodologically unproblematic – the anticipated future state is constitutive of the purpose, plan, stratagem, decision-scheme, etc. (including 'intention' where used as a synonym for 'plan'), and the cause is the antecedent mental state of Admiral Tryon, or whoever, which can in turn be explained by reference to the influences which made it so. The more difficult teleological explanations are those which invoke an end-state but are at the same time non-purposive. They may no longer be problematic in biology, where they are generally accepted as fundamental to the mode of reasoning on which the theory of natural selection depends. But sociological evolution is a different matter from biological evolution, and arguments of the form 'without X, no Y, therefore X because Y' may have to be differently construed.

The necessary distinction to be drawn at the same time as that between purposive and functional explanations is that between explanations of the origin of an institution or practice and of its modification or persistence. The literature of sociology is full of reports of behaviour which is shown either to reinforce or to adapt the wider pattern of social relations in the society in question independently of the agents' purpose or plan or even awareness that it should do so. When Malinowski reports the Trobriand Islanders as strengthening the social bonds between them in the course

---

* On which I have found Larry Wright, 'Functions', *Philosophical Review* LXXXII (1973), particularly helpful.

of their periodic co-operation in the building of their canoes, he does not claim that they are to be understood to be building canoes for the purpose of strengthening their social bonds. But once they do co-operate in the building of canoes, their so doing has the observable consequence of strengthening their social bonds and thereby helping to maintain their society in equilibrium. Arguments of this kind are, moreover, just as straightforward where the original cause no longer applies but the behaviour generated by it persists as an apparent vestige or survival, whether as a matter of deliberate policy or because of an ancillary gratification of which the agents may or may not be consciously aware. Thus, if Firth is right about the continuing treatment of the Tikopia chiefs as *tapu* even after the suppression of the belief which originally caused them to be so, it is to be explained, at least in part, by the sense of solidarity which it fosters among the Tikopia at a time when their sense of identity as a people is coming increasingly under threat. This sort of explanation is admittedly difficult to test conclusively. But there is nothing in it to conflict with the methodology of scientific explanation in general.

'But if teleological explanations in sociology are so readily compatible with scientific explanation in general, why has so much controversy been generated by their use?' This is as fair a question as why such heavy weather should be made over value-judgements, and the answer is, as it happens, in part the same. Because purposive explanations invoke a sought-after end-state and functional explanations an adaptive or equilibrating mechanism, those who employ them have often been accused by theorists from rival schools of allowing their hypotheses to be dictated in reverse by their evaluative presuppositions about the particular end-state which they regard as desirable; and it is perfectly possible, as I implied already in Section 5, that many of these accusations are well-founded *ad hominem*. But there is also a more serious methodological point. The temptation which these explanations pose is not only to allow explanatory presuppositions to merge with evaluative: it is also to allow an explicitly validated claim that X can be explained by reference to the fact of Y to elide into a claim *not* explicitly validated that X is the case because and only because it does produce or generate Y. In the examples which I have given, both conditions are fulfilled. But can we say the same about, for example, rules of residence and marriage? The function which they serve may be readily demonstrable. But does it follow that that is why they are there? No anthropological school pretends, so far as I am aware, that the rules of residence and marriage reported by competent fieldworkers for the Kachin, Mara, Karadjeri,

Aluridja, Ashanti, Bemba, Nayars and all the rest are the result of a conscious decision on the part of their founding fathers. However well, therefore, the consequences of a particular set of rules may now suit the members of the society in question – whether they are aware of it or not – it is at most their persistence which is thereby explained. Even if it is also true that patrilineal-cum-matrilocal societies are a null class because of the tensions to which the operation of such rules would inevitably give rise, this is no answer to the question why the other three boxes in the diagram in Section 22 of Chapter 2 are filled as they are. Or again: it is demonstrable alike for ancient Greece and for mediaeval Europe that urbanization performed the function of serving the needs of trade. Indeed, the rise of towns and the expansion of trade in particular regions and at particular times coincide so closely that it would hardly be possible to deny a causal connection between them. But is that why towns appeared? Yes, when they were deliberately founded, as many of them were, by rulers with an interest in tolls and taxes and control of the movement of the commodities in question. But this could only occur after other towns were there to be the models for the new royal or baronial foundations or the colonies sent out from the established Greek *poleis*; and it is no explanation of these other towns to point to the consequence of their presence in serving the needs of trade, however consistent the correlation between the two.

Functional explanations of modification or persistence which ignore the question whether an institution or practice which results in a designated end-state is at the same time there because and only because it does result in that end-state are sometimes defended by a dismissal of the quest for 'origins' as neither useful nor necessary. But without some reference to origin, no teleological explanation can convincingly rule out the alternative hypotheses which may be offered by theorists of rival schools. Perhaps it is fruitless to try to trace the origins of the first *poleis* of Archaic Greece back into the mists of the eighth century B.C. where neither the fleeting literary references nor the fragmentary archaeological record yield the reports against which the needed hypothesis could be tested, just as the stages of primitive social evolution from the early pair-bonding within a system of open communities inherited from our apelike ancestors to the elaborate rules of exogamy documented by modern anthropology may have to remain irretrievably conjectural. But the question how the institution or practice identified as functional came into being in the first place is not a matter of irrelevant antiquarian curiosity. The answer to it, where unobtainable, may be dispensable for the time being in the way that strong theoretical grounding for an otherwise well-attested causal hypothesis may be dispensable. But the origin of social institutions and practices whose presence is invoked to explain an end-state cannot be treated, even for convenience, as unproblematic. Particularly where a teleological explanation along these lines is entirely functional and not at any point purposive, it needs explicitly to map the path by which the initial determinants and unintended consequences of the agents' behaviour led, and were bound to lead, to the end-state in question. There has, in other words, to be elaborated a model linking the functional hypothesis to a theory adequate to ground the claim that the institution or practice invoked wouldn't be there at all if it didn't result in the modification or persistence of whatever it is by which the end-state is constituted.

There are, in fact, several possible models of this kind which could fit the examples which I have cited. For the purpose of the methodological argument, moreover, it does not matter which can be better or less well validated: they still serve to show that teleological explanation can be legitimate in sociology even where no conscious purposes are involved. Thus in the example of towns, it has been argued both for ancient Greece and for mediaeval Europe that following periods of widespread disorder and anarchy, settlements tended to cluster round the more defensible strongpoints, so that when trade revived merchants and craftsmen established themselves in the vicinity of a castle or citadel which itself was often sited where there had originally been a Roman (in Europe) or Mycenaean (in Greece) settlement. The military protectors of these enlarged communities saw the advantages to themselves in encouraging trade and manufacture to expand *in situ*, and however little they may have foreseen – let alone planned – the eventual consequences for their successors, they so behaved as to encourage those groups who would one day demand the citizen rights which mark off the towns and cities of Europe from the urban communities of the ancient Near East, or Islam, or Imperial China, or Japan. On this account, there is nothing para-doxical in the explanation of the rise of towns by reference to an as yet unrealized future, since their function in serving the needs of trade independently of a deliberate plan that they should can be seen to originate in the different antecedent motives of the two sets of agents whose joint behaviour generated the process which furnishes the explanation.

No similar process can be outlined which would fit the example of marriage and residence rules. But a functional explanation can still be formulated which likewise fulfils without paradox the requirement that the institution or practice which results in a designated end-state should be there because and only because it does so. One such possible explanation is, admittedly, the reductionist one whereby instinctual behaviour-patterns are hypothesized as the determinants of exogamous social organization and the necessary grounding is furnished by the theory of natural selection itself. But even at the sociological level a non-reductionist functional explanation in the Durkheimian tradition can be formulated which might in principle turn out to be valid. Suppose it is the case that certain constraints are imposed on possible alternative forms of social organization by what is consistent with a prior need for symbolic classification of the membership and non-membership groups between whom women can be systematically exchanged. In that event, it will be true to say that rules of residence and marriage are there because of their consequences even though the consequences are not perceived as such by the agents for whom the rules have come to have the force of unquestioned custom. There has still to be elaborated a model of the process by which this comes about, and a biological grounding may still be invoked to explain the need for orderly symbolic classification as a universal inborn proclivity of the human mind. Furthermore, the process may be one of quite unconscious trial-and-error whereby the particular rules adopted out of the possible range are those whose persistence is felt – but not realized – to promote the most comfortable degree of integration. But whatever the answer on which anthropologists of rival schools may one day be brought to agree, a hypothesized explanation of this form is perfectly compatible with the methodology of scientific explanation in general.

There is, accordingly, nothing in teleological explanations in sociology, whether purposive or functional, which prevents their being fitted into the same common schema of hypothesis, model, theory and presupposition. If their grounding differs from that of explanations of the more straightforwardly historical kind, it is not because of the difficulty of locating it but because of the temptation to look for it *ex post facto* and not, therefore, strictly to test a preferred hypothesis against those put forward by theorists of rival schools. To say of a society that it had to evolve a specified set of institutions and practices if it was to arrive at an end-state which we know from observation that it did is not to license the invocation of the end-state to explain their adoption by itself. The motives and dispositions underlying the evolution cannot themselves be claimed to be the results of social selection any more than the agents of change of genetic frequency can themselves be claimed to be the results of natural selection. True as it may be that not only the rise of towns but formally free labour, double-entry book-keeping, capital accumulation, extractable energy resources, scientific rationalism and commercial law were all necessary conditions of the Industrial Revolution, their consequences cannot be invoked to explain its inception. Whatever the agents involved can accurately be reported as doing, they cannot be reported as 'creating the Industrial Revolution': only after the first time could it be a goal because and only because of which the institutions and processes necessary to *re*create it might be brought into being. To cast the explanation of the first industrial revolution in teleological form is, therefore, inevitably to commit what is sometimes called the fallacy of 'affirming the consequent'. Whatever the theory which claims to ground the hypotheses in which the appropriate causes, constraints and initial conditions are connected to the behaviour constitutive of industrialization, be it a Marxian theory of social relations of production, a Weberian theory of rationalization, a Durkheimian theory of the progressive division of labour, or any other, it has to be interpreted by way of a model which does more than narrate a chosen sequence of steps assumed without test against possible alternatives to have led inevitably to the end-state.

Yet at the same time, the very same feature of teleological explanations which poses the temptation to commit the fallacy of 'affirming the consequent' also licenses the attribution of 'functional equivalence' to a model which, when it *is* tested against its rival, turns out to be compatible with it. Once industrialization has come to be seen as an attainable end-state by the rulers of pre-industrial societies, it is not only possible but likely that they will either choose or have forced upon them different paths to it which will be equally 'functional'. Not only is it likely that different rulers of different societies, although all pursuing the goal of industrialization with the same conscious purpose in mind, will pursue it in different ways according to their different circumstances. It is also likely that some of them will be so placed that either of two or more alternative paths would lead the evolution of their society's institutions and practices in the same direction. Even within a single case-history, two or more rival models can embody a different set of causes and conditions of the end-state, either of which would operate in the absence of the other. For the explanation to rule out any competitors which might be put forward by theorists of rival schools, the chosen model would need to specify in detail the interrelations between technology, urbanization, literacy, population growth, mobility of labour, fiscal policy, form of political organization, industrial discipline, internal communications, patterns of landownership, secularization of traditional religion or whatever other variables the interpretation of the underlying theory requires;

and in the present state of our knowledge, it cannot yet be claimed that we have a validated theory of industrialization any more than we have a validated theory of rules of marriage and residence. But this is a failure of substantive sociology. It is not a methodological one.

§ 16. Is there, then, a distinctive form of explanation appropriate to, and characteristic of, human history itself? If it makes no difference, methodologically speaking, that it is both human and a history, the answer must in one sense be no. If neither the contrast between self-conscious actions and inanimate events nor that between narrative sequences and time-reversible conjunctions poses any special problem of explanation, the differences in procedure which are dictated by differences in subject-matter are differences only of technique. But the claim that sociological theory is evolutionary has proved considerably more contentious than it would be if this point alone were at issue. The further difficulty cannot merely be the possible intrusion of value-judgements. It is true that the notion of social evolution carries as unmistakable a leftward bias in its Marxian version as it carries a rightward bias in its Spencerian version. But as I have pointed out already, it is perfectly possible without inconsistency to accept Spencer's conception of the survival of the fittest while rejecting his disparagement of 'injudicious charity', or to accept Marx's conception of a dialectic between the forces and social relations of production while rejecting his utopian vision of a future communist society. Nor can it merely be the uncomfortable overtones held to attach to 'Victorian' presuppositions of the inevitability of 'progress'. Dated and complacent as they may have come to seem, theories of a unilinear progression from militant to industrial society, or from an Asiatic to an ancient to a feudal to a bourgeois to a socialist mode of production, or from a theological to a metaphysical to a positivist age, or from promiscuity to polygamy to monogamy, or from status to contract, or from animism to science could perfectly well have turned out to stand up better than they have against the reported evidence now available. If evolutionism in these forms is no longer acceptable in the eyes of later-twentieth-century sociologists, anthropologists and historians, that is not a reason for the concept of social evolution to be contentious as such.

Its contentiousness is, however, more readily explicable in the light of the methodological difficulties raised, as we have just seen, by teleological, and particularly functional, explanations. To invoke evolution as a theoretical concept capable of generating better explanations of human institutions and practices than can be generated without it is to invite the objection that it cannot isolate any particular sequence of stages as 'the' evolutionary sequence except *ex post facto*. The objection is not that evolutionary explanations are not properly causal. Even a self-styled evolutionist who explicitly subscribes to the presupposition that evolution is a 'temporal sequence of forms' in which one 'grows out of' another in accordance with an 'irreversible and non-repetitive process'* cannot dispute that a hypothesis that stage B was bound to follow from stage A has to be grounded in a theory which explains what it was about A at time t which guaranteed that B would follow it at $t + 1$. But the grounding is not, and cannot pretend to be, nomothetic. An evolutionary explanation carries, like any other, the implication that if the same antecedent conditions were to obtain elsewhere the same sequence of cause and effect would again be repeated. But this is of as little explanatory value as any other *ceteris paribus* generalization of cause and effect at the sociological level. The trouble is not that the course of history cannot be predicted in advance: no more (as I remarked already in Section 4 of Chapter 1) can the evolution of species. It is that adequate grounding of a hypothesis which attributes a reported change in institutions or practices to selective pressures identified only with hindsight depends on a model which not only links the hypothesis to the underlying concept of evolution but at the same time invalidates any rival hypotheses which may also be consistent with the observations reported. If this is problematic already in the testing of hypotheses which seek to explain rules of marriage and descent by their function in promoting social harmony, or the rise of towns by their function in serving the needs of trade, how much more problematic will it be in the grounding of hypotheses about the Fall of the Roman Empire or the Industrial Revolution in some would-be general theory of competitive selection under evolutionary pressure?

This question, however, pertinent though it is, risks confusing the generality of an explanans with the complexity of the explananda on which it is brought to bear. Just because it is enormously more difficult to explain the collapse of the Roman Empire in the West than the expansion of the Merina kingdom in nineteenth-century Madagascar, it does not follow that there is a special methodological problem in the Roman case; and just because a model of selective pressures is easier to construct in contrasting the political interests and therefore allegiances of the richer peasants of the Western Sarthe with those of their poorer counterparts to the East than in contrasting the early industrialization

---

* These phrases are taken from Leslie A. White, *The Evolution of Culture* (1959), Ch. 1.

of Western with the later industrialization of Eastern Europe, it does not follow that the notion of selective pressure has no application to the problem of the relatively slower economic evolution of Eastern than Western Europe between the fourteenth and nineteenth centuries. It would be absurd to suggest that the concept of evolution is a magic key which will unlock all the mysteries of comparative macro-sociology. Of course it is not. But even in the absence of an understanding (in the secondary sense) of human psychology comparable to that which we have of population genetics, it can provide an adequate grounding on which there can be based at least some hypotheses both testable and worth testing.

In case even this modest claim is thought to call for an illustration, let me revert yet again to the example of slavery and to the contrast between its functions in the Roman and the Ottoman Empires. In its Roman form, it functioned primarily to provide the labour necessary to man the primary sector of the economy. Although doctors, bankers and naval captains might all be slaves, and although increasing numbers of slaves came to be employed domestically by the urban rich, it was chiefly the slaves of the late Republic and early Empire who tilled the fields and quarried the mines while free men, whether levied, conscripted or hired, fought the wars of conquest which replenished the supply of slaves. The origin of the process is, admittedly, still in dispute among specialists. It seems implausible to hypothesize a purely purposive explanation, since there is no evidence of a conscious design of these institutions and practices by the senatorial aristocracy who were the principal beneficiaries. But once under way, the process could be predicted to evolve, broadly speaking, as it did under both endogenous and exogenous pressures until such time as the costs of its continuance became prohibitive. In its Ottoman form, by contrast, the analogous functions were performed by the opposite categories of subjects and the homologous groups performed quite different functions: slaves fought the wars, and non-servile peasants tilled the soil. But a similar evolution can be held to have been similarly predictable in view of the different endogenous and exogenous pressures observable in the Ottoman case. The Roman flow-chart reproduced in Section 7 has to be replaced by one in which there are specified both the internal connections between political and religious institutions peculiar to Islamic societies and the external presence of the residual Byzantine Empire which involved the Sultans in an unremitting *jihad* against the Christian infidels. But these different pressures can be invoked with equal validity in the explanation of an equally successful evolution of an empire founded on conquest.

To this summary comparison it might be objected that I have merely imposed on the two case-histories the jargon of analogues, functions and so forth in the hope of lending them a spurious conviction borrowed from the much more rigorous theoretical grounding on which evolutionary explanations in biology can be shown to rest. But jargon or not, the imposition can be vindicated by appeal to the reported evidence. Whatever uncertainties remain on points of detail, and however many further questions may still call for an answer, the two empires did both expand as they did because, among other things, they adapted the institution of slavery in their different ways in response to the pressures acting upon them. Comparison with biological theory does not undermine the methodological point. On the contrary, it confirms it. Sociologists are often resistant to such comparison because of their well-entrenched suspicion of attempts to reduce sociological to biological theory. But the contention that similarities and differences between human societies can be explained by reference to an underlying theoretical concept of social evolution analogous to the concept of natural selection still leaves the question of reduction entirely open. To apply the concepts of analogues and homologues, or exogenous and endogenous pressure, to a comparison of Roman and Ottoman slavery involves no necessary commitment whatever to the presuppositions of ethological sociobiology. It is true that there underlies any evolutionary theory, whether sociological or biological, a presupposition of the inevitability of competition itself. But that does not require that struggles for survival should be construed within sociological theory as special cases of the struggle for biological survival. It merely offers a successful example, as far as it goes, of the common mode of reasoning. An evolutionary theory succeeds, if it does, in grounding particular hypotheses about the direction of change because the selective pressures identified with hindsight can be shown to have had the effects attributed to them for reasons which the theory provides. Success may be harder to achieve in sociology than in biology; and even in biology, an enormous amount of patient observation and disappointed conjecture is likely to be necessary before it is. But although there are many societies in the historical and ethnographic record of which we shall never know quite why they are characterized by one rather than another type of institution or practice, this is not because the attempt to answer the question within a recognizably evolutionary framework is methodologically unsound once across the boundary between nature and culture.

§ 17. There remains one last objection which might be mounted of a methodological kind. To vindicate the claim that a distinctively evolutionary social theory really *is* a theory – that is, a body of ideas testable in principle – it is not enough just to lay down a directive that statements of it are to be construed as such. Nor is it enough just to conduct the search for the causes of specified effects within a long-run historical sequence so defined that the notions of analogues, homologues and functional adaptation can plausibly be applied to it. It is necessary also to be able to show how an *un*successful evolutionary theory can come to be displaced by a better one. If substantive explanations of changes from one set of institutions and practices to another are to escape the dilemma that if they are distinctive they are only trivially 'evolutionary', then their testability must be a matter not merely of the awkward evidence which might emerge from a further study of Roman, Ottoman or any other society's archival or archaeological record but of its awkwardness in relation to the body of ideas of which a non-trivial notion of evolution, and therefore of analogues, homologues, etc., is an indispensable part.

To meet this objection, however, it is enough to go back once again to the theories of Spencer and Marx. Controversial as some aspects of their writings may be, there can be extracted from them arguments which illustrate not only the way in which evolutionary explanations may have to be modified but also the way in which their modification itself marks a recognizable theoretical advance. As throughout this volume, it is immaterial whether the summary which I give is a strictly accurate representation of what they or their disciples would agree that they meant: the methodological moral to be drawn remains the same.

Spencer's presuppositions are no more capable than Marx's of being tested directly. His conception of 'General Evolution' as a process of increasing complexity and differentiation across the whole of the physical, biological and social world is not refuted simply by pointing to apparent counter-examples of simplification or regression. But nor is he to be dismissed for that reason as a speculative system-builder whose citations of empirical research are no more than parables on which to hang the exposition of a metaphysical dogma. When it comes to his account of the origins and development of political organization, he advances a theory derived, it is true, from his overall presupposition, yet so interpreted as to postulate not only specific causal connections between environmental pressure and selective adaptation but also reasons for holding them to be genuinely causal. This is particularly clear in his account of the role of war. Given that societies compete with each other and come into conflict over access to scarce resources, Spencer believed that war is 'the' prime cause of the evolution of 'governmental structures' in which progressively more powerful leaders come to dominate their fellows and thereby make their societies progressively more capable of resisting or vanquishing their competitors. This trend is not merely asserted as inevitable and then exemplified with selective citations from the ethnographic and historical record. The underlying idea of competition within and between societies is interpreted in terms of a structural-cum-functional model which generates specific hypotheses about the conditions under which we would expect to find such institutional and behavioural patterns as chiefdoms, absolute kingship and what Spencer calls 'narrowing of the compound political head'. Nor can the theory be criticized as illegitimately teleological. It may be that in practice the processes by which societies come originally to select their 'warrior-chiefs' have to be taken for granted. But there is no reason to suppose that any more detailed familiarity with these processes would undermine the theory. Those early societies which succumbed to their neighbours did so because they failed to develop the institutions necessary to defend themselves; those which succeeded did so because their leaders recognized the need for discipline and obedience and possessed the means of imposing it; and the apparent exceptions can be accommodated without circularity by pointing to the influences – notably, in Spencer's theory, the geographical ones – which favour the continuing independence of smaller and less hierarchically organized political units.

Persuasively as I have tried to put it, this theory has been invalidated. But its invalidation has no more to do with the untestable nature of its explanatory presuppositions than with the contestable nature of the evaluative presuppositions from which Spencer derived his ancillary doctrines about the virtues of unfettered competition and the duty of right-minded citizens not to interfere with the natural elimination of the unfit. The theory fails because the evolution of political institutions is more complex than it allows. Undoubtedly, there are some societies in which a form of hierarchical organization develops in response to, or even in direct imitation of, the military pressure of an already hierarchically organized neighbour.* But there are also cases where it is the *prior* emergence of *non*-military hierarchical organization which makes the society warlike. This possibility is not allowed for by Spencer's theory. Nor can his theory be reconstrued as a presupposition from which a more successful alternative theory can then be derived, since the distinctive contribution of the theory is precisely the stress on war as cause rather than consequence of the evolution of bands into states. The range of

---

* Cf. e.g. R. A. Levine and W. G. Sangree, 'The Diffusion of Age-Group Organisation in East Africa: a Controlled Comparison', *Africa* XXXII (1962).

alternative sequences by which this critical transition can come about is still not fully understood (in the secondary sense). 'The Origin of the State' is still a controversial topic on which I shall be offering some views of my own in Volume II.* But subsequent theories, while both less schematically conceived and more elaborately modelled than Spencer's, can still be seen to be grounded in an underlying conception of social selection analogous to natural selection; and it is, accordingly, a merit of Spencer's theory, methodologically speaking, that it was capable of invalidation and supersession in this way.

The same holds for the central theory of so-called 'classical' Marxism – the theory, that is, of the evolution of capitalist industrial societies into socialist societies by way of a proletarian revolution as a result of the increasingly uncontainable contradiction between their forces and social relations of production. This theory, while resting no less evidently than Spencer's on untestable presuppositions of its own, can at the same time be interpreted by way of a rigorous model of the relations between the classes of which capitalist industrial society consists and of the role of the declining rate of profit, the progressive immiseration of the proletariat and the absorption of the intermediate classes by the proletariat. Its invalidation, therefore, just as in Spencer's case, has no more to do with its derivation from untestable presuppositions than with its contingent connection with strongly-held value-judgements about the preferability of a socialist to a capitalist form of social organization. It fails because capitalist industrial societies have evolved in a way different from that predicted by it, and for reasons which cannot be accommodated within it: in particular, the progressively accelerating polarization of the two mutually exclusive classes has not occurred, and no alternative model of the 'classical' theory can allow for this in a way which preserves it intact. There do remain from it a number of causal hypotheses which all rival theorists are likely to accept – for instance, on the effects under certain specified initial conditions of investment in increasingly capital-intensive technology. What is more, there are other theories of the evolution of capitalism deriving from recognizably Marxian presuppositions which have not yet been invalidated and perhaps never will. But the 'classical' version of the theory has the same merit, methodologically speaking, as Spencer's theory of primitive state-formation: it has shown itself capable of supersession by other still recognizably evolutionary theories testable in their turn by reference to further quasi-experimental contrasts which history either has provided or can be expected one day to provide.

* See my 'Origins of States: the Case of Archaic Greece', *Comparative Studies in Society and History* XXIV (1982).

From the viewpoint of the historian of ideas, there is no doubt an irony in the need for a reassertion of evolution as the *idée maîtresse* of sociological theory a hundred years after Spencer and Marx. But to reassert it is not to dissent from either the methodological or the substantive criticisms which have been heaped upon 'social Darwinism' and 'vulgar Marxism' alike. However well justified they have been, it does not follow from them that any and all theories which rest on a concept of social evolution are incapable of being modelled in a testable form. The tests do, of course, have to be performed: the quasi-experimental contrasts need to be formulated and the evidence which might invalidate the particular hypotheses, or undermine their grounding, to be reported to the satisfaction of all rival observers. But there is no methodological barrier in the way of doing so. The mode of reasoning is fully as defensible in sociological as in biological theory, however large the substantive differences between them may be. The sense in which there is a form of explanation peculiarly appropriate to the study of human history is not one which requires the notion of explanation itself to be differently construed.

CONCLUSION

§ 18. The answers which I have now given to the four questions about explanation in social theory to which this chapter has been addressed have each in their way revealed how dissimilar are the problems by which sociologists, anthropologists and historians are faced to those faced by researchers in either physical or biological science. But I hope also to have said enough to show that there is nothing in either the answers to them or the techniques by which those answers are arrived at which conflicts with my opening claim that the problems of explanation in social theory are not, methodologically speaking, special ones. The difference of subject-matter imposes differences of technique, as it does between one science and another on both sides of the frontier between nature and culture. But it does not impose a requirement on social scientists either to adopt different criteria of validity or to disclaim a capacity to achieve it at all. It is true that there is a difference in the level at which theoretical grounding is to be sought. But again, it is a difference which can be paralleled within the natural sciences as well as between the natural and the social; and it is still a difference within a common mode of reasoning.

This conclusion will seem no more than obvious to readers already committed to a presupposition of the unity of scientific method. But it may leave those who are not so committed with a residual doubt. For if I am right, then it must seem puzzling that the controversies between theorists of rival sociological schools should be quite so intractable and so acrimonious as they evidently are. Why, after all this time, are Marxists and Durkheimians, Structuralists and Historicists, Behaviorists and Phenomenologists still at one another's throats? A part of the answer is to be found, as we have seen, in the degree to which their moral and political values incline them to one preferred explanation as against another – a state of affairs which will only be remedied when our understanding (in the secondary sense) of human behaviour has so far advanced that their values become as irrelevant to their substantive conclusions as the doctrines of the Papacy became to the conclusions of rival astronomers about the number of Jupiter's moons. But is there really no more to it than that? To this, my reply can only be that I have yet to find a sociological theory whose contentiousness can be shown to derive from anything in or about it which cannot be accommodated within the methodology set out in this volume. To those readers who regard this chapter as provocative but unconvincing, I can only say: show me an example on which my methodology breaks down. To those who regard it as sensible but obvious, I can only say: wait and see what is distinctive about the substantive theories of my own which it has helped me to formulate.

4
Description in social theory

TERTIARY UNDERSTANDING

§ 1. To the question 'what is still lacking in a sociology consisting only of reportage and explanation?' the answer 'description' or 'understanding in the tertiary sense' can be made convincing only by an analysis of selected examples. No single example can serve as a paradigm for the whole range of events, processes or states of affairs which sociologists, anthropologists or historians may wish to describe to their readers. But as a first illustration, consider the force of the term 'understand' as it is applied in the sixth line from the end of the poem reproduced below. The poem, 'Only Lovers', is one of a set entitled *Japanese Snapshots*, by Angela Carter, and its author's purpose, as I construe it, is precisely to convey how an alien culture impinges on a participant-observer in what is generally taken to be the most intimate of social relationships. Here is the poem in full:

Only lovers use this hotel, therefore
our presence here defines our status.
He checks the price per hour.
It is not unreasonable.
'Come in, come in!' says the smiling landlady.
What a cosy room! A pleasant
watercolour of a cockerel hangs
beside a capacious wardrobe which silently
reminds us to hang up our clothes tidily.
On the dresser are paper towels, a comb
and a jar of lubricating fluid. Chips
of mica glitter in the walls. The maid
brings tea and very sweet small cakes.
She wears a starched apron. She
is a model of propriety. Such a respectable brothel!
How clean the towels are. And the crisp sheets
smell of soap.
Ah! Now I understand!
This is not an illicit bedroom at all.

It is a safety-net in which the death-
defying somersault of love may be performed
with absolute propriety.
That is the custom of the country.

Notice first the exclamation-mark which follows 'I understand'. It
serves the same function as the exclamation-mark which conventionally
follows 'eureka'. But where 'eureka!' is prompted by the sensation of
having arrived at a scientific discovery, it is a sensation of awareness
rather than discovery which prompts 'I understand!' It is true that
reportage and explanation are still, as they always are, bound up with the
description of what the author has come to be aware of: read as an
ethnographic monograph, which in part it is, the poem offers one kind
of answer to the question why rooms of this kind are furnished as they
are in Japan – European *chambres à l'heure* or North American motel
cabins not being furnished in quite the same way. But the understanding
which justifies the exclamation-mark is an understanding not of the
reasons for the difference so much as of the poet's own realization of its
nature. The awareness which she seeks to convey in turn to the reader
is an awareness, or understanding in the tertiary sense, of what the
Japanese attitude to non-conjugal sexual relations is – to her – like.

Analysis of the example is, however, complicated by the need to
distinguish between the understanding which the poet has of what she
is describing, the understanding which she has of her own reactions to
it and the understanding which the reader of the poems has of her
description both of it and of her own reactions to it. It is quite possible
for a participant-observer to understand in the tertiary sense what an
event, process or state of affairs is like for those directly involved in it
and yet be incapable of transmitting that understanding adequately to
someone else. In the example which I have chosen, the participant-
observer may be misdescribing what the practice of non-conjugal sexual
relations is like to the Japanese themselves; or she may be misdescribing
her own reaction in such a way as would require her to confess that her
awareness of what the practice is like to them, and therefore by contrast
to her, has been inadequately expressed; or she may simply be failing to
word the description in a way sufficiently illuminating to convey what
she has chosen to try to describe. But in all three cases, the nature of the
understanding required is the same. What is required in the observer and
the reader alike is at once more than a primary understanding of the
meaning of the terms which are used in the description – whether the
terms are 'ours' or 'theirs' – and less than a literal recreation of the
experiences in question. The practical test of it is whether the person who

claims to have arrived at it can talk back to the persons whose experiences are those described in such a way as will elicit their agreement that that is indeed what the event, process or state of affairs was like for them. It is, of course, seldom an all-or-nothing affair. Tertiary understanding may still be partial and fragmentary and the attempt to press it too far may lead only to the feeling that the words being used for the purpose are, as it were, dissolving in the attempt – whence, perhaps, a recourse to poetry. Nor is it possible to specify just how much experience, and of what, is necessary before someone can claim to have progressed beyond the stage of primary understanding of the terms used to a capacity to appreciate all the nuances of thought and feeling which may be there to be conveyed. All that can safely be said in the case of the poem just quoted is that, on the one hand, it would not be understood in the tertiary sense by a child of five, however well educated, and that, on the other hand, it can perfectly well be understood in the tertiary sense by readers who have not themselves ever been to a Japanese hotel of this kind, or even to Japan, or to a hotel of this kind, at all.

Even this cautious claim may be disputed by those who subscribe to the presuppositions of either Behaviorism on the one side or Pheno-menology on the other. But for the purposes of this chapter, their competing objections cancel each other out. To the Behaviorist, the inability of a child of five to understand the poem is an inability deriving simply from the lack of sufficient conditioning in regard to the relatively complex terms used: it is a difficulty no different in kind from what it would be if the example were not drawn from human behaviour at all but from chemistry or physics. But in the face of this objection, the Phenomenologist is entitled to retort that the assimilation of an under-standing of art or ritual to an understanding of textbooks of natural science must, whatever the merits of Behaviorist psychology as an explanatory theory, be a misdescription since it is demonstrably incon-sistent with the comparisons and contrasts drawn by the members of the culture under study themselves. Conversely, if the Phenomenologist goes so far as to object that nobody can understand Angela Carter's experience in the tertiary sense except Angela Carter herself, the Behaviorist is entitled to retort that in seeking to describe her experiences she is necessarily appealing to the possibility of external verbal or other criteria for internal emotional states. No doubt it is easier for a woman to understand another woman's experience in the tertiary sense than it is for a man, and perhaps there comes a point beyond which even the best description will fail to convey just what an act of sexual intercourse is like for a member of the opposite sex to the reader's. But is still a very long way from accepting the self-defeating conclusion that nobody can arrive at a tertiary understanding of anyone's experience but their own and that the meaning of Angela Carter's poem must be so inaccessible to 'us' as to make it pointless for us to read it except for the bits of reportage and explanation which it happens to contain.

It may, admittedly, not be possible to specify the conditions of success. Once it is conceded that there is somewhere a point beyond which only a woman can understand what another woman's experience is like, then is there not somewhere a point beyond which only a Bushman can totally understand a Bushman's, only a Catholic a Catholic's, only a musician a musician's and only a sociologist a sociologist's? And are there not, indeed, states of mind which exclude the possibility of being conveyed to other people without being modified in the process? How, for example, can a Tikopia traditionalist either frame or accept a description of what it is like to be a Tikopia traditionalist without implicitly accepting the possibility of a *non*-traditional view of the chiefs and their treatment as *tapu* which, for a 'real' traditionalist, is literally inconceivable? But these barriers to some unattainable ideal of total understanding in the tertiary sense have to be treated as technical difficulties to be surmounted as best they can: they are not barriers to the possibility of any success in description whatever. Every person capable of primary understanding of what other people say and do is capable of some degree of tertiary understanding simply by virtue of the faculty of imagination with which all human beings are endowed. It may be that no amount of further research will enable me fully to understand what it is like to believe in an omnipotent and benevolent God because I am in some way as ineluctably incapable of seeing it as believable as a Tikopia traditionalist of seeing the belief that the spirits of the chiefs are assimilated to the gods after death as anything other than self-evident. But even these gaps in the understanding achievable by one person of another can be bridged by the metaphors, similes and analogies and the ancillary reports and explanations which it is the business of the sociologist, anthropologist or historian concerned to describe 'their' experience to provide.

The more fundamental methodological difficulty arises from the claim that the practical test of understanding in the tertiary sense is in the responses of those whose experiences have been described. It arises not because it is mistaken to concede to agents themselves a fundamentally privileged position in describing what their experiences are like, but because this concession has at the same time to be reconciled with the possibility that their own description could still be bettered by a rival observer. Since description necessarily involves more than the mere repetition of what 'they' say about their experiences, the researcher who succeeds in framing a description whose terms and implications are acceptable to 'them' is, in effect, *re*interpreting the meaning to 'them' of the experiences so described. What is more, that description may itself be capable of improvement. Angela Carter, in her poem, is describing something about the sexual mores of Japan which, let me assume for methodology's sake, would be agreed by the Japanese to be consistent with the rather different terms in which they would themselves describe their own view of their mores. At the same time, however, her poem itself invites commentary from readers who may wish to proffer a further description of *her* reactions to which *she* would in principle assent and which would, therefore, amount to a more successful description than the first. But the agreement of the person whose experience is described cannot itself be put forward as a sufficient condition of success, since if an earlier agreed description has been shown to be capable of improvement it must likewise be possible that a later one will be too. Not only is it impossible to lay down the conditions under which agents will, or could, be brought to accept a redescription of what they say it is like for them to do, say, think and feel what they do. In addition, any redescription can in principle be corrected by another, and that by another in its turn, so that there opens out an infinite regress of possible redescriptions of redescriptions of redescriptions of what someone's experience is like.

Yet dismaying as it may be to acknowledge that there is in principle no limit to the sociologist's, anthropologist's or historian's descriptive task, it would be a mistake to conclude that no description can serve its purpose unless further redescribed *ad infinitum*. All descriptions are partial, just as all explanations are provisional. But the impossibility of perfection is no more a reason for abandoning altogether the attempt to say what other people's experience is like than for abandoning the attempt to say why they do, say, think and feel what they do. It is true that, as I have already remarked in Section 12 of Chapter 1, there is literally an infinity of reports which could be put forward about the event, process or state of affairs being described which neither assert anything which could be shown to be untrue nor phrase anything in such a way that the agents themselves would not in principle accept it. But in practice, the researcher can content himself with a description which is deliberately restricted in two ways: first, by confining it to that aspect of the agents' lives which he has chosen in advance as being of interest to him and – in due course – his readers; second, by testing it against the agents' view of what is important to *them* about the aspect of their lives which he tells them is of interest to *him*. This is not as restrictive as it may sound, for it does not rule out even such ambitious undertakings as the attempt to convey 'the totality of their social experience' or 'the essence of their world-view'. On the contrary, what makes such things feasible objects for description is that they are defined in terms of the researcher's interest in the agents' scale of priorities, so that the success of the observer's description depends not on the breadth or depth of detail by itself but on the degree to which he is able to encapsulate in a summary of his own an account which 'they' could be brought to accept of what they would say themselves if required to consider their social experience or world-view 'as a whole'. No description will ever be perfectly complete. But it is still possible to distinguish between good descriptions and bad, even of describenda as large and complicated as these.

§2. Good descriptions, no less than good explanations, have to be grounded in a theory – that is, some underlying body of ideas which furnishes a reason for both readers of them and rival observers of what they describe to accept them. Moreover, as with explanatory concepts, the concepts in which descriptions are grounded are unlikely to be those used by the agents whose behaviour is being described unless they happen themselves to be trained practitioners of descriptive sociology (or, perhaps, natural adepts at understanding in the tertiary sense). But within that general similarity, descriptive theoretical concepts will be of a markedly different kind and serve a markedly different function.

Consider as an example the term 'Machiavellian'. To twentieth-century readers, and for those of several centuries before, it is a term rich in overtones whose resonance all derives, however indirectly, from what Machiavelli either meant or is thought to have meant in his injunctions to princes. Whether or not the picture of early Renaissance politics which *The Prince* conveys is an authentic description of Florence under the Medici or anywhere else, the term now carries a whole set of related descriptive implications: the unremitting intrigue, the deliberate treachery, the relentless ambition, the ruthless but calculating use of force, the contempt for moral rhetoric coupled with a cynical willingness to exploit it, all amount to a picture of what certain forms of institutions and practices are, or could be, like for those involved in them. There are at the same time explanatory implications about how a set of such institutions and practices might work and evaluative implications about the wickedness, at least in orthodox moral and political theory, of such a way of behaving. But its principal function is to select and emphasize certain aspects of behaviour in such a way as to imply a view of political life which not only penetrates beneath the superficial conceptions of participants and observers alike but also brings together ostensibly dissimilar periods and milieux under a common rubric of, so to speak, *Realpolitik à l'outrance*. Its value as a concept does not, therefore, lie in its use in reportage, since what it does is to assemble a chosen set of reports already accepted by rival observers as accurate. Nor is the test of its value its actual currency among 'them', since it may be of as much value or more when applied to the institutions and practices of a society whose members have never heard of Machiavelli or Machiavellism. The concepts of a descriptive theory, as of an explanatory one, *re*conceptualize 'their' account of what they think, say and do but with the difference that instead of reordering 'their' ideas about their own experience in terms of presumptive causal connections they reorder them in terms of a presumptive relation to a latent *Weltanschauung*.

No such descriptive theory can be cited as a paradigm from the writings of any sociologist, anthropologist or historian, 'classical' or modern, for the simple reason that none of them has formulated the distinction between reportage, explanation, description and evaluation in the terms on which its exposition would have to depend. But it is not difficult to reconstruct one out of what they have said for other purposes and in other terms. Thus, there is implicit in the writings of Marx, Weber and Durkheim alike a view of what it is like to be a member of a society which works in the way that they argue societies in general to work under conditions stipulated by their explanatory theories; and nothing prevents either the rival observer or the reader of their works from agreeing with that implicit view while rejecting both the explanations from which it derives and the evaluations ancillary to it. There is no inconsistency in rejecting both Marx's explanation of why capitalist industrial societies have evolved the structure which they have and his evaluation of them as indefensibly exploitative while at the same time accepting the authenticity of the passage in the *Economic and Philosophic Manuscripts of 1844* in which he seeks to convey what it is like for the worker to feel himself alienated and diminished by the sense of being, as it were, 'emptied' into his product in such a way that his labour becomes an object existing independently of himself and standing in opposition to him; or in rejecting both Weber's explanation of the rise of bureaucracy in terms of an inherent process of 'rationalization' and his evaluation of it as inimical to innovation and leadership while at the same time agreeing with the passage in *The Protestant Ethic and the Spirit of Capitalism* in which he describes the spirit of a bureaucratic age as one of a 'mechanized petrifaction' in which the specialists have lost all sense of vocation; or in rejecting both Durkheim's explanation of social cohesion by reference to the influence of the *conscience collective* and his evaluation of violent change as pathological while at the same time conceding to the notion of a 'collective consciousness' a capacity to convey the feeling of a sense of membership of a social and ideological community whose norms one accepts. Indeed, there is no inconsistency even in going so far as to maintain that although a sociologist's explanations are indisputably invalid and his evaluations untenably incoherent, nevertheless his descriptions of the society he has chosen to study are to be accepted because its institutions and practices are such that its members do feel *as if* those explanations and evaluations were the right ones.

Behind the methodological difficulties in framing and testing a descriptive theory lie, once more, the philosophical problems of justifying the possibility of such a theory at all; and there is the additional problem that whereas in the case of explanatory theory there is if anything a too abundant philosophical literature, in the case of descriptive theory there is no literature at all which bears directly on the topic as formulated here. Much has, however, been written which bears on it indirectly; and even the most empirically-minded researchers are likely to find that they have something to learn from writers in the Phenomenological tradition. A Wittgensteinian claim that 'the understanding of a human society is closely connected with the activities of the philosopher'* is altogether more plausible if it is tertiary, not secondary, understanding which is taken to be meant. Much of what Wittgenstein says in Part II, Section xi of the *Philosophical Investigations* is immediately relevant to the problem of attaining and justifying an insight into what another person's experiences and perceptions are like. The notion of 'aspect blindness' and its kinship to the lack of a musical ear, the assertion that seeing something *as something* is subject to the will, the example of whistling a theme with the right expression to illustrate what is meant by understanding 'fine shades of behaviour', and the celebrated remark that 'the given is, so to speak, *forms of life*' all help to illuminate what is involved in the analysis and comparison of *Weltanschauungen*; and it is hard to see how it could be disputed that here, in Wittgenstein's own words, '*Unser Problem ist kein kausales, sondern ein begriffliches.*' But whatever the merits of Wittgenstein's or Collingwood's (or Husserl's or Croce's or Rickert's or Merleau-Ponty's) philosophies, the resolution of the practising sociologist's methodological problem does not depend on an informed appraisal of them any more than on an assessment of the

---

*Peter Winch, *The Idea of a Social Science* (1958), p. 91.

relative merits of the various techniques of fieldwork and participant-observation by which tertiary understanding can most efficiently be pursued. It depends on arriving at serviceable criteria for establishing whether or not a description has succeeded in achieving the purpose for which it was framed.

§ 3. Initially, at least, it is likely to be more rewarding to analyse what makes descriptions bad than what makes them good. This is partly because, as I have admitted, it is impossible to analyse the notion of tertiary understanding in such a way as to yield a set of sufficient conditions of perfect success in achieving it; and it is partly because it is in the nature of sociology, as of science generally, that its practitioners can more readily be told by methodologists what procedures will guarantee failure than what alternative procedure will guarantee success. In Section 13 of Chapter 1, I listed some of the pitfalls of description as contrasted with explanation – oversimplification, ahistoricity, ex-aggeration and ethnocentricity – and the list can be extended a good deal further than this. But the overall distinction to which any such list needs to be subordinated is the distinction between failings of omission and commission. It is difficult to find the right general terms with which to draw the distinction in this context. But for want of better, I shall use *misapprehension* for the first and *mystification* for the second. 'Mystifica-tion' may suggest a deliberate intention to misdescribe which is some-times but by no means always present, and in adopting it I am not seeking to imply that a sociologist who is guilty of it is necessarily compromising his academic integrity in the service of his political purposes or ideals. I do, however, intend it to carry the implication that more is at issue than a simple failure to perceive what those whose thoughts, words and deeds are being described would regard as deserving of inclusion. Mystification is done when the sociologist does not merely fail to see what 'they' see but when he supposes that they see it in a way which is pre-emptively dictated by a descriptive theory of his own.

As an example which will bring out the force of this distinction while at the same time further illustrating the nature of understanding in the tertiary sense, I have chosen the discussion by an American professor of literature writing in the 1970s about what he calls 'the British experience on the Western Front from 1914 to 1918'.* His particular concern is with what he calls the 'literary dimensions' of that experience – that is to say, the way in which the literary forms and conventions of the time them-

* Paul Fussell, *The Great War and Modern Memory* (1975).

selves influenced the way in which the war in the trenches was experienced, and those experiences described, by those who took part in it. As usual, the work in question is concerned to explain as well as to describe: the hypothesis that the literary forms and conventions did have an influence of this kind is one which, while not in broad terms controversial, needs to be supported by empirical evidence and grounded in a provisionally adequate explanatory theory in just the same way as does any other hypothesis about the influence of ideas on other ideas and the behaviour sanctioned, encouraged or imposed by them. But this chapter is concerned only with the issues of tertiary, not secondary, understanding which the book raises. In terms of the distinctions already drawn, these issues subdivide neatly into six. First, there is the question whether Fussell's subjects in their own descriptions themselves either misapprehended or mystified (or both) their own experience; second, there is the question whether Fussell either misapprehends or mystifies (or both) their own descriptions; and third, there is the question whether I am guilty of either misapprehension or mystification (or both) in what I am about to say to you, the reader of *this* book, about Fussell's. On the last, I can only leave you to judge for yourself. But consideration of the first two may help to define the criteria for badly (or *relatively* well) grounded sociological description more precisely than I have done so far.

The description of their experiences by the men who fought in the trenches and Fussell's description of their descriptions are inevitably interwoven with one another. Their descriptions, as presented to the readers of his book, are already selected and edited by him, and whatever he says about them which goes beyond simple reportage of their authorship and provenance carries an implication, however tentative, about the kinds of inferences which might be drawn from them. At its extreme, this elaboration of views about views about views reaches the point where, for example, I find myself wanting to dispute Fussell's description of Philip Larkin's description (in a poem of the 1960s)* of a crowd photographed as opposite outside a recruiting station (in August 1914) as part of Fussell's own more general description of the (to him) 'innocence' of what (to them, according to him) were 'intact certainties'. But there are less intricate themes developed in the book which serve adequately to illustrate the same distinction. Specifically, it offers examples of the risks both of misapprehension and of mystification in relation both to their own accounts of their experience and to his.

---

* 'MCMXIV', in *The Whitsun Weddings* (1964).

Where their own misapprehension is at issue, the difficulty lies in recognizing and assimilating the assumptions which underlay their own view of their experience in a way of which they were not themselves aware. Fussell cites the episode in which Captain Nevill of the East Surreys presented each of his four platoons with a football and offered a prize to whichever first dribbled its ball up to the German front line in the attack on the Somme. Fussell implies that to him, whose own experience of war was against the same enemy in the same area some thirty years later (he dedicates the book to a fellow-infantryman killed beside him in France on March 15, 1945), the idea of so doing is 'preposterous'. But he recognizes also that to a generation in which Sir Henry Newbolt's 'There's a breathless hush in the close tonight . . . "Play up! Play up! and play the game!" ' could be recited with a straight face it was not preposterous at all; and he pertinently quotes in illustration a poem written after the episode and preserved on the border of a field concert programme in the Imperial War Museum in which Newbolt's poem is unmistakably echoed (' "True to the land that bore them – The Surreys play the game" and so on for two more stanzas'). He can, therefore, fairly claim to understand their unspoken assumptions better than themselves, and in this sense to put their own misapprehensions right in the light of a theory of his own.

Where, by contrast, their own accounts actually mystify their experience, it is because the literary conventions of the time are so far accepted by them as to amount to a distortion of the experiences interpreted in terms of those conventions. Fussell draws up a table illustrating what he calls the 'system of "high" diction' in which, for example, the enemy is the 'foe', danger is 'peril', soldiers are 'warriors', horses are 'steeds' or 'chargers', to die is to 'perish', to show cowardice is to 'swerve' and the dead are the 'fallen'. He does not, of course, suggest that those who were fighting and dying thought literally in these terms. Indeed, they were – as no doubt their counterparts have been since the time of Homer – appropriately cynical about the rhetorical fictions of the politicians, the war correspondents and the authors of the official communiqués. Yet there seems no doubt that the literary conventions did sometimes serve to distort their own descriptions of their experience, and were even recognized by some of the more articulate and self-conscious of them as doing so. But an awareness of the risk is not necessarily enough to ensure that the diarist or memoirist who seeks to describe his experiences in such a way as will authentically convey 'how it really was' in the trenches will succeed in doing so; and it is therefore one of the tasks of the historian or sociologist who later reads the diary or memoir to judge how far he has.

But then what about the misapprehension and/or mystification which may unwittingly be introduced by the historian or sociologist himself? Fussell, it seems to me, does in part misapprehend the assumptions and outlook of the English officer class of 1914, chiefly because he leaves out of account the possibility that they were just as aware as himself of how exceptionally long a time it had been since their country had last been engaged in a Continental war. Of course they did not foresee how different the World War of 1914–18 was going to be from the Franco-Prussian War of 1870–71. But what of it? To attribute to them an 'innocence' about war on *these* grounds is to go beyond the necessary and legitimate attempt to recapture their attitude to the writings of Newbolt, E. H. Henty and Rider Haggard into a judgement of hindsight of another and more questionable kind. Fussell is quite right when he says that the appeal of Ian Hay's best-selling *The First Hundred Thousand*, published in 1915, was to readers already appreciative of Kipling's *Stalky & Co.* But when he describes *Stalky & Co.* as a 'fantasy of school high-jinks' he reveals how far he has failed to understand, in the tertiary sense, the attitudes of those who went from schools such as United Services College, Westward Ho!, to the risks of mutilation and death anywhere from the Orange Free State to the North-West Frontier. Whatever your view of 'Stalkyism', a comment which conveys a much fuller understanding of it is this, by an English novelist born in 1913, on the First World War story 'Sea Constables' in which Kipling depicts a naval officer, Portson, refusing to take a dying American blockade-runner, whom he has run aground, to England and a doctor:

> When Portson says, 'I wasn't in this job for fun. It was business.', he echoes exactly the creed of *Stalky & Co.*, a creed designed to teach the young what is business in life and what is fun – not at all the same distinction as that made by conventional moralists. I find the Stalky code repulsive, but, if it is not acceptable in wartime and 'Sea Constables', it is hard to see when it ever could be.*

A misapprehension of this kind becomes a mystification when it reaches the point at which, in effect, the charge that 'they' mystified their own experience rebounds. Here, for instance, is Fussell's description of a three-minute playlet called 'The Attack' from a popular gramophone record of the period:

> The suspense is well managed, and the effect is surprisingly exciting. 'The Attack' must have constituted a sort of folk war-memoir for many thousands of households, allowing veterans when the need was on them to replay vicariously the parts they had once played in actuality. Their instinct, if pitiful, was sound: they sensed that so theatrical a war could well be revisited theatrically.†

Here, the mystification does not consist in the explicitly pejorative 'pitiful', but in the claim that 'they' can be said to have 'sensed'

---

* Angus Wilson, *The Strange Ride of Rudyard Kipling* (1977), p. 313.
† Fussell, pp. 229–30.

something which I am quite sure they did not. I do not dispute that the theatricality of war, and perhaps the peculiar theatricality of war as fought on the Western Front, is reflected in the way in which it was subsequently described both by those who fought in it and by those who did not. Nor do I dispute that the popularity of a record of this kind is a testimony to the wish, and perhaps the need, of many of those who had taken part in just such attacks to 'replay vicariously the parts they had once played in actuality'. But to describe this wish in terms of a sense of the particular theatricality of the experience recreated is to read into it a gloss which is Fussell's own. There are, after all, plenty of parallels to it in areas of experience wholly remote from trench warfare: think merely of the many readers of illustrated advertisements in newspapers and magazines who, as market researchers have found, look chiefly at the advertisements for those products which they already possess. Fussell has allowed himself to be so far persuaded by his own descriptive theory as to be taken in; the demystifier is remystifying what he describes.

As I have implied, my description of Fussell's descriptions may itself misapprehend, or mystify, or both, what he is doing in them. But even if this is so, it is immaterial to the methodological point. They illustrate it particularly well because the argument in the course of which they are put forward is an argument about the way in which descriptions of experience themselves relate to unspoken conventions about what the experience described is supposed to be like. But it holds across the whole range of descriptions of thought, feeling and behaviour. The twin spectres of misapprehension and mystification haunt the sociologist, the anthropologist and the historian just as unrelentingly as they haunt the biographer, the memoirist, the would-be realistic novelist and the literary critic.

AUTHENTICITY AND ITS OPPOSITES

§4. If there is any single term for what a 'good' description ought to aspire to, it is *authenticity*. But once again, it is much easier to say what isn't authentic than what is. Authenticity consists above all in the active and sustained avoidance of what Dr Johnson called 'cant', George Orwell called 'humbug' and I shall call, in the idiom of my own period and milieu, 'bullshit'. To illustrate it as briefly as I can, I have chosen two sentences from Flaubert's *Madame Bovary*. *Madame Bovary* is of course a work of fiction. But works of fiction, or at any rate of realistic fiction, furnish better examples for methodological discussion if only because the technical problems of research into the *vie intérieure* of living persons can be assumed to have been overcome. It would be no less appropriate to cite such well-known works of descriptive sociology as John Dollard's *Caste and Class in a Southern Town* (1937), William Foote Whyte's *Street Corner Society* (1943), Erving Goffman's *Asylums* (1961), Oscar Lewis's *The Children of Sanchez* (1961), or an attempted historical reconstruction such as Emmanuel Le Roy Ladurie's *Montaillou: Village Occitan de 1294 à 1324* (1978), or the descriptive sections of Malinowski's *Argonauts of the Western Pacific* (1922).* But not only do all these authors, even where drawing on their own observations rather than inferring what they describe from documentary sources, have to rely on inferences from outward behaviour to inner states of consciousness which the rival observer might dispute; in addition, they all have some further explanatory purpose in mind of a kind which a non-academic observer like Flaubert does not. What is important for the purpose of this chapter is that Flaubert's authenticity has been praised even by critics unwilling to concede authenticity to any other 'realistic' novelist of the nineteenth century.† As I remarked in Section 7 of Chapter 1, novels *are* sociology to the extent that their authors make them so; and it is worth remembering also that the sub-title of *Madame Bovary* is 'Moeurs de Province'.

Flaubert's achievement lies in part in his mentioning of the hitherto unmentionable, but I am not here concerned with that aspect of it except in that it makes him a better example for the purpose of this chapter than, say, Thackeray or Hardy. Nor am I concerned with Flaubert's meticulously accurate reportage of the outward details of French provincial life, remarkable though it is. The aspect of his achievement which makes him a paradigm of descriptive authenticity is, above all, his ability to redescribe what the life of a person like Emma Bovary was like better than such a person could describe it to herself. This is in part a function of his better knowledge both of her period and milieu and of the life of those other, superior milieux of which she daydreams, and it is no doubt true of all the real-life Emma Bovarys, then as now, that they lack the kind of informed sociology of their own circumstances which even a less gifted observer than Flaubert could bring to bear. But it is also a function of a tertiary understanding which permits him to say just where *her* self-description is inauthentic without himself remystifying it in his turn. When he says of Emma that '*toute l'amertume de l'existence lui semblait servie sur son assiette*' he is not saying that this is what the reader is to

---

* Cf. p. 517: 'What interests me really in the study of the native is his *Weltanschauung...*'

† See e.g. Nathalie Sarraute as cited by Lionel Trilling, *Sincerity and Authenticity* (1972), p. 100.

suppose that Emma said to herself. as one celebrated commentator says of this passage, 'she doubtless has such a feeling; but if she wanted to express it, it would not come out like that'.* Flaubert's description, however, carries conviction because the reader can accept that *if* it were put to her this way she would agree to it. Where, by contrast, he says of her that she *'confondait, dans son désir, les sensualités du luxe avec les joies du coeur, l'élégance des habitudes et les délicatesses du sentiment'*, it must follow that she would dispute it. But she would be wrong – not, of course, wrong about what she actually felt, for here the agent's account is absolutely privileged over the observer's, but in failing initially to see that the way in which she was describing her feelings to herself could be bettered. It might, of course, happen that she would continue to dispute the redescription because she was too far self-deceived for the self-deception to be put right merely by reading what Flaubert has to say about her. But if Flaubert can show that she could, in principle, have been brought by him to the point of coming to share his view that she had previously misapprehended and/or mystified her own experience, then his redescription does qualify as authentic.

At this point, readers may object that although the example of Emma Bovary may serve to illustrate the methodological point whether or not I am right in attributing to Flaubert an authenticity which I denied to Fussell, the two still differ in that the suggested test of a 'good' description cannot in actual practice be applied in the case of a fictional character. The rival observer who disagrees with Fussell's description of 'their' descriptions of their own experiences can in principle go and ask them: if, when the veterans who are listening to the recorded playlet of 'The Attack' are asked whether they are 'sensing that so theatrical a war could well be revisited theatrically' they reply 'yes', then I shall have no option but either to withdraw or to call them liars. But Flaubert has constructed a character of which he is not only the creator but the judge: he is free to authenticate his theory for himself. To say that *Madame Bovary* is a model of sociological insight is to say that Flaubert is a novelist of remarkable gifts, but it cannot be to say that sociologists, anthropologists or historians can have recourse to artistic invention. The true criterion of authenticity, therefore, has to be sought not in fiction, even of the most realistic kind, but in autobiography – that is, in the description of things which actually happened by the person to whom they happened for the explicit purpose of conveying to other people to whom they did not happen what it was like for the person to whom they did.

* Erich Auerbach, *Mimesis* (Eng. trans., 1953), p. 427.

It is certainly fair to say that autobiographies furnish the severest test – almost constitute the touchstone, as it were – of *in*authenticity, since if a person misdescribes his or her very own experience there cannot be the excuse which the sociologist has to fall back on that he has been misled by what his native informants have told him. But the methodological point remains the same: when the autobiographer either misapprehends or mystifies his or her own experience, the misapprehension or mystification is of no different a kind whether or not it is (to you or me) less forgivable because it is his or her own experience which is at issue. And it remains equally difficult to specify what is, rather than what isn't, authentic. It is not simply that autobiographers must not tell lies or suppress unflattering episodes or seek to present their motives in a too favourable light. Montaigne passes these tests so successfully as to make him, for Emerson, 'the frankest and honestest of all writers'. But then Rousseau put him, for his pains, '*à la tête de ces faux sincères qui veulent tromper en disant vrai*'; and Rousseau was in turn dismissed for *his* pains by the anti-hero of Dostoievski's *Notes from Underground*, quoting Heine, as distorting his *Confessions* out of vanity in order to impress the reader with his candour. The more determined the pursuit of authenticity, it would seem, the more self-conscious it becomes, and the more self-conscious the less authentic.

My own impression, for what it is worth, is that Heine is right about Rousseau, and Rousseau wrong about Montaigne. But Montaigne was very self-conscious about what he was doing, and if we accept that self-consciousness heightens the risk of inauthenticity, then it is the *un*self-conscious observer of his society and himself whom we must try to find. There is, admittedly, a suggestion of paradox here, for to observe oneself at all is to be self-conscious by definition, and the quest for the innocent eye of an observer whose authenticity is guaranteed by his naivety is likely to lead only to another sort of bullshit of its own. But unselfconsciousness in this context need not mean either ignorance or naivety so much as a lack of concern with what the reader will make of the self-description given. The readiest example is Pepys. 'To whom', as Robert Louis Stevenson asked (who did not even have the complete edition before him), 'was he posing in the Diary, and what, in the name of astonishment, was the nature of the pose?'* What indeed? Pepys's purpose in writing the diary remains obscure.† He was not writing it for publication, although he must in a sense have been writing for posterity or he would

---

* 'Samuel Pepys', in *Familiar Studies of Men and Books* (n.d.), p. 266.
† See the 'Introduction' by the Editors (Robert Latham and William Matthews) to Volume I of the Complete Edition (1970).

not have preserved it as carefully as he did. Nor was he writing it for himself in any straightforward sense, for he seems hardly ever to have referred back to it, and he never used it, although he lived quite long enough to do so, as the basis for a later historical or biographical memoir. Nor was he writing it for his intimate friends, for although he did not wholly conceal its existence from them they never read it either during his lifetime or after his death. It was written in shorthand, but a shorthand which could have been deciphered without difficulty by anyone who had wanted to do so. All that can be said is that whatever the motives which caused him to do it, Pepys was fitted by his temperament, his talents and his circumstances to leave a description of his life over a decade which comes as near to avoiding inauthenticity as it is plausible ever to expect. It is not that he was wholly without bias, as emerges clearly enough in his account of his dealings with Sir William Penn, whose interests were often and for obvious reasons at odds with his. But he is never misled by his bias into bullshit about his own thoughts and actions (as is, by contrast, the Duc de Saint-Simon in his 'historical memoirs' of the reign of Louis XIV, superb though his descriptions of other people are). He writes as though his purpose was nothing other than to convey to posterity what his life was like. If he is boasting on the one hand, or confessing on the other, it is only to himself, and he knows that he is doing it, so that the reader comes to know him in the end even better – if possible – than Flaubert's Emma, or Dostoievski's anti-hero, or Rousseau or Montaigne.

§5. But there is yet another difficulty. Autobiography may furnish the severest test of authenticity. But the autobiographer, in conveying to his readers what his life and times were like, is conveying only what they were like to him. That is precisely what makes him an autobiographer as opposed to a sociologist, anthropologist or historian. Yet a description of a whole society, or even of a sub-culture or milieu or class or faction or clique or group within it, must describe what it was like not just from the standpoint of a single observer. In this larger context, the quest for authenticity leads straight into the additional problem of selection and emphasis which faces the sociologist who wants to include whatever is significantly relevant to his theme but in order to do so has first to decide whose criteria of relevance he will accept as privileged. Macaulay says somewhere that 'Those are the best pictures and the best histories which exhibit such parts of the truth as most nearly to produce the effects of the whole.' But this only raises the further question: effects on whom?

Once more, the question can only be answered by a negative. There is no uniquely privileged participant-observer against whose reactions the researcher can test his description and its grounding. There are only participants any one of whom may be able to point out to him that something which he ought from their point of view to have put in has been left out; and if the purpose of his description is such that their point of view should have been a part of it, then he is guilty at best of incompleteness (which is a kind of misapprehension) and at worst of suppression (which is a kind of mystification). And since whatever event, process or state of affairs he is seeking to describe will have been experienced by a multiplicity of participants all of whom will have viewed it differently from each other, how will he ever be able to rebut the charge that he has failed to include what he should?

To answer this, let me again begin with an example from fiction – or rather, from the accusation levelled by one celebrated writer of fiction against another. Here is E. M. Forster charging Henry James with *suppressio veri* amounting to mystification in his delineation of his characters who, says Forster,

> are incapable of fun, of rapid motion, of carnality, and of nine-tenths of heroism. Their clothes will not take off, the diseases that ravage them are anonymous, like the sources of their income, their servants are noiseless or resemble themselves, no social explanation of the world we know is possible for them, for there are no stupid people in their world, no barriers of language, and no poor. Even their sensations are limited. They can land in Europe and look at works of art and each other, but that is all.*

The accusation is not, to be sure, fair, or even meant to be. It invites the obvious retort not merely that Forster has chosen to forget that James wrote *The Princess Cassimassima* but that not all the characters of Forster's own novels are always bursting with explicit carnality or even fun. But the more constructive defence which can be made to it rests on the observation that the limitations which Forster imputes to James's vision of human nature were, rather, limitations on the overt expression of carnality and the rest imposed on persons such as James is concerned to describe by the conventions of the period and milieu in which they lived. It is simply not true that Chad Newsome in *The Ambassadors*, Morton Densher in *The Wings of the Dove* or Prince Amerigo in *The Golden Bowl* are incapable of carnal fun. On the contrary, James makes it perfectly clear that they both have it and give it. But they do not talk about it in other people's hearing; and nor does James.† The themes of

---

* *Aspects of the Novel* (1927), Ch. 8.
† Cf. his letter of February 23, 1888, to Paul Bourget, in *Letters III, 1883–1895* (ed. Edel, 1980).

lust, cupidity, betrayal and renunciation which are acted out in these three novels can be claimed to be rendered authentically precisely because they are rendered in the terms appropriate to the conventions – or, if you like, the hypocrisies – by which such matters were regulated among persons of the period and milieu in which they are set. The omissions are not merely justified but positively demanded because they are – if they are – representative of these.

§ 6. This notion of *representativeness*, which I here introduce for the first time, has a twofold importance for the practice of descriptive sociology. First, it suggests a way of answering the question about completeness of description not in terms of an all-embracing inclusion of divergent perspectives such as is in any event impossible, but rather of perspectives which are themselves shared by the multifarious persons covered by the description independently of variations of individual temperament. Second, it implies in consequence that the number of different perspectives of which the sociologist has to take account is a function not of the size of the institution or society which he is describing but of the conflicts of view within it. In sociology (or anthropology or history), authentic description requires both a demonstrable correspondence with the reactions of actual persons which is irrelevant to the novelist and a defensible criterion of selection and emphasis which is irrelevant to the autobiographer. If the test of the first is whether those whose thoughts and deeds are being described could in principle be brought to accept the description as 'what it was like', the test of the second is whether they would agree that the divergent points of view of distinguishable groups or categories within their institution or society have all been taken into account.

In practice, the relatively limited range both of researchers' concerns on the one hand and of ideological conflicts within human societies and institutions on the other helps to make the ideal of representativeness much more easily attainable than the infinite range of possible descriptions which neither misapprehend nor mystify might appear to imply. Not only does the sociologist of kinship terms not need to concern himself with differences of viewpoint over music any more than the sociologist of music needs to concern himself with differences of viewpoint over kinship terms; but in neither case are there so many differences as to make it impossible for both of them to include all the relevant viewpoints – at the social, as opposed to the individual, level. No doubt in every society there are as many political ideologies as there are citizens, as many religions as there are believers, as many aesthetics as there are connoisseurs and as many codes of domestic morality as there are families. But the number of ideologies in the orthodox sense – the sense, that is, that ties them by definition to groups as opposed to persons – in any society is so far from infinite that it is rare, even in the largest and most differentiated societies, for there to be more than literally a handful of them. It may be an exaggeration to say of the Prologue to Chaucer's *Canterbury Tales* that 'it is the concise portrait of an entire nation'.* But if you believe that a description of English society as a whole is quite impossible, read Halévy's *England in 1815* and then write down a list of what has been left out which ought to have been put in. No doubt you will come back with a list. But it will not be a long one. Halévy is perfectly aware that his work is incomplete in the sense that on many of the topics with which it deals it could profitably be supplemented or, indeed, corrected by results of specialist studies. But that is a different point. Authenticity, and the representativeness which it requires, is not compromised simply because a description might usefully be supplemented by the inclusion of reported observations not available to the sociologist, anthropologist or historian at the time of writing. What does compromise it is a pre-emptive omission or suppression of the experience and/or viewpoint of a group or category of persons who did hold a distinctive and relevant, even if confused and unarticulated, point of view of their own.

I do not wish to minimize the difficulties which face the researcher when he comes in practice to decide what to include and what to omit. Even if he is satisfied with the adequacy of his underlying theory, he still faces the task of establishing criteria of selection and emphasis within the group or category to be described. Where and how is he to ground his decision as to which of its members is the authentic spokesman for the rest, which of the things said and done by different persons within it are to be claimed to be typical or what degree of self-awareness is to be imputed to those least prone to try, unless prompted, to formulate a description of their own experience to themselves? The technically experienced fieldworker learns, among other things, how to test his own provisional descriptions against the most immediate criticisms to which a failure to surmount these difficulties would expose him. But even after a whole career of participant-observation he will not have arrived at a copybook procedure for so doing. How far I am from having done so myself will become apparent to the reader on arriving at Chapter 4 of Volume III, in which I offer a description of my own society in my own

---

* As is claimed by Nevill Coghill in the Introduction to his edition of them (1951), p. 15.

lifetime along the lines of the methodological directives which the present chapter sets out. It is, however, safe to say at least that the goal of authenticity in sociological description is not wholly unattainable in principle, however difficult in practice; that the criteria of authenticity are capable of definition, if only negatively; and that for the practising sociologist, anthropologist or historian, they not only need to but can be supplemented by a criterion of representativeness by reference to which it can be shown that there have been included in the description all those divergent points of view which are collectively held by identifiable sub-groups or categories distinguished by a qualitatively different perception of their common experience in relation to the society of which they form a part.

§7. The analysis of misdescription needs, however, to be taken beyond the broad distinction between sins of misapprehension on the one side and of mystification on the other. Misapprehension needs to be broken down in greater detail under the three headings of incompleteness, oversimplification and ahistoricity, and mystification under the three headings of suppression, exaggeration and ethnocentricity. These headings are neither rigorous nor exclusive. But they do make it possible to differentiate between the most important of the different ways in which descriptive sociology may fall short of the twin standards of representativeness and authenticity, even where the description neither includes any demonstrably inaccurate report nor presupposes any demonstrably invalid explanation.

Incompleteness typically arises from the neglect by the observer of an aspect of the institutions and practices of the society he is studying which is only peripheral to his own theoretical interests but is of much closer significance to 'them'. Consider for example a survey of the population of Greater London in 1970 concerned, among other things, with leisure – both the amount of it and the use to which it was being put.* Respondents were asked how they spent their time when not at work, a 'time budget' was applied in which 'activity' was broken down among 99 coded categories, and tables were drawn up showing the frequency with which different sports, hobbies and pastimes were indulged in by the members of different age groups and social classes. The figures shown cannot of course hope to be strictly accurate: even if respondents are telling the truth about how often they visit museums or polish their cars (and the recording angel will quickly confirm that they are not), their estimates of the time involved will be rough approximations at best. But

* Michael Young and Peter Willmott, *The Symmetrical Family* (1973).

this is not the point at issue. What is remarkable about the tables and supporting text is that there is no mention of sexual activity whatever. One code in the time budget which covers 'Private activities, non-specified, others' is allowed to include 'any time expenditure the respondent is unwilling or unable to give information on'. But nothing is said even to hint at the possibility that for many Londoners in 1970 the anticipation, pursuit and enjoyment of sexual relations may have been an, or even the most, important single use of leisure time. Now the authors of the survey might well reply that they were not in fact interested in the sexual behaviour of their sample and that for their purpose 'leisure' was operationally defined to exclude it. But it is still an odd definition of 'leisure' from the standpoint of their respondents themselves. Even if, once given their definition, the authors are not asserting anything demonstrably untrue, they have offered a demonstrably incomplete description of life and leisure in London as experienced by those about whom they have chosen to write.

Oversimplification typically arises when the researcher has failed to realize that the beliefs and practices connected with the behaviour which he is describing are more complex than his account of it, accurate as it may be, would suggest. This was the failing of many of the travellers' tales on which knowledge of 'primitive' cultures was based before the development of systematic participant-observation as the basic technique of social anthropology. Often, no doubt, the accounts of explorers, missionaries or castaways contained inaccurate reportage either because their own observations were vitiated by misunderstandings in the primary sense or because their native informants had misled them. But often their failure was simply that they assumed that there was nothing further which they needed, for their purposes, to record although their native informants, if pressed for a description in *their* terms, would have elaborated further. Oversimplification can equally well arise when the observer is confronted with a more, rather than less, complicated way of life than he has been led to expect: it is not simply a product of underestimation of the intelligence, subtlety and application of the members of an allegedly 'simple' society by observers from an ostensibly 'advanced' one. But the readiest illustrations are of this kind. It is now a commonplace among anthropologists that people living at an economic and technological level far below 'ours' are nevertheless quite capable of having formulated precise and extensive taxonomies within which the animals, vegetables and minerals in their environment are distinguished in detail. A trained fieldworker will no longer be surprised to discover that several hundreds of varieties of a species are separately named or that techniques of selective breeding or astronomical observation are practised with accuracy and success. He may well be no more interested in zoology or botany or astronomy as such than the explorers, missionaries or castaways who preceded him. But he will recognize, as they did not, that a well-grounded description of the way of life he is studying must not fail to bring out the significance to 'them' of their careful and elaborate classification of the natural world.

Ahistoricity typically arises where the researcher forgets that a set of reports about the behaviour of the members of an earlier society all of which may be perfectly accurate as they stand will be a misdescription if so presented as to imply that they were capable of conceptualizing their own experiences to themselves in the idiom of a later one. As we have seen, the use of terms which 'they' did not have is not necessarily a misdescription: 'Machiavellians' can authentically be described as such who have never heard of Machiavelli, and a description of Emma Bovary's feelings which uses terms that she does not can be illuminating for the very reason that it thereby puts what she will agree that she felt better than she could. But if, for example, a historian of political thought summarizes the views of Plato and Aristotle on slavery by selecting and emphasizing passages of their writings which parallel the views on slavery of eighteenth- or nineteenth-century slaveowners in Brazil, the Caribbean or the Southern United States, this cannot but misapprehend them: theoretical grounding for a description in these terms is simply not there. Whatever parallels there may be in conceptions of innate inferiority attributed to subordinate categories of persons, the attitudes of the ancient Greeks cannot authentically be described as 'racist' in the modern sense, and it is demonstrably ahistorical to leave a modern reader with an impression that they can.

Suppression, by contrast, typically arises where the researcher deliberately fails to include reports which would make the description which he presents less favourable to his chosen cause. But it need not, any more than mystification generally, imply deliberate bad faith. It is not the researcher's motive which makes it suppression. It is the fact that 'they' would feel that their experience was being described in such a way that, whether or not the researcher's values are the same as their own, something important to their own view of their experience has been presented through the researcher's eyes rather than theirs. Here, for example, is a sentence from an American sociology textbook written by an author who, for all I know, was thoroughly sympathetic to the cause of those about whom he was writing and had not the least desire to misdescribe anything to anybody:

The right to vote is virtually universal, and almost everywhere there are competing parties or factions trying to garner votes. Even such groups as the Negroes in the South, whose legal right to vote is often denied in practice, have pressure groups, such as the National Association for the Advancement of Colored Peoples, that have demonstrated their not inconsiderable political effectiveness. Moreover, there is no large segment of the population that is everywhere deprived of the vote. The votes of Northern Negroes can and do benefit Southern Negroes to some extent.*

Now this may, as it stands, be a piece of accurate reportage; and even if it is not, let me assume for methodology's sake that it is. But as a description of what it is like to be an American Negro in the 1950s it is a mystification because it omits what those described would most want the reader to be aware of – the frustration and bitterness felt by Negroes in a White-dominated society *despite* the amelioration which had also come about since the Second World War.

Exaggeration, likewise, typically arises when the researcher overstates a description to make a case for purposes of his own; and exaggerated descriptions often include reports which turn out on investigation to be inaccurate. But again, they need not do so. The mystification may derive simply from a too eager striving for authenticity. To illustrate it, here is a passage about the line bureaucrats of San Francisco City Hall from Tom Wolfe's *Mau-mauing the Flak-Catchers* (1971):

> Who else is left to understand the secret bliss of the coffee break at 10.30 a.m., the walk with one's fellows through the majesty of the gold-and-marble lobby and out across the grass and the great white walkways of City Hall Plaza, past the Ionic columns and Italian Renaissance façade of the Public Library on the opposite side and down McAllister Street a few steps to the cafeteria, where you say hello to Jerry as he flips the white enamel handle on the urn and pours you a smoking china mug of coffee and you sit down at a Formica table and let coffee and cigarette smoke seep through you amid the Spanish burble of the bus boys, knowing that it is all set and cushioned, solid and yet lined with velvet, all waiting for you, as long as you want it, somewhere below your consciousness, the Bourbon Louis baroque hulk and the golden dome of the City Hall, waiting for you on the way back, through the Plaza and up the steps and into the great central court, and you stop and talk with your good buddy by the door to the Registrar's or by the bust of Mayor Angelo Rossi, both of you in your shirtsleeves but with your ties held down smoothly by a small-bar tie clip, rocking back on the heels of your Hush Puppies, talking with an insider's chuckles of how that crazy messenger, the one with the glass eye, got caught trying to run football-pool cards off on the Xerox machine because he couldn't see the Viper standing there on his blind side for five minutes with his arms crossed, just watching him ...

* H. M. Johnson, *Sociology: a Systematic Introduction* (1960), p. 385.

There is more in the same vein and it is all, of its kind, splendid stuff. There is no reason why a journalist like Wolfe, any more than a novelist like Flaubert, should not be capable in his chosen *genre* of conveying what other people's experience is like better than they can themselves. But what do the line bureaucrats of San Francisco City Hall have to say themselves when they read it? I assume (and even if my assumption is wrong, it again does not undermine the methodological point) that they would dismiss it as rhetorical and overwritten, not because Wolfe has misunderstood their behaviour in either the primary or the secondary sense, but because he imputes to them, for the sake of a perlocutionary effect, attitudes and feelings not quite as experienced by themselves.

Ethnocentricity, lastly, typically arises where the assumptions of the observer's own period or milieu are read into the experience of the members of another in which they do not in fact have any place. It is particularly likely to arise when the description is of 'their' values and these are interpreted by the observer with implicit reference to values of his own which 'they' do not share. But it may equally arise when the description is of their view of their experience independently of value-judgements of any kind. An example of the kind where values are involved is an account of the moral standards of the peasants of a Southern Italian village by an American anthropologist which depicts their loyalty in patron–client relationships and their hostility in inter-familial ones in terms of an implicit comparison to an ideal of community co-operation which is wholly foreign to anything in their upbringing and experience.* An example where values are not involved is an account of the beliefs of the early Middle Ages by a twentieth-century historian which depicts the preoccupation of the thinkers of the time with the mystical meanings held to reside in the properties of the natural world in terms of an implicit comparison to the historian's own taken-for-granted distinction between the natural and the supernatural.† In both cases mystification has crept in. It is not just misapprehension, for what these researchers have done is not merely to fail to add or include what 'they' would have added or included if the description had been checked with 'them'. They have done more: they have imputed to 'them' – whether they realize it or not – a theoretical presupposition of their own which 'they' would disavow.

These six types of inauthenticity are not the only ones. Nor is their

---

* See the comments of Colin Bell and Howard Newby, *Community Studies* (1971), pp.150ff., on E. C. Banfield, *The Moral Basis of a Backward Society* (1956).
† Cf. the remark of Bloch (*Feudal Society*, p.84) on historians unable 'to lay aside the spectacles of men of the nineteenth and twentieth centuries'.

avoidance all that a good description needs. But one which can pass the
test is at least halfway to the degree of tertiary understanding, and the
success in conveying that understanding to the reader, to which practising sociologists, anthropologists and historians can realistically aspire.

PUTTING DESCRIPTIONS ACROSS

§8. There have now to be more closely examined, however, the means
by which tertiary understanding can best be conveyed. Descriptions
must be both authentic and representative. But they must also be so
framed that they do then succeed in conveying to the reader just what
the experiences described were (authentically and representatively) like.
Descriptions are not merely reinterpretations *to* 'them'; they are also
reinterpretations *for* 'us'.

Again this is not a problem of translation. It is true that many
sociological descriptions are written and disseminated in a language
different from that of the people whose thoughts, feelings, words and
actions are being described. But the problem is the same irrespective of
barriers of language. These may make description more difficult, just as
it may be more difficult when it is a past generation of the researcher's
own society whose experience he seeks to understand in the tertiary sense
and convey to readers who are contemporaries of his own. But the
linguistic difficulty will have had already to be overcome before the
methodological problem which concerns us here can arise at all. Describing to an English-speaking audience what '*mana*' means to the Poly-
nesians, or '*virtu*' means to Machiavelli or '*ujama*' means to President
Nyerere of Tanzania requires of him neither more nor less than describing what 'divine right' means to Charles I or 'equality' means to the
Levellers or 'democracy' means to the citizens of the twentieth-century
United States. In all of these examples, the common problem is to bridge
the divide between the reader's experience and the experiences of the
people whom the researcher wishes to describe to him, and this can only
be done by appealing at some point and in some form to what the reader
is presumed already to understand in the tertiary sense. This is equally
true where the description is of the reader's own experience and author
and reader are members of a common culture as it is where those whose
experience is being described are as different in language, outlook and
mores from either author or reader, or both, as it is possible for human
beings to be. It is for this reason that the effect of a good description on
the reader can aptly be described itself as an 'enlargement' of the reader's
experience. I remember a schoolfriend of mine describing to me the

effect on him of reading *The Brothers Karamazov* at the age of sixteen: before he had read it, he told me, his vision of life had been like *this* (and he held out his hands joined at the palms at a narrow angle); but now (widening the angle as far as his wrists would let him) it was like *this*! He assumed, of course, that Dostoievski was both authentic and representative. But what he was trying to convey to me was that he had been enabled to see 'their' reported behaviour as understandable, in the tertiary sense, in 'our' terms, however different might be the beliefs and attitudes of Dostoievski's characters (and the language in which they expressed them to themselves) from those of a twentieth-century English sixteen-year-old from a 'good' home and school.

Conversely, a description, even if authentic and representative, will fail to bridge the divide between the understanding achieved by the observer and the understanding of comparable experience attributed to the reader if the author reinterprets it through a misplaced invocation of theoretical presuppositions imputed to 'us'. How, for example, is a film-maker to proceed who wants to convey what he has come to understand in the tertiary sense about what it was like for the inhabitants of ancient Rome as the barbarian invaders surged across the Rhine and the Eternal City came to feel itself under threat for the first time since Hannibal encircled and destroyed the army of Aemilius Paullus and Terentius Varro at Cannae? One way *not* to do it is to make the characters speak in the mock-archaic diction of the Hollywood epic which turns 'I do not know' into 'I know not', and 'Hurry!' into 'Make haste!'. Yet to succeed, the description has also to avoid the alternative error of using so up-to-date an idiom that 'I do not know' becomes 'Search me!', and 'Hurry!' becomes 'Get your skates on!' or 'Move your ass!' It is possible, in such cases, that there are some aspects of an intended description which simply cannot be conveyed directly, and it may for this purpose be an inherent disadvantage of the cinema as a medium that there cannot be insinuated into it the commentary which the writer can insinuate into his narrative without breaking its flow. But if the conveying of understanding in the tertiary sense is the film-maker's purpose, he should be able to turn his skill with the medium, together with his grasp of 'our' idiom into which 'their' experiences need to be rephrased, to achieving that purpose as well as or better than can be done by the written word alone. Unlike the Hollywood epic, a fictional documentary* may very

* Or a non-fictional one: a film such as John Marshall's *The Hunters* (1956) – which I have not myself seen, but is widely admired among practising anthropologists – may convey what the life of the !Kung Bushmen is like better than any fieldworker's monograph.

well succeed in authentically and representatively conveying the institutions and practices of another period and milieu to its audience, even though the actors are not expected by either the film-maker or the audience to reproduce exactly how 'they' looked, talked and behaved. Provided that the conventions of the medium are respected by the filmmaker and accepted by the audience, there is no reason in principle why such a film should not succeed in enabling the audience to understand 'their' life and times in the tertiary sense just as well as Flaubert, Malinowski, John Dollard, William Foote Whyte, Erving Goffman, Oscar Lewis or Emmanuel Le Roy Ladurie.

§9. Understanding of this kind must not, however, be equated with 'valuing' or even 'reacting to'. When Collingwood looked at the Albert Memorial and realized that he did not understand, in the tertiary sense, how it could be to 'them' the memorial to build, he did not have to come to share their admiration of it, but only to relate the seeing of it to some other aesthetic experience. This might or might not be easier for him than to come to understand the art of a culture more remote in either time or place from his own: that is still not the point. The point is that he had, although finding the Albert Memorial hideous, to come to bridge the divide between mid-Victorian and early twentieth-century taste by means of the right analogy between it and other works of art of which he *did* have a tertiary understanding. To stop seeing a memorial, artefact, sculpture, building or indeed a whole architectural and artistic style as 'dated' requires, just as Wittgenstein says, an act of will. But it cannot be performed just by trying. It needs the help of the sociologist, anthropologist or historian who has already succeeded in both enlarging his own tertiary understanding and suspending his own evaluative presuppositions.

The same holds where it is not literally seeing as, but hearing as. To come to understand, in the tertiary sense, an unfamiliar musical idiom is in the same way more than being able to report and explain it and less than coming to like it (although one may). Suppose that Collingwood has remedied his incomprehension of the Albert Memorial only to be confronted for the first time in his life with the sound shown overleaf.* Now he has – or let me for methodology's sake assume so – a thorough knowledge of musical theory and an explanation with which he is satisfied of the nature and development of twelve-note music: he can at once, for example, understand in the secondary sense the need for the predictable

* The example of the Webern Variations (op. 27) is borrowed from Roger Scruton, *Art and Imagination* (1974), p. 172.

G sharp of the final bar of the sequence by reference to the fact that the melodic line has previously exhausted all but one of a twelve-note series, and he has in no way failed to understand in the primary sense what Webern was doing in stringing symbols together on paper in this way. But his explanation is neither necessary nor sufficient for understanding in the tertiary sense, and his primary understanding, although obviously necessary, is equally obviously very far from sufficient. What he needs if he is to understand it in the tertiary sense – let alone to convey that understanding by an appropriate *re*description in the book which he wishes to write for a *non*-specialist audience about European music of the twentieth century – is to be able to relate his experience of twelve-note music to the experience of classical music which he brings to it in such a way that he could, in principle, pass the standard practical test – that is, by giving an account of it to Webern himself which Webern would accept as authentic. He may still find Webern's music unsatisfying or even positively distasteful and he may, for his own pleasure, return from it to Mozart or Vivaldi as eagerly as he returns from the Albert Memorial to the cathedrals of Durham or Chartres. But he has, by that time, heard them and seen them as they could have been described as being heard and seen by their creators, whether he admires them or not.

§ 10. But now suppose that there appears to be lacking *any* idiom in terms of which the researcher can relate his readers' presumptive experiences to those which he wishes to describe to them. What is he to do when he wants to convey what an institution or practice is like which he suspects they will find radically unintelligible in the tertiary sense?

Dazzled by so many and such marvellous inventions, the people of Macondo did not know where their amazement began. They stayed up all night looking at the pale electric bulbs fed by the plant that Aurelio Triste had brought back when the train made its second trip, and it took time and effort for them to become accustomed to its obsessive *toom-toom*. They became indignant over the living images that the prosperous merchant Bruno Crespi projected in the theatre with the lion-head ticket windows, for a character who had died and was buried in one film and for whose misfortune tears of affliction had been shed would reappear alive and transformed into an Arab in the next one. The audience, who paid two cents apiece to share the difficulties of the actors, would not tolerate the outlandish fraud and they broke up the seats. The mayor, at the urging of Bruno Crespi, explained in a proclamation that the cinema was a machine of illusions that did not merit the emotional outbursts of the audience. With that discouraging explanation many felt that they had been the victims of some new and showy gipsy business and they decided not to return to the movies, considering that they already had too many troubles of their own to weep over the acted-out misfortunes of imaginary beings. (Gabriel Garcia Marquez, *One Hundred Years of Solitude*)

So – what is Bruno Crespi to say to those who, although they have understood in the primary sense that the machine is portraying actors, not people, still fail to understand the practice of cinema-going in the tertiary sense as it is understood by the ordinary run of habituated cinema-goers in the rest of the modern world? It will be no good his accusing them of 'irrationality', for it is they who regard the practice as irrational by a standard presumptively common to both him and themselves. Nor will it be any good telling them to try again, for they have. Nor will it be any good telling them about the history of photography, or persuading them to read *Cahiers du Cinéma*. They cannot, and by now don't care to, understand how anyone can seriously want to spend two cents in order to weep over the acted-out misfortunes of imaginary beings.

The example, it is true, is another fictional one. But it draws sufficiently closely on the author's own upbringing in a small, declining town in the Atlantic region of Colombia in the 1920s not to belong to the realm of fantasy. What *is* Bruno Crespi to say? There really doesn't seem to be anything he can say which will bring them back into the cinema there and then; and the Mayor's proclamation, like many such, appears to have had an opposite effect from what its instigator had in mind. Yet we know that the people of Macondo will come round to movie-going in the end. They may not care for Bruno Crespi's original choice; they may come still later to desert the movie theatre for the television screen in their own homes; there may always be other pastimes which most or all of them prefer. But an account of a town in Colombia whose inhabitants *went on* reacting to the cinema in the way that the inhabitants of Macondo are described as doing would be as much of a fantasy as the Wise Men of Gotham whom I dismissed along with Wittgenstein's eccentric wood-valuers in Section 8 of Chapter 1. Bruno Crespi's difficulty is not a symptom of the inherent incomprehensibility, in the tertiary sense, of the practice in question, but simply of its novelty. The initial lack of understanding lay not in a failure to understand in the primary sense what was being portrayed – *that* the audience understood if anything too well –

but in a failure to see it as the point of the cinema that it should indeed, as the Mayor told them, be a machine of illusions which for that very reason does not merit the emotional outburst appropriate to the portrayal of an actual death (and subsequent resurrection), whereas it does perhaps merit two cents of expenditure for the entertainment it provides.

To this, 'they' might still reply that it is only worth two cents to go and see if it *is* also worth an emotional outburst: if the machine of illusions is portraying merely the representation of things which never happened to people pretending to be people who never existed in the first place, how can anyone want to waste their time on it at all? But this question itself has a detectable touch of rhetoric. The implication that people's emotions are not aroused except by reports of what they believe to be true is not merely demonstrably incorrect, but also presupposes a clear-cut distinction between true and false and a pervasive significance attaching to it which goes well beyond, and therefore belies, the simulated naivety of the question. The person who does understand in the tertiary sense what the cinema is all about should, admittedly, be prepared to accept the initial astonishment of those who don't. Of course they will react to it in a different way from those who came to understand it as a part of the culture into which they grew up as children. But their reactions would only be puzzling if they were to continue to profess themselves as baffled by it after long familiarity as they were at the outset. It would then be as though an ethnographer were to return from the field complaining that, say, the representational art of the Kwakiutl Indians was as baffling to him at the end of two years' fieldwork as it was on the day he arrived. It may well be that in the course of his fieldwork he will have *pretended* a continuing bafflement. He may well have asked his native informants what point anyone can possibly see in a painting of a split and distorted representation of a killer whale on the front of a house in the same sort of tone of voice as the inhabitants of Macondo might continue to pester Bruno Crespi with mock-innocent questioning about the point of his machine of illusions. But the point of these questions is that they are already part of standard sociological technique. They express not an incurable bewilderment but a curiosity to explore the full implications of an institution or practice whose meaning to those involved in it the researcher is not yet sure of understanding as fully as he might. They are asked in the spirit in which I might ask a fellow-member of my own society 'Didn't you feel when you watched the film of the Queen's coronation that it was an embarrassingly silly piece of play-acting?' or 'What on earth is the pleasure you get by having eleven people trying to prevent you and ten other people kicking a ball in between two sticks set up at their end of a field?' The ethnographer from an alien culture who asks me questions about mine of the form 'How can you possibly ...?' or is moved to exclamations like 'Don't tell me you really ...!' or 'How absurd that you should ...!' is not yet, unless his own attitude is entirely simulated, in a position to start describing it to the members of his own. But that is not because it is radically unintelligible. It is only because he is – quite naturally – still finding it a little odd, and thus seeking to elicit from his informants some further response to questions or exclamations of a deliberately rhetorical kind. 'How can you possibly ...?' is not a request for a cause; 'Don't tell me you really ...!' is not an accusation of inaccurate reportage; 'How absurd that you should ...!' is not the assertion of a value-judgement. They are all technical devices adopted for the purpose and in the hope of enlarging the researcher's tertiary understanding.

Oddity, therefore, is a difficulty in the way of effective description not because it leads the sociologist to conclude that there is *no* idiom in which he can convey to his readers what an alien culture is like for those brought up in it but because it makes it that much harder for him to know what kind of parallels he should be choosing for the purpose. To the extent that he is concerned with describing as distinct from either explaining or evaluating, he is concerned to give his readers an answer that will satisfy *them* in the form of a statement that 'it is like ...' – well, what? If he is describing a culture of vegetarians to the members of a culture of meat-eaters, he can say 'their feelings about eating the flesh of animals are like your feelings about eating the flesh of human beings'. If he is writing for an American audience about the feelings of Durkheimian solidarity which animate the songs and dances with which the scattered Arunta tribespeople celebrate the periodic festivals at which they come together, he can remind them of the singing of 'I am an American' on specified days in their own schools. If he wants to convey to those brought up to believe in twentieth-century Western medicine the ambiguous attitude of the professional sorcerer to the techniques by which he effects his apparent cures, he can cite the cases where Western practitioners admit to the apparent efficacy of psychosomatic techniques which they cannot themselves explain. There may not always be parallels as close as these. But there will always be a parallel of some kind. The danger is merely that where it isn't a close one, the researcher may pitch the analogy at so general a level that tertiary understanding will not be enlarged after all. Thus, it will scarcely do if he illustrates his monograph on Kwakiutl painting with photographs of a further set of objects which will strike his readers as equally alien to their taste and offers no further

comment than they are another example of 'their' form of art. Nor will
it necessarily help – although it may – if his illustrations are accompanied
by a detailed explanation of the history and function of the symbolism
and of the motives which have caused it to be given expression in this
form. This kind of secondary understanding will sometimes be enough
to reduce the gap between the cultures to the size of a gap within the
same culture – that is, to the gap which left Collingwood on one side and
the patrons of Sir George Gilbert Scott on the other. But this is the very
gap which raises the difficulty of tertiary understanding in its acutest
form. The reader has still to be brought to see 'their' art as the sociologist,
anthropologist or historian has been brought to see it, even if still finding
it just as ugly as Collingwood found the Albert Memorial.

What is needed, accordingly, is not so much the one right parallel as
the supplementation of an adequate parallel with the right selection of
descriptively relevant reports about 'their' culture. The reader must be put
in the position of being able to talk to the artist as sympathetically as the
researcher has been able to do by the end of his fieldwork or study of
the documentary sources; and this means, as in the example of twelve-
note music, being put in the position of seeing how the work of art relates
to other aspects of the culture in question in the artist's mind. Indeed,
this may be more enlightening than the obvious parallels. Suppose that
you express yourself thoroughly baffled by the painted faces of Caduveo
women as described by travellers since the seventeenth century and
photographed by Lévi-Strauss in 1935. I might be tempted to suggest
to you the parallels of make-up as practised by most modern Western
women and of tattooing as practised by some modern Western men. But
to leave it at that would be to *mis*describe the practice of Caduveo women
to you, even if it gave you, as it might, a feeling of diminished puzzlement
amounting at least to the beginning of tertiary understanding. Of course,
there is *a* parallel between all forms of bodily decoration across all
cultures. But for the purpose of description, differences within that
category are all-important. 'Face-painting' is a theory-neutral term; but
'making up', in this context, is not. A description of Caduveo face-
painting cannot hope to convey to the reader from a different culture
what the practice is like for the Caduveo themselves unless it makes clear
that first, the women do it to each other's faces, and second, they are not
tattoos but paintings done with a wooden spatula dipped in juice. We
have only to ask ourselves the question whether Caduveo women, if
sufficiently well informed about other cultures where make-up and
tattooing are standard practice, would agree that that is what their own
practice of face-painting is like to realize that they would reject the

parallel as inauthentic. The divide between the cultures needs to be more circuitously bridged, possibly by way of extending the idea of decorative painting of inanimate objects to the painting of one's own person in the same kind of way. I say 'possibly' because I do not have a theory adequate to enable me to say what further reports on the attitudes and behaviour of the Caduveo would be the best with which to supplement the parallel. But however peculiar the practice may seem to you, I am quite sure that it would not continue to seem so if you were yourself to go and do the fieldwork and then convey your tertiary understanding of it to me and your other presumptive readers in a considered sociological description.*

THE USES OF ANALOGY AND DETAIL

§ 11. Where a description does succeed through pointing an apposite parallel, the resemblance on which it rests may be of any one of several different kinds and at any one of several different levels. In explanatory contexts, analogies take the form of a matrix in which the vertical relations are causal ones, as – to give a simple natural-scientific example – with

$$\text{echo} \leftrightarrow \text{reflection}$$
$$\uparrow \qquad \uparrow$$
$$\text{sound} \leftrightarrow \text{light.}$$

---

* For comparison and commentary, see Robert Brain, *The Decorated Body* (1979), Ch. 2 ('The Painted Body'). The photograph is taken from Claude Lévi-Strauss, *Structural Anthropology* (Eng. trans., 1963), Ch. 14.

In descriptive contexts such as only arise in the human sciences the vertical relations are not necessarily causal, but may be so if that is the kind of analogy which in the given instance best serves the descriptive purpose. Thus in the analogy argued by Radcliffe-Brown to hold between the subservience to ritual found in 'primitive' societies and the subservience to technology found in 'modern' ones, the vertical relations are causal even though the purpose of the argument is to persuade the 'modern' reader that the 'primitive' man's ostensibly puzzling acceptance of ritual prohibitions is just like his own acceptance of the authority of science. Schematically, the argument is that

$$\begin{array}{ccc}
\text{subservience to technology} & \leftrightarrow & \text{subservience to ritual} \\
\uparrow & & \uparrow \\
\text{respect for scientific laws} & \leftrightarrow & \text{respect for moral laws} \\
\nwarrow & & \nearrow \\
& \text{fear of transgressing the pre-ordained} &
\end{array}$$

and that, by implication, if the reader accepts the explanation as valid it is as understandable in the tertiary sense what it is like for one of 'them' to be careful not to kill a cicada as for one of 'us' to be careful, say, with an electric plug.

In other instances, however, the vertical relations are not causal at all; or even if they are, it is not that aspect of them which gives the analogy its point. In the example 'their feelings about eating the flesh of animals are like your feelings about eating the flesh of human beings', there is a presumptive common explanation in terms of the psychological aversion engendered by the idea of killing for food and the idea of eating a fellow living creature. But the success of the analogy does not depend on the invocation of the explanation. It depends on the reader's awareness that the values of 'our' culture are such that, for whatever cause, we too have an inbuilt aversion to the killing of some living creatures for food, although not necessarily the same ones as 'they'.

Now, however, consider a more complicated example, from a book review by Malcolm Muggeridge written in the 1970s: 'Is not today's Etonian or Harrovian in his proletarian fancy-dress, with his talk of avoiding the rat-race and eschewal of the mores and attitudes of his forbears, a Beloved Vagabond *de nos jours*?' It is more complicated than the example from Radcliffe-Brown not because the attitudes of Etonians and Harrovians of the 1970s on the one hand, or 'Beloved Vagabonds' of the 1910s on the other, are more difficult to describe than ritual prohibitions among so-called 'primitive' people, but because there underlies the analogy drawn a covert claim that *plus ça change, plus c'est la même chose.* Again, there is a causal story built in: the same sorts of influences are being argued to produce the same forms of behaviour then as now. But the resemblance is not being argued by appeal to the explanation; and the purpose for which it is drawn is not only to convey a tertiary understanding but also to convey the evaluative implication that the privileged English schoolboys of today are neither as original nor as daring in their attitudes and behaviour as they and possibly the reader (if not suitably alerted) may suppose. Schematically, therefore, the analogy is something like the diagram below.

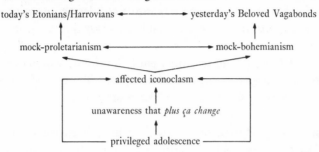

Here the vertical relations are not, except for the lowermost, causal, but a mixture between symptoms-of-a-common-condition and genus-to-species, coupled with a horizontal relation of resemblance which I have compressed into the term 'mock'. The reader who fails to find it persuasive is not, or at any rate need not be, disavowing a secondary understanding of why the social and psychological influences which lead privileged young men to affect iconoclastic attitudes recur from generation to generation. The justification for scepticism is rather that the resemblance is being exaggerated (overdone, made too much of, pressed too far): it cannot be grounded in an adequate descriptive theory. The reader (or rival observer) who feels that the juxtaposition as it is presented misdescribes either or both today's Etonians/Harrovians and yesterday's Beloved Vagabonds is voicing reservations about the emphasis which has been given to a resemblance which covers only a limited aspect of the total way of life of those described; and this amounts to a suspicion that the twin standards of representativeness and authenticity have been covertly breached for the sake of a pejorative insinuation about the spoilt young men of the writer's own period and milieu.

Such scepticism may be well founded even where the vertical relations within the matrix of the analogy are acceptable. It is surely difficult not to agree both that mock-proletarianism and mock-bohemianism are two kinds of affected iconoclasm and that affected iconoclasm and an awareness that *plus ça change* ... may both, under certain conditions, be among the symptoms of a privileged adolescence. But may not Muggeridge, by so insisting on it, be conveying 'their' experience a little too much through his own eyes and, therefore, mystifying it? And may not the apparent implication that a whole generation of privileged young men and their way of life can be described in this way leave too far out of account the likelihood that there were very many members of both the two sub-cultures in question who were not only less eccentric but also more self-aware than the description suggests? The criticism is not that the analogy is inapposite. Indeed, it could plausibly be elaborated through further association of ideas into a still larger and more complicated diagram. But there is immediately a danger that the gain in impact on, and persuasiveness to, the reader will be outweighed by a loss in either authenticity or representativeness (or both) which can only be made up by yet more reportage of other aspects of 'their' behaviour which are also relevant to the purpose of the description.

§ 12. But how is this to be done? And by what criteria is it to be assessed? We appear to be back with Macaulay's dictum: the aim in introducing the reportage of such additional facts as will strike the reader as particularly vivid or illuminating is, presumably, to 'exhibit such parts of the truth as most nearly to produce the effects of the whole'. But just as there is no one privileged observer who can be asked to pronounce on either the authenticity or the representativeness of a description, so equally there is no one privileged reader whose reactions can be used to test whether a description includes a sufficient selection of sufficiently vivid and illuminating details to provide adequate grounding for the analogy intended to bridge the divide between 'their' experience and 'ours'.

Here a further distinction needs to be made, for which the terms *vivid* and *illuminating* may as well be allowed to stand. There are two slightly different purposes for which a sociologist, anthropologist or historian (or autobiographer or novelist) may wish to introduce an extra graphic touch. The first is to bring to life (hence 'vivid') an institution, practice or attitude of mind which the reader might otherwise find it difficult to picture. The second is to make less obscure (hence, 'illuminating') a mode of thought or behaviour with which the reader might otherwise find it difficult to sympathize. Both, of course, may be intended to serve an explanatory and/or evaluative purpose as well. The graphic touch may at the same time help the reader to understand why the agents in question thought, said or did what they are reported as having thought, said or done or to share the researcher's view of it as good or bad. But for the purely descriptive purpose, there are two distinguishable (although often overlapping) criteria of success.

As an example of the vivid, here is Bloch's description of the attitude to time of the 'men of the two feudal ages'. Notice that he comments explicitly on their 'remoteness' from 'us': it is this which the reported behaviour of the lawcourt at Mons is intended to illustrate. The remoteness, however, is not of the kind which will leave the reader with a sense of unresolved puzzlement. Bloch is not searching for an anecdote which will diminish an otherwise radical incommunicability, but for one which will bring home to the reader the implications for feudal society of a lack of the respect for numerical accuracy and of the inbuilt awareness of the passage of hours such as 'we' nowadays take for granted.

> These men, subjected both externally and internally to so many ungovernable forces, lived in a world in which the passage of time escaped their grasp all the more because they were so ill-equipped to measure it. Waterclocks, which were costly and cumbersome, were very rare. Hour-glasses were little used. The inadequacy of sundials, especially under skies quickly clouded over, was notorious. This resulted in the use of curious devices. In his concern to regulate the course of a notably nomadic life, King Alfred had conceived the idea of carrying with him everywhere a supply of candles of equal length, which he had lit in turn, to mark the passing of the hours, but such concern for uniformity in the division of the day was exceptional in that age. Reckoning ordinarily – after the example of Antiquity – twelve hours of day and twelve of night, whatever the season, people of the highest education became used to seeing each of these fractions, taken one by one, grow and diminish incessantly, according to the annual revolution of the sun. This was to continue till the moment when – towards the beginning of the fourteenth century – counterpoise clocks brought with them at last, not only the mechanization of the instrument, but, so to speak, of time itself.
>
> An anecdote related in a chronicle of Hainault illustrates admirably the sort of perpetual fluctuation of time in those days. At Mons a judicial duel is due to take place. Only one champion puts in an appearance – at dawn; at the ninth hour, which marks the end of the waiting period prescribed by custom, he requests that the failure of his adversary be placed on record. On the point of law, there is no doubt. But has the specified period really elapsed? The county judges deliberate, look at the sun, and question the clerics in whom the practice of the liturgy has induced a more exact knowledge of the rhythm of the hours than their own, and by whose bells it is measured, more or less accurately, to the common benefit of men. Eventually the court pronounces firmly that the hour of 'none' is past. To us, accustomed to live with our eyes turning constantly to the clock, how remote from our civilization seems this society in which a court of law could not ascertain the time of day without discussion and inquiry!*

* *Feudal Society*, pp. 73–4, citing Gislebert of Mons (ed. Pertz), pp. 188–9.

As an example of the illuminating, here is W. L. Burn's description of the attitude to God's will of the believing Christians of the educated classes of mid nineteenth-century England. Notice here that the explicit comment is not in terms of remoteness but of implications which 'one' (i.e. the historian or sociologist of the twentieth century) might suggest to be 'fantastic'. The behaviour reported by way of illustrating 'their' attitude first seems to invite, but then is used to rebut, this suggestion because the anecdotes chosen by Burn are such as to bring out the way in which 'their' literal belief in a last judgement dictated an attitude to natural misfortune which was not, therefore, 'fantastic' at all. Here, explanation is explicitly invoked in the service of description. But a page or two earlier, Burn has raised the pure descriptive question whether 'they' were not mystifying their own attitudes and beliefs: 'Was all the talk about "duty" and "prayers" and "religion" hypocritical humbug? ... Was the whole age a hollow sham?' His answer is that it was not, or at any rate not for 'the country as a whole', and that what may appear to be bullshit to us needs to be understood in the tertiary sense by reference to the nature of the beliefs which the kind of people he has in mind did actually hold. Hence the clue to be followed in 'their' use of the word 'lesson'.

> ... Another word much used was 'lesson'. God 'taught' lessons and it was the duty of men to learn them; as it was the duty of schoolboys to learn what their masters sought to teach them. The colonial and garrison chaplain of Sierra Leone wrote in 1850 of the drowning of his predecessor and three other officials on an occasion when three other intending passengers had been at the last minute prevented from joining the boat party. 'The over-ruling ways of Providence are wonderful and sometimes exemplified in so striking a manner that it is impossible not to see in them an intention to teach the living a lesson they are too apt to forget ... Such was the Will of Him whose mercies are inscrutable, yet merciful and just.'
> When the Revd John Bowen (1815–59) was invited in 1857 to accept the bishopric of Sierra Leone he felt that he dared not refuse. But he was convinced that he must go out as a married man and he only succeeded at the last moment in his urgent desire to marry. 'A light has shone on my path and an excellent Christian woman has been given to me.' When Mrs Bowen died in child-bed in the next year her husband noted, 'I have had a severe chastisement to bear. May it teach me the intended lesson!' It reminded him, a man of some standing, that he too was mortal. 'After all,' he reflected, 'I may have a very short time to stay.' And he was right; he died in 1859. A Caithness doctor, James Mill (1810–73), said on the death of his eldest child at the age of fourteen, in 1859, 'Truly I know the bitterness of mourning over a first-born son. May I as fully realize and mourn over my own sin against God, for I was never more convinced of anything than of my need of this trial. Without trial how should we bear

in mind that we are strangers and pilgrims here?' On the death of another son in 1870 he said, 'perhaps it is better and we must and ought to submit with adoring reverence, for God does all things well'. Not so very long afterwards he himself fell ill and as he approached death, 'he saw great reason for thankfulness that he was not glurd (glued) to the world, and could think of leaving it without regret. He said he believed it was James's death that loosened him from the world and showed him its vanity as a portion.' At the end, 'When the cough was very harassing some nights ago he said, "This will soon wear me out but I do not wish to murmur or complain. I know the Hand that sends it." '

One could ask questions about these 'lessons' and suggest that the implications drawn from some of the events described were fantastic. Might not 'Providence' have taught its lesson without the loss of four lives in that West African river? Alternatively, would not the loss of the other three have made the lesson the more impressive? Was there anything remarkable in an English girl dying in child-bed in West Africa in 1858? It may seem, too, today, that some of the emotions which the deaths generated could have been usefully transferred into attempts to avert the deaths; that the men who were drowned ought to have been more careful, that Bishop Bowen was callously selfish in taking his wife to Sierra Leone; that 'the hand of Providence' could in many instances be translated into foolhardiness, bungling surgery, incompetent nursing, foul working conditions, defective drains. But the fact that we can, properly, ask such questions shows how wide is the gap between that age and ours. To ask them at all, perhaps, is to miss the point – *their* point – not ours. Death, to them, was not the end. But it was the gate to Heaven or Hell, the awful preliminary to the final, all-important divine judgement. Lessons, even such lessons as the death of a beloved relative, were things to be grateful for if they assisted the survivors so to order the remainder of their own lives as to gain eternal bliss and escape eternal damnation. It is not irreverent to liken such lessons to the warnings which a schoolmaster might give a boy before his GCE examination or a trainer give to an apprentice about to ride in his first big race: 'You're pretty safe with your geometry but you'll have to be careful with your algebra'; 'Keep four or five lengths behind the favourite till you get to the turn'; 'Remember what happened to Tom Smith'.*

I have quoted both these passages at some length because it is impossible to judge the contribution of a set of chosen reports to the success of a description without including the context in which they are presented. But let me assume once again, for methodology's sake, that the two passages are both authentic and representative. Their success in each case rests on the choice of the vivid or illuminating detail which can be related to the appropriate equivalents in 'our' culture. In Burn's case, there is an explicit resemblance drawn between the lessons which 'they'

* W. L. Burn, *The Age of Equipoise* (1964), pp. 44–6.

thought God taught and those which 'we' might expect from a coach or a schoolmaster; in Bloch's there is an explicit contrast drawn between 'their' inexact reckonings by the sun and 'our' exact reckonings by the clock. Yet it is not the balance between the similarities and differences between 'them' and 'us' which is decisive, but their presumptive grounding in a theory adequate to vindicate the similarities and differences alike. The temptation which attends the invocation of the graphic detail in the absence of an adequate theory is the temptation to use it to serve a purpose other than that of description itself. Even where accuracy of reportage is strictly maintained, there is always a risk that the researcher may select for his description those aspects or episodes which are likeliest to entertain, provoke or stimulate the reader rather than simply to convey as authentically and representatively as possible what the institution, practice or attitude being described was like to 'them'.

In this respect, Bloch's description stands in striking contrast to the use of anecdotes from a similar historical period made by, for example, Pareto. Pareto's *Trattato di Sociologia Generale* is full of well-attested reports from a variety of places and times, including the Middle Ages, which are introduced to illustrate his explanatory theory about the relation of variable cultural forms to underlying psychological constants. But in telling his chosen anecdotes he is concerned not merely to illustrate and describe, but to ridicule. When he recounts, for example, the prosecution of leeches for trespass by order of the Court of Berne in the year 1451, or the defence of the rats of Autun by the celebrated advocate Barthélémy Chassanné, he is doing so not for the purpose of helping the reader to understand in the tertiary sense what it was like to subscribe to a set of beliefs from which the bringing of lawsuits in due form against animals could appear naturally to follow but for the purpose of making those who did so look silly.* No doubt it is conceivable that the perlocutionary effect of these passages in Pareto's *Trattato* is to convey to the reader a more vivid and illuminating sense of what the Middle Ages were like to those who lived through them while at the same time convincing him that Pareto's own explanatory theory of 'derivations' and 'residues' is not worth taking seriously. But that, if it happens, still does not furnish

---

* Vilfredo Pareto, *The Mind and Society* (Eng. trans., 1935), § 1502; although the further purpose of these anecdotes becomes clear only in § 1503, where he adds that 'There were jurists and theologians who thought that the procedures used against rational beings could not be extended to brute creatures, and among the theologians stood St Thomas Aquinas, no less. But nothing of that sort could put an end to such trials; any more than in our own time demonstrations of the utter inanity of the "social contract", of "solidarity", "peace through law", "Christian Science" and other such vagaries can put an end to their respective derivations.'

an argument for claiming that Pareto is as good as Bloch at describing the attitudes of the people of those days. A good description is one which successfully conveys to the reader what 'their' experience was like to *them*; and if a description of the Middle Ages framed for the sake of supporting the presuppositions of a militant, doctrinaire rationalist of the early twentieth century does convey it, it can only be by coincidence.

Similarly, Burn's description stands in striking contrast to the way in which, for example, Macaulay portrays the members of a chosen group or class in the England of a hundred years before his own time. Here he is in characteristic form, in his essay on the Earl of Chatham in the *Edinburgh Review* of January 1834, on the Tory members of the House of Commons in the 1730s:

> The Tories furnished little more than rows of ponderous foxhunters, fat with Staffordshire and Devonshire ale, men who drank to the King over the water and believed that all the fundholders were Jews, men whose religion consisted in hating the Dissenters and whose political researches had led them to fear, like Squire Western, that their land might be sent over to Hanover to be put into the sinking fund.

The reader is not, to be sure, meant to take the final assertion quite literally. But nor is the description entirely spurious. The 'little more' of the opening line signals a deliberately polemical exaggeration, but it does not caricature the Tory members to the point of fantasy. The failure of a passage like this as a sociological description lies rather in its having a little bit too much conscious literary merit to be counted even under the most generous rubric as social science. Unlike the example from Burn, it makes up in rhetoric for what it lacks in theoretical grounding.

§ 13. Yet it is no more a vice in a sociological description that it should be literary than it is a virtue that it should be literal. One of the distinctive characteristics of descriptions as opposed to either reports on the one hand or explanations on the other is the role of metaphor and simile within them. This is a separate matter from the use of analogies to point a resemblance in the reader's mind between 'them' and 'us', as in the example of the 'Beloved Vagabonds *de nos jours*'. The justification for the use of metaphors and similes within a description from 'their' point of view derives, as in the example of Flaubert saying of Emma Bovary that '*toute l'amertume de l'existence lui semblait servie sur son assiette*', from the strength of the theory underlying the implied claim that the person described *might as well have* felt, thought, said or done something other than what he or she ('literally') did.

There is a substantial philosophical literature on metaphor. But just as practising sociologists, anthropologists or historians do not need to be able to say what an explanation is but only what counts as one, so do they not need to be able to say what a metaphor is but only where and how it can best perform a descriptive function. Aristotle's original dictum that the value of metaphor lies in giving two ideas for the price of one says most if not all of what needs to be said for their purpose. The result of the association generated, or even forced, between the second idea and the first is that the reader's tertiary understanding is enlarged to the degree that the second adds something to the first – provided always that the metaphor would be acceptable in principle to the person whose behaviour or attitude is being described with the help of it.

The value of metaphors and similes is particularly striking where without them the problem of radical unintelligibility would otherwise be more serious than it already is. It may possibly be true, as I conceded in Section 8 of Chapter 1, that some of those who are, or by the criteria of the psychological medicine of today would have been, diagnosed as insane are beyond the reach of understanding in even the primary sense. But by no means all are: *pace* Weber, it is simply not true that sociologists are bound to leave psychopathology entirely to the psychopathologists. Consider the following example of a patient aged 46 who was being treated in 1966 with the drug laevodihydroxyphenylalanine, which appeared at the time to be of therapeutic value in the treatment of the survivors of the epidemic of *encephalitis lethargica* of 1916 to 1927. Before the application of the drug, 'Leonard L.' (as he is labelled by the doctor who was administering it to him) was not only speechless but incapable of any voluntary movements other than very small movements of the right hand which enabled him to spell out messages on a letter-board:

> At the end of my first meeting with Leonard L. I said to him: 'What's it like being the way you are? What would you compare it to?' He spelt out the following answer: 'Caged. Deprived. Like Rilke's "Panther".'*
> And then he swept his eyes around the ward and spelt out: 'This is a human zoo.' Again and again, with his penetrating descriptions, his imaginative metaphors, or his great stock of poetic images, Mr L. would try to evoke the nature of his own being and experience. 'There's an awful presence', he once tapped out, 'and an awful absence. The presence is a mixture of nagging and

*Sein Blick ist vom Vorübergehn der Stäbe
So mud geworden, dass er nichts mehr hält.
Ihm ist, als ob es tausend Stäbe gäbe
Und hinter tausend Stäben Keine Welt.

(His gaze from going through the bars has grown so weary that it can take in nothing more. For him it is as though there were a thousand bars, and behind the thousand bars no world.) 'Leonard L.' is case no. 20 in Oliver W. Sacks, *Awakenings* (1973).

pushing and pressure, with being held back and constrained and stopped – I often call it "the goad and halter". The absence is a terrible isolation and coldness and shrinking – more than you can imagine, Dr Sacks, much more than anybody who isn't this way can possibly imagine – a bottomless darkness and unreality.'

Notice here the effectiveness of the combination between the claim that 'we' could not possibly imagine what Mr L.'s experience is really like and the invocation of a literary parallel. In contrast to the examples in the previous section, no extra circumstantial detail is reported. The tacit appeal to 'our' experience presupposes only that we have all seen a caged panther, or similar animal, in a zoo. The recourse to poetry – in this case, to a stanza written by someone whom Mr L. takes by implication to be a major poet – serves the purpose of science because, unlike the rhetoric of Pareto about mediaeval lawyers or of Macaulay about foxhunting Tories, it is had by Mr L. solely in order to convey as authentically as he knows how the answer to Dr Sacks's question 'What's it like being the way you are?'

This example does not, perhaps, have any very close relevance to the kind of substantive social theory which I shall be concerned to expound in Volume II. But it illustrates very well the way in which the purposes of description can usefully be served by answering the question 'what is/was it like?' by saying 'it is/was as though ...' instead of, or as well as, by adding the extra vivid and/or illuminating detail. I have said that the value of metaphors and similes is particularly striking where there is a problem of radical unintelligibility. But they can be equally valuable, even if less strikingly so, where the experience being described can be presumed to be much less remote from the reader's than in the case of the unhappy Mr L. In the example with which the first section of this chapter began, the experience which Angela Carter sought to describe in her poem is not under any definition of psychopathology an abnormal one. But to convey to the reader what it was like for her she needed both to include the graphic touches (the watercolour, the mica chips, the maid's starched apron, the jar of lubricating fluid) and the literary metaphor of the 'safety-net' in which the 'death-defying somersault of love' is to be performed. And in this case, as I pointed out, there *is* a sociological as well as a psychological dimension to the experience, for part of what she seeks to convey is the kind of thing which is typically conveyed in an ethnographic monograph.

It is, accordingly, fair to say that description in sociology calls for an exercise of imagination on the sociologist's part which is not involved in either reportage or explanation or, therefore, in the practice of natural science at all. This implies neither that imagination is not otherwise called for in science, whether social or natural, nor that descriptive sociology belongs on the far side of the frontier between science and art. But description in sociology, although constrained in the ways which it is the principal purpose of this chapter to analyse, not only permits but often requires the formulation of theoretical concepts which can still less be said to be given to the sociologist by his data than can those which he may frame in order to explain them.

It is not that the concepts most helpful to the success of a description are necessarily or particularly likely to be neologisms: they may or may not be. It is sometimes as well to be reminded that there was a time when not only 'Machiavellian' but also 'baroque', 'folkloric', 'Jesuitical', 'neo-classical', 'middle-class' and 'radical chic' among many, many others did not exist for the purpose of description or anything else. But not only may a description call for the invention or adaptation of one more concept than has yet occurred to the sociologist seeking to frame it. In addition, there may always be one more detail whose reportage might make the portrayal yet more graphic, or one more metaphor or simile which might help to convey still better to the reader what 'their' experience was like. No doubt the need for supererogatory feats of imagination will vary from one topic to another as a function both of the researcher's aspiration to come as close to total success as he can and of the presumptive sensibilities and experiences of those to whom his description is addressed. Some readers may have been helped to a tertiary understanding of the affected iconoclasm of mid twentieth-century Etonians or Harrovians by being asked to think of the Beloved Vagabonds of an earlier period, or of the caged and deprived state of mind of 'Leonard L.' by being quoted Rilke's Panther, whereas others may not have needed any such help at all. But no more in description than in explanation are sociologists, anthropologists or historians to assume that their readers may already have anticipated their hard-won results for themselves. It is better to elaborate a description which the reader may then pretend to find obvious than to run the risk of misapprehension or even mystification which is involved in leaving reportage, accurate as it may be, to speak for itself.

§ 14. Descriptive inference, accordingly, has a logic of its own, not in a strict technical sense (although formal logicians may perhaps come to devise one) but in the informal sense that within a description an added proposition when conjoined with the rest serves to license a further conclusion. Trivially, it licenses the conclusion that the social context within which the added proposition holds is such that the agents in question could in principle be brought to agree that it helps to convey what the context is like to and for themselves. Less trivially, it licenses a conclusion of the form informally covered by such phrases as 'enlarging the understanding', 'adding insight' or 'further illuminating ...' (the social context, the workings of the institution or practice, the nuances of the relationship, etc.). At this point, we are no longer concerned only with the use of analogies to the presumptive experience of the reader. Descriptive inference is internal to sociological descriptions of events, processes and states of affairs as observed and reported, and it needs to be analysed under the two separate headings of the (vivid or illuminating) detail and the (vivid or illuminating) metaphor or simile. Both add something to the degree of tertiary understanding conveyed, but in different ways.

It might seem tempting to consider descriptive inference of both types in terms initially of *depiction* – that is, to assume that the function of description is that which a picture would best serve. But this would be to put the matter back to front. It is true that, as we shall see in a moment, pictures can be effective as a descriptive technique. But this is not because they are the paradigm under which all other techniques should be subsumed. Where an illustration (to borrow a phrase from another book review) 'complements the text with a revealing visual flash', this is because it functions as an aid to reportage rather than description. Words are notoriously less effective than pictures for the purpose of conveying appearance in the literal sense: if I want you to meet my daughter, whom you have never seen, at the railway station I shall show you a snapshot from the family album rather than recite her colour of hair, set of eyes, etc., and if you ask me what an okapi looks like I shall offer you an illustrated textbook of wildlife rather than recite its size, gait, etc. Sociological description, on the other hand, is a matter of selection and emphasis of aspects of attitudes and behaviour and the *Weltanschauung* behind them. It may be that this calls on occasion for reportage of the kind that a picture will do best as, for example, where illustrated fashion magazines are used to document changes in styles of dress which the sociologist wishes to relate to the mores of different social classes as these are described by him. But this is reportage by pictorial means serving the purposes of description. It is not a reduction of description to pictorial reportage.

Where it is an extra detail rather than a metaphor or simile which adds something not already implicit in a description, it is because it is (to adapt a phrase of Henri Pirenne's) *un détail qui se répercute*. But the extent to which it adds to the description – the degree of repercussion, as it were – is not necessarily a function of its importance to those whose institutions and practices are being described. On the contrary, it is often the trivia *qui se répercutent*. For example: in 1954, when a force of some 80,000 British troops was occupying the Suez Canal Zone under treaty, the roneoed sheet given out to the officers of the Irish Guards who were to be stationed there included the suggestion (it was not quite an order) that they should take with them a 'Sunday-in-the-country suit'. I well remember not only my own incredulous amusement but that of a friend of mine to whom I subsequently related it and who assured me that I must on no account fail to record it for my memoirs. As a detail of the behaviour of the agents in question it was in itself insignificant to 'them'. Yet how much it says about the mores of the *corps d'élite* of the British officer class! How inconceivable it would be in the American army, or the Australian, or the French! A trivial detail of behaviour, if you like: but as illuminating in its way as the diaries of the mid-Victorian clerics reported by Burn or the deliberations of the Court of Mons over the time of day reported by Bloch.

In this example, no picture is called for. You have no need to be shown the recording angel's videotape of the officers of the First Battalion of the Irish Guards assembling for Sunday lunch, for the point of the description is that this was a set of mores such that what 'they' actually called 'Sunday-in-the-country suits' were prescribed, or at least recommended, wearing. But to see the way in which a picture, and only a picture, *can* serve the purposes of description on the same sort of theme, let me revert to 'Ian Hay', the author of *The First Hundred Thousand*, to whom I referred in Section 3 because he was cited by Professor Fussell in his description of the way in which 'the British experience on the Western Front from 1914 to 1918' was described by those who took part in it. *The First Hundred Thousand* is without question an important primary source for this purpose. But to be able to assess it – to be in a position, that is, to describe to the reader what it, as a description of that experience, is itself like – we need to know something about the describer. It will help to know that he did fight in the trenches himself (even though we may not need to know that his regiment was the Argyll and Sutherland Highlanders). It will help to know something about his own social background (even though we may not need to know that his real name was John Hay Beith). And it will also help to have an idea of what he looked like. Of course, to be able to make descriptive inferences of any value from his appearance you have already to have a fairly full understanding of his period and milieu. But if I may assume that you have, then does it not further enlarge your tertiary understanding, as it did mine, to discover that he looked like this?

To be sure, the inferences to be drawn are not to be drawn from those features of his appearance which are genetically rather than culturally determined. It is rather the cultural *gestalt* – the suit, the pose, the moustache, the haircut, the handkerchief in the breast pocket. It is as inconceivable that this should be a photograph of Norman Mailer, author of an important literary source for the American experience in the Pacific from 1942 to 1945 (*The Naked and the Dead*) as that an American regimental adjutant should have issued an instruction about a 'Sunday-in-the-country suit' to officers posted to the Suez Canal Zone in 1954. I do not suggest that a photograph of the author of *The First Hundred Thousand* adds more than a small extra touch to what Professor Fussell and many others can tell us about him and his writings in order to convey what the period and milieu were like of which he was a representative spokesman. But that much it does, and vividly.

A metaphor or simile, on the other hand, although it too may fulfil a quasi-pictorial function in helping to indicate what something or someone literally looked like, normally adds to a sociological description by an association of ideas which is still further removed from a mode of inference for which the relation of photograph to original could stand as the paradigm. The illuminating simile or metaphor typically licenses an inference which authentically and representatively conveys more of (to use what is itself a metaphor) the *flavour* of 'their' sense of what it was like to them. Often, a good description proceeds by first giving the vivid details which license the inference to 'their' experience of them and then suggesting the simile or metaphor which licenses the inference to the kind of experience 'they' could themselves be brought to agree to having had.

Angela Carter's poem once again serves as an example: first the detail to help convey what her experience was like, then the metaphor to help convey her own attitude to that experience.

Indeed, a simile is in one way the most obvious of all techniques of description. For if description consists in saying what an event, process or state of affairs was like, the most obvious answer to give to a request for a description must be 'it was like X': eating meat, for a vegetarian, is like eating human flesh for a meat-eater; Arunta festivals are like 'I am an American' day; doing sorcery is like psychosomatic healing; listening to the crooning of Frank Sinatra (a New York bobby-soxer told a newspaper reporter) was like being stroked all over by a hand covered in cold cream; being a sailor (said Dr Johnson) is like being in a jail with the chance of being drowned; the style of London toilette universal in 1864 (wrote Henry Adams) was grotesque, like Monckton Milnes on horseback in Rotten Row; being the way he is (Leonard L. told Dr Sacks) is like Rilke's panther; and so on. Just as the details which may be added to make a description more vivid (or illuminating) can be extended indefinitely, so can the similes which may be added to make it more illuminating (or vivid). These similes may be elaborate or simple, far-fetched or obvious, grave or gay, lively or severe. The only test of their value is their capacity to enlarge the reader's tertiary understanding of what the experience was like in such a way that those who had the experience could in principle be brought to agree that it does.

CONCEPTUALIZATION AND NARRATION

§ 15. Although it still remains easier to say what makes a description bad than what makes it good, it begins by now to be possible to say something about the nature of the skills which the researcher must possess if his descriptions are to be as good as his reports and explanations allow. Receptivity to 'their' criteria of selection and emphasis is a first prerequisite: but this already requires a feel for their underlying *Weltanschauung* which goes beyond what can be directly learned from what 'they' say when questioned by 'us'. For as we have seen, there is always present the possibility that 'they' are misapprehending or mystifying their own experience. In one sense, therefore, descriptive sociology continues to require a more open mind than explanatory, since descriptive theories must not override the agents' own privileged interpretation of their intentions and beliefs in the way that explanatory theories can and usually should. But in another sense, it requires a greater willingness to impose the criteria brought to it by the sociologist himself, since he must be prepared, in effect, to accuse 'them' of having less open minds than he does. When, for example, E. M. Forster is credited by his biographer with an 'expert sense of suburban class-values' this involves in turn crediting him with the gift of a 'supersensitive ear for tone of voice – for the imperceptible tones that betray bad faith and self-deception',* or in other words with a combination of a feel for nuances acquired during his years of participant-observation in the institutions and practices of the villas of Weybridge, Tonbridge and Tunbridge Wells and a capacity to analyse those nuances in the light of a theory and its interpretation which can sift the authentic from the inauthentic in 'their' own behaviour in, and attitudes to, those institutions and practices. It is true that in Forster's case, as in many others, the criteria of selection and emphasis are not purely descriptive; there is an evaluation implicit, and sometimes explicit, in his portrayal of 'them'. But here, as always, the evaluative element can be disentangled from both the descriptive and the explanatory. The rival observer whose moral standards are different but sociological standards the same can agree with Forster's perception that 'they' are deceiving themselves and therefore by definition in a state of 'bad faith' without being thereby committed to an evaluation which makes them, as moral agents, on that account 'bad'.

Even the most gifted researcher, however, may be led astray into misdescription if his feel for nuances and capacity to analyse them are not supported on the other side by a potential, at any rate, for valid explanations as well. These explanations need not be at all profound. They may contribute nothing to the formulation and testing of those wide-ranging and powerful hypotheses which characterize significant theoretical progress. But to claim to have detected self-deception among representative members of the surburban middle class in Edwardian England is to claim also to have arrived at a secondary understanding of the presumptive causal connection between internalized social constraints and 'imperceptible' (that is, imperceptible to all but Forster) differences in tone of voice. This cannot but imply some possibility in principle of a predictive test whereby if, under quasi-experimental conditions, a representative member of the suburban middle class did not come out with the self-deceiving tone of voice which Forster expected, then Forster's description of the pervasive feel of suburban bad faith would itself be shown up as self-deceiving. Not that any number of such quasi-experiments, however successful, can by themselves confirm the theory from which Forster's criteria of selection and emphasis are

* P. N. Furbank, *E. M. Forster: A Life* I (1977), p. 74.

derived. But if descriptions such as those to be found in Forster's novels are to rank as authentic, two conditions must be fulfilled: first, the reports which the descriptions contain must be such as could be matched by real-life examples; second, the divergences between his account of what 'their' experience was like for them and their own must be able to withstand the claim of a rival observer, or themselves, that it presupposes the validity of causal connections which would not stand up to attempted invalidation with real-life subjects.

This volume, as I have said several times, is an essay on methodology, not a manual of technique, and the arguments of this chapter do not depend on a particular view of the relative value of laboratory experiment, field study, documentary analysis or participant-observation in either explaining or describing – let alone evaluating – the kind of social behaviour which Forster, or Flaubert, or Malinowski, or Bloch, or Burn (or John Dollard, or William Foote Whyte, or Erving Goffman, or Oscar Lewis, or Emmanuel Le Roy Ladurie, or who you please) describes best. They do, however, depend on a view of the relative value of one rather than another interpretation of an underlying descriptive theory. The merit of a good description does not lie merely in the choice of the adjectives, similes and metaphors used to convey an understanding in the tertiary sense of what 'their' experience was like for 'them'. It lies also in the prior conceptualization of the period and milieu within which the describendum occurs. What, for example, licenses Bloch's description of early vassalage as having what his translator renders as a 'sort of cosy domestic flavour' (*comme une odeur de pain de ménage*)?* It goes beyond mere reportage such as could be checked against the recording angel's archives; it is not a description which 'they' will have used themselves; and we might even be wise to suppose that they would initially have rejected it if put to them. Yet it serves authentically to convey what it was like for them in a demonstrably significant respect – significant because Bloch's sources support the claim that the tie between lord and commended man had, at that stage, residual overtones of companionage such that the half-conscious sentiments surrounding it partook not merely of homage on the one side and protection on the other but also of the fellow-feeling of the small band of warriors who, like the ancient German *comites*, still lacked any sense of a hierarchy of social classes which in other contexts might be expected to permeate the practice of commendation. It is for this reason that an adjective like 'cosy', or a simile like that of the *odeur de pain de ménage*, even if at first sight inappropriate

---

* *Feudal Society*, p. 236.

to the rude and brutish mores of an age of brigandage, rapine and anarchy, gives a well-grounded answer to the basic descriptive question 'what is/was it like?'; and it does it all the better because it combines an outstandingly skilled researcher's feel for 'their' experience with his sense of what will most effectively convey it to the presumptive reader to whom the contrast between 'their' period and milieu and 'ours' gives it an initial air of paradox.

§ 16. I have tacitly assumed thus far that sociological description is in principle static, and that although it must of course relate to some particular period and milieu it has still to be analysed as a set of propositions couched for the most part in the ethnographic present. But as in reportage itself, sequences need to be described as such, and the criteria of selection and emphasis which underlie a descriptive narrative raise further methodological problems of their own.

In Section 14 of Chapter 2, I used as an example of a descriptive narrative the obituary of a Nigerian born in the early years of the twentieth century and killed in 1966 whose experiences, although hardly typical in themselves, were at the same time such as could serve authentically to convey something of what it was like for a member of that country's commercial and political élite to live through the successive transitions from colonial dependence to independent statehood to civil war. So bare a summary of a life can hardly be more than a prolegomenon to a description adequate to fulfil the tasks outlined in the previous sections. But a full-length biography whose subject has been chosen for his or her representativeness of a period and milieu should come as near to adequacy as it is reasonable to ask. The reports of successive events of which it consists must of course be accurate, and the temptations to incompleteness, oversimplification, ahistoricity, suppression, exaggeration and ethnocentricity withstood. If, however, these conditions are fulfilled, the merits of the biography as a description of the period and milieu will then depend on how far the biographer's interpretation of his underlying theory leaves the reader with those, and only those, reported episodes which are authentically representative of them and expressed by means of adjectives, similes, metaphors and analogies which so convey them to 'us'.

Yet this leaves unsettled the very problem posed by the telling of the story of a life: how to describe the passage of time itself. The life of a society is the sum of the lives of its members over the period chosen for study as these work themselves out from birth to death. But not every day, or week, or month, or year has equal significance. Once having chosen the person (or family or group) representative of the period and milieu which he wishes to describe, the sociologically-minded biographer will try to narrate that life or set of lives in such a way as to reflect the standards and priorities of the period and milieu. But how is he to choose? I said in Section 4 that the number of ideologies in even a large and complex society is still sufficiently limited to be manageable. But the significance of the passage of time – and the elasticity, as well as the selectivity, with which it is subsequently recalled – is something much more personal. How, therefore, are these multifarious and conflicting individual priorities to be reconciled or synthesized in such a way as to yield the authentic and representative criteria of narrative sequence for a period and milieu viewed as a whole?

Conventional biographical criteria, appropriate though they may be in the individual case, may be a positive impediment to descriptive sociology. 'Born on such-and-such a date, son of so-and-so and so-and-so, he was educated first at X and then at Y and proceeded from the post of this to the post of that ending with so many years at the Ministry of Whatever, where he carried through the influential reforms for which his name is celebrated but whose effect, as a result of his untimely death in office on such-and-such a date, he did not live to witness.' This *may* do quite well, if these landmarks and the intervals between them are indeed those to which he and his contemporaries attached significance. Is not, for example, the second Marquis of Rockingham, born in 1730, authentically representative of his period and milieu in having gone from Westminster School to St John's College, Cambridge, succeeded to the marquisate in 1750, served as lord of the bedchamber from 1751 to 1762, fallen out of favour in 1762, presided over a coalition ministry in 1765, been dismissed twelve months later, led the opposition in the House of Lords from 1768 to 1781 and become once again Prime Minister in 1782, the year of his death? But however well such a summary may serve to describe, within its limits, the career of a representative Whig nobleman of mid eighteenth-century England, the sequence which it follows and the duration of the intervals between one selected episode and the next cannot be imposed automatically on the biographies of his contemporaries whose priorities were different from his own. A standard chronology is apposite for descriptive use only to the degree that the society in question approximates to the ideal type of an age-set society where every person passes through a common set of predetermined roles and statuses lasting for stipulated periods and marked by visible rites of passage. All societies have some such features: the transition from childhood to adulthood, however quickly or slowly made and however publicly or privately symbolized, is significant in the biography of every single person who has lived long enough to become an adult in any society whatever. But to the degree that transitions of status are fluid, age-categories variable and careers haphazard, different lives all have different intervals of time appropriate to their narration and the sociologist describing them has to be able to provide theoretical justification for his choice.

At the same time, his choice will still be constrained by evidence for priorities of 'theirs' rather than his own. He is not to exchange the misapprehensions of the *Dictionary of National Biography*, accurate as its details may be, on the one hand for the mystifications of Proust, authentic as his observations may be, on the other. I cited Proust in Section 4 of Chapter 1 as an example of an author whose work enables the reader to arrive at a tertiary understanding of the mores of the period and milieu of which he wrote. But Proust is an author whose view alike of science and of art is enmeshed in a *Weltanschauung* peculiar to himself of which the analysis, rewarding as it would be, would stretch too far a chapter already required to embrace within a discussion of the sociological imagination an account of its similarities to and differences from the imagination of the artist, and would involve, in the attempt authentically to describe that view of life, so penetrating yet at the same time so hermetic, not merely a capacity to elucidate a perspective as foreign to an ethnographer of alien races as to a historian of France herself but even an ability to parody the convoluted style in which, for page after page, it is expressed.

The decision, accordingly, which the narrative sociologist has to take is how to combine a description of the priorities of his chosen subjects with a description of the priorities in terms of which their lives were, or would have been, assessed by representative members of the other groups or kinds of people in their same society. The scope which this gives even in the biography of a single person representative of a homogeneous and clearly delimited period and milieu is already vast: think only how remote are the chances that two different biographers, even though they share common presuppositions and purposes, will produce biographies which match each other in more than the outline reportage of the events most important (by the criteria of the *Dictionary of National Biography*) in the subject's public career. But it would be a mistake to underestimate for that reason the degree of success with which a biography, long or short, *can* convey both authentically and representatively the priorities of subject, milieu and period. Here, for example, is a single tiny vignette taken in its entirety from *The Times* in 1977:

MAN OF TWO CAREERS

Mr. Cecil Ernest Rogers, who has been responsible for the safekeeping of scores of thousands of Criminal Appeal files, retired after 61 years in the public service. He is 76.

The Lord Chief Justice, bidding farewell to him in the Court of Appeal, Criminal Division, said that Mr. Rogers was a tidy minded man: he had divided his public service into two neat parcels – some 30 years in the Royal Navy and 30 years in the Royal Courts of Justice. His record was of the utmost distinction. As a boy seaman, aged 17, in the Royal Navy, he had been torpedoed, during the First World War, and he had served in cruisers, destroyers, sloops and for a time, in the aircraft carrier Indomitable.

After leaving the Navy in 1945 he came to the Law Courts, and in 1973 was awarded the MBE for his services.

For good measure, in his spare time, he had been a great supporter of the Inns of Court Mission, where he was loved and his hand was to be seen in many of their activities.

'We shall miss you', his Lordship told him. 'We wish you well.'

It is true that to extract the descriptive implications which are there the researcher has already to have some tertiary understanding of the workings of English society in the twentieth century. To use it in this way is already to presuppose an underlying theory with which a rival observer might wish to take issue. But how vividly it captures the flavour of rites of passage characteristic of the career of a certain kind of subordinate public servant in twentieth-century England! And how illuminatingly it reveals the ideology of the relations between such servants and the institutions and persons whom they served! The reported facts of Mr Rogers's career – the 30 years of naval service, the 30 years keeping criminal files, the award of the Medal of the British Empire in 1973, the spare-time involvement (and the way it is told!) in the Inns of Court Mission – are as descriptively valuable as the watercolour, the mica chips, the maid's starched apron and the jar of lubricating fluid in Angela Carter's poem.

At the same time, the use of the occasion of retirement, together with the ritual address by the Lord Chief Justice himself which marked it, to convey the priorities and values of Mr Rogers and his masters alike parallels the use in ethnographic description of gatherings and ceremonies in which the *conscience collective* is, as it were, made manifest before the eyes of the visiting fieldworker. Whatever may be the inadequacies for the purpose of explanation of the concept of a *conscience collective*, it does come into its own in descriptive theory; for it is at their communal festivals and celebrations that a group, a tribe, a coterie, a following, a sect, even a people or (if small enough) a whole society may indeed be seen to behave *as if* its members were animated by a single common set of attitudes and values. What is more, it is characteristic of such occasions that participants will say that they feel *as if* the passage of time between this festival or celebration and the last had been swifter, and the events which took place in that interval of less significance, than the passage of time during the festival or celebration itself. Such occasions are the favourites of ethnographers, whether or not they would call themselves adherents of the Durkheimian school, and rightly so. They are valuable not merely for the opportunity which they afford of observing what it is that goes on when the group, tribe, etc. is assembled for a common purpose and perhaps of framing and testing an explanation of some aspect of it, but also for the opportunity of testing a descriptive theory of what the rituals and ceremonies to which 'they' attach particular importance are like for 'them' to participate in. And in the same way, it is relevant to Proust's achievement as (in part) a sociologist of a section of French society and its mores in the *belle époque* as well as a novelist with a particular view of the workings of the memory and its relation to the *recherche du temps perdu* that he can devote so much attention, in a narrative extending over several decades, to a description of what happened in the course of an afternoon party.

To the extent, moreover, that the purpose of a narrative is descriptive, it can well happen that the priorities thereby imposed on the sociologist are not only at variance but in contradiction with what is required for the purpose of explanation. An example directly relevant to the account of twentieth-century England which I shall be giving in Volume III is the significance of the First World War. An explanatory account of the period is likely to attach much less significance to the fact of the beginning of the War in 1914 or its end in 1918 than did those who lived through it. Undoubtedly, many changes were hastened, and some initiated, by the events of the War with results both intended and unintended by those who brought them about. But there are strong grounds for arguing that the changes (or lack of them) between 1918 and, say, 1940 can more often be traced to causes which not merely antedated the War but would have continued to determine the course of subsequent events in much the same way even if the War had never happened. Descriptively, however, the War and the dates at which it began and ended have to be seen as important to the extent that British people of all ages, classes and conditions felt them, for the rest of their lives, to have been so; and it is for this reason that Chapter 4 of Volume III ('The Case Described'), but not Chapter 3 ('The Case Explained'), begins in the conventional manner on the evening of 11 November 1918, when David Lloyd George and Winston Churchill dined together alone listening to the celebrations of the crowd which had earlier included, among others, Leonard and Virginia Woolf wandering about in the rain in the area of Trafalgar Square feeling steadily more depressed.

It would be foolish to deny that the life, even over a limited period, of a large society is so enormously more complex than that of a selected one of the persons who belong to it that if two biographers of a common subject agree only in outline, two historians of a common society are bound to produce descriptive narratives which diverge in their treatment of the passage of time, as well as everything else, at numerous points. But their discretion, wide as its scope must be, is still not untrammelled. The descriptive sociologist's priorities are never just his own. The stories which he chooses to tell and the manner in which he chooses to tell them are to reflect 'their' priorities, not his; and although he may presume to describe their experiences for them in terms other than those they do, or would ever, use it must still be only for the purpose of improving them. This applies as much to self-consciously literary narrative historians as it does to sociologists and anthropologists who conceive of themselves as engaged in creating a 'natural science of society'; and it applies whether or not the description is one which includes overtly evaluative terms.

THE RELATION OF DESCRIPTION TO EVALUATION

§ 17. Evaluative terms are inescapable in sociological description, and in narrative descriptions more so than elsewhere. How can you possibly tell the story of a person's life in such a way as to convey what his or her experiences as a member of a given society in a given period and milieu were like without confronting the questions whether he/she was brave or cowardly, wise or foolish, dutiful or intransigent, virtuous or vicious, a success or a failure? To be sure, the methodologically proper way to use terms like these in social-scientific writing is to apply them to the hero or heroine of the story by reference to his or her own values or the values of the persons by whom he or she would have been judged during his or her own lifetime. In principle, there should be no difficulty in distinguishing the reportage of 'their' evaluation of the subject's conduct from the evaluation of the biographer, whether or not it agrees with 'theirs'. But the distinction is not always so easy to maintain, not because the examples which are offered by biographical writing impugn the validity of the distinction between description and evaluation but because, as we have seen time and again, the same term can serve either or both a descriptive and/or an evaluative function. When, in Section 15, I referred to E. M. Forster's 'supersensitive ear for the tone of voice – for the imperceptible tones which betray bad faith and self-deception', I went on to remark that the evaluative element could, as always, be separately distinguished: it needs a further argument grounded in a theory of a different kind to show that the bad faith and self-deception of the subjects, if such they be, are to be morally condemned. But suppose that the sociologist, out of a proper concern to convey a potentially dislikeable aspect of 'their' attitudes and behaviour to 'us', seeks actively to engage 'our' sympathy on behalf of 'their' values. Does not the distinction then become deliberately blurred?

I am not here thinking of the apologias which biographers may make on behalf of their subjects where explanation is invoked explicitly in the cause of evaluation or exculpation, as for example when Lockhart says that 'of all Burns's failings, it may be safely asserted that there was more in his history to account and apologize for them, than can be alleged in regard to almost any other great man's imperfections'.* This is quite different from the invocation of evaluation in the cause of description, where an appeal is made to the reader's own presumed moral standards in order to help in the understanding in the tertiary sense of conduct with which 'we' might otherwise find it difficult to sympathize. Here, for example, is a comment in the form of a rhetorical question in a magazine article by a professor of philosophy of left-wing political sympathies about the self-styled 'Angry Brigade', a group of young people responsible for the bombing of the house and car of the British Secretary of State for Employment, Mr Robert Carr, in January 1971:† 'Can one not imagine someone seriously arguing that if Mr Carr or Mr Davies is responsible for the unemployment of a million people and the misery that this involves, his life is forfeit – that in such circumstances killing is no murder?' The comment is primarily descriptive. But it succeeds, if it does, by first soliciting the reader's acquiescence in the suggestion that the killing of persons responsible for the conscious infliction of suffering on a large scale is not necessarily to be condemned as 'murder' and then persuading the reader that to 'them' (the members of the Angry Brigade) the economic policy of the government of which Mr Carr was the minister responsible for employment was an appropriate case in point. How, therefore, if the success of a description directly depends on conveying a tertiary understanding of the agents' own moral and political

---

* J. G. Lockhart, *Burns* (1828), p. 136, quoted by A. D. J. Cockshut, *Truth to Life* (1974), p. 26.
† On whom see Gordon Carr, *The Angry Brigade: the Cause and the Case* (1975).

standards, is it possible to continue to claim that description and evaluation can be kept apart?

The answer, however, is not that in cases of this kind description and
evaluation have to be conflated. It is that the relation between them
involves the risk of two further kinds of mystification beyond the three
which I listed in Section 6. The first, for which I shall use the term
derogation, involves the description of the thoughts and actions of a
person or group in such a way that the reader is left with a pejorative
implication beyond what is warranted by the reportage of their evaluation
by 'them'. The second, for which I shall use the term *hagiography*,
involves describing them in such a way that the reader is left with an
implication which is too favourable. In cases where the illocutionary
burden is carried by one or more explicitly evaluative terms, the test is
simply to ask whose are the values by reference to which the term is being
applied – the agent's, the representative members of the agent's period
and milieu, or the researcher's own. But just as a set of accurate reports
containing no explicitly descriptive adjective, simile or metaphor may
still function as a description which is not, after all, authentic, so may
a set of accurate reports containing no explicitly evaluative terms
function as a description which is, after all, cloaking an evaluation of the
author's and not of 'theirs'.

As an example of derogation, here is another example from fiction
together with the comments of a reviewer who, for the purpose of the
argument, I assume to be authentic in his own description of the fictional
work:

> At the end we observe Colonel Macready reflecting: 'He had lost his son,
> his wife and his chauffeur.' A simple statement of fact. But the innocent
> bathos which counts dead son, estranged wife and absentee chauffeur as
> equivalently 'lost' belittles the Colonel irretrievably, and could not have
> done so with such effect had more words been expended.

We must, as always, assume for methodology's sake that the recording
angel would confirm that the Colonel did at that moment mutter to himself
precisely the words: 'I have lost my son, wife and chauffeur.' But as the
reviewer correctly points out, the very baldness of the reportage, with
its implication that that was *all* that the Colonel had to say to himself
about the event, is what serves to make him appear ridiculous in the
reader's eyes. Perhaps it will become evident, when a fuller description
of his state of mind has been given, that the colonel did reflect on his
experience in such a way that to the reader who shares the author's values
he has indeed been deservedly belittled. But if the derogation is to stand
in for the description, there should first have been asked and answered

a question of the very form of 'Can one not imagine ... ?' What might there not be of irony, or self-awareness, or even of what we might want to call 'genuine' innocence in the Colonel's character which would lead us to conclude that this disingenuously succinct report of what he said to himself at one particular moment had seriously misdescribed it?

As an example of hagiography, here is a representative piece of *Times* obituarese:

> Weller, affectionately known as 'Sam' to all his friends, though shy and reserved, hid a warm and generous personality behind a slightly aloof manner. He enjoyed the cut and thrust of a dialogue between experts (and his college often reaped the benefit of his ability to spot the weak points of his opponent's defence) but had little taste for the small talk of a common room, and little sympathy for the occasional excesses of under-graduates. Yet those who sought his help were never refused and found him ready and eager to assist.

Again, we must assume that the recording angel would confirm that those who sought Weller's help *were* never refused (What, never? Well – *hardly* ever). But even so: are we not being solicited to view a disdainful old curmudgeon in a more favourable light than would quite accord with the value-judgements of those who actually encountered him? Would the undergraduates and colleagues who sought his help themselves describe him as 'ready and eager to assist'? No doubt an understanding, in the tertiary sense, of his conduct requires that there should be reported not only his manifest distaste for common-room small talk and his polemical vigour in debate but also the greater warmth and generosity which he disclosed on other occasions. But the suspicion remains that the obitu-arist has sought to leave the reader with a more favourable impression than could be shown to be authentic by reference to 'their' standards as opposed to his own.

The test is thus the same in these examples as in the case of the philosophy professor's description of the attitude of mind of the members of the Angry Brigade. If his way of putting it, whether or not they so put it themselves, is such as they could in principle be brought to accept as authentic, then it is immaterial whether or not his values are such that this serves to condone their bombing the Minister's house; it counts in any event as a contribution to the reader's tertiary under-standing of their behaviour. But if he is seeking to condone their behaviour by reinterpreting, in terms of his own values, an attitude of mind which cannot authentically be described as a serious conviction that a failure to find work, as opposed to welfare benefits, out of government funds for a million unemployed is rightly punishable by death, then he is guilty of hagiography. And conversely, if he *is* guilty of hagiography, then he can authentically be described by his readers as indulging in the sort of sentimental condonation of violence characteristic of 'radical chic'; but if he is not, then to describe him as though he were is derogation of *him*.

§ 18. In these examples, the charge of hagiography or derogation rests on the description of the behaviour or attitude of mind of one or a very few designated persons. Often, however, the entanglement of description with evaluation runs through the account given by the sociologist, anthropologist or historian of a practice, institution or a whole society over what may be a whole epoch or era. For this, the most obvious general term is *romanticization*. Its merit is that it covers any and all cases where a description is framed to elicit an evaluation by the reader out of proportion to the evaluations of the representative participants in the practices, institutions or societies described. It arises whenever the researcher, for reasons of his own, selects and emphasizes reports which, when taken together, exaggerate the degree to which what is described accords with the criteria to which he, but not 'they', attaches priority. Thus researchers of various theoretical schools can, and have, romanticized the courage of the Spartiates, the egalitarianism of the panchayats of village India, the savagery of the North American Indians, the hardheartedness of the Lancashire mill-owners of the early Industrial Revolution, the depravity of the rulers of the Italian city-states, the *douceur de vivre* of the *ancien régime* and many more besides. The methodological problem is not that they are guilty of misreportage, for if they are their mistakes can in principle be put right. Nor is it that they have incidentally passed their own evaluative judgements on the conduct of those whose mores they are describing, for they are as free to do so as the reader is free to reject them. Rather, the problem is that the reader is given no means other than his own congenital scepticism of assessing the degree to which the selection and emphasis of the reports presented has been pre-empted by the researcher's wish to present a description dictated by an evaluative theory of his own.

There is an instructive and entertaining discussion of one aspect of this problem, although not under the same name, in Burn's *The Age of Equipoise* from which I have already quoted at some length in Section 11. One of the examples which Burn uses* to illustrate what he aptly calls the game of 'selective Victorianism' is a photograph of a mid-Victorian

* *Op. cit.*, pp. 26ff.

rectory showing the family group on the lawn on a perfect summer afternoon: there is the handsome and gentlemanly rector with his serene-looking wife, his prettily-dressed daughters and his muscularly-Christian young son, his gnarled, respectable coachman, and his butler, cook and maids 'half-abashed and half-delighted at being photographed with the family', the whole looking as if the camera 'had caught in one moment all the peace, the deep security, the kindly and dignified affluence of English life'. And yet how differently could the same scene be described: the rector unintellectual and indolent, his wife evidently encumbered with a large and uncomfortable rectory which they cannot afford to maintain and serene-looking only by virtue of the opium contained in Batley's Sedative Solution, the daughters ill educated and (by the standards of their social superiors) equally ill dressed, the son rebellious and exasperating, the coachman drunken and dishonest, the servants slack and casual (which, considering how they are treated, could hardly be otherwise). To the extent that rival descriptions of what the photograph is claimed to depict rest on inferences from it which the recording angel could confirm or reject, we are of course dealing with questions of reportage rather than description. But to the extent that the photograph is being used to convey what life was like in an English country rectory in the 1850s or 60s, the historian's task is to present it to his readers in such a way as will make it sound neither more nor less agreeable to its inhabitants than can be shown to be authentic, and neither more nor less representative than the experience of others like themselves would confirm. As Burn is at pains to point out, 'in choosing the rectory for the scene of our photograph we have chosen a setting which admitted of more variation than any other'. It is thereby the more difficult to use any one piece of evidence, however vivid and illuminating, without romanticizing it one way or the other. It should be easy enough, in practice, to avoid the obviously inauthentic and unrepresentative extremes, whether Dean Burgon's hagiographic account of the incumbency of the Revd H. J. Rose at Houghton Conquest ('The best traditions of an English country parsonage were to be witnessed at Houghton in perfection. Real learning and sound Divinity, pure taste and graceful hospitality flourished there and abounded. Within doors there was an unfailing loving-kindness; without there was (with all their faults) a God-fearing, a well-disposed and affectionate peasantry.') or the *Saturday Review's* derogatory comment on the state of Chesham ('Fornication and adultery, incest and murder, abortion and poisoning – all the tangled annals of the poor – this is "Our Village" at work – this is Christian and happy England.'). As Burn says, 'The Dean was making the best of

things; the *Saturday Review*, as usual, was making the worst of them.'
But how are we to tell when we have got it right?

It is not enough to say 'by being without presuppositions of one's
own'. For myself, so far as I can judge, I have no motive or disposition
whatever to take a more or less favourable or unfavourable view by the
standards of their own time of the rectors, their families, their servants
and their parishioners in the England of the 1860s. But lack of motive
to adopt the wrong criteria of selection and emphasis is no guarantee of
adopting the right ones. And what is worse, the determination to avoid
romanticization in the cause of the active and sustained avoidance of
bullshit in which authenticity chiefly consists carries with it a subtler
temptation still: the temptation to that variant of mystification which
may be labelled 'no-bullshit bullshit'. This, if anything, is the failing of
Flaubert himself. Even given that he has, as a novelist, the privilege
denied to the sociologist, anthropologist or historian of being his own
recording angel, can he not still be charged with being just a little bit too
cynical about his unhappy Emma?

As always, the descriptive element has to be disentangled from both
the explanatory and the evaluative, and for this purpose the term
'cynicism' is not quite right. It catches the flavour, perhaps, of a certain
kind of determinedly anti-romantic description. But what it usually
denotes is not a misdescription so much as an explanation (or misexplana-
tion) deriving from presuppositions at the same time explanatory and
evaluative. It manifests itself in a disposition to attribute the behaviour
of people to bad motives rather than good ones, whether the standards
of good and bad are those of the researcher, his subjects, or both; and
where the researcher is committed already to one of two sides, it is apt
to be compounded by a deliberate denial of the benefit of the doubt to
the other. How many histories have there not been written in which the
explanations advanced attribute more consistently discreditable motives
to landlords than peasants, employers than employees, Catholics than
Protestants, Frenchmen than Englishmen and so on? An explanation is
not, to be sure, necessarily mistaken because it is inspired by a presupposition of cynicism. But its validity must be assessed separately from
the assessment of the authenticity of a perhaps *too* anti-romantic description of the behaviour which has been cynically explained. It is a matter
not of showing why the rectors, their families, their servants and their
parishioners behaved as discreditably as they did, but of establishing the
extent to which their behaviour is to be described as 'hypocritical',
'complacent', 'unfeeling', or indeed 'un-Christian', independently of the
researcher's own chosen moral, political or aesthetic theory.

Let me assume, then, that the researcher has somehow chosen a representative sample of mid-Victorian parishes and that he can supplement the photographs which we have of the rectors and their families by as much documentary evidence as he needs. To avoid romanticization, he must ask not only how far the rector's own account of his attitudes may be inauthentic but also how far the descriptions of other rival observers, whether Dean Burgon or the *Saturday Review*, may be inauthentic too. But how easy it is, in doing so, to go too far the other way – to let knowledge of the period and milieu slide into knowingness, detachment into superiority, impartiality into an automatic and undifferentiating scepticism! Suppose that the rector's wife was indeed a regular consumer of measured quantities of Batley's Sedative Solution and that its soothing influence provides a valid explanation of what Burn describes as 'the dignified composure with which she faces the camera and what remains of her life' (for she is suffering from cancer). What sort of attitude to this state of affairs should be incorporated in the description? It must be relevant to report, for a start, that the practice was quite widespread, that the state of medical science was by 'our' standards rudimentary, that the mores of the time denied to women the solace of alcohol which was permitted to their husbands and fathers, and that those of their husbands or fathers who found them out did their best to make them feel ashamed of themselves.* But just what are the terms in which to convey the subtler nuances of what the rector and his family felt on the question whether his wife's consumption of opiates was excusable? By 'our' standards, the educated classes of mid-Victorian England had an exaggerated inclination to moralize, and a description of their attitudes calls for a tertiary understanding not merely of their belief in God and His part in human affairs, such as Burn conveys so well, but also of their related views of what it is or is not seemly to do in private or talk about in public. All rival observers will agree that these views, as they related to the consumption of opiates, were ambivalent. But that ambivalence itself has somehow to be conveyed to the reader in a way which carries no hint of hagiography or derogation.

In practice, I do not know how this kind of exercise can better be done than along the lines that Burn does; and it may be that he does it so well because he is writing not only a century after the period he describes, but a generation after G. M. Young had written *Victorian England: Portrait of an Age* (1936) in reaction to Lytton Strachey's reaction, in

---

* See Virginia Berridge and Griffith Edwards, *Opium and the People: Opiate Use in Nineteenth-Century England* (1981).

Eminent Victorians (1918), to what Strachey saw as the Victorians' own hagiography about themselves. Certainly, Strachey failed to get it right: whatever the best way to describe General Gordon's reported habit of retiring to his tent with a Bible and a bottle of brandy, it is not this: 'But the Holy Bible was not his only solace. For now, under the parching African sun, we catch glimpses, for the first time, of Gordon's hand stretching out towards stimulants of a more material quality. For months together, we are told, he would drink nothing but pure water; and then ... water that was not so pure.' This sort of thing is at best no-bullshit bullshit, and at worst the kind of derogation authentically describable as bitchiness. But then not even G. M. Young gets it quite right either. His well-known injunction to go on reading until you can hear 'them' talking is as sound a piece of advice to historians as Malinowski's injunction to get out and do your own fieldwork is a sound piece of advice to anthropologists. But there is a catch to it: not by any means all of 'them' were writing, or even reading, or being listened to by those who were. Young, who once said of himself that if he could be born when he chose he would have wished to be an English country rector in the very period of Burn's suggested photograph, gives a description of the age which reflects this preference just a little too strongly. It is an admirable antidote to Strachey. But nowhere in it will the reader be able to find a portrayal of the standards and attitudes of the representative member of the *un*respectable classes as sympathetic as the portrayal of those of the respectable.

Yet Young *could* have done it; Henry Mayhew did it in his *London Labour and the London Poor*; E. P. Thompson does it – perhaps to the point of romanticization – in *The Making of the English Working Class* (1963); and Burn does it too, at least in part. It may be that I am myself exaggerating the authenticity and representativeness of Burn's description of the 'age of equipoise'. But to argue that I am is to accept that it is not impossible in principle to convey the experience of representative members of a chosen period and milieu and therewith the evaluative standards applied to it both by themselves and by the members of the other milieux within their society. No doubt there can never be a perfectly authentic and representative portrait of an age. But there can never be a perfectly accurate report or a perfectly valid explanation of it either.

§ 19. We are, however, confronted with yet a further methodological danger when 'their' moral, political or aesthetic values are directly likened to those of the sociologist's, or his presumptive reader's, own period and milieu. As we have already seen, analogies from one culture to another are the stock-in-trade of descriptive sociology, since description of 'them' is at the same time description to, and for, 'us'. But where the parallel drawn is between one set of values and another, there is the risk that it may be drawn by reference to ostensibly descriptive criteria which have in fact been pre-empted by the researcher's own moral, political or aesthetic presuppositions.

First, let me cite an example where there is a parallel which I believe to be of significant help in enlarging the presumptive reader's tertiary understanding. In the speeches of the Athenian orators which have come down to us, there are two different ways in which rich people are designated. One is by the use of the standard Greek term for the 'rich': *plousioi*. The other is the phrase *hoi tas ousias echontes*, which is literally 'they having goods', or, more idiomatically, 'persons of means'. Now I am not an expert in the forensic technique of lawyers either ancient or modern. But I am confident in accepting the authority of A. H. M. Jones* for the suggestion that the differences in evaluative overtones in the two ways of referring to the rich are the same in the two cultures. Counsel on the opposing side is as unlikely in ancient Athens as in modern London to use the phrase 'person of means' except in irony. But Counsel on behalf of his client may well. Any rival observer will accept that money, like sex and drugs, is one of the topics about which 'they' were ambivalent, just as we are; and to someone in our culture who wants the ancient Greeks' ambivalence about money described to them, I can think of no better parallel to draw for a start than this one. It may be that I am mistaken, and that if I were to go back to do such vicarious fieldwork as is possible through a rereading of Demosthenes, Lysias and the rest I should find myself compelled to qualify my claim. But even if so, it would not have anything to do with whatever *my* values about money may happen to be.

Now, however, let me cite a different parallel, drawing again on Dodds's *The Greeks and the Irrational*. There was, in Athens, a dining-club whose members called themselves *kakodaimonistai*, or 'devil-worshippers', in an obvious parody of the antithetical name *agathodai-monistai* sometimes adopted by dining clubs of the most respectable kind; and the obvious parallel which springs to mind (or at any rate, sprang to *my* mind when I first read of them) is the so-called 'Hell's Angels' of my own day. But there is not a descriptive parallel to be drawn between them of the kind that a purely evaluative comparison might suggest.

* See his *Athenian Democracy* (1957), p. 36.

Readers whose moral theories dictate either an approval of those whom they incline to describe as spiritedly mocking the conventional forms of their period and milieu or, on the other hand, a disapproval of those whom they incline to describe as anti-socially flouting the customary decencies will be equally guilty of misdescription if they allow the parallel to stand. For what was shocking to their contemporaries about the *kakodaimonistai* was not that they were anti-social but that they were impious, whereas what is shocking to their contemporaries about the 'Hell's Angels' is not that they are impious but that they are anti-social. A descriptive parallel too readily drawn between them by inference from the dictionary meaning of their titles and a presumption that readers will judge them equally bad will not, on closer inspection, pass the test of authenticity. There *are* people in 'our' society who are like the *kakodaimonistai*. But they are people of the sort who ostentatiously flout customary superstitions or religious taboos rather than the sort who join motorcycle gangs for the pleasures of gang fights and gang rape. A more authentic parallel to the 'Hell's Angels' are the 'Mohocks' of early eighteenth-century London – aggressive young men who roamed the streets in groups after dark beating up casual strangers and who would, one may assume, have been delighted to be able to do it on the Hell's Angels' motorcycles if only they could have had the opportunity. If, by contrast, I search for authentic examples of *kakodaimonistai* from my own period and milieu, I find that I first recall from my early schooldays a boy who on one occasion, to the horrid excitement of the rest of us, poured ink on his Bible and kicked it round the dormitory floor. By now, although I can still recreate my response to the episode in a way of which Dilthey and Collingwood would thoroughly approve, I have not the least disposition to pass a value-judgement on it one way or the other, any more than on the habit of the original *kakodaimonistai* of deliberately holding their meetings on what conventional Athenians regarded as 'unlucky' days. But if I did now feel as shocked by it as I undoubtedly did at the age of ten (at a school at which a boy was actually beaten with six strokes of the cane for saying 'God damn you!' to another), this would make me not more qualified but less so for the assessment of the authenticity of the different descriptive parallels which may be drawn between the different ways in which self-consciously and ostentatiously anti-conventional groups may choose to defy the accepted values of their period and milieu.

The test of the authenticity of a parallel which rests on explicitly evaluative terms is thus not the coherence of the evaluation, whether in 'their' terms or 'ours'. It is still the standard practical test for authenticity (could 'they' have been brought in principle to accept it?) and behind that the standard practical test for accuracy of reportage (are there any good grounds on which the rival observer might seek to designate their observed actions differently?). A parallel drawn by reference to the researcher's own values is likely to distort both – that is, not only to misdescribe one or other set of behaviour and attitudes, but also to misreport it. For to describe 'their' behaviour as, for example, 'impious' is to imply both that people's judgements of it were like those of impiety at other places and times and also that it can accurately be reported as having been impious in intention and belief. There is a wide variety of circumstances in which the researcher may very well have failed to understand an ostensibly impious act in the primary sense; and the risks of doing so will only be compounded if he has allowed his own agreement or disagreement with 'their' evaluation of impiety to influence the terms in which he seeks to convey it to his readers.

HOW GOOD CAN DESCRIPTIONS HOPE TO BE?

§ 20. How, then, after all this, is the practising sociologist, anthropologist or historian to choose or construct the theoretical concepts – or 'ideal types', if that is what they are – in which his descriptions can best be grounded? Where should they come from? The extreme by relation to which the meaning of a descriptive concept is to be fixed must be intelligible by reference both to what 'their' experience is like to themselves and to the analogous experiences of others to which it is being likened. It can, however, equally well be done from either end. It can be formulated either as a hypothetical set of circumstances, or form of behaviour, or mode of attitude or feeling from which an adjectival concept is then derived, or as an adjectival concept implying an extreme instantiation which would be applicable if, and only if, a hypothetical state of affairs, etc. were to be observed. Thus, for example, extremes of personality can be formulated either in the manner of a Theophrastus character ('the sort of person who feels that he ought always to sit next to his host at dinner, takes his son to Delphi for his first haircut, has to have an Ethiopian for a houseboy, insists on new coins for his payments in silver, has a tombstone carved with an inscription on it when his lapdog dies', etc.) who can then be encapsulated in an adjective (*microphilotimos*) or by coining an adjective (like 'Micawberish') which implies an extreme disposition to behave in certain ways (always credulously optimistic, always expecting 'something to turn up', etc.). Either way, we have an ideal type which is 'ideal' in the sense of never being actually observed.

We are not asked to believe that any petty-proud Athenian ever behaved in every one of the ways which Theophrastus enumerates any more than that any actual person is of a consistently Micawberish disposition under all circumstances. But we have been given a yardstick against which claims that 'his/her behaviour was like . . .' can be assessed and compared.

This yardstick, however, although ideal in one sense must at the same time be real in another. For there must be nothing impossible, in the light of currently accepted explanatory theory, in the set of supposed observations implied by the ideal type. Indeed, it could even be said that the descriptive ideal type needs to be less of a fiction than the explanatory. An explanatory theory involves ideal types as limiting cases unrealizable in the world but logically required by extrapolation from a model of the theory which fits the world as revealed to our observations in the light of it. A descriptive theory, on the other hand, involves ideal types as extrapolations from observed institutions and practices to states of affairs which *could* be experienced, however exotically improbable they may be, and thereby furnish the necessary basis of comparison between one person's experience and the next's. Descriptions in sociology given in the form of 'it is/was like . . .' are not inviting the reader into a world of science fiction. If, say, the reader is asked to imagine someone else's experience by reference to what it would be like to be an entrepreneur operating in a market of perfect competition and nil information costs, this will be no help whatever in enlarging his tertiary understanding, however useful the notion of such a market may be in the grounding of counterfactual hypotheses in a powerful and well-tested explanatory theory. Even the licence to describe 'as if . . .' cannot be extended to impossible worlds. It might still be said that the state of affairs implied by a descriptive ideal type is often as remote from the experiences which it is invoked to help describe as is the explanatory ideal type from the observations which it is invoked to help explain. But the caricatures, if such they are, by which tertiary understanding is conveyed are caricatures in the pejorative sense only if the ideal type is incapable of realization even 'as if . . .'. To revert to the example of 'Machiavellism': there is certainly an element of caricature in the description of manoeuvres for power on, say, the committee of a golf club or the board of a university faculty as 'Machiavellian'; but it helps to convey the flavour of them because, and only because, they can to some degree be authentically likened to the conditions of unremitting intrigue, deliberate treachery, etc., which did obtain among the rulers of the Italian city-states whose behaviour Machiavelli so observantly reported, so cynically explained and so vividly described.

At the same time, it follows from this difference that the formation of ideal types in descriptive theory is in one way more creative, even if in another way less fictional. The ideal types of descriptive theory are generated by extracting, or even forcing, a similarity between observations which, as reported, could not be seen of themselves to fall under the common rubric. Philosophers will no doubt continue to debate whether metaphors should be analysed as reflecting or as producing similarity. But whichever answer is correct, the process is demonstrably a different one from that whereby ostensibly disparate observations are brought within the scope of a set of causal hypotheses all grounded in a single explanatory theory. In both cases, the researcher has either constructed or borrowed a concept with which to lay hold of his chosen portion of the ceaseless flux, seamless web, etc., of human history. But where the ideal-typical concepts of a good explanatory theory will be broad in scope, general in content, free in operation and simplifying in effect, those of a good descriptive theory may, but need not, be any of these. To serve the purpose of conveying a resemblance between one event, process or state of affairs and another as experienced by the persons involved in it, ideal-typical descriptive concepts may be at the same time parochial in scope, specific in content, restricted in operation and complicating in effect.

As an example, consider the description of the novel collaboratively written by Andrew Lang and Rider Haggard about the adventures of Odysseus and Helen of Troy in Egypt under the title *The World's Desire* as 'a piece of gorgeous Cecil B. De Mille hokum'.* The parallel drawn is not merely to a later period but a different art form. It is parochial in its reference to one chosen Hollywood director; specific in its evocation of the particular kind of technicoloured hokum which De Mille purveyed; restricted by its limitation to the swashbuckling melodramas characteristic of an evanescent era in the history of the cinema and of popular taste; and complicating in its effect by forcing a comparison not merely between one historical romance and another but between hokum in print and hokum on film. Yet it succeeds for those very reasons; and it can be shown to be more than adequately grounded, for there is evidence enough to suggest that those very qualities which, some decades later, elicited the neologism 'hokum' to describe them were felt to be present in Lang and Haggard's writing by the qualified critics among Lang's contemporaries. Gross quotes Henry James, in a characteristic turn of phrase, taking Lang posthumously to task for his '*cultivation*,

---

* John Gross, *The Rise and Fall of the Man of Letters* (1969), p. 136.

absolutely, of the puerile imagination and the fourth-rate opinion', and although neither you nor I are therefore required to accede to a derogatory evaluation of Lang – if according to your values *The Prisoner of Zenda* is a better novel than *The Golden Bowl* you will presumably be on Lang's side – it seems difficult to contest that 'gorgeous Cecil B. De Mille hokum' describes it pretty well.

It is, perhaps, arguable that vivid and illuminating as it may be, it describes the genre of *The World's Desire* no better than could be done by the use of an ideal type extrapolated directly from 'their' terms. If the author of a piece of gorgeous Cecil B. De Mille hokum describes his own purpose in his Preface as being, say, to 'tell a stirring tale of derring-do in the good old days of yore', this may convey its flavour to 'us' quite adequately. But the theoretical concepts most useful in descriptive sociology have, as we have seen, a capacity to bridge a presumptive divide between the culture of those whose thoughts, words or deeds are being described and that of the presumptive reader and/or the sociologist himself. They posit a resemblance between 'their' experience and somebody else's, and the degree to which it is vivid and illuminating does not directly depend either on how widely its scope extends or on how large a difference it spans between one culture and another. The ideal-typical concept to which the resemblance appeals may, therefore, be either of 'theirs' or of 'ours'. Whichever it is, however, the methodology of description remains the same: to posit a resemblance between one set of experiences and another is to ascribe to both of them at least one common property by virtue of which the resemblance holds, and the function of descriptive theory is to formulate the concepts in which such resemblances can best be grounded for their purpose.

§ 21. But what is the practical test not merely of adequacy but of excellence? It is not just the avoidance of misapprehension or mystification, for one description can be more vivid and/or illuminating than another even where both are neither inauthentic nor unrepresentative. But descriptions are discretionary, as we have seen, in a way that explanations are not, even where the reportage of the events, processes or states of affairs described is not in dispute between rival observers. Where a rival observer questions a well-validated explanation, it can only be on the grounds that an alternative and perhaps more general theory can give still stronger support to the counterfactual conditionals which it implies. But to question a description, however vivid and illuminating, is to suggest in a quite different sense that there is, literally, more to it than that.

The difference is that no two authentic, well-grounded descriptions are ever incompatible. They can simply be added together to make a third. If one of them contains either a report or an accompanying simile, metaphor or analogy which the other does not and which renders it more vivid or more illuminating, then nothing prevents it from being introduced into the rival description which, perhaps, is more vivid or illuminating in some other respect. It is true to say that rival explanations are not always incompatible either: one theory may, in the course of research, come to be incorporated into another more general one as a special case. But two different explanations cannot both be of equal validity except as answers to different requests for secondary understanding dictated by a different selection of possible causes, conditions and constraints. Different descriptions, on the other hand, can be of equal authenticity, even where both are given in answer to a request for tertiary understanding of the same aspect of the same event, process or state of affairs. To say this may seem either paradoxical or naive in the face of the shelves upon shelves laden with descriptions of the same aspects of the same society, period and milieu by sociologists, anthropologists and historians of rival schools which differ so much from each other that the reader who comes to them with no presuppositions of his own might be forgiven for wondering if it really is the same aspect of the same reported society, period and milieu which is being described. But this is because in any full-length work of sociology, anthropology or history description is always intertwined with explanation on the one hand and evaluation on the other. Alternative descriptions based on accurate reports which any rival observer is bound to accept are not exclusive of one another as, in their different ways, both alternative explanations and alternative evaluations are.

It is true that in practice disputes about authenticity and representativeness are bound to continue between researchers from rival theoretical schools if only because, lacking access to the recording angel's videotapes, they continue to quarrel over the accuracy of each other's reports. But this is a technical difficulty only. It is not intrinsic to the methodology of description. It is a function of the imperfection of the sources with which sociologists, anthropologists and historians have to work as best they can. It is particularly acute where there is doubt, as there often is, about the standing of the chosen informants. A claim that a work of even the most meticulous participant-observation is authentically representative of 'their' institutions and practices can be disputed not merely by appealing to a different set of theoretical concepts whereby 'their' modes of thought are to be conveyed but also by casting doubt on the assumption that they and their preoccupations have been adequately sampled by the reliance on native informants whose accuracy cannot be tested beyond a certain point. But once two researchers have agreed on the accuracy of the sampling procedures which have yielded the particular selection of reported observations from which their different descriptions are then constructed, they have no further reason to insist that the reader has to choose between them. Whereas in matters of reportage and explanation, practising sociologists, anthropologists and historians have no choice but to accept some sort of correspondence theory of truth, in matters of description they have no choice but to accept as it were a coherence theory: whatever their differences, they are bound to accept each other's contributions as jointly constituent parts of a common whole.

But excellence is not, as this might seem to imply, a simple function of length. Essential though it is that every relevant viewpoint should be covered, and probable though it may be that there is still a further graphic detail or a further vivid or illuminating simile or metaphor which would merit inclusion, there is at the same time a virtue in economy no less in description than in explanation. The more shortly the job can be done the better. There will always be room for dispute about what is redundant and what is not if only because different researchers will have different ideas about how much, and of what kind, needs to be said to their presumptive readers for tertiary understanding to be conveyed. But in practice, there operates a rough-and-ready law of diminishing marginal returns. Haunted as the researcher may be by the fear of what a rival observer (or, more often, participant) may show his description to lack, he can do no more to exorcize it than ask himself what else he could possibly have been expected to include in addition to what he has already done; and eventually, even in the most ambitious work of *histoire totale*, the next thing which might be added will not make enough difference to the description as constructed already for its inclusion to be mandatory.

§ 22. Then is there, finally, any one methodological route by which the researcher may hope to ascend from adequacy to excellence? Although I have said that participant-observation is only one technique among several, nevertheless it is unlikely to be disputed that there can be no better qualified observer than one who has actually spent a lifetime in the field. What Malinowski called 'open-air anthropology, as opposed to hearsay note-taking' can hardly fail to yield better opportunities to capture the *détail qui se répercute* or to conjure up the vivid or illuminating simile or metaphor. How can the armchair sociologist presume to pronounce on the experience of people to whom he has never spoken, in whose institutions and practices he has never played a part, and whose manners and mores are far removed from his own? How often has not Frazer been criticized for writing *The Golden Bough* without ever setting foot among the people on whose beliefs he passes judgement, or Zola for writing *Germinal* after only a week spent among the miners of Anzin? And what would the historian of ancient Rome not give to be able to spend even a single day in the forum or along the Appian Way face-to-face with a cross-section of the very people whose modes of feeling and thought he has sought to reconstruct and convey to his twentieth-century readers?

Yet not even the most committed disciple of Malinowski could claim that sufficiently intensive and protracted participant-observation is a guarantee of tertiary understanding by itself. As every aspirant field-worker knows, you cannot do fieldwork except in a role of your own, even if that role is neither more nor less than that of a visiting anthropologist, and your relations with the people whose institutions and practices you are seeking to describe are inexorably conditioned thereby. This need not compromise the accuracy of the reports, validity of the explanations, or coherence of the evaluations which you choose to make. But the consequence for your descriptions is that both their authenticity and their representativeness will have to be warranted by appeal to further testimony than your own. We are all, after all, participant-observers of many years' experience in our own societies, if no other. But which of us would venture to claim that our own participant-observation, even if consciously informed by a desire for both authenticity and representativeness, is privileged over that of everybody else? Indeed, the more detailed the description which any one participant-observer gives, the more likely it is to be challenged either by rival observers or by those whose experience it pretends to describe. In practice, this is often because of the intrusion of rival evaluations: even if rival observers refrain from applying rival criteria of good and bad, the inhabitants of the Deep South, 'Cornerville', asylums, the slums of Mexico City, mediaeval Montaillou or the Trobriand Islands are bound to be sensitive to what they will regard as underemphasis of their virtues and overemphasis of their defects. But even where neither hagiography nor derogation is at issue, the effect of intensive and protracted fieldwork is to thrust authenticity and representativeness into competition with each other, for it is the vivid and illuminating details of the participant-observer's own experiences which are most likely to invite the objection that other people's experiences of the very same events, processes and states of affairs are altogether different from his.

If this competition between the two were indeed irreconcilable, there could be no hope of a description even of the simplest and most homogeneous society which could ever be acceptable to all rival observers. But if the argument of the previous section is correct, it is not. For the best descriptions are those in which it too is accommodated – in which, that is, the fieldworker has recognized that his own experiences need to be supplemented by those of others, that no single category of native informant is to be relied on exclusively, that representativeness may well require an accumulation of mutually irreconcilable perspectives and that not even the most penetrating insight into the most revealing of a society's collective ceremonials or focal rituals can substitute for the further descriptions which 'they' give only to and among themselves. If this in turn suggests that it is only the simplest and most homogeneous society which is therefore describable, the answer is that the more complex the society, the more helpful its members are likely to be in furnishing the literary and other materials from which an authentic and representative description of it can be put together. The technical difficulties will not correlate uniformly with either its size or its sophistication. The description of a large and complex society is in practice made easier, even if more time-consuming, by the plethora of autobiographies, novels, memoirs, diaries, letters, interviews and the rest by which participant-observation can be not only supplemented but refined. It would no doubt be absurd to suppose that a solitary researcher, however gifted, could even after a lifetime in the field present to his readers on the basis of his direct observations alone a description as authentic and representative of, say, twentieth-century Indian as of Trobriand society. But if he has supplemented and refined the participant-observation of many years with the rich documentary sources, ranging all the way from Kipling's *Kim* and Forster's *Hill of Devi* to the Government of India's official publications, to the ethnographers' numerous monographs on the *jāti* system, to the 'Philosophy, Religion and Yoga' section of the list of UBS Publishers and Distributors of New Delhi, to autobiographies and memoirs as diverse as Sita Ram's *From Sepoy to Subadar* and Wavell's *Viceroy's Journal*, to the writings and speeches of Gandhi, Nehru and Lal Bahadur Shastri and their followers and opponents, to the novels of Paul Scott, R. K. Narayan, Ruth Prawer Jhabvala and Salman Rushdie, he may well be entitled to feel not only that the description of India which he then presents to his readers can stand comparison with Malinowski's of the Trobriand Islands but also, perhaps, that he has succeeded in understanding its institutions and practices better in the tertiary than the secondary sense.

Excellence of description, therefore, even if it cannot be mastered by any single strategy or assessed in degrees of success or failure with the precision that the success and failure of explanations can, is both attainable and recognizable. The agreement at which rival observers can hope to arrive will not be such as can be as clearly and schematically set out as when they come to agree that a good explanatory theory has been so modelled as to furnish the necessary grounding for a validated causal hypothesis. But it would be wholly mistaken to conclude from this that disagreements over a description's excellence or lack of it are, so to speak, extra-sociological. In the first place, the disagreement may be one which persists simply in the absence of evidence which rival observers could agree to be decisive; just as different researchers will continue to prefer one rather than another not yet conclusively tested causal hypothesis because they hope, for whatever reasons, that one rather than another underlying explanatory theory will turn out to be the right one, so may they continue to prefer one rather than another not yet fully authenticated description. In the second place, even when all rival observers are satisfied with the sufficiency of the evidence, it is only by appeal to that evidence, and in particular to 'their' own view of that evidence, that the claim for the superiority of one description over another can be sustained at all. A self-confirming *Weltanschauung* which can reinterpret whatever 'they' say in the light of the observer's own untestable presuppositions will render his descriptions no less trivially circular than a pseudo-causal hypothesis which has been immunized by a self-confirming explanatory theory against any possible counter-evidence. It may be that in descriptive sociology the nature both of the researcher's activity and of the skills which it requires are in some sense more 'philosophical' and 'literary' than in explanatory sociology alone. But sociologists, anthropologists and historians who include description as well as explanation among their aims need be no less confident not only that they know what they are trying to achieve but also that if they succeed in achieving it they will, in the end, be acknowledged to have done so even by the partisans of rival theoretical schools.

CONCLUSION

§ 23. Some readers may perhaps be disposed to ask why something as important and yet in some ways as obvious as what I have called 'tertiary' understanding should not have been expounded and analysed many times already, given the amount that has been written by now on the methodology of the sciences of man. I am by no means sure of the answer, and it does not in any case affect the strength of the arguments of this chapter one way or the other. But four considerations suggest themselves. First, many of the issues raised in this chapter *are* already familiar, but to students of literature and biography rather than to sociologists, anthropologists or historians. Second, much of the philosophical literature has been preoccupied with the traditional dichotomy between facts and values. Third, the philosophers and sociologists who have devoted most attention to the concept of understanding in relation to human behaviour have done so by contrasting it directly with the understanding of natural events rather than by asking themselves how far and in what sense it is or is not common to both. Fourth, the problems of explanation in the social sciences have been sufficiently controversial, and their potential implications for substantive research sufficiently far-reaching, for them to take up the attention of writers interested in methodology to the exclusion of a set of problems which many of them may continue to regard as marginal. But whatever the reasons may be, it remains the case that the problems of description as here defined have up to now received far less attention than they deserve from philosophers, methodologists and practitioners of the social sciences alike.

5

Evaluation in social theory

THE INESCAPABILITY OF EVALUATION

§ 1. Any reader who, like myself, was brought up on what was then regarded (at least in England) as the humorous classic *1066 and All That* will remember how hard its authors played the joke about whether a historical person or happening was to be classified as a Good Thing or a Bad Thing. The joke drew its point from the sort of schoolbook historiography in which a succession of kings, battles, treaties, geographical discoveries and technical inventions was chronicled from the standpoint of an unblushing chauvinism and a simple-minded conviction that at the end of the day the Good Things, in Britain if nowhere else, thoroughly outweighed the Bad. But the range of historical, anthropological and sociological writings to which the caricature could equally well be applied extends a great deal further than the schoolbooks of the heyday of the British Empire. Since it is undeniable that everyone has and cannot help having moral, political or aesthetic views of some kind or other about what states of society are or aren't to be preferred to others, it must be doubtful if there has ever been a work of substantive social theory in which there is not somewhere a turn of phrase which was written, whether consciously or not, as an expression of a value-judgement to which the author subscribes. The extent to which it may obtrude on the reader varies, of course, widely. At one end, there is the kind of sober narrative and dispassionate analysis in which causes and consequences are presented *sine ira et studio*, and the author's preferences camouflaged almost to invisibility. At the other end, it is obvious at a glance that narrative and analysis are alike subordinated to the overriding purpose of persuading the reader to share the author's view of Good Things and Bad. To the purists of value-neutrality, any moral, political or aesthetic judgements whatever should be excised from the sciences of man if they are to continue to claim the title of sciences. But although they can be, do they have to? Might it not be possible here, too, to preserve a distinction between presuppositionlessness and theory-neutrality?

Whatever the right answer to these questions, detachment by itself will not be enough. It is sometimes suggested that a researcher who seeks as far as possible to excise, or at least to discount, any possible bias will succeed to the degree that he is remote from the events, processes and states of affairs which he is concerned to report, explain and describe. Thus Tacitus himself, when he announces it as his plan to treat of the events from the end of the principate of Augustus to the end of that of Tiberius *sine ira et studio*, adds that he stands well removed from what might otherwise occasion him to give way to one or both of those temptations (*'quorum causas procul habeo'*). But there cannot be a single reader who, on coming to the end of the *Annals*, would be willing to agree with him. Indeed, the values of historians may inform their writings with just as much passion when they are dealing with the long distant past as when they are dealing with their own lifetimes, as the state of ancient historiography nearly two millennia after Tacitus is enough to show. For example: equally pre-emptive mistranslations of a single short passage of Diodorus Siculus about ownership and redistribution of land in the Lipari Islands in the sixth century B.C. have been put before their readers by competent scholars who are partisans of the virtues of primitive communism on the one side and of the sanctity of private property on the other.* It may be that for discussion *ad hominem* it is better to use examples about which strong views are unlikely any longer to be held: readers of this volume will, I assume, be better able to consider *sine ira et studio* the execution of Charles I in 1648 and the contrasting attitudes of Hume and Macaulay to it than they will the waging of war by the United States in Vietnam in the 1960s and the rival analyses of its rationale by 'left-wing' or 'right-wing' historians. But the methodological issues raised are the same irrespective of either the immediacy of the events or the strength of the prejudices of those who either read or write about them. They are not resolved simply by the passage of time.

Nor will theory-neutrality be achieved by taking up a position equi-distant from the extremes. It is, perhaps, a plausible assumption that where debate over whether a person, policy, institution or regime is a Good Thing or a Bad Thing is polarized between authors of left-wing and right-wing persuasions, the risks of wilful misreportage, question-

---

* For references, see M. M. Austin and P. Vidal-Naquet, *Economic and Social History of Ancient Greece* (Eng. edn., 1977), pp. 236–8.

begging explanation and hagiographic or derogatory description are not significantly lower at the one pole than the other. But the solution does not lie in trying to find a mid-point between them. In the first place, it has quite often been the case that a pre-emptive evaluation has, in the event, helped to guide sociologists, anthropologists or historians to a re-explanation and/or redescription of old evidence or a reportage of new which comes to be accepted even by those on the opposite side; and in the second, to compromise on principle between conflicting evaluations is itself to adopt a bias of another kind. Once it is accepted that there is no logical, but only a contingent, relation between moral, political and aesthetic values and the values of science, then however strongly infected with the researcher's evaluative presuppositions a work of sociology, anthropology or history may be, the methodologist can always reconstruct it in such a way that the value-judgements are sifted out and the explanatory and/or descriptive content is left behind.

It is true that *1066 and All That* itself could not seriously be counted as a contribution to social science once the value-judgements had been sifted out of it. But nothing prevents reports, explanations and descriptions assembled for the purpose of persuading the reader that Henry VIII was a Bad Thing from being analysed by just the same criteria of accuracy, validity and authenticity as if they had been assembled for an article in the *English Historical Review* about the implications of his involvement in a continental war in 1543 for the future dependence of the English crown on parliamentary consent to taxation. Even good old-fashioned rhetorical diatribes in the style of 'We accuse him of having given up his people to the merciless inflictions of the most hot-headed and hard-hearted of prelates' (Macaulay) or 'The spoliation of the Church's property, the fraudulent alienation of the state domains, the robbery of the common lands, the usurpation of feudal and clan property under circumstances of reckless terrorism' (Marx) may contain reports as accurate, explanations as valid and descriptions as authentic as a scholarly monograph in a social-scientific journal. Neither diagnosis of researchers' purposes nor construal of their terminology is a simple matter, and their readers will do as well to be as suspicious of protestations of theory-neutrality as of blatantly pre-emptive appeals to conscience. But the same distinctions hold good at either extreme and the same disentaglement can, however laboriously, be performed. If the purists of value-neutrality are right, the single methodological rule to be followed is to perform the disentanglement in any and all cases. But this is not the only conclusion consistent with their premise. It is precisely because evaluation can, if necessary, be disentangled from reportage, explanation and description that it may not always be necessary to do so.

§ 2. Lord Acton to Bishop Creighton, 5 April, 1887: 'If men were truly sincere, and delivered judgements by no canons but those of evident morality, then Julian would be described in the same terms by Christian and pagan, Luther by Catholic and Protestant, Washington by Whig and Tory, Napoleon by patriotic Frenchmen and patriotic German.' We all know very well that they are not so described. But before concluding that practising sociologists, anthropologists and historians are therefore obliged to excise from their writings any possible hint of approval or disapproval of one or the other side, it is worth remembering the extent to which there is, all the same, agreement on a 'canon of evident morality'. Much of the argument between Christian and pagan, Catholic and Protestant, Whig and Tory or Frenchman and German is not in fact about the standards by which the actions of Julian, Luther, Washington and Napoleon are to be judged so much as about whether those actions were really as much of a Good Thing or Bad Thing as their admirers or detractors have claimed.

The reason is simply that sociologists, anthropologists and historians of all schools do share some sort of tacit, if unspecific, commitment to the value of benevolence. Whatever the particular evaluative theory to which they may subscribe, they will not repudiate without further argument any hint of approval of persons, policies, institutions and regimes which can be shown to have promoted the well-being as they interpret it themselves of the members of the society under study, whether by increasing the supply of material goods or services made available to them, freeing them from unnecessary compulsions or restraints, or promoting a culture in which the gratification afforded to them by the arts or sciences is enhanced or diffused. Likewise, whatever the other criteria by which they may also apportion praise or blame, none of them will be found unequivocally to applaud rulers who can be shown to have permitted, encouraged or even actively promoted avoidable hardship or distress for its own sake. It is true that some of the defences which are offered by appeal to an 'evident canon' of benevolence are remarkably implausible. But the search for apologias is itself a testimony to the need of those who put them forward to appeal to one. When Boswell sets out the basis of his disagreement with Johnson about the slave trade and argues that 'To abolish that trade would be to "... *shut the gates of mercy on mankind*"', he is claiming, however implausibly, that 'African Savages' are happier transported to the West Indies than they would be if left to 'massacre or intolerable bondage' in their country of origin.* The transparency of such an apologia merely reveals the more clearly its attempted grounding. The more transparent, indeed, the apologia, the less of a methodological problem there is. The nature of the connection between reportage and evaluation is straightforward: if Boswell were right, any 'African Savages' who had experienced it would have said, on reflection, had an enquiring sociologist asked them, that they too thought the slave trade a Good Thing from the point of view of their own well-being.

The connection is equally straightforward in those cases where personal good faith is being impugned. For example: I have in my possession a copy of a letter written by Albert Speer in answer to a correspondent who queried his claim that he did not know what was going on in Auschwitz. It is not that Speer seeks to dispute the canon of evident morality any more than Boswell did. On the contrary, he admits that 'This deliberate blindness outweighs whatever good I may have done or tried to do in the last period of the war.'† The question left in the reader's mind is simply whether to believe that it was really a blindness. Did a Minister of War Production notorious alike for his attention to detail, his economy in the allocation of strategic materials and his interest in the use of Jews and others as forced labour on projects of his own really know nothing of what Auschwitz was for? His reply is that the allocation of rail wagons was outside his concern ('*Ich hatte andere Sorgen*') and that he associated the place-name Auschwitz with a chemical works; and he goes on to observe that even in the democratic United States, Truman knew nothing about the atomic bomb and the 'Manhattan Project' until he became President on Roosevelt's death. The connection between reportage and evaluation, accordingly, is as uncontentious here as in Boswell's defence of the slave trade. The difference is only that here it is a matter of whether Speer is, in Acton's phrase, being 'truly sincere' or not, and he is the only person other than the recording angel who knows.

The connection is not, perhaps, quite so straightforward when the evaluation is bound up with an explanation which is itself controversial. But even here, the methodological difficulty is not that facts and values are inextricably intertwined. It is that so many of the explanatory hypotheses which tacitly appeal to an evident canon of benevolence are not only contentious but untestable. It makes no difference whether the

* See the passage in Boswell's *Life* relating to September 23, 1777, where Johnson's views and his own are both set out at some length.
† *Inside the Third Reich* (Eng. trans., 1970), p. 507.

researcher advances a judgement of this kind because of having come to accept one rather than another explanatory hypothesis as valid or whether, on the contrary, he is readier to uphold a chosen hypothesis against its rivals because he is already committed to a preference for the one state of society over the other. Nor does it make any difference whether the judgement about a better or worse state of society is explicitly formulated or camouflaged to invisibility. Where the argument is a political polemic in support of one or another faction or party, the connection is, as a rule, clearly visible: 'if the such-and-such party had remained in office and its policy been consistently pursued the nation would now be enjoying a period of unrivalled prosperity' is a hypothesis testable in principle against what the population would in that event have said about their own prosperity, even if it has only been formulated at all for the purpose of persuading the reader what a Good Thing the such-and-such party is. But the same holds with, for example:

> There was, of course, poverty amidst this growing plenty, as the investigations of Charles Booth and Seebohm Rowntree made abundantly clear, and the tide of depression left its flotsam of bankrupts as well as of unemployed; but, for all the justifiable alarms which attended the years of trade depression, it was only the unfortunate few who were not appreciably better off in 1895 than they had been twenty years earlier.*

There is no overt claim here that the population was enjoying the best of possible worlds. Yet the sentence has an unmistakably complacent ring; and its complacency resides in the implication, signalled by the opening 'of course', that the changes between 1875 and 1895 were, in the technical sense, Pareto-optimal and that an evaluation which focussed on the continued ill-being of the unfortunate few would therefore be mistaken. Thus even here, where the value-judgement to which the reader's assent is solicited is not directly formulated as such, its relation to the reported observations and implied counterfactual conditionals is as straightforward as where an appeal to benevolence is more outspokenly voiced and a comparison with alternative possible states of society more explicitly made. Notice, moreover, that the appeal to benevolence is presupposed in both examples to be uncontentious in itself. It is only the question whether the group or category of persons in question is or would have been better off by their own presumptive standards under one or

* Arthur J. Taylor, 'The Economy', in Simon Nowell-Smith, ed., *Edwardian England 1901–1914* (1964), p. 127.

another set of conditions which is contentious; and this, even if it cannot be conclusively answered, is a sociological question, not a philosophical one.*

BENEVOLENCE AS A PRESUPPOSITION

§ 3. Here, already, the purists of value-neutrality are likely to mount two immediate counter-arguments. First, it is surely the case that the well-being of any one group or category of the population of any society is in some ways and to some degree in conflict with that of others, so that any comparison between alternative states of it must be pre-emptive of a weighting of different preferences of 'theirs'. Second, there are surely many sociologists, anthropologists and historians who do not appeal to the 'well-being', whatever that means, of those whose institutions and practices they have reported, explained and described, but to some quite other criterion of evaluation. But both these can be conceded without its following from either of them that no hint whatever of a presupposition of benevolence should be allowed to stand in sociological, anthro-pological or historical writing except in indirect speech.

That the wants and preferences of different members of any society are in conflict with one another is undeniable, and it raises both technical questions about the possibility of their reconciliation and philosophical questions about the grounds on which one type of want ought or ought not to be given priority over another. But it does not raise any methodo-logical difficulty about a presupposition of benevolence as such. Where the members of a definable group or category are all agreed that a change is an improvement in their well-being as they see it, and the researcher cannot find any respect in which anyone else's well-being is diminished in consequence, is he not entitled to present it to his readers not merely as an 'improvement' but as an improvement? Only to a rival observer who is avowedly malevolent is it not an improvement, even *ceteris paribus*, that the sick should be cured and the starving fed. To all other observers, whatever theory they may accept which in a given context overrides the *ceteris paribus* clause, it will be incontestable that the sick ought to be cured and the starving fed if there is no countervailing reason against it. The conflicts of values and priorities in any actual society may be such

---

* The definition of 'benevolence' itself is of course a philosophical matter; but for the purpose of this chapter, I take it to mean simply a desire that other people's desires should be fulfilled unless there is some reason against it – which is at the same time less than 'love of another' (Bishop Butler) and more than 'an interest in one another's interests' (John Rawls, *A Theory of Justice* (1971), p. 148).

that even so innocuous a judgement as this one can seldom be made. Moreover, even where unanimity of preferences does obtain, other things seldom if ever *are* equal: an appeal to benevolence alone will yield few if any practical inferences for the conduct of public policy even in the smallest and simplest society. But none of this amounts to an argument for saying that no conceivable change in a society could ever bring about what could be accepted as an improvement by any researcher willing to endorse benevolence as a value. It amounts only to a reminder that uncontentiously demonstrable improvements are fewer and farther between than may sometimes be assumed.

Likewise, it is not in dispute that many sociologists, anthropologists and historians do appeal to values other than benevolence in soliciting their readers' approval or disapproval of the persons, policies, institutions and regimes which they have reported, explained and described. In particular, many of them appeal to the overriding priority attached to a patriotic or nationalistic cause. The blind *Lobpreisen der Heimat* which Burckhardt so deplored in the writings of other historians may less often be found in the twentieth century than the nineteenth: even 1066 is no longer debated with the passion which informed Edward Augustus Freeman's almost lifelong championship of the Saxons (Good Thing) against the Normans (Bad Thing).* But consider only how many histories of the origins of either the First or Second World Wars can be classified as pro- or anti-German, or how deeply permeated is the debate about the 'modernization' of the 'Third World' by implicit acceptance or rejection of the United States as the model for success or failure, or how many mediaevalists can be shown to side either with or against the Papacy. Yet examples like these are entirely compatible with an acceptance of the presupposition of benevolence coupled with an insistence on theory-neutrality beyond that point. For either the claim for the superiority of one nation, cause, movement or creed over another is grounded in an appeal to the enhanced well-being of the people concerned as they view it themselves, in which case it may be accepted as uncontentious as far as it goes, or it appeals to some further moral, political or aesthetic ideal which has then to be argued against its rivals on extra-sociological

---

* See his *History of the Norman Conquest* (1867–79), whose readers must judge for themselves how far the claim in the Preface to Volume v that 'I can say in all honesty that I have laboured for truth' (p. x) squares with the claim in the Preface to Volume I that the Conquest 'did but communicate to us a certain foreign infusion' (p. viii). To David C. Douglas and George W. Greenaway, eds., *English Historical Documents II*[2] (1981), p.4, 'It is particularly unfortunate that Freeman's fine erudition, and his exhaustive knowledge of the chronicles of the age, should have been coloured by such partisanship ...'

grounds. Nothing, admittedly prevents a researcher from refusing to assign any value whatever to what the members of the society which he is studying regard as their well-being: if he wants to persuade his readers that war, pestilence and famine are Good Things because they strengthen and ennoble the characters of the citizens of those nations subjected to them and that the best nation is one whose rulers instil in its citizens a patient endurance of their sufferings and a humble submission to the will of God, he is free to try. But that is not a methodological argument against allowing benevolence as a presupposition which has then to be overruled, if the researcher so holds, on other grounds. Examples of that kind only show all the more clearly the usefulness of drawing a line between an initial tacit appeal to benevolence which rests on the evidence of people's own view of their own well-being and an appeal to any and all other values including those which have least regard for conventional notions of what it is normal for human beings to desire. Let us by all means excise the judgements which rest on a presupposition that Christians (or pagans), Catholics (or Protestants), Whigs (or Tories), Frenchmen (or Germans) are bound to be in the right (or wrong). But let us thereafter be all the more willing to leave as they stand judgements that it is, other things equal, a Good Thing that the starving should be fed and the sick cured, independently of their religious or national status.

The objection may still be raised that these judgements, even if all practising sociologists, anthropologists and historians would be willing to subscribe to them, presuppose more than the existence of shared sentiments of sympathy and goodwill such as the notion of benevolence implies. For to say that the starving *should* be fed and the sick cured is not just to say that the researcher feels sorry for people who, he finds, have not enough to eat or suffer from painful and debilitating ailments but to imply that it is the obligation or duty of the responsible authorities to try to feed and cure them, or that they have a right or entitlement to be fed and cured; and this presupposes that there is a moral theory of some kind from which propositions about obligations, duties, rights and entitlements could be derived. But it is quite possible to assent to the proposition that a society which satisfies more of its members' desires, other things equal, than one which does not is therefore a better society without being committed to any moral or political theory on which there might be grounded a judgement of policy about either how, when or by whom the improvements ought to be brought about, if at all. The *ceteris paribus* clause has precisely the force of allowing 'their' reported desires still to be revalued on a whole variety of possible grounds. The 'evident canon' of benevolence enjoins merely that the researcher has to *have* a reason for denying that it would be a Good Thing rather than a Bad Thing if their reported desires were somehow or other met. It does not compel him in endorsing it to offer any view of the merits or demerits of the various theories from which such a denial, or its repudiation, might be derived. Still less does it compel him to lay down which of 'their' various possible desires are to count as needs or deserts or which of the various possible components of their stated 'well-being' are to be ranked above others. It merely permits him, subject to certain methodological conditions which it is the principal purpose of this chapter to set out, to leave 'their' stated preferences to stand free of inverted commas as grounds on which, if they were to be met, the state of their society could be pronounced better, other things equal, than if they were not. The purists of value-neutrality will, no doubt, still insist that any such judgement is the business of the philosopher, not the social scientist. But if they do, they are still free to reinstate the inverted commas for themselves and to turn the researcher's conclusion that he has observed an improvement in the state of 'their' group, category or society back into a conclusion that he has observed only an ' "improvement" to "them" '.

§4. This suggested endorsement of benevolence as an 'evident canon' may, however, be criticized as a methodological rule no less by the opponents than by the purists of value-neutrality. For (they will say) if any value-judgement is to be admitted at all into social science, why stop there? Whatever the particular evaluative theories to which different sociologists, anthropologists and historians may happen to subscribe, they surely will all agree that a presupposition of *ceteris paribus* benevolence says very, very much less than there is to be said about human institutions and practices from a moral, political and aesthetic point of view.

This also is incontestable; and if that is what practising sociologists, anthropologists and historians want to do, it is not for the methodologist to tell them that they may not. But it *is* for the methodologist to make clear to them the point at which they have crossed the frontier of social science into the territory of philosophy. Readers who look to them for reports, explanations and descriptions of the societies which they have chosen to study will no doubt want their reports, explanations and descriptions to furnish them with evidence on which to decide by the lights of their own evaluative theories how far those societies' institutions and practices are a Good Thing or Bad Thing. But they will not want that decision pre-empted by the researcher's presupposition that *his* preferred evaluative theory is the right one. They will want to have been told about 'their' evaluation of their institutions and practices, about the extent of unanimity or conflict of values among them, the nature and scope of their grievances and aspirations, the intensity with which they seek to pursue claims of what they conceive as justice or right against one another, and the extent to which they themselves regard it as a duty to act benevolently. But they will recognize that their decision to endorse or reject the evaluations which one or another group or category of 'them' is reported, explained and described as having made cannot be arrived at by reference to those reports, explanations and descriptions alone.

A variant of the same objection from a similar standpoint is that although social scientists are right to abstain from pronouncing on what is good or bad about the behaviour which they have chosen to study, they ought nevertheless, since they all *do* subscribe to some evaluative theory or other, to confess to their readers what their values are, if only to help them to detect and repudiate their possible effects. If even the most detached academic observers of human institutions and practices are bound to admit that they would, if pressed, have to declare whose side they are (or would have been) on, then is it not better that they should announce their moral, political or aesthetic judgements and the theories in which they are grounded as explicitly and coherently as they can rather than pretend to their readers and themselves that they have none? But once given that their evaluations can always be disentangled from the reports, explanations and descriptions within which they are presented or to which they apply, it will be better still that the researcher should either keep them to himself or argue for them as what they are. Suppose I tell you at the opening of Volume II that my values are those of a Christian, Protestant, Whig, Francophile or whatever they may indeed happen to be, and that my preferences are, for me, adequately grounded in my preferred moral, political or aesthetic theory. This will not by itself bring you anywhere closer to sharing my views than you are already. If my purpose is to persuade you of them, I must do more than simply announce them; and if it isn't, I have no need to mention them at all. Merely to alert you to the bias which I may not have succeeded in discounting for myself is more or less to invite you to resist my explanatory and descriptive conclusions if your preferred evaluative theory is not the same as mine. If at the end of the day there is no substantive social theory which is not Christian (or pagan), Protestant (or Catholic), Whig (or Tory), Francophile (or Germanophile), etc., social theory, then the whole attempt to arrive at explanations and descriptions of reported behaviour whose validity and authenticity have been established to the satisfaction of all rival observers should have been abandoned before it was begun.

The methodology recommended in this chapter corresponds, accordingly, to that of Chapters 2 to 4 in requiring of the practising sociologist, anthropologist or historian the same mixture of sympathy and detachment appropriate to his position relative to the agents whose behaviour he is studying on the one side and the readers to whom he wishes to present his conclusions on the other. In acknowledging that he subscribes to a presupposition of benevolence, he is committing himself to taking seriously the wants, grievances and aspirations of the members of the society concerned, however alien from his own. But in refusing at the same time either to appraise their values and preferences in the light of his own, or to take sides as between different groups or categories of 'them' whose values and preferences conflict, he is preserving the independence from moral, political or aesthetic judgement without which any claim to be offering the reader a work of social science and not of philosophy or propaganda (or both) would be impossible to sustain.

FORMS OF MISEVALUATION

§ 5. This, however, still leaves open the possibility that the researcher who presents 'their' stated values and preferences to his reader can – and if he can, should – pronounce upon them from within the frontier which divides social science from moral, political or aesthetic philosophy. Just because he abstains from emending or rejecting them by reference to an evaluative theory of his own, it does not follow that he cannot correct them on other, non-pre-emptive grounds. He can, to be sure, simply let them stand without any further comment; but this will be almost as much of an abdication from what his readers are likely to feel entitled to expect as to refrain from any attempt to replace 'their' explanations and descriptions of their own institutions and practices with better ones. There is the same three-way relation between the researcher, those whose institutions and practices and attitudes to them he is studying, and the presumptive reader whose curiosity about those institutions, practices and attitudes to them he wishes to satisfy. Just as 'they' can, within certain limits, be shown to have not only misexplained but sometimes misdescribed what they say and do, so can they sometimes be shown to have misevaluated it by failing to meet a defeasibility condition which is independent of any evaluative theory of the researcher's own. Such misevaluations may be of either or both of two kinds, for which I propose to use the two terms *false consciousness* and *bad faith*.

'False consciousness' is a term already so contentious that to use it in this context may seem to invite just the kind of irreconcilably partisan argument which this whole volume has sought to circumvent. But it can be so defined that its use in correcting what 'they' say about their preferences is not methodologically but only substantively contentious. So restricted, it is evaluatively theory-neutral. The moral and political implications which it may carry in Marxist or any other theory are neither pre-emptively assumed nor ruled out of court. The methodological difficulty which attends its use under this definition is of another kind. To say that agents can be mistaken about their assessment of their own well-being and the tacit appeal to the observer's benevolence which it implies is to claim that under certain conditions they would, or could be brought to, assess it differently. But what conditions? Where is the line to be drawn between 'if I had known what harm such a measure would do to the cause which I hold dear I would not have lobbied in support of it' and 'if I had been suitably brainwashed by my captors I would willingly have accepted a lifetime of slavery'? 'Imagine yourself to be a Trobriand Islander' may, as we have seen, be a useful maxim where description is at issue. But for a sociologist to say to you, his reader, true though it may be, 'if you were a Trobriand Islander, your assessment of your well-being would be very different from what it is' is not to correct your values and preferences but to speculate about somebody else's. When J. S. Mill says* that the same causes which make a man a Churchman in London would have made him a Buddhist or Confucian in Peking, he is asserting what is virtually a truism of comparative sociology; but although it can be used, as Mill uses it, to argue for an evaluative theory on which to ground an appeal for toleration of unorthodox opinions, it cannot be used to persuade the London Churchman to accept the doctrines of the Buddhist or Confucian in preference to his own. There has to be drawn a line at the point where it ceases to be plausible to speak of a person differently conditioned as the same person.

This can only mean, if theory-neutrality is to be preserved, that 'they' must in principle be capable of being brought to change their own evaluations without their circumstances being changed for the purpose. For their consciousness to be 'false' in the restricted sense here proposed, they must be making a mistake by a criterion which they are themselves willing to accept, not one which the sociologist, anthropologist or

* In Ch. 2 of *On Liberty* (1859).

historian can argue, however convincingly, that they could have been conditioned to accept but weren't. These mistakes then fall into two sub-categories: first, mistakes of the kind where the misevaluation derives from their honest misstatement of their own preferences; second, mistakes of the kind where the misevaluation derives from misinforma-tion. Observers of what they say and do may still wish to go further in correcting their stated preferences, and may wish to use the term 'false consciousness' in a less restricted sense in doing so. But they can do so only by appeal to a theory which will have to be defended against its rivals on other grounds.

A good example of honest misstatement of preferences is to be found in the experimental literature on 'ethnic' attitudes. People may say and believe that it is their preference that segregation should be enforced by law and/or custom, yet be unaware that they do not, in the event, behave consistently with that stated preference. For example: an American sociologist, in a paper published in the mid 1930s,* reported that he and his wife had visited a great number of restaurants and hotels in the company of a Chinese couple and been refused service only once; yet when he sent out questionnaires to the proprietors of the establishments which had accepted them asking whether they would accept a person of Chinese race, over 90% both of them and of a control group replied 'no'. How far such discrepancies may be generalizable or replicable is a matter for further research and debate. But the example still serves to illustrate the methodological point. If the attitudes and actions of the hoteliers and restaurateurs have been accurately reported, their assertion as to what would make the institutions and practices of their society more of a Good Thing from their point of view is not to be accepted as it stands: there is no obligation, even *ceteris paribus*, either on the benevolent observer to do what they ask or on the reader of the sociologist's report to accept at face value what they say.

The easiest examples of the second kind of misevaluation, where it derives from simple misinformation, are those where the information has a strictly deductive implication. As I remarked in the discussion of inference within reportage in Section 23 of Chapter 2, the conclusions of arithmetic are as inescapable in sociology as anywhere else. If in a monetarized society the members of any group or category of people whose well-being is avowedly tied to their cash income have simply miscalculated the size of the gap between their net current income and what they tell the enquiring sociologist they need to satisfy them, then

* See R. T. Lapière, 'Attitudes vs. Actions', *Social Forces* XIII (1934).

they are guilty of false consciousness in an almost trivial sense which no rival observer will dispute. It is true that such examples are not always quite as trivial as they may seem. To confront 'them' with a paper on the logic of social choice from the *Journal of Economic Theory* which proves them to be voicing preferences inconsistent with their own stated interests may be no more immediately persuasive in changing their assessment of their own well-being than a copy of *Cahiers du Cinéma* in changing the attitudes of the inhabitants of 'Macondo' to Bruno Crespi's 'machine of illusions'. But in the absence of special explanation of 'their' refusal to accept an inference according to rules acknowledged by them and the observer alike, the observer can correct an evaluation which they have made of their society's institutions or practices without appealing to any moral, political or aesthetic theory of his own.

The more contentious examples are those where the information which, it is alleged, would change 'their' view of their well-being is of an empirical kind. 'If I had known what harm the realization of my stated preference would do ...' may be a concession readily made with hindsight. But the enquiring fieldworker, even if strongly persuaded on the basis of independent study that this was just what would happen, would have had no business to lay charges of 'false consciousness' at the time when the agent's original assessment was made unless the agent could have been persuaded by him then and there. Arguments appealing to disputable predictions are the very ones which generate the most acrimonious controversy because of the strong contingent connections between the preferred explanations and evaluations alike of sociologists, anthropologists and historians and of those whose institutions and practices they study. But to the extent that evidence acceptable to all rival observers supports him, a researcher is in principle as fully entitled to tell his readers that 'they' were wrong in assessing their own prospective well-being as they did as to tell the ancient Romans who progressively withdrew the corn supply from the hands of private contractors that they were unwittingly creating an increasingly artificial cost-benefit imbalance between regions.

§6. 'Bad faith' is likewise a term which can be and has been defined within and for the purposes of a particular evaluative theory. Indeed, it has come to be associated with the theory advanced in *Being and Nothingness* by Jean-Paul Sartre as closely as 'false consciousness' with the theories of Marx and Engels. But it too can be more restrictively, and thereby non-pre-emptively, defined. It does still imply something more than an honest misstatement which further reflection or information would be sufficient to correct. But it can do so in two distinguishable, but not mutually exclusive, ways without violation of theory-neutrality. In the first, the researcher can correct 'their' assessment of their well-being relative to that of others by showing that it has been weighted in their own favour; in the second, he can correct 'their' conception of what is to count as benevolence by showing that it is incoherent in their own terms.

The second may invite the objection that the diversity not only of morals but of theories of morals is so notoriously wide that to charge 'them' with incoherence is to impose an ethnocentric criterion of 'ours' which holds only for ourselves. But the notion of acting benevolently is understandable in the primary sense in any and all societies, including the Ik of Section 19 of Chapter 2. It is not in dispute that some or all of the members of many known societies do so evaluate their own conduct that they regard it for their own reasons as a Good Thing *not* to act benevolently. Indeed, it would be unwarrantably ethnocentric for any sociologist, anthropologist or historian automatically to assume bad faith on the part of the Spanish Inquisitors, the Aztec priests who practised human sacrifice, the Covenanters who, massacred their Highland prisoners, children included, after the Battle of Philiphaugh to the cry of 'Jesus and no quarter!', or the Nazis who were responsible for the systematic genocide of the Jews. But the diversity of morals and theories of morals, although it may be an argument against cognitivist ethical theory, is not an argument against the claim that there is no society whose members are incapable of assessing their behaviour towards each other, or the members of other societies, in the light of whether they are treating them as they wish to be treated. The Konyak Naga who has bought a young boy for the express purpose of cutting off his head makes no pretence that he is acting benevolently; his claim is only that it has to be done because the shedding of blood is necessary to maintain the fertility of the soil, and one anthropologist who has done fieldwork among them reports a Naga expressing overt pity for his intended victim whose misfortune it was to have to perform that necessary function.*

A charge of bad faith, therefore, can be vindicated only by a demonstration that the native informants are not to be believed in saying either that they *are* acting benevolently according to their lights or that they are acting *un*benevolently only in the cause of some overriding evaluative theory. Such charges are by no means easy to press to the satisfaction

---

* See Christoph von Fürer-Haimendorf, *Morals and Merit: a Study of Values and Social Controls in South Asian Societies* (1967), p. 114.

of all rival observers, and it is all too tempting to deny the benefit of the doubt to agents who are in no position to answer back. But a critical examination of 'their' stated evaluation of their actions is not outside the role or the competence of the sociologist, anthropologist or historian. If the inquisitor doesn't really believe that he is saving the heretic's soul by sending him to the stake, or the Naga headhunter doesn't really believe that the shedding of his victim's blood is necessary to maintain the fertility of the soil, then the reader of an account of their behaviour is entitled to be told so. This is not a violation of the maxim that all agents are to be taken seriously. To convict 'them' of bad faith is neither to dismiss out of hand the beliefs and attitudes which they claim to hold nor to pronounce them indefensibly wicked. It is only to show that they cannot justify their actions to themselves in the way that the reader might otherwise, and mistakenly, assume.

The same holds where the charge of bad faith attaches in the first type of context – that is, where it is claimed by 'them' that the privileges which they enjoy are to the benefit of their ostensibly less fortunate fellow-citizens. The *locus classicus* for an argument on these lines is the speech which Sarpedon makes to Glaucus in Book XII of the *Iliad*: those who are mighty in battle and fight in the front rank deserve the superior life-style which they enjoy because of the risks and burdens which they bear on behalf of the non-combatants at home. There are again two possibilities: it might turn out on closer enquiry either that Sarpedon would not, in the event, repudiate his privileges if he were not a front-rank fighter or that his too easy view of the non-combatants' view of their benefit is not in fact shared by them. In either case, the reader is entitled to have it pointed out to him; and if the researcher is able to do so, the reader will have no choice but to accept that Sarpedon's claim is not to be taken at face value. But this will not entail the conclusion that Sarpedon was wicked or the institutions and practices of his society a Bad Thing: that is still up to you.

Imputations of bad faith under either heading evidently involve more than mere reportage: correction or rejection of 'their' stated values and preferences on these grounds may require both a test of explanatory hypotheses about their motives and an assessment of the authenticity of the descriptions of themselves and other people to which they assent. They are accordingly likely to require of the researcher who ventures to make one not only a keen eye for a plausible counterfactual conditional but a keen or even supersensitive ear, such as we have seen E. M. Forster's biographer attribute to him, for the 'imperceptible tones' in which bad faith is betrayed. But they are still not pre-emptive of whatever evaluation may follow from his chosen moral, political or aesthetic theory. It is still only a matter of sociological, not philosophical, judgement whether 'their' protestations should be passed on at face value to the reader or not; and the reader who feels that they have been when they ought not to have been is still only charging the researcher with bad sociology, not with bad ethics.

APPEALING TO THE 'FACTS'

§7. Restrictive as they may be, these methodological rules also furnish a workable criterion by which the reader can construe appeals made to the 'facts' of evaluatively contentious behaviour, whether the appeal is made by 'them' and passed on to him in *oratio obliqua* or made in *oratio recta* by the researcher on their behalf. These 'facts' will, like any others, be so only under a presupposition defining them as such. But here the methodological need is to distinguish between those which can and those which cannot be presented at face value to the reader without pre-empting an evaluation which goes beyond a presupposition of benevolence alone.

Any such appeal also raises the by now familiar difficulty that the initial construal must have regard to the purpose and not merely the syntactical form of the appeal which has been made. Thus, when Johnson is reported by Boswell as saying of Lady Diana Beauclerk 'The woman's a whore and there's an end on't', it would be a mistake for the historian of eighteenth-century England to pass it on to his readers as a report when it is, on the contrary, an evaluation. But when the same historian himself tells his readers that John Wilkes was a rake – as Johnson would have been the first to agree – it would be an equal mistake for the reader to construe it as an evaluation, unless explicitly made so, for the historian may well, far from disapproving of Wilkes's libertinism in the way that Johnson did, think him a thoroughly Good Thing on just that account. But there is no special methodological problem here. It makes no difference whose side either the historian or the reader is on. Once it has been established that it is more than a mere report which has been made, the difficulty is merely to establish whether it presupposes only a tacit appeal to benevolence or whether it is to be construed as appealing instead, or as well, to some other moral, political or aesthetic theory either of 'theirs' or of the researcher's own.

Here, first, is an easy example: General Huerta's letter to the acting President of Mexico in September 1911, asking for permission to proceed against the followers of Emiliano Zapata on the grounds that 'The facts show me the necessity to work resolutely and without mercy. These people are all bandits.'* Partisans of any and all theoretical schools will, I take it, agree that this invocation of the 'facts' does not in fact make it a matter of reportage that the Zapatistas were 'bandits'. It is a highly prejudiced evaluation grounded, if at all, in a theory which denies legitimation to either or both the Zapatistas' demands for land reform and their recourse to arms in support of them. Nor, in any case, is it plausible on any interpretation to clear General Huerta of the charge of bad faith: far from being willing himself to negotiate before resorting to violence, he was planning a coup d'état on his own account. Readers whose evaluative theories incline them against Zapata remain perfectly free to argue that Huerta's use of force was justified, just as readers disposed to take Zapata's side remain perfectly free to judge him a hero and (in due course) a martyr and his opponents as oppressors and tyrants. But they can hardly disagree with the purists of value-neutrality that although it is a fact that to Zapata's opponents his followers were 'bandits', the researcher presenting that fact to his readers will need to leave the inverted commas firmly in place.

But now consider an example which is not quite as easy, taken from an article by a British sociologist (Robert Moore) about race relations in Britain in the late 1970s:

> During the last 16 years successive governments have promoted racist attitudes, reduced the security of the black community, threatened the black community through their immigration policies and, in general, have defined blacks as a problem. Whether this was an intended or an unintended consequence of a series of 'moral panics' about immigration, it is a fact nonetheless.

A fact? Some readers will have reacted already against what they may well feel can be construed as a no less prejudiced evaluation of the British government's attitudes and policies than General Huerta's of the Zapatistas'. It is quite clear where the author's values and preferences lie, and it is only under some moral theory which makes racially discriminatory attitudes a Bad Thing in themselves that a government which unintentionally exacerbates the hostility of indigenous whites to immigrant blacks is to be unequivocally condemned. Yet even the purists of value-neutrality will be bound to agree that the feelings and attitudes of the black community are a matter of reportage, explanation and/or description, and that the explanatory hypothesis that they are the product

---

* The letter is quoted by John Womack, Jr, *Zapata and the Mexican Revolution* (1968), p. 121.

of successive governments' policies is a matter for empirical test. It is true
that the language in which the relevant propositions are stated or implied
cannot pass the test of transposition *salva veritate*. It is not interchange-
able with the terms preferred by rival observers who hold that the
successive British governments were wholly justified in what they did.
But the disentanglement of the evaluative content can, as always, be
performed. It may be no more a 'fact' that successive British governments of the 1960s and 1970s 'promoted racist attitudes' than that the
Zapatistas of 1911 were 'all bandits'. But if the technical difficulties of
performing the necessary research could be overcome, observers of all
theoretical schools could be brought to accept that the governments in
question had (or had not) increased (or diminished) by their policies the
sense of insecurity among blacks and of hostility among whites, and that
if they had, indeed, increased them then so far as the black population's
well-being is concerned their policies were – other things equal – a Bad
Thing.

From this, it is only one step further to examples in which appeal to
the 'facts' can safely be construed as wholly non-pre-emptive of an
evaluation by any other criterion than benevolence alone. The following
and final example is taken from a rejoinder in an exchange in the
correspondence columns of an American literary magazine about the care
of the old in the mid twentieth-century United States:

> Speaking as a historian I [Lawrence Stone] am reasonably certain that
> these two facts are correct: first, that no society in the world has ever spent
> more of its gross national product on the old; second, that the lives of the
> aged poor, despite the ravages of inflation and the depredations of callous and
> dishonest nursing-home operators, are generally far less horrible than they
> were in the past.

The purists of value-neutrality will no doubt object to 'horrible' as a term
which has no place in an argument spoken 'as a historian', even though
they can have no quarrel over the status of the first of the two 'facts'.
But they will have to concede that it is not pre-emptive of any evaluation
which goes beyond the presupposition that if elderly Americans find a
given set of arrangements for their care less disagreeable than the arrangements which preceded it then the change is a Good Thing, other things
equal, on that account. 'Depredations', 'callous' and 'dishonest' are not,
of course, theory-neutral terms. But in this context, 'horrible' is. The
criterion to which it appeals is no more (although no less) than the
improvement, as they experience it, in the conditions under which
elderly Americans live, and it is only the reader who is not prepared, even
ceteris paribus, to accept it as an improvement who will deny Professor

Stone his claim to be 'speaking as a historian'. The purists may still insist that it is not a matter of 'fact' of the same order as 'copper expands on heating' and 'the Battle of Hastings was fought in 1066'. But this is not because it is not in principle susceptible to test. It is only because it cannot be tested accurately; and this is not a reason not to allow it to stand in *oratio recta* as the claimed conclusion of a historian's (as opposed to a philosopher's) research.

§ 8. A different objection which might be mounted at this point by the purists of value-neutrality is that my proposed methodology will in practice, despite the apparent innocuousness of a presupposition of benevolence, encourage sociologists, anthropologists and historians to solicit the agreement of their readers to an acceptance or rejection of the *prima facie* benevolent case and thereby to descend, as it were, from the practice of social science to that of political propaganda. But where this can be shown to occur – as it often can – the moral to be drawn is not that social scientists are wrong to admit benevolence as a presupposition. It is that they are wrong to use it for a further purpose which can only be vindicated by a further argument of a different kind.

Boswell's breathtaking appeal to 'the gates of mercy' in defence of the Atlantic slave trade is not, perhaps, a sufficiently academic example against which to test a methodological rule. But George Fitzhugh's *Sociology for the South, or the Failure of Free Society*, published in Richmond, Virginia, in 1854 is, as its title suggests, a sustained attempt to enlist the criteria of social science in the cause of slavery. Fitzhugh's purpose is to persuade his readers that the ante-bellum South is less of a Bad Thing than they might suppose, because the slaves on the planta-tions are much better off, and the formally free workers in the Northern cities much worse off, than Northern detractors of slavery are prepared to concede. There is no reason to doubt that his advocacy is 'truly sincere': his dislike of industrial capitalism is as deeply felt, although from the opposite end of the political spectrum, as Marx's. But sincere as it may be, the advocacy is so blatantly partisan as to be bound to bring the so-called social science into discredit.* The purists of value-neutrality can plausibly claim that a 'sociology' so evidently committed in advance to arguing the 'failure' of the 'free' society of the Northern States only goes to show how necessary it is to keep any and all value-judgements out of sociology entirely. They may agree that the canon of evident morality to which Fitzhugh seeks to appeal is indeed that of

---

* To give just one example (p. 253): 'At the slaveholding South, *all* [my italics] is peace, quiet, plenty and contentment.'

benevolence. But in the face of what rival observers have convincingly reported, explained and described about the treatment of Southern slaves the appeal is as demonstrably implausible as Boswell's, and it would be very much more helpful to the advancement of social science if it had not been made at all.

Yet this argument too can be turned the other way. For Fitzhugh's demonstrable partisanship reveals in its turn that benevolence cannot be used to pre-empt an evaluation sustainable, if at all, only by the support of a theory which deploys other and altogether more contentious values. The claim that slavery can be justified to non-Southerners because slaves are happier on the plantations than they would be as formally free wage-workers in the factories of the industrial North is, as it were, the homage which political propaganda is compelled to pay to social science. Indeed, it may well be that the purist's case is stronger where the appeal to benevolence is less obviously transparent than in a white Southerner's defence of plantation slavery. The very outrageousness of Fitzhugh's ostensibly benevolent appeal to 'contentment', or Boswell's to 'the gates of mercy', makes it easy both to detect and to discount their bias. But the examples by which the purists of value-neutrality will have the most reason to be inflamed will be those passages of pretended sociology in which the presentation of matters of ostensible reportage is dictated by a pre-emptive evaluation deliberately concealed behind a superficially uncontentious account of what has or hasn't promoted 'their' well-being. In the two examples set out below, the authors are demonstrably committed to mutually irreconcilable evaluations. But they neither permit themselves openly to avow them nor present their evidence in terms which could be directly construed as pre-emptive of them.

> 1. For the mass of the population, material conditions of life – improving more or less regularly though they have been for a long time – are still governed primarily by the terms on which people sell their labour during their working lives. And for most of them – for manual workers, and many low-grade white collar workers who have lost the advantage in the labour market which once supported their claims to modest 'middle class' status – the life cycle usually follows a curve fairly close to a flat line. It rises to a low hump in early adulthood, improvements over time in the average level of living apart; and slopes downwards through middle into old age. The contrast is clear with the upward, incremental and promotional life cycles characteristic of members of the middle-range salariat – run-of-the-mill executives and officials, the lower and auxiliary professions. There is a still sharper contrast with the life cycles of people at the top, who share control of the dominant institutions of economy and society or enjoy the security of the established professions.
>
> Economic position and power at the top, moreover, are firmly

buttressed by property ownership. Private capital is massively concentrated in the hands of a small minority, though it is now more dispersed within the families of the wealthy than in the past, as a protection against taxation. Some 1 per cent of the adult population have as large a share of all income after tax as the poorest 30 per cent or so. Two fifths or more of their income comes from investments: a matter of little surprise, since they alone own about 30 per cent of all private wealth, and four-fifths of all company stock in personal hands. Private property, individual and corporate, is the pivot of capitalist economy, as much in its 'welfare' form as before. It is for that reason above all that, despite its expansion of production, capitalism can make no claims to a steadily more equal spread of wealth. Inequality is entrenched in its institutional structure. (John Westergaard and Henrietta Reisler, *Class in a Capitalist Society* (1975), pp.118–19)

2. The distribution of consumption goods also tends to become more equitable as the size of national income increases. The wealthier a country, the larger the proportion of its population which owns automobiles, telephones, bathtubs, refrigerating equipment and so forth. Where there is a dearth of goods, the sharing of such goods must inevitably be less equitable than in a country where there is relative abundance. For example, the number of people who can afford automobiles, washing machines, decent housing, telephones, good clothes, or have their children complete high school or go to college still represents only a small minority of the population in many European countries. The great national wealth of the United States or Canada, or even to a lesser extent the Australasian Dominions or Sweden, means that there is relatively little difference between standards of living of adjacent social classes and that even classes which are far apart in the social structure will enjoy more nearly similar consumption patterns than will comparable classes in Southern Europe. To a Southern European, and to an even greater extent to the inhabitant of one of the 'under-developed' countries, social stratification is characterized by a much greater distinction in ways of life, with little overlap in the goods the various strata own or can afford to purchase. It may be suggested, therefore, that the wealthier the country, the less is status inferiority experienced as a major source of deprivation.

Increased wealth and education also serve democracy by increasing the lower classes' exposure to cross-pressures which reduce their commitment to given ideologies and make them less receptive to extremist ones. (S. M. Lipset, *Political Man* (1958), p.65)

I have chosen these two passages to quote at some length because the first is as blatant a piece of 'left-wing' as the second of 'right-wing' advocacy. There are, as it happens, one or two things with which rival observers might wish to take issue in both of them. But let me assume for methodology's sake that neither contains a report which is demonstrably inaccurate nor implies an explanation which is demonstrably invalid. The difference between them is then that the evidence presented in the first has clearly been chosen in order to persuade you that the material condition of the mass of the population in mid twentieth-century capitalist industrial societies is not such a Good Thing as it is made out to be, whereas that in the second has been chosen in order to persuade you that it is. The purists of value-neutrality will at once conclude that this is enough by itself to prove them right, since if even such ostensibly 'scientific' claims as these two passages contain can be shown to be a function of mutually incompatible evaluative theories, the folly of allowing even the most uncontentious-looking appeal to benevolence to intrude into rival explanations and/or descriptions of industrial capitalism is made plain. But once more the argument can be turned the other way. For if both are appealing in the name of the same 'evident canon' to an implicit common standard of well-being, then the presupposition of benevolence is theory-neutral between them. If the authors of either or both these two passages are to be criticized for the intrusion of their political values into their practice of social science, it is not because they ought not to be trying, if that is their purpose, to persuade their readers that the representative members of the relatively worse-off groups or categories of the populations of capitalist industrial societies are, or would be, better off by their own material standards under some institutional arrangements than under others. It is because they have chosen their reports, explanations and descriptions to illustrate rather than to test an answer to which they are pre-emptively committed in advance. It is not the presupposition which is methodologically improper, but its use.

EVALUATION WITHOUT PRE-EMPTION

§9. Properly used, therefore, there are numerous words and phrases with an unmistakably evaluative content which can nevertheless be left safely to stand in direct speech in a passage of sociological, anthropological or historical writing. 'Successful reform', 'discernible progress', 'enlightened policy', 'beneficent influence', 'heightened well-being', 'amelioration of condition', 'diffusion of prosperity', 'increase in welfare' (or their opposites) can all be applied to persons and regimes whose actions have been reported, explained and/or described without the researcher who does so laying himself open to the charge of having trespassed into moral philosophy or descended from the practice of social science to that of political propaganda. To apply them is not to pre-empt the conclusion either that the agents concerned were necessarily right (or wrong) to do what they did or that the outcome of their doing it was necessarily a Good (or Bad) Thing.

As an illustration, let me revert to the example of the Industrial Revolution. To the purists of value-neutrality, the notion that an academic researcher should pronounce on it as a Good Thing or a Bad Thing is not only improper but even absurd. No doubt much that took place in the course of it was of a kind to arouse strong moral, political and aesthetic reactions, then as now. No doubt, too, we could all be made in theory to take sides in accordance with the principle outlined in Section 11 of Chapter 1, since we could all have put to us the hypothetical but not meaningless question what policy we would have chosen to adopt in regard to it if in a position to do so. But what contribution could anyone's answer make to substantive social theory? How are those who are, as we can all be made to be, 'concerned with making some judgement of value upon the whole process entailed in the Industrial Revolution, of which we ourselves are an end-product'* to do so except in the light of a pre-emptive philosophy of history which will be at best irrelevant to and at worst subversive of the would-be accurate reports, valid explanations and authentic descriptions which are the social-scientific researcher's concern? Even where the attempted evaluation is limited to a particular group or category, how can it be made without invoking some extrinsic moral standard of the researcher's own? Is it or isn't it an 'improvement' for the agricultural labourer of the late eighteenth century to exchange lower wages and the relatively better sanitation of the countryside for higher wages but a greater chance of the death of a larger proportion of infant children in the town? How much weight is to be attached to the unpleasantness of the discipline of timekeeping imposed by even the most benevolent factory-owner on workers unprepared for and resistant to it? How far should the presumptive improvement in well-being reflected in the statistics for increased per capita consumption of beer and spirits be offset by evidence for the need to have recourse to alcohol to assuage feelings of exhaustion, degradation and despair? And what happens when comparisons between different categories, groups and generations are made, as they surely have to be? Can the improvement in the welfare of a half-starved crofter's son living on potatoes in a hovel in a rain-swept Highland glen who has become a skilled cotton operative living in a four-roomed house in Glasgow and eating meat every Sunday be said to compensate for the decline in the welfare of a hand-loom weaver of the previous generation from a once-prosperous Yorkshire dale who ended up coughing his lungs out in a filthy cellar in Leeds after being driven to pawn the tools of his only available livelihood?

* E. P. Thompson, *The Making of the English Working Class*, p. 444.

Yet just because questions like these are irretrievably contentious, it does not follow that all such questions are. Nor does it follow from the evident prejudices which animate the 'optimists' and 'pessimists'* that none of their differences can be settled except within the pre-emptive conclusions of some shared evaluative theory. Suppose, for example, that an 'optimist' and a 'pessimist' are in dispute over the improvement – if such it was – in the real wages of British coalminers between 1790 and 1840.† 'Real wages' are defined in terms of annual net cash earnings relative to price indices acceptable to them both, and neither disputes the accuracy of the sources. The pessimist accordingly agrees with the optimist that miners' real wages did demonstrably increase over the period. But he then further points out – again, let me assume, with the support of the recording angel's statistics – that the increase was only achieved at the cost of demonstrably longer hours at the coalface. Was it therefore an improvement or wasn't it? The answer must depend, other things equal, on whether the miners themselves thought the longer hours sufficiently compensated by the higher wages. For those who did, the increase was an improvement; for those who did not, it was not; and neither the optimist nor the pessimist will be in a position to contradict them unless they can demonstrate either false consciousness or bad faith. They will, no doubt, continue to disagree over other aspects of the miners' conditions as well as over the policies of mineowners and governments towards them. But they can nevertheless agree both that the increase in real wages was or was not (other things equal) an improvement and that no evaluative theory going beyond the shared presupposition of benevolence is involved in their reaching agreement on that point.

Much, as always, depends on the context and the purpose for which a term of this kind is deployed. But 'improvement' and its cognates are safely admissible in direct speech in even the most scrupulously detached piece of social-scientific writing if (but only if) certain conditions can be shown to hold. If their use is based on accurate reportage, valid explanation and authentic description; if the persons to whose assessment of their own well-being they appeal cannot be convicted of either false consciousness or bad faith; if no one person's, group's, category's or society's well-being is weighted against another's; and if there is no tacit appeal to any moral, political or aesthetic theory by which a further evaluation could be held to have been pre-empted – then, the sociologist, anthropologist

---

* For whom see the references given by E. J. Hobsbawm, 'The Standard of Living Debate: a Postscript', in his *Labouring Men* (1964), p. 120 n.1.

† The example is taken from Thompson, *The Making of the English Working Class*, p. 211.

or historian who uses them cannot be charged with incorporating into his research any other presupposition than the sympathy which, together with the necessary detachment, he brings to his study of any and all institutions and practices, however much of a Good Thing or a Bad Thing they may be to him on other grounds.

§ 10. Another objection remains, however, which may be mounted from the other flank. I have said that the proper attitude of the researcher towards the people whose institutions and practices he is studying is a mixture of sympathy and detachment – which in the present context is in effect to say of benevolence and impartiality. But an appeal to benevolence and impartiality is (or so it might be alleged) a covert pre-emption in favour of the particular evaluative theory which claims to find adequate grounding for judgements of social choice in them and them alone: Utilitarianism. It is all very well to say that talk of Pareto-optimal improvements in well-being can be put before the reader in direct speech because final judgement on whether or not 'they' ought to have what they believe will best accord with their preferences is left open to be settled on other grounds. But to start from 'their' preferences is, it might be said, to concede a *prima facie* legitimacy to them and therefore to put non- or anti-Utilitarians in the position of having first to show that Utilitarian theory is inadequate as a grounding for judgements of social choice before arguing the merits of rival alternatives, Whig, Catholic, Marxist, Burkean, Nietzschean or whatever they may be.

But the answer is simply that no pre-emption is involved, covert or not. Just because one of the many rival theories of social choice claims to be grounded in benevolence and impartiality alone, it does not follow either that social-scientific researchers ought not to view those whom they study benevolently and impartially or that in doing so they are committing themselves to the theory which holds that no further criterion is needed for deciding what differentiates Good Things from Bad. The researcher who is impartial and benevolent towards those whose institutions and practices he has explained and described is still free to endorse all the criticisms of Utilitarian theory which its opponents have made. There is no inconsistency in his accepting the methodological rules set out in this chapter while at the same time denouncing the doctrines of Bentham and his successors as manipulative, élitist, psychologically implausible, insensitive at best to the complexities of ethical choice and at worst conducive to repressive and authoritarian government. No doubt there are many practitioners and many readers of social science who subscribe to evaluative theories in whose terms appeals to either impartiality or benevolence are irrelevant if not downright wicked, and who regard the exposure of oppression and injustice as defined by their chosen theories in overt opposition to any of the several variants of Utilitarian theory as the purpose which the reportage, explanation and/ or description of human societies ought to serve. But their objection can still only be to the use to which appeals to impartiality and benevolence are put. It is perfectly true that such appeals are often made for the purpose of disarming the committed adherents of the theoretical school to which the researcher is opposed. But theory-neutrality is not violated by the making of them in itself. It is violated only by the pre-emption which may be implicit in their application for a further purpose; and this the rival observer remains free to discount, here as anywhere else.

At the same time, the researcher who subscribes to a presupposition of benevolence but disavows the further claim that impartiality and benevolence alone furnish adequate grounding for a theory of social choice need not be implying an ability actually to refute the arguments of those who do. It is simply not his business to argue the question one way or the other. In admitting to taking an impartially benevolent view of the pains and pleasures, desires, hopes, fears, preferences and values of those whom he studies, he is conceding that it would be odd to present them to his readers at all if he did not, just as it would be odd to present his readers with a chosen set of ostensibly explanatory conditions antecedent to the behaviour which he reports if he did not subscribe to a presupposition of causality, or to present them with a set of descriptions of the kind analysed in Chapter 4 if he did not subscribe to a presupposition of the mutual communicability of subjective human experience. But once having satisfied himself that 'their' stated view of their own well-being can be passed on to the reader at face value – that is, as clear of false consciousness, bad faith or conflict with the preferences of other members of the designated category or group – he is not required to pronounce in any way on whether or not their wishes amount to justified claims on Utilitarian or any other grounds. That is a matter for readers to decide for themselves.

§11. I conclude, therefore, that the line between presupposition and theory can be no less clearly and firmly drawn in evaluation than in explanation and description, and that a presupposition of benevolence is so widely shared, and can be so innocuously applied, as to license a minimal and (if thought necessary) reversible intrusion of one kind of value-judgement into sociological, anthropological and historical writing. But the test of this, as of any other, suggested methodological rule is its usefulness. The examples which I have cited so far are perhaps too easy ones: what serious harm could conceivably be done to the progress of substantive social theory by researchers telling their readers in direct speech that it is, other things equal, better that the starving should be fed, the sick cured and coalminers paid higher real wages rather than lower ones? But it is not by any means so easy where the stated preferences of the members of the society, group or category under study are such as, perhaps, to cast doubt on the supposed uncontentiousness of the value of benevolence itself.

Such cases are, indeed, familiar in philosophical discussion, for it is one of the severest tests of any theory of how human societies ought ideally to be organized to imagine as stark as possible a choice between painful liberty and contented servitude: is it not better, as Rousseau saw, to know one's chains for what they are than to deck them with flowers?* It may be that the deliberately awkward examples of a 'Brave New World' kind discussed among philosophers are rather far-fetched even by the standards of the most eccentric institutions and practices in the ethnographic record: the likelihood that, for example, an anthropologist will in fact come upon a tribe of contented sado-masochists or of lotus- or 'soma-' eaters is at least as remote as that he will in fact come upon the villagers of Gotham with their hands joined round a thorn bush to keep a cuckoo in it. But the dilemma is real enough;† and the institution of slavery provides, once again, an instructive and at the same time realistic example. If a researcher finds that even those who are, or may become, slaves regard slavery as preferable to its abolition, and if he can find no grounds on which to impute to them either false consciousness or bad faith, then how (according to my suggested rule) is he to present his findings to his readers?

Let me accordingly revert to the Ila, among whom (as I reported in Section 6 of Chapter 2) the essence of slavery is‡ absorption into the owner's kinship group and designation as born outside the village. There is no ground for the rival observer to claim that Ila slaves are not 'real'

---

*The question in this form is borrowed from Isaiah Berlin's Introduction to his *Four Essays on Liberty* (1969), p. xxxix.

†In Aldous Huxley's own words (*Brave New World*, Ch. 17): ' "But I don't want comfort. I want God, I want poetry, I want real danger, I want freedom, I want goodness, I want sin."

"In fact", said Mustapha Mond, "you're claiming the right to be unhappy."

"All right then", said the Savage defiantly, "I'm claiming the right to be unhappy." '

‡ I use the ethnographic present: slavery was in fact abolished by the British in 1917. The account is based on that of Arthur Tuden in the volume on *Social Stratification in Africa* from which I also took the example of the *iddir* of the Shoa Galla in Section 21 of Chapter 2.

slaves: they are not tied tenants, or indentured apprentices, or prisoners, or conscripts or kidnapped pawns held for ransom; they are bought from overpopulated neighbours who are willing sellers; and they are regarded as the property of their owners. But although the status of slaves is always acknowledged as such, it is considered ill-mannered to use terms which are disparaging of it; slaves undergo the same initiation rites as free Ila, they are presented by their owners with cattle in a deliberate reinforcement of the symbolism of kinship affiliation, they are free to marry non-slaves and they perform the same economic tasks as free Ila. They call their owners 'uncle'. They risk being sold in payment for debt in times of hardship, but free Ila are then liable to be sold into slavery too. A disability which they suffer is that they are debarred, as pseudo-kinsmen, from the rules of exchange with and inheritance from distant relations. But they share fully in inheritance within the small agnatic groups, three generations in depth, which are the basic structural unit of Ila society. Moreover, they benefit from reverse discrimination in their favour: owners are at pains to be seen to treat them no less well than authentic kinsmen. They are subject to harsh physical penalties if they disobey their owners, but so are authentic kinsmen. Because they are relatively freer of kinship ties than other Ila, their support is actively sought by leaders of village factions and they serve a useful and gratifying function as a sort of floating vote. There is tacit manumission for those who remain in the village for long enough and are then, as we have already seen, specifically referred to by other Ila as 'not property'.

Now I have, as you may have suspected, again doctored the record a little for methodology's sake. This account suppresses, in particular, the Ila practice of keeping single slave women available on demand for sexual intercourse with guests or kinsmen of their owners. But it is not too fanciful to suppose that this might have come to be remedied along with a general improvement in the position of women without the institution of slavery being abolished. Suppose that a competent fieldworker who had studied their society in detail both before and after 1917 had found that the free Ila, the slave Ila and the parents of the slave Ila all agreed they were unhappier after abolition than before. He might well feel (I am sure I should myself) that they were in some sense wrong to be unhappier, even if they were right to say, as well they might, that they found the experience of manumission disturbing. Yet is not this reaction not merely patronizing but irrelevant? Does it not pre-empt a blatantly paternalistic judgement grounded, if at all, in a highly contentious theory of determinate human needs? Would not its intrusion into the account of Ila society put before the prospective reader be at best as inappropriate as an exposition of the researcher's religious beliefs within an account of Ila religion and at worst a direct violation of both the sympathy and the detachment that it is the academic duty of the fieldworker to cultivate and preserve? The good faith of the native informants is not in doubt. Their consciousness is not false in the sense either that they are misstating their preferences or that they lack the information which might modify them. They are unanimous. There is nobody else who would be threatened or distressed if their form of slavery were to be reinstituted at their request. So what else is the researcher entitled to say to his readers except that slavery was, for the Ila, a Good Thing in the circumstances and that the reader, if benevolent, will be bound to agree that it ought, other things equal, to be restored?

Now of course there is a great deal which, if confronted with such a finding, the researcher would still be perfectly entitled to say to his readers. But he would not be entitled to claim theory-neutrality for it, and he would need to make it clear in saying it how far the theory in question was explanatory, descriptive or evaluative. Whichever the case, it could well be a theory which invoked a concept of 'false consciousness' in a less restricted sense than that advocated in Section 5. Explanatorily, it might be plausible to argue that if certain ecological and cultural conditions had obtained, the Ila (which is to say, the very different Ila which they would then be) would not have preferred slavery. Descriptively, it might be plausible to argue that the Ila were misapprehending or mystifying their own experience of slavery through a failure to consider it in a way which could, but had not yet, been put to them. Evaluatively, it might be plausible to argue that they ought to prefer freedom because of an intrinsic value discernible to anyone whose moral intuitions are unclouded by pre-existing interests. But none of these arguments would be arguments against the presupposition of benevolence underlying the presentation of the original finding that the Ila *did* regard slavery as a Good Thing for themselves. Indeed, it is only because the presupposition of benevolence is tacitly endorsed that there arises the problem to which an explanatory, descriptive or evaluative theory of 'false consciousness' could be held to be called for in response. Only because their non-defeasible preference for slavery is more difficult for the researcher to accept as a preference to be passed on to the reader at face value does he have reason to treat it differently from a preference for their sick to be cured and their starving fed.

Arguments of this kind are, to be sure, notoriously difficult, whichever form they take. Moreover, part of the difficulty is that explanation, description and evaluation are particularly easy to confuse with one another in such contexts. Ila society has, as all societies do, a set of concepts, beliefs and values in terms of which its members explain, describe and evaluate their own institutions and practices, and by virtue of so doing they help to maintain those institutions and practices in the form in which the enquiring fieldworker discovers and reports them. When, therefore, he tells his readers that 'their' explanations, descriptions and evaluations are in need of correction, he inevitably becomes involved in a second-order exercise in which *his* explanations, descriptions and evaluations have to be related to one another as well. This raises some well-known philosophical difficulties about the nature of the relationship between beliefs and values and the institutions and practices which stand in a reciprocal causal (and not only causal) relationship to them.* But these difficulties are not such as to undermine the methodological distinction between reportage, explanation, description and evaluation. They are, on the contrary, such as to bring out once again the need to preserve it. The researcher who refuses to pass on at face value the Ila preference for slavery must, at the least, tell his readers whether this is because a defeasibility condition holds, or because on some explanatory or descriptive theory their consciousness can be shown to be false in some further sense, or because he is so convinced of an evaluative theory which overrides any preference for slavery that he cannot refrain from admitting it into his account over and above his initial conclusion that by the criterion of benevolence alone slavery was a Good Thing for 'them'.

THEORY-NEUTRAL USES OF EVALUATIVE TERMS

§ 12. If, accordingly, there is after all one limited kind of evaluation which sociologists, anthropologists and historians can properly submit to their readers, it follows that both explanation and description can, and to this extent should, be subordinated to it when the argument so requires; and this implies the admissibility of theoretical terms which retain an avowedly evaluative as well as explanatory and/or descriptive content. There is, it is true, the continuing difference that the evaluative content is restricted in a way that the others are not. If the resulting explanation can be shown to be valid, or description authentic, there is no room for a rival explanatory theory which does not incorporate it, or a descriptive theory which cannot admit it as complementary, whereas

---

* On which I have found J. L. Mackie, 'Ideological Explanation', in Stephan Körner, ed., *Explanation* (1975), particularly helpful.

the evaluation will still leave rival observers as free as ever they were to override a purely benevolent endorsement of 'their' non-defeasible desire for what they see as their own well-being. But there is no need to disavow the inbuilt implication that some institutions and practices are preferable to others by the criterion of benevolence alone.

As an illustration, consider first the term 'parasitic' as used by geographers and economists analysing the relation between towns or cities and their surrounding countryside.* It is a term pre-emptive of explanation by reference to a theory of the reciprocal flow of goods and services interpreted by a model specifying the conditions under which the flow will be asymmetrically in favour of the city. But 'parasitic' is at the same time a metaphorical term suggestive of the debilitation of a productive countryside for the support of a wasteful and luxurious urban élite and its own unproductive servants, retainers and hangers-on. To the purists of value-neutrality, its use is therefore a perpetuation of the long tradition of denunciations of urban life by preachers and moralists concerned to uphold the virtues of innocent rural frugality and to denounce the temptations and corruptions of Babylon. Yet they cannot deny that some of the hypotheses of economic geographers about the causal connections between agglomeration of population and specialization of function, or between acceleration of urban-rural exchanges and reinvestment of capital in agriculture, are valid (or not) quite independently of their proponents' views of a more or less one-sided flow of goods or services as a Good or Bad Thing. Nor can they deny that it is no more a moral, political or aesthetic evaluation in itself to calculate the net economic gains or losses than it is to calculate the nutritional gains or losses between a parasitic plant or animal and its host organism. The calculation *can*, to be sure, be put to use in the service of a moral denunciation, or political programme, or exposition of an ideal of the good society. But equally, the force of 'parasitic' as a social-scientific term *can* be restricted within the presupposition that economic 'benefits', as conventionally defined, are a Good Thing for those who receive them to the extent that they are desired and nothing else impedes or overrides their desirability.

The same holds for a term whose theoretical content is descriptive rather than explanatory but which also carries, as normally used, at least some mildly evaluative overtone. As an illustration, consider 'harmonious'. Just as 'parasitical' cities have been denounced as wicked since at least the time of St Bernard, so have 'harmonious' ones been held

* See e.g. E. A. Wrigley, 'Parasite or Stimulus: the Town in a Pre-industrial Economy', in Philip Abrams and E. A. Wrigley, eds., *Towns in Societies* (1978).

up as ideals since at least the time of Solon. 'Good order' – the Greeks' *eunomia* – is obviously defined by appeal to an ethical norm of some kind and not merely by reference to observable degrees of consensus about, and conformity to, whatever may happen to be a particular society's existing rules. But if construed as a descriptive term whose evaluative overtones are restricted within the presupposition of benevolence, it need involve no commitment to the moral value of a lack of mutual antagonism among fellow-citizens beyond its desirability, other things equal, to those who feel that their society (or community within it) is, indeed, a harmonious one. The whole notion of a social consensus by which differences of opinion or condition are somehow reconciled within a higher affinity which brings them into an as it were musical accord raises questions of political philosophy which revolve once again round the conflict between happiness and freedom.* But that conflict can once again be left to readers to resolve in the light of their own evaluative theories without the researcher having to disavow the implication that if a group or category of people do prefer to be in agreement with one another, a society in which they feel as if in musical accord is to that extent better, other things equal, than one in which they do not.

I have chosen these two examples because the one term is predominantly explanatory and the other predominantly descriptive. But the same methodological rule can be applied to the same effect to any or all of the terms which I cited in Section 13 of Chapter 1 as equally capable of explanatory, descriptive and evaluative use: 'democratic', 'alienated', 'prejudiced', 'deviant', 'bourgeois', 'tribal', 'charismatic' and 'imperialist'. How they are to be construed, and to which purpose they are being put, can only be settled case by case. But even where it turns out that the explanatory and/or descriptive use is for an overtly evaluative purpose, it does not follow that the argument in question is to be ruled out of court on that account as an improper intrusion of moral and political philosophy into matters of social science. Parasitic cities, harmonious social arrangements, democratic constitutions, alienated workers, prejudiced ethnic groups, deviant adolescents, bourgeois lifestyles, tribal loyalties, charismatic leaders and imperialist policies can innocuously be spoken of as better or worse than their alternatives provided that theory-neutrality is – as it can be – preserved, and no other criterion invoked in *oratio recta* than the desire for what they see as their own well-being on the part of groups or categories of people who agree among themselves and cannot plausibly be charged with either false consciousness or bad faith.

* See e.g. Barbara Goodwin, *Social Science and Utopia* (1978), Chs. 5 and 6.

§ 13. The same rule also licenses, within the same constraints, what may be labelled *optative* sociology: that is, claims about the institutions and practices of a society which are of the form neither of 'if . . . then . . .' nor of 'it is/was as if . . .' but of 'if only . . . !'.

Such claims cannot but imply a value-judgement: a researcher cannot coherently voice to his readers a desire that some event, process or state of affairs should happen or be the case while in the same breath denying that it would be a Good Thing if (only!) it did or were. What is more, many such claims function in practice not merely as advocacy, but as special pleading of a shamelessly pre-emptive kind. But there is no need categorically to deny them a place in social science, if they can be so construed that theory-neutrality is preserved. Since they too stand in varying relations to the explanations and/or descriptions on which they rest, it is useful to classify optative sociology under two headings: first, *utopian* sociology, which rests primarily on explanatory arguments and relates typically, but not necessarily, to the future; second, *nostalgic* sociology which rests principally on descriptive arguments and relates typically, but not necessarily, to the past.

As an example of utopian sociology, here is a passage from Theo Nichols and Huw Beynon, *Living with Capitalism* (1977):

> Now by its very nature the book that we have written cannot hope to offer a view of an alternative socialist society. But what it does seek to do is to look at things as they are: thereby indicating the tendencies that are becoming clear in large corporations, and the way they are affecting the people who work in them. What becomes clear from this – and what we came up against time and time again while we were at ChemCo. – is the immense waste of human potential that is locked up within capitalist factory production. This experience strengthened our central political conviction that the need for a fundamental restructuring of British society is both a desirable and urgent one.

Despite the claim to be looking at 'things as they are', this appeal to the notion of 'wasted human potential' will rightly be construed as preemptive evaluation both by purists of value-neutrality, for whom such notions have no place in a work of sociology at all, and by adherents of rival evaluative theories, for whom the conclusion to be drawn from a study of capitalist factory production is its evident superiority over socialist factory production. But both will agree that on any definition of 'waste', the claim that an institution or practice is wasteful appeals to an implicit counterfactual conditional: differently used, the human or other resources in question would bring about a different state of affairs.

Nothing, therefore, prevents a utopian optative of the form of 'if only the resources had been better spent!' from being so framed as to be theory-neutral within the presupposition of benevolence. It just so happens that this one also appeals to a further evaluative theory. The methodological difficulty which it poses is not its tacit resort to the optative mode, but its tacit pre-emption of what is implicitly to count as a good use of 'human potential'. It goes beyond an impartial and benevolent presentation of 'their' ascertainable preferences to a theory of what constitutes a good or bad organization of factory work which no purely sociological evidence can compel rival observers of different theoretical persuasions to accept.

As an example of nostalgic sociology, here is a passage from David Cecil's *The Young Melbourne*[2] (1954):

> Here we come to their outstanding distinction. They were the most agreeable society England had ever known. The character of their agreeability was of a piece with the rest of them; mundane, straightforward, a trifle philistine, largely concerned with gossip, not given to subtle analyses or flights of fancy. But it had all their vitality and all their sense of style. It was incomparably racy and spontaneous and accomplished; based solidly on a wide culture and experience, yet free to express itself in bursts of high spirits, in impulses of appreciation, in delicate movements of sentiment, in graceful accomplishments. For it had its grace; a virile classical grace like that of the Chippendale furniture which adorned its rooms, lending a glittering finish to its shrewd humour, its sharp-eyed observation, its vigorous disquisitions on men and things. Educated without pedantry, informal but not slipshod, polished but not precious, brilliant without fatigue, it combined in an easy perfection the charms of civilization and nature.

Here, despite the ostensibly straightforward appeal to descriptive criteria for what 'they' were like, both the purists of value-neutrality and the adherents of rival evaluative theories will at once take objection to both 'most agreeable' and 'easy perfection'. No doubt 'they' might be willing – perhaps too willing – to pass the description as authentic. But rival observers are still free to argue that in the light of the evaluative theory to which they subscribe this was a thoroughly bad set of people. Again, however, it is not the nostalgia itself which poses the methodological difficulty. 'If only the combination in an easy perfection of the charms of civilization and nature were still with us today!' is no more necessarily objectionable because of its recourse to the optative mode than 'if only the human potential had not been wasted!'. It just so happens that in this case 'agreeable' and 'perfection' are both evaluatively pre-emptive beyond what could be construed as no more than an impartially benevolent presentation of the values of the Whig aristocracy of the period of Melbourne's youth.

Within the optative mode, a whole range of permutations is possible. The two examples just given are typical of two familiar variants and styles. But explanation and description, reference to a hypothetical future or an idealized past, desire for change or attachment to the status quo, and praise or blame at a macro- or micro-sociological level may be combined in any of the many different ways which these distinctions entail without any modification of the methodological rule. However worded, expression of the desire for a different state of society from that in fact reported, explained and/or described cannot but be construed as propaganda, not science. But if the value to which it appeals is benevolence alone, it can in practice be accepted, *ceteris paribus*, by all rival observers, however different their own chosen theories, who accept the explanations and descriptions on which it rests. Emotive and rhetorical as it may be, talk of wasted opportunities, tragic blunders, radiant futures or golden pasts does not have to be excised completely from any would-be academic work of sociology, anthropology or history. If there is no need in practice to insulate within inverted commas any work or phrase which implies that it is – other things equal – a Good Thing that people's desire for what they see as their own well-being should if possible be gratified, then there is no need to insulate a stated preference or even longing for a state of society in which that is more rather than less nearly achieved.

§ 14. Theory-neutrality, finally, can likewise be preserved – although it often isn't – at the opposite pole, where the sociologist's, anthropologist's or historian's purpose is to persuade the reader not that a state of society could be more of a Good Thing than it is but that it is more of a Bad Thing than it seems. For this type of argument, the obvious label is *exposure*. It is true to say that both explanation and description, even if undertaken for no evaluative purpose, involve exposure of a kind. Well-validated explanations involve the laying bare of hidden causal regularities not perceptible at the level of reportage. Well-authenticated descriptions involve the laying bare of subtler implications and nuances than can be directly observed in what people do and say. But exposure in the stronger sense – the sense, if you like, of an '*exposé*' – involves the use of explanations, descriptions, or sometimes reports by themselves to dispel the comforting illusions by which agents have deceived themselves and/or researchers their readers.

Where reports by themselves are so used, the mode of reasoning is strictly *ad hominem*. It is the context within which the reader, or the rival observer, is addressed which makes the recital of matters of (mere) reportage into an *exposé*. Here are two anecdotal examples from public debates where the technique was used to equally good effect: in the first, a speaker from the South African Embassy in London defending his government's racial policies was answered by a bald recital of laws affecting the well-being of non-white South Africans enacted since the Nationalist Party's electoral victory in 1948. In the second, a French academic Marxist attacking Swedish Social Democracy as indistinguishable from alternative variants of capitalist exploitation was answered by a bald recital of Acts of Parliament affecting the well-being of Swedish workers and their dependents enacted since the Social Democratic Party's electoral victory in 1932. In both cases the methodological moral is in part the familiar one that assertions which cannot themselves be construed as other than reports may still be so deployed as to serve an explanatory, descriptive or, as here, evaluative purpose; and in neither case does it make a difference whether that purpose is left-wing, right-wing or neither. But notice, in addition, that the purpose is essentially *counter*-pre-emptive. There can be no exposure except of something which has been disguised or concealed. No doubt the South African Embassy spokesman is 'truly sincere' in subscribing to a theory which, for him, legitimates his government's pretendedly benevolent treatment of non-whites, as is the French academic Marxist in subscribing to one which, for him, discredits the Swedish Government's pretendedly benevolent treatment of its working class. But the bald recitals achieved their effect because without them the audience would have been left with an account acceptable only to those of its members who already accepted the same evaluative theory as had been pre-emptively assumed by the platform speaker.

Where explanations and/or descriptions perform a counter-pre-emptive function, the argument is still *ad hominem* to the extent that it attributes to presumptive readers a susceptibility against which they need to be better protected than they could otherwise protect themselves. If the purpose of an explanation is to dispel the hopes and fears which you might otherwise entertain about how much better or worse for 'them' things might have been, or of a description to immunize you against a potential romanticization of how good or bad for 'them' they are or were, the passage in question can hardly be construed as impersonally 'scientific'. But even in those contexts where the jibe that 'sociology specializes in unveiling the illusion that has deceived no-one'* is most likely to strike home, the explanations and descriptions presented to the reader who claims not to need them still stand or fall by the same criteria. They are open to criticism on methodological grounds only if the counter-pre-emption of some suspected evaluative theory is taken to the point at which it becomes a re-pre-emption of its own.

No doubt the purists of value-neutrality will still object that none of this should be allowed any place in social-scientific writing at all. Even if they concede that nothing prevents the use of sociological evidence to provoke guilt, outrage, pity or dismay in the audience to whom it is presented, they will still insist that it is a *mis*use of it to do so. Yet precisely because explanatory or descriptive arguments so used (or misused) can be assessed separately from their perlocutionary effects, there is no occasion for methodological concern. As we have just seen, there are some contexts in which the bald recital of matters of pure reportage can function by itself to counter-pre-empt a pre-emptive evaluation, and it cannot be held to compromise their status as reports that they are so used. Indeed, they can only be so used with success if their status as reports can*not* be compromised; and in the same way, the use (or misuse) of explanations or descriptions to achieve such effects depends on their capacity to withstand attempts to invalidate or inauthenticate them. They can safely be left to carry an implication that a given institution or practice is, was, might be, or might have been more or less of a Good Thing, other things equal, by the criterion of benevolence alone. The effect which they may then have on the evaluations which their readers make is an entirely separate matter to be resolved at their own discretion in the light of their own ideals and the moral, political or aesthetic theory which grounds them.

CONCLUSION

§ 15. This concluding chapter has, in a sense, been no more than an Appendix to what I announced at the outset to be the principal argument of the volume as a whole. Evaluative theories are different in kind from either explanatory or descriptive; the methodological problems which they pose have nothing to do with the analysis of the concept of understanding on which the distinction between reportage, explanation and description rests; and they are in any case immaterial to the relation

---

* Nathan Glazer, 'The Ideological Uses of Sociology', in Paul F. Lazarsfeld *et al.*, eds., *The Uses of Sociology* (1967), p. 76.

between the sciences of man and of nature. It is true that they cannot simply be ignored in a methodology which claims to be of relevance to practising sociologists, anthropologists and historians, if only because such a methodology must at the very least show how evaluation can be distinguished from reportage, explanation and description, and why it should. But as I have conceded throughout, nothing prevents those engaged in research into human institutions and practices from incorporating into their research the ideas which they cannot help having about what makes one form of social organization either better or worse than another. If they wish to expound to their readers their theories of justice or freedom, or their vision of the good society, neither their readers nor any passing methodologist can stop them. All the methodologist can do is to make clear to them, if they are not aware of it already, that in seeking to vindicate their evaluations against those of rival theoretical schools they are appealing to fundamentally different criteria from those to which they appeal in seeking to vindicate their reports as accurate, their explanations as valid and their descriptions as authentic.

This being so, there is an obvious rationale for a methodology which denies evaluation any place in social-scientific writing at all. But it is not, I have sought to argue, either the only one or the best, partly because of the hopeless impracticality of seeking actually to implement it and partly because of the alternative possibility of applying to evaluation the same distinction between presuppositionlessness and theory-neutrality already applied to explanation and description. Since evaluation is, and always will be, discretionary to a degree that explanation and description are not, this suggestion itself must be differently construed from those put forward in Chapters 2 to 4: a researcher who repudiates the presupposition of benevolence does not thereby defeat the purpose of studying behaviour at all. But if the arguments of this chapter are well founded, it follows from them that despite all the irreconcilable conflicts between rival moral, political and aesthetic theories, there are two methodologically proper uses of evaluative terms within the writings of sociologists, anthropologists and historians. First, as even the purists of value-neutrality will accept, judgements of good and bad can and must feature as having been observed to play a part in the behaviour of those whose institutions and practices are under study; second, however, they can safely be presented to the reader in direct speech with such tacit endorsement as is implied by a presupposition of benevolence alone provided that no defeasibility condition holds and no moral, political or aesthetic judgement has been pre-empted about what exactly ought or ought not to be or have been done by the agents concerned.

Beyond this point, there is nothing further that can usefully be said from a methodological point of view. But if the argument of this chapter is of a different kind from my opening claim that it is the problems of description which pose special methodological difficulties for the sciences of man, its underlying purpose is still the same. The justification of any methodological discussion is pragmatic. If this volume makes no contribution – and it does not – to the resolution of either the technical or the philosophical problems posed by the practice of substantive social theory, its success can only be judged by the degree to which practitioners who read it agree that it can help them to report, explain, describe and evaluate human institutions and practices better than they would other-wise have done. It has, in other words, not only to have laid down criteria for distinguishing good theories from bad, but to have done so in such a way as will, if its injunctions are followed, lead to better ones.

Index

348 INDEX

Pantomine, 72, 73, 118
Paraguay, 171
Pareto, Vilfredo, 264 and n, 265, 267
Pareto-optimal(ity), 306, 327
Patis, 21, 28, 108, 177
Patron-client relations, 134–5, 248
Peasantry, 95, 125–6, 142, 174–5, 193, 215, 248, 285, 286
Peculium, 19
Penn, Sir William, 240
Pepys, Samuel, 239–40
Perfect competition, 5, 292
Perlocution, perlocutionary effect, 39, 112, 248, 264, 339
Persia, Persians, 80, 96, 170, 180, 191
Petrarch, 88
Petronius, 53, 54
Phenomenology, 28, 41, 67, 99, 144, 222, 225, 230
Philiphaugh, Battle of, 316
Philippine Islands, 158
Phrenology, 5, 167n
Physiocrats, 11, 12
Physiology, 5, 28, 153, 162, 176, 194
Piero di Cosimo, 159, 160, 163, 166, 182, 183, 184, 204
Pigou, A. C., 90–91 and 90n
Pirenne, Henri, 269
Plato, 246
Plautus, 53, 54
Plotnicov, Leonard, 128
Political science, 3, 154, 180
Porphyria, 7, 151
Portugal, Portuguese, 171
Positivism, 2, 4, 5, 36, 144
Potlatch, 75–6, 77
Potter, Stephen, 114
Power, Eileen, 137n
Price, John, 129n
Principes, 128
Proust, 21, 277, 279
Prussia, 103, 104, 105
Psychoanalysis, 64, 147, 152
Psychology, 28, 29, 31, 32, 44, 45, 49, 108, 148, 151, 162, 163, 167, 168, 176, 185–6, 202, 207, 216, 225, 258, 259, 264

Quesnay, François, 10, 12
Quine, W. V., 66–7
Quintilian, 88

Race, racism, 44, 72, 73, 80, 96, 115, 246, 314, 318–19, 338
Radama, 172–3, 174, 175
Radcliffe-Brown, A. R., 2, 131, 132, 258
'Radical chic', 268, 284
Rain-dance(ing), 60–62, 63, 67, 69, 76, 105, 118, 161, 183
Ram, Sita, 298

Rationality, 21–6, 52, 65, 83, 163, 253, 264n, 265
Rawls, John, 307n
'Recording angel', 96–9, 100, 109, 110, 126, 136, 140, 158, 180, 184, 197, 244, 270, 274, 282, 283, 285, 286, 295, 305, 326
Reduction(ism), 29–31, 55, 166, 212, 217, 269
Reisler, Henrietta, 323
Relativism, 7, 8, 9
Religion, 4, 31, 67, 82, 83, 110, 111, 126, 213, 242, 262, 298, 309, 331
Renaissance, 5, 87–9, 92, 96, 159, 163, 182, 204, 228
Rickert, Heinrich, 230
Rilke, 266, 268, 272
Ritual, 68, 69, 70, 83, 85, 225, 258, 278, 279, 298
Rockingham, 2nd Marquis of, 276
'Role distance', 62, 63
Roman à clef, 70
Rome, Romans, Roman Empire, 13–14, 19, 20, 21, 41, 53–4, 78–81, 88, 90, 119, 120, 126, 128, 129, 157, 161, 178–9, 180–81, 188–93, 197, 215–18, 250, 297, 315
Roniger, Louis, 135n
Roosevelt, Franklin D., 305
Rose, Rev. H. J., 285
Rosselón (Roussillon), 101
Rousseau, 239, 240, 329
Rowntree, Seebohm, 306
Royal Anthropological Institute, 120n, 121
Rubinstein, W. D., 140n
Ruse, M. E., 165n
Rushdie, Salman, 298
Russell, Bertrand, 103
Russell, Lord John, 161
Russia, Russians, *see* Soviet Union
Ruwet, Nicolas, 158

Sacks, Oliver W., 266n, 272
Sacrifice, 71, 78, 170
Saint-Simon, Comte de, 167
Saint-Simon, Duc de, 240
Salomon, F., 75n
Sangree, W. G., 219n
Saracens, 170
Sarpedon, 317
Sarraute, Nathalie, 237n
Sarthe, 174–5, 176, 215
Sartre, Jean-Paul, 315
Saturday Review, 285, 286, 287
Scaliger, 158
Schizophrenia, 5, 7, 146, 151
Scotland, 101, 122, 169
Scott, Sir George Gilbert, 16, 18, 256
Scott, Paul, 298
Scutari, 105
Seaman, L. C. B., 161n
Self-deception, 28, 238, 273, 281, 337